The Role of Social Capital in Development
An Empirical Assessment

In recent years the role of social capital – defined as the institutions and networks of relationships between people, and the associated norms and values – has risen to considerable prominence in programs of poverty alleviation and development. Although development practitioners have long suspected that social capital affects the efficiency and quality of most development processes, this book is the first to provide the rigorous empirical results needed to confirm that impression and translate it into effective and informed policymaking. Based on a large volume of newly collected data, the book relies equally on quantitative and qualitative research methodologies to establish new approaches for measuring social capital and its impact. The book documents the pervasive role of social capital in accelerating poverty alleviation and rural development, facilitating the provision of goods and services, and easing political transition and recovery from civil conflicts.

Christiaan Grootaert is Lead Economist in the Social Development Department at the World Bank, and Manager of the Social Capital Initiative. His research centers on the measurement and analysis of poverty, risk, and vulnerability; education and labor markets; child labor; and the role of institutions and social capital in development in Africa, Asia, the Middle East, and Eastern Europe. Recent publications include *The Policy Analysis of Child Labor: A Comparative Study* (with H. Patrinos). He is co-author of the *World Development Report 2000–2001: Attacking Poverty*, and has contributed articles to various journals, including the *Journal of Development Economics*, *Journal of Development Studies*, *World Development*, and *Journal of African Economies*.

Thierry van Bastelaer is Director of the Integrated Financial Services Team at the IRIS Center at the University of Maryland and Research Coordinator of the Social Capital Initiative. As a political economist, he has worked in a number of areas, including private sector policy reform, legal and regulatory reform for microfinance, policy priorities for electronic commerce, small enterprise development, and corruption. His research has focused on the political economy of reform, social capital, and microfinance. He has published widely and has traveled extensively in South Asia.

The Role of Social Capital in Development

An Empirical Assessment

Edited by

Christiaan Grootaert and Thierry van Bastelaer

With a foreword by

Robert D. Putnam

CAMBRIDGE
UNIVERSITY PRESS

PUBLISHED BY THE PRESS SYNDICATE OF THE UNIVERSITY OF CAMBRIDGE
The Pitt Building, Trumpington Street, Cambridge, United Kingdom

CAMBRIDGE UNIVERSITY PRESS
The Edinburgh Building, Cambridge CB2 2RU, UK
40 West 20th Street, New York, NY 10011-4211, USA
477 Williamstown Road, Port Melbourne, VIC 3207, Australia
Ruiz de Alarcón 13, 28014 Madrid, Spain
Dock House, The Waterfront, Cape Town 8001, South Africa

http://www.cambridge.org

First published 2002

Printed in the United Kingdom at the University Press, Cambridge

Typeface Times 10/12 pt.   *System* LATEX 2$_\varepsilon$ [TB]

A catalogue record for this book is available from the British Library

Library of Congress Cataloguing in Publication data

The role of social capital in development : an empirical assessment/edited by Christiaan
Grootaert and Thierry van Bastelaer; with a foreword by Robert D. Putnam.
      p.   cm.
Includes bibliographical references and index.
ISBN 0-521-81291-7
1. Social capital (Sociology)   2. Poverty.   3. Economic development.   4. Rural
development.   I. Grootaert, Christiaan, 1950–   II. van Bastelaer, Thierry 1962–
HM741 .R65   2002
302–dc21   2001043594

ISBN 0 521 81291 7 hardback

Contents

Figures and maps

Tables

Boxes

Notes on Contributors

ROBERT H. BATES is Eaton Professor of the Science of Government and Faculty Fellow of the Center for International Development at Harvard University. Specializing in the political economy of development, he concentrates on Sub-Saharan Africa. His most recent books include *Analytic Narratives* (Princeton University Press, 1998, co-authored with Avner Grief, Margaret Levi, Jean-Laurent Rosenthal, and Barry R. Weingast), and *Prosperity and Violence* (W. W. Norton, 2001).

ANTHONY J. BEBBINGTON is Associate Professor of Geography at the University of Colorado at Boulder where he also co-directs the Program in Developing Areas Research and Teaching. His research is concentrated in Latin America, particularly the Andean countries, and has focused on: rural poverty and livelihoods; peasant and indigenous organizations; NGOs, the state and rural development; and small farm agriculture. He has been a Fellow at the Center for Advanced Studies in the Behavioral Sciences at Stanford, and has also worked at the Social Development Department of the World Bank, the International Institute for Environment and Development (UK), the Overseas Development Institute (UK), and the University of Cambridge.

THOMAS F. CARROLL is Professor Emeritus of Economics and Regional Planning at George Washington University, Washington, DC. His original discipline is agricultural economics. He was a staff member of the Food and Agriculture Organization in Rome and a senior official of the Inter-American Development Bank in Washington, DC. He has written widely on land reform, cooperatives, rural development, and regional planning, and carried out field assignments for development agencies around the world. During 1986–7, he taught at the John F. Kennedy School of Government at Harvard University. His current research interest is externally assisted local institutional development.

NAT J. COLLETTA is Research Professor and Co-Director of the Institute for Peacebuilding and Development at the Elliott School for International Affairs, George Washington University. His area of expertise is post-conflict management. He was Manager of the World Bank's Post Conflict Unit which coordinated the Bank's policy toward assistance in war to peace transitions.

PAUL COLLIER is Director of the Development Research Group of the World Bank. He is on leave from the University of Oxford where he is Professor of Economics and Director of the Centre for the Study of African Economies. For four years he held a joint appointment with the Kennedy School of Government, Harvard. He has published around eighty articles and books with a predominant focus on Africa.

MICHELLE L. CULLEN is a post-conflict consultant for the World Bank specializing in social assessment, study implementation, and project monitoring and evaluation in conflict-affected countries. She has written reports for the World Health Organization, the US National Institute for Mental Health, and the Commonwealth of Australia, and has worked with the Carter Center on its human rights and conflict resolution programs. She is co-author of *Violent Conflict and the Transformation of Social Capital: Lessons from Cambodia, Rwanda, Guatemala and Somalia* (with Nat Colletta). She obtained her masters degree in anthropology from the University of Melbourne in Melbourne, Australia.

MARCEL FAFCHAMPS is Reader in the Department of Economics and Professoral Fellow at Mansfield College in the University of Oxford. He is Deputy Director of the Centre for the Study of African Economies. Prior to joining Oxford University, he taught at Stanford University for ten years. He has also worked for the World Bank and for the International Labour Organization. He holds a PhD from the University of California at Berkeley and a law degree from the Université Catholique de Louvain in Belgium.

DANIEL O. GILLIGAN is a graduate student at the Agricultural and Resource Economics Department of the University of Maryland. His research interests include the role of information asymmetries in agricultural labor market contracts and the design of effective poverty alleviation programs. He has worked for the Harvard Institute for International Development in Cambridge, Massachusetts, and in Jakarta, Indonesia. He has an MA from the Fletcher School of Law and Diplomacy at Tufts University.

CHRISTIAAN GROOTAERT is Lead Economist in the Social Development Department at the World Bank and Manager of the Social Capital Initiative. His research centers on the measurement and analysis of poverty, risk, and vulnerability; education and labor markets; child labor; and the role of institutions and social capital in development in Africa, Asia, the Middle East, and Eastern Europe. Recent publications include *The Policy Analysis of Child*

Labor: A Comparative Study (with H. Patrinos). He is co-author of the *World Development Report 2000–2001: Attacking Poverty*, and has contributed articles to numerous journals.

MARY KAY GUGERTY is Assistant Professor of Public Affairs at the Evans School of Public Affairs at the University of Washington. She received her PhD in political economy and government from Harvard University and holds an MPA from the John F. Kennedy School of Government at Harvard. Her recent research examines the organizational design of rotating savings and credit organizations in developing countries, and the impacts of ethnic diversity on collective action in local organizations.

MAINUL HUQ works as an international consultant for the World Bank and other donor agencies, especially in the South Asian region. He is also CEO of Development Policy Group, a research-based consulting firm based in Bangladesh. Prior to this, he worked as an economist for the World Bank at its headquarters. He has worked and published extensively in the area of industrial pollution policy.

JONATHAN ISHAM is Assistant Professor of Economics and an affiliated member of the Environmental Studies Program at Middlebury College, Vermont. Previously, he has held positions at the Center for Institutional Reform and the Informal Sector (IRIS) at the University of Maryland, and at the World Bank, and served as Peace Corps volunteer in Benin from 1984 to 1987. He holds an MA from the Johns Hopkins School of Advanced Inernational Studies, and a PhD from the University of Maryland. He is the co-editor of the forthcoming volume *Social Capital and Economic Development: Well-Being in Developing Countries* (Edward Elgar).

SATU KÄHKÖNEN is a Senior Economist at the World Bank. Prior to joining the World Bank, she was Associate Director of the Center for Institutional Reform and the Informal Sector (IRIS) at the University of Maryland. In addition to conducting research on institutional aspects of economic development, she has undertaken field work in a number of developing and transition economies. She is the author and co-editor of *A Not-so-Dismal Science: A Broader View of Economies and Societies*; *A New Institutional Approach to Economic Development*; and *Institutions, Incentives and Economic Reforms in India.*

STEPHEN KNACK is a Senior Research Economist in the World Bank's Development Research Group. He has published widely on the social and political determinants of growth and effective governance. Prior to joining the World Bank in 1999, he was a Research Associate at the Center for Institutional Reform and the Informal Sector (IRIS) at the University of

Maryland, and Assistant Professor in the American University's School of Public Affairs. He received a PhD in economics from the University of Maryland in 1991.

MICHAEL KREMER is Professor of Economics at Harvard University and Senior Fellow at the Brookings Institution. He received his PhD from Harvard University in 1992. He is a 1997 recipient of a MacArthur "genius" fellowship, and in 1996 he received a Presidential Early Career Award for Scientists and Engineers. His research focuses on the economics of developing countries, including: incentives for research and development on malaria, tuberculosis, HIV, and other diseases affecting developing countries; the epidemiology of the AIDS epidemic; the economics of elephant poaching; payroll taxation and youth unemployment; economic sanctions and international relations; and income distribution dynamics.

ANIRUDH KRISHNA teaches at Duke University in the public policy and political science departments. He holds a PhD in government from Cornell University and masters degrees in international development and economics from Cornell University and the Delhi School of Economics. Before taking up an academic career, he served for a number of years in the Indian Administrative Service.

BART MINTEN is a Senior Research Associate at the Cornell Food and Nutrition Policy Program at Cornell University. He currently resides in Madagascar and is the lead researcher for a USAID-financed economic research program. He holds a doctorate in agricultural and environmental economics from Cornell. Prior to this position, he was a consultant for the World Bank, a post-doctoral fellow at the International Food Policy Research Institute, and Assistant Professor at the Katholieke Universiteit Leuven, Belgium.

SHEOLI PARGAL is a Senior Economist in the Policy Support Division of the World Bank's Corporate Secretariat. She joined the Bank through the Young Professionals program and has worked in Bank operations in Latin America as well as in the Bank's Research Department. Her research interests and publications cover institutional frameworks for utility regulation, empirical firm-level research on the control and regulation of industrial pollution, and explorations of the potential of community pressure as an "informal" regulatory device. She received a PhD in economics from Northwestern University in 1992.

ROBERT D. PUTNAM is Malkin Professor of Public Policy at Harvard University. He is a member of the National Academy of Sciences, a Fellow of the British Academy, and in 2001–2 President of the American Political Science Association. His books include *Bowling Alone: The Collapse and Revival of*

American Community (2000); *Democracies in Flux: The Evolution of Social Capital in Contemporary Society* (2001); *Disaffected Democracies: What's Troubling the Trilateral Countries?* (2000); *Making Democracy Work: Civic Traditions in Modern Italy* (1993); and *Double-Edged Diplomacy: International Bargaining and Domestic Politics* (1993). He has taught at the University of Michigan and served on the staff of the National Security Council. He is currently working on a multi-year project to develop practical strategies for civic renewal in the United States.

NORMAN UPHOFF is Director of the Cornell International Institute for Food, Agriculture, and Development and Professor of Government and International Agriculture at Cornell University. He has served on the Research Advisory Committee of USAID and the South Asia Committee of the Social Science Research Council, and is currently chair of the external advisory committee of the College of Rural Development, China Agricultural University, Beijing, and Honorary Professor at the Post-Graduate School of Agriculture and Rural Development, University of Pretoria, South Africa. His research and advising activities overseas have focused on Ghana, Nepal, Sri Lanka, Indonesia, and Madagascar. He holds a PhD in political science from the University of California, Berkeley.

THIERRY VAN BASTELAER is Director of the Integrated Financial Services Team at the Center for Institutional Reform and the Informal Sector (IRIS) at the University of Maryland and Research Coordinator of the Social Capital Initiative. As a political economist, he has worked in a number of areas, including private sector policy reform, legal and regulatory reform for microfinance, policy priorities for electronic commerce, small enterprise development, and corruption. His research has focused on the political economy of reform, social capital, and microfinance. He has published widely and has traveled extensively in South Asia.

IRENE YACKOVLEV is a graduate student in political science at the Massachusetts Institute of Technology. She specializes in formal theory, statistical methods, and the political economy of development, with special emphasis on Latin America.

Acknowledgments

We would like to express our thanks to all researchers who participated in the Social Capital Initiative. Their successful completion of the studies of the Initiative has produced a unique body of evidence on the importance of social capital for economic and social development. We also thank our colleagues on the Social Capital Team for their many contributions: Susan Assaf, Gracie Ochieng, Gi-Taik Oh, Tine Rossing Feldman, and Casper Sorensen.

We acknowledge gratefully the guidance of the Steering Committee, and the leadership of Ian Johnson, Vice-President, Environmentally and Socially Sustainable Development, and Steen Jorgensen, Director, Social Development Department. We would like to pay tribute to Ismail Serageldin whose vision led to the creation of the Social Capital Initiative. We also honor the memory of Mancur Olson whose ideas and contributions shaped the early phases of the Initiative.

Finally, we thank Chris Harrison and four anonymous referees at Cambridge University Press for many valuable comments and suggestions for the book as a whole and for the individual chapters.

The Social Capital Initiative received generous funding from the Government of Denmark.

CHRISTIAAN GROOTAERT
THIERRY VAN BASTELAER

Foreword

During 1993 several workshops on social capital and economic development were held in Cambridge, Massachusetts, at the American Academy of Art and Sciences with support from the Rockefeller and Carnegie Foundations and at Harvard's Center for International Affairs with support from the World Bank. Many of the definitional and conceptual issues that have subsequently preoccupied this rapidly growing field of study were at the center of the agenda of those initial conferences:

- What does "social capital" mean, and is the analogy to other forms of capital useful?
- How can we distinguish between the "good" and "bad" effects of social capital?
- Through what mechanisms might social capital affect development?
- How might social capital be influenced by, or interact with, public policy?

The pioneering workshops revealed little consensus on any of these issues. In the ensuing decade "social capital" has become one of the hottest concepts in social science globally. Although conceptual battles continue, much progress has been made. Some of the progress has reflected theoretical refinements. For example, experts in the field are now converging toward a "lean and mean" definition of *social capital*, focused on social networks and the associated norms of reciprocity and trust. All sides now understand that (like other forms of capital) social capital can be put to both good and bad purposes.

However, as this volume itself illustrates, most of the progress in this rapidly advancing field has come from a very far-reaching expansion – virtually an explosion – in the range of systematic empirical evidence about the forms, causes, and consequences of social capital.

We have developed much more comprehensive inventories of measures of social capital. We recognize that formal voluntary associations (emphasized out of practical methodological necessity in some early work on social capital) are merely one sub-species in a much more diverse universe of forms of social capital.

We have much richer, fuller, and more systematic evidence of the consequences of social capital. While early work had focused primarily on government
performance, macroeconomic rates of growth, and (in closely related work)
school performance and job placement, we now are beginning to see how
social capital can influence everything from infant mortality rates to solid waste
management to communal violence.

Finally, we have developed a much more capacious sense of the factors that
influence stocks of social capital. While some early work was understood to
imply that stocks of social capital were immutable except on a time-scale of
centuries, we now are beginning to explore ways in which individual behavior
and collective choice can have important effects on social capital over even
relatively short periods.

All these advances in our knowledge are well exemplified in this important
new volume. The volume itself marks a substantial expansion in the evidentiary
basis for continuing conceptual refinement. The richness and diversity of the
empirical case studies reported here are unmatched in the existing literature
on social capital, making the volume an important addition to our stock of
intellectual capital.

April 13, 2001   ROBERT D. PUTNAM

Introduction and overview

Christiaan Grootaert and Thierry van Bastelaer

As economics and other social sciences improved their analytical apparatus throughout the twentieth century, it became increasingly clear that, despite major technical refinements, their tools were not able to account entirely for observed variations in cross-country levels of economic development. Indeed, these tools – in particular as used in neoclassical growth theory – were not fully successful at explaining why countries with similar endowments of natural and physical capital experienced vastly different rates of growth and levels of *per capita* income. At the same time, development practitioners in the field were observing variations in project performance that could not be fully explained by differences in the quality and quantity of the inputs. Equally surprising was the observation that apparently similar communities exhibited very different track records in managing common resources or organizing for the common good.

By the mid-1960s researchers and practitioners had come to recognize that the quality of the labor factor of production was as critical as its quantity in assessing the impact of human input on growth and development (see Becker 1962, Schultz 1963). Although the subsequent search for a scientifically satisfying definition and measure of "human capital" was only partly successful, the concept has since been largely accepted by the academic, practitioner, and policymaking communities.

The addition of this new construct to the social scientists' toolkit only partly filled the conceptual and empirical gap in the understanding of the sources of growth and differences in project success. Beginning in the 1980s, a new focus on the role of personal interactions (at the micro and meso levels) and institutions (at the macro level) decisively advanced efforts to account for differences in cross-country and field project performance. Acceptance of this concept of "social capital" by the scientific community has been hampered by the absence of a body of research that rigorously demonstrates the empirical relevance of social capital in its three dimensions – micro, meso, and macro – across a variety of segments of economic life. Governments and donor organizations, which quickly understood the relevance of social capital in poverty alleviation, have had to rely on a very small body of evidence to justify incorporating

1

social capital in their anti-poverty programs.[1] This book aims to increase this body of evidence by presenting the results of a uniquely large empirical investigation of the role of social capital in economic development and poverty alleviation.

The scope, forms, and channels of social capital

The concept of social capital has developed along three dimensions. They are its *scope* (or unit of observation), its *forms* (or manifestations), and the *channels* through which it affects development.

The scope of social capital

Although there are distinct traces of the concept in earlier writings, the analysis of social capital at the micro level is usually associated with Robert Putnam (1993).[2] In his seminal book on civic associations in Italy, Putnam defines social capital as those features of social organization, such as networks of individuals or households, and the associated norms and values that create externalities for the community as a whole. Putnam originally envisaged these externalities as being only of a positive nature, but he and others have since recognized that negative externalities can result from interpersonal interactions, as demonstrated by certain interests groups – or, in extreme cases, malevolent organizations such as the Mafia in Italy or the Interahamwe in Rwanda. In such situations, social capital benefits members of the association, but not necessarily nonmembers or the community at large.

By expanding the unit of observation and introducing a vertical component to social capital, James Coleman (1990) opened the door to a broader – or "meso" – interpretation of social capital. His definition of social capital as "a variety of different entities [which] all consist of some aspect of social structure, and [which] facilitate certain actions of actors – whether personal or corporate actors – within the structure" (p. 598) implicitly considers relations among groups, rather than individuals. This definition expands the concept to include vertical as well as horizontal associations and behavior within and among other entities, such as firms. Vertical associations are characterized by hierarchical relationships and an unequal power distribution among members. Like micro-level social capital, association-based social capital can create positive or negative externalities.

---

[1] For a brief discussion of several of these studies, see Grootaert (1997), Woolcock and Narayan (2000).

[2] Woolcock (1998) identifies Lyda Judson Hanifan (1920) and Jane Jacobs (1961) as the first proponents of the modern concept of social capital.

The third and most encompassing view of social capital includes the social and political environment that shapes social structure and enables norms to develop. In addition to the largely informal, and often local, horizontal and hierarchical relationships of the first two concepts, this macro view also includes the most formalized institutional relationships and structures, such as the political regime, the rule of law, the court system, and civil and political liberties. This focus on institutions draws on the work of Douglass North (1990) and Mancur Olson (1982), who have argued that such institutions have a critical effect on the rate and pattern of economic development.

There is a strong degree of complementarity between horizontal and hierarchical associations and macro institutions, and their coexistence maximizes the impact of social capital on economic and social outcomes. For example, macro institutions can provide an enabling environment in which local associations can develop and flourish; local associations can sustain regional and national institutions and add a measure of stability to them. A certain degree of substitution is also inherent to the interlocking aspect of the three levels of social capital. For example, a strengthening of the rule of law that results in better-enforced contracts may render local interactions and reliance on reputations and informal ways of resolving conflict less critical to enterprise development. Although the resulting loosening of social ties at the local level would suggest that micro-level social capital has been weakened, this effect must be weighed against the counterbalancing effect at the national level. Accordingly, the empirical results offered in this book assess the impact of social capital in development through its channels at the household, community, and national levels.

The forms of social capital

Whether at the micro, meso, or macro level, social capital exerts its influence on development as a result of the interactions between two distinct types of social capital – structural and cognitive. Structural social capital facilitates information sharing and collective action and decisionmaking through established roles and social networks supplemented by rules, procedures, and precedents. As such, it is a relatively objective and externally observable construct. Cognitive social capital refers to shared norms, values, trust, attitudes, and beliefs, and is therefore a more subjective and intangible concept. Anirudh Krishna and Norman Uphoff elaborate on these two forms of social capital in chapter 3.

The two forms of social capital can be, but are not necessarily, complementary. Cooperation between neighbors can be based on a personal cognitive bond that may not be reflected in a formal structural arrangement. Similarly, the existence of a community association does not necessarily testify to strong personal connections among its members, either because participation in its activities is not voluntary or because its existence has outlasted the external factor that led to its creation. Social interaction can become capital through the persistence of its effects, which can be ensured through both cognitive and structural channels. For example, a sports association embodies the values and goals of the social interaction that initiated it, but the cognitive social capital created by the repeated social interaction can survive the end of the sports season and have lasting effects among, and even beyond, the original members.

The channels of social capital

Any form of capital – material or nonmaterial – represents an asset or a class of assets that produces a stream of benefit. The stream of benefits from social capital – or the channels through which it affects development – includes several related elements, such as information sharing and mutually beneficial collective action and decisionmaking. These benefits, in turn, can lead to higher incomes for households, communities, and nations. This approach is elaborated on in chapter 1 of this book, in which Paul Collier suggests that social interaction generates three types of externalities: information about others' behavior, knowledge about the nonbehavioral environment, and collective action that overcomes the free-rider problem.

Several case studies in this book highlight the role of information sharing. Social capital can lower information uncertainty by spreading knowledge about the state of the world or by making the behavior of others more predictable. The study of agricultural traders in Madagascar by Marcel Fafchamps and Bart Minten in chapter 4 is a good example: better-connected traders have better information on prices and on the credibility of clients, and as a result they enjoy larger sales and gross margins on their transactions.

In addition to acting as forums for information exchange, networks and associations facilitate collective action and decisionmaking by increasing the benefits of compliance with expected behavior or by increasing the costs of noncompliance. The case studies in this book document this channel of operation of social capital in a wide range of geographic and sectoral settings.

Is it capital?

The concept of social capital has met with significant skepticism, particularly from some academicians who have questioned the use of the word *capital* to capture the essence of social interactions and attitudes. Indeed, social capital exhibits a number of characteristics that distinguish it from other forms of capital. First, unlike physical capital, but like human capital, social capital can accumulate as a result of its use. Put differently, social capital is both an input into and an output of collective action. To the extent that social interactions are drawn on to produce a mutually beneficial output, the quantity or quality of these interactions is likely to increase. Second, although every other form of capital has a potential productive impact in a typical Robinson Crusoe economy, social capital doesn't (at least not until Friday emerges from the sea); creating and activating social capital requires at least two people. In other words, social capital has public good characteristics that have direct implications for the optimality of its production level. Like other public goods, it will tend to be underproduced because of incomplete collective internalization of the positive externalities inherent in its production.[3]

Social capital shares several attributes with other forms of capital, however. Foremost, it is not costless to produce, as it requires an investment – at least in terms of time and effort, if not always money – that can be significant. The trusting relationships among the members of a sports club or professional organization often require years of meeting and interacting to develop. As Putnam shows in his analysis of civic associations in Italy, embodied social capital can take generations to build and to become fully effective. And as the many examples of civil conflict around the world testify, trust is more easily destroyed than (re)built. Thus there is a distinct maintenance expense to social capital, usually in the form of time.

The key attribute of capital, however, is that it is an *accumulated stock* from which a stream of benefits flows. The view that social capital is an asset – that is, that it represents genuine capital – means that it is more than just a set of social organizations or social values. On the input side this additional dimension lies in the investment required to create a lasting asset; on the output side it lies in the resulting ability to generate a stream of benefits. The case studies in this book – and the empirical literature elsewhere – document that social capital can directly enhance output and lead to higher productivity of other resources, such as human and physical capital.

A word of caution is in order, however. There could be a temptation to extend the concept of social capital too broadly, turning it into a catch-all category designed to capture any asset that does not fall under the conventional categories of natural, physical, and human capital. A concept that encompasses too much is at risk of explaining nothing. The challenge for research, therefore, is to give meaningful and pragmatic content to the rich notion of social capital in each context and to define and measure suitable indicators.

---

[3] Where negative externalities are present (as in the case of crime syndicates), "too much" social capital will be generated relative to the social optimum (which presumably is zero for this example). We share the reluctance expressed by Uphoff and others to use the term "negative social capital" to describe social interactions and values used to increase inequity or decrease welfare. Using such a term is as nonsensical as describing an illegal gun factory as "negative physical capital." Expressions such as "damaging" or "harmful" social capital are more meaningful, as they imply an assessment of the effects of a certain kind of social capital.

Social capital: from concept to measurement

All of the chapters in part 2 of this book, which examines the impact of social capital on development, view social capital as an asset that can be accumulated and that yields a flow of benefits. The nature and recipients of these benefits can differ. In Krishna and Uphoff's analysis of the watersheds in Rajasthan (chapter 3), the benefit is collective action to manage a common resource effectively. In Fafchamps and Minten's observation of traders in Madagascar (chapter 4), social capital reduces transactions costs and acts as an informal channel for acquiring insurance against liquidity risk. In Jonathan Isham and Satu Kähkönen's study of water projects in Indonesia (chapter 5), social capital increases the ability of villagers to organize to design and manage water supply systems. Sheoli Pargal, Daniel Gilligan and Mainul Huq's study of solid waste removal in urban neighborhoods in Bangladesh (chapter 6) finds a similar organizational benefit. These case studies make it clear that the benefits from the stock of social capital can flow either to communities (villages in Rajasthan and Indonesia, urban neighborhoods in Bangladesh) or to individuals (traders in Madagascar).[4]

Like human capital, social capital is difficult, if not impossible, to measure directly; for empirical purposes the use of proxy indicators is necessary. Years of education and years of work experience have a long tradition as proxies for human capital and have proven their value in numerous empirical studies. No such acquired consensus yet exists for the study of social capital, and the search for the best proxy indicator continues.

This book aims to make a contribution in this critical area. The measurement challenge is to identify a contextually relevant indicator of social capital and to establish an empirical correlation with relevant benefit indicators. As the case studies in this book demonstrate, these social capital indicators differ both geographically and sectorally. Krishna and Uphoff rely primarily on membership in networks as a measure of structural social capital. Fafchamps and Minten use the number and types of relations among traders as their main indicator. Isham and Kähkönen measure the prevalence of social networks and the patterns of social interaction among water users. They construct variables capturing the density of membership in water users' associations, the extent of meeting attendance and participation in decisionmaking in these associations, the extent of social interaction among neighbors, and the number of collective village activities. To try to measure the cognitive dimension of social capital, they construct

---

[4] This issue is related to – but nevertheless distinct from – the question of collective versus individual ownership of social capital. Both positions have been advanced in the literature, with Putnam (1993) perhaps the most noted proponent of the view that social capital is a collective asset. Others, such as Portes (1998), suggest that social capital may well be individually owned, although they acknowledge that the creation of social capital requires interaction between at least two individuals. Thus the process of asset creation should be distinguished from its ultimate ownership.

a neighborhood trust index, Pargal, Gilligan, and Huq also use a combination of indicators for structural and cognitive social capital. Structural social capital is proxied by associational activity; cognitive social capital is proxied by measures of trust and the strength of norms of reciprocity and sharing. The selection of the proxy variables in each of these case studies was inspired by the specific manifestations of social capital or the specific vehicles (associations, social networks) through which social capital is acquired.

The choice of indicators to measure social capital is also guided by the scope of the concept and the breadth of the unit of observation used. The chapters in part 3 of the book demonstrate how measurement proxies of social capital can be tailored to the unit of measurement. At one end of this spectrum, Mary Kay Gugerty and Michael Kremer study the impact of NGO funding on social capital formation in rural women's groups and primary schools in western Kenya (chapter 7). In the case of women's groups, social capital is measured by labor input and participation rates, community interaction, and group solidarity and composition. In the context of schools, social capital is reflected in parental attendance at school meetings, parent contribution of labor and in-kind inputs to school projects, and the level of effort and attendance among teachers.

Anthony Bebbington and Thomas Carroll use a broader unit of measurement in their study of poor people's organizations in the Andes of Bolivia, Ecuador, and Peru (chapter 8). They examine the role of indigenous supracommunal federations in organizing community-based groups around shared economic, political, or cultural interests. To describe the social capital in these federations, they examine five types of variables. Internal relations are captured by measures of neighbor- or kin-based networks and intercommunity networks within the federation. External relations are captured by indicators of the links with higher-tier indigenous organizations, municipal and regional institutions, and support agencies.

At the other end of the spectrum, Nat Colletta and Michelle Cullen (chapter 9) and Robert Bates and Irene Yackovlev (chapter 10) use national-level and cross-country measurement units, such as the ethnic composition of the population and indicators of conflict and governance. These studies examine the role of social capital in leading to, or preventing, ethnic conflict and identify when ethnic competition can lead to political conflict. These studies, which focus on the macro dimension of social capital, complete the progression from within-community local groups (chapter 7) to supracommunity federations (chapter 8) to a country-level (chapter 9), and cross-country perspective (chapter 10).

The structure of the book

The ten studies included in this book were undertaken as part of the World Bank's Social Capital Initiative, with generous support from the Government of Denmark. They reflect the threefold objective of the Initiative, which aimed

Table I.1   *Classification of chapters by scope, forms, and channels of social capital*

Chapter	Topic	Scope	Form	Channel
1	A microeconomic perspective of social capital	Micro/meso	S, C	I, CA
2	Macroeconomic social capital, growth, and income distribution	Macro	S, C	I, CA
3	Watershed management in India	Micro/meso	S, C	CA
4	Agricultural trading in Madagascar	Micro	C	I, CA
5	Access to water in Indonesia	Micro/meso	S, C	CA
6	Solid waste collection in Bangladesh	Micro/meso	S, C	CA
7	Women's groups and primary schools in Kenya	Micro/meso	S, C	CA
8	Farmer federations in the Andes	Meso	S	I, CA
9	Civil conflicts in Rwanda and Cambodia	Meso/macro	S, C	I, CA
10	Ethnic conflicts and politics in Africa	Macro	S, C	I, CA

Note: I = information, CA = collective action, S = structural, C = cognitive.

to assess the impact of social capital on development outcomes, identify cases in which outside assistance facilitated social capital formation, and develop indicators for monitoring social capital. An important aim was to ensure that geographic coverage was broad and a wide range of quantitative and qualitative methods was used.

Most of the studies in this volume take a micro- or meso-level approach to analyzing social capital. The exceptions are Stephen Knack's review of the macro-empirical literature on the effect of social capital on economic growth (chapter 2), Colletta and Cullen's analysis of the role of social capital in preventing or allowing civil conflicts (chapter 9), and Bates and Yackovlev's cross-country study of ethnicity and policy formation (chapter 10).

Most of the studies measure both structural and cognitive forms of social capital. The exceptions are the chapters by Fafchamps and Minten (chapter 4), who focus exclusively on cognitive social capital among Malagasy traders, and by Bebbington and Carroll (chapter 8), who investigate supracommunal federations as a specific manifestation of structural social capital in the Andes.

Although an unambiguous classification of the concept of social capital according to its scope, forms, and channels is somewhat artificial – the reality is one of a continuum over these three dimensions – table I.1 indicates the main orientation of each chapter.

We have grouped the chapters into three parts. Chapters 1 and 2 in part 1 of the book provide an overview of the social capital concept at the micro/meso and macro levels. Part 2 of the book consists of four case studies (chapters 3–6) that document empirically the importance of social capital for key areas of development. Part 3 (chapters 7–10) presents evidence on the accumulation and destruction of social capital in diverse settings and investigates whether these processes can be influenced by policy and donor interventions.

In chapter 1, Paul Collier presents a microeconomic framework for understanding the channels through which social capital operates. He proposes a classification of social capital based on the economically beneficial results from three types of externalities it generates. First, social capital facilitates the transmission of knowledge about the behavior of others, reducing the problem of opportunism through repeat transactions that establish trustworthiness and reputations. Second, it facilitates the transmission of knowledge about technology and markets, reducing market failures in information. The transmission of knowledge can occur by pooling information in the context of networks and clubs or by copying behavior, which requires only one-way interaction. Third, by relying on norms and rules, social capital reduces the problem of free-riding, thereby facilitating collective action. Collier argues that the distributional implications of social capital can be expected to vary according to this typology. The process of copying may be intrinsically equalizing, for example, whereas networks may tend to exclude the poor because they have less knowledge to pool.

Chapter 2 takes these efficiency and distributional considerations to the macro level. Stephen Knack reviews the cross-country evidence of the impact of macro-level social capital variables on economic performance. His review highlights the impact of legal mechanisms for enforcing contracts and protecting personal and property rights as well as informal mechanisms (common values, norms, informal networks, associational memberships) that can complement or substitute for legal mechanisms. Although each individual measure of macro-level social capital suffers from some shortcomings, taken together the body of literature points to a significant and positive effect of social capital on economic growth.

Knack also presents new empirical results, which indicate that the impact of social capital is *progressive*: higher levels of social capital are associated with subsequent improvements in the distribution of income. He hence suggests that the micro-level evidence presented later in this volume is consistent with the results from the macro-level comparative studies.

The four case studies presented in part 2 (chapters 3–6) provide concrete evidence of the impact of social capital on development. In chapter 3, Krishna and Uphoff describe how farmers address the critical problem of managing watersheds, which requires collaboration to be successful. The authors isolate the social factors that account for the degree of success observed in sixty-four villages in the Indian State of Rajasthan. They develop a social capital index that combines an equal number of structural and cognitive factors representative of the social environment in the region (informal networks, established roles, solidarity, mutual trust). They then show that this index, along with political competition and literacy, has a significant and positive association with both watershed management and broader development outcomes. They also find that demographic characteristics and household attributes, such as education, wealth, and social status, are not systematically associated with the level of social capital within households. In contrast, several community attributes associated with participation, such as experience in dealing with community problems, positively affect the social capital index. The largest increments in social capital occur where beliefs in participation are reinforced by the existence of rules that are clear and fairly implemented. This is a good example of the mutually reinforcing role of structural and cognitive social capital.

The case study presented in chapter 4 suggests that cognitive social capital – in the form of trust emanating from personal contacts – can increase incomes of agricultural traders and their families. Fafchamps and Minten show that traders in Madagascar rank relationships higher than input prices, output prices, and access to credit or equipment in terms of their importance for success in business. Better-connected traders enjoy significantly higher sales and gross margins than less well-connected traders, after controlling for physical and human inputs as well as entrepreneurial characteristics. This social capital enables traders to conduct business with one another in a more trusting manner, thereby reducing the costs of securing and providing credit, finding reliable price information, and carrying out quality inspections. Traders who do not develop the appropriate social capital do not expand their businesses. The authors argue that social capital embodied in networks of trust has characteristics similar to other factors of production, such as physical capital and labor. Like these inputs, social capital is accumulated over time and improves economic performance.

In addition to directly enhancing the main source of livelihood of rural farmers or traders – as demonstrated in chapters 3 and 4 – social capital helps the poor in both rural and urban settings by increasing access to goods and services, in particular those that exhibit public good characteristics. Chapters 5 and 6 seek to identify the role played by social capital in the community-based provision of water services and waste collection. Because these activities involve positive externalities, incentives for individual action are limited and the activities are usually underprovided. The studies suggest that social capital can help internalize these externalities and provide incentives for collective action.[5]

---

[5] Although a private good, credit is rarely available to households that cannot provide collateral or have no easily accessible credit records. The vast literature on microfinance suggests that personal relations among borrowers, embodied in joint responsibility lending groups, can offer a powerful substitute for collateral and credit history. See van Bastelaer (1999) for a critical review of the role of social capital in the provision of credit to the poor.

In chapter 5, Isham and Kähkönen examine community-based water services in the Central Java province of Indonesia and analyze why some services have succeeded there while others have failed. The answer depends on the extent to which the demand-responsive approach embedded in community-based projects was actually implemented. In villages with high levels of social capital – in particular villages with active groups and associations – household participation in design is likely to be high and monitoring mechanisms are more likely to be in place. In those villages, households are accustomed to working together, and social ties deter free-riding. This is especially important in the case of piped water systems, whose design and monitoring are more dependent on collective action. In villages selecting piped systems, high social capital led to more favorable impacts at the household level. This suggests that the type of water delivery system most appropriate for a given community should be a function of the level of social capital in the community, as different technologies require different levels of collective action. Also, the type of institution embodying social capital affects the efficiency of the delivery system. In some villages, water users' committees prove to be the best channel through which to coordinate use and maintenance of the water system; in others the mere presence of a water committee does not lead to improved performance, and the key to success lies in other institutional arrangements.

Waste collection services are rarely provided adequately by municipalities in developing countries. In response, some neighborhoods choose to undertake collection themselves. In chapter 6, Pargal, Gilligan, and Huq explore the characteristics of those neighborhoods of Dhaka, Bangladesh, in which the community successfully organized voluntary waste management services. The authors develop measures of trust and norms of reciprocity and sharing among neighborhood residents as proxies for cognitive social capital; they use indicators of associational activity to estimate structural social capital. Their analysis shows that these variables have a large and significant impact on the probability that a neighborhood will organize for refuse collection. Homogeneity of interests and points of view as well as education levels also increase the likelihood of collective action. While the analysis suggests a coproductive role for the government, it does not indicate that policymakers can easily affect the level of social capital. Rather, the authors argue, the study's main policy implication is that the introduction of public–private partnerships or self-help schemes is more likely to be successful in neighborhoods with high levels of social capital. Thus social capital proxies or determinants can be used as predictors of success when targeting neighborhoods for social or public goods interventions.

Part 3 of the book changes the focus of analysis to identifying the circumstances in which social capital accumulates or decreases and determining whether this process can be affected by donor interventions and policy. In chapter 7, Gugerty and Kremer analyze the results of an unusual experiment of randomized aid allocation by an NGO in Kenya. Women's community groups and community primary schools were divided into sets of comparable groups, among which aid was randomly allocated. The advantage of randomization is that it avoids the usual problems of endogeneity and self-selection in assessing program impacts (that is, the fact that groups with more social capital obtain more funding). In the case of women's groups, the authors find that over the study's time horizon of one year (a relatively short time in which to build social capital), funding had little effect on social capital formation, and may have encouraged the participation of less disadvantaged women and the entry of men into group membership and leadership. In the case of primary schools, a centralized top-down program of textbook provision had similar effects to a more participatory program of grants to school committees: neither program substantially affected school committee and parent participation, but both improved teacher attendance and effort. This experiment suggests to the authors that social capital is not easily created: assistance specifically designed to strengthen cooperation and participation appears to have had very limited effects in the short run. The form of assistance may nonetheless influence social capital. Individuals may choose to invest more in institutions receiving outside assistance, but that investment could take the form of either rent seeking or productive investment. Project design may influence that choice. When program inputs are not easily diverted to other uses and when beneficiary institutions have a clear collective rationale, outside assistance may more naturally produce effective programs and social capital.

In chapter 8, Bebbington and Carroll reach more encouraging conclusions about the possibility of creating specific forms of structural social capital. The Andean federations they study are supracommunal organizations linking community-based groups around shared economic, political, or cultural interests. Their importance stems from their ability to transcend the limits of strictly local groups and to forge ties with otherwise distant regional and national institutions. The role and functioning of these organizations can be properly understood only if a clear distinction is made between internal and external relations. Bonding, or integrating, relationships take place within the group and facilitate interaction and collective action within it. Bridging, or linking, relationships strengthen linkages between the group and other organizations. These external relationships are a critical element in stimulating this type of social capital by third parties, such as NGOs or the government. On the basis of detailed case studies and the results of a larger survey, the authors find that the strength and quality of social capital varies considerably among different organizations but that those with strong social capital have contributed to more inclusive forms of municipal governance, helped build local negotiating capacity and linkages with product and input markets, and in some cases fostered cultural revitalization. The study also concludes that federations constitute an important form of social capital that can be induced and reinforced by purposeful forms of external intervention. The requisite strategy involves building on existing or latent social resources, and finding incentives of common interest. The key to success is the simultaneous strengthening of the internal capacity of the federations and the forging of effective links with external actors (government, churches, or NGOs).

The last two chapters in part 3 move the analysis to the macro level by focusing on the role of social capital in preventing or contributing to political conflict and change. In chapter 9, Colletta and Cullen examine how the genocides in Cambodia and Rwanda destroyed social capital and how it is being rebuilt after the end of hostilities. The distinction between *bonding* and *bridging* social capital, introduced in chapter 8, constitutes the framework for the study. This dimension interacts with the horizontal/vertical aspects of social capital. Horizontal social capital is measured by indicators of trust and cross-cutting networks (the existence of informal associations, the extent of intermarriage, and mutual aid); vertical social capital is measured by such factors as state and market penetration at the local level. High levels of social cohesion occur where vertical social capital is strong, as reflected in an open, accountable relationship between the state and individuals and communities, and where bridging social capital predominates. Such a society will be inclusive and law abiding and will have an open media and noncorrupt government. In contrast, weak vertical links combined with strong bonding social capital (dominated by kin-based or ethnic links) will lead to low levels of social cohesion. The society will be marked by exclusion, inequity, and oppression. Colletta and Cullen describe just such a situation in Cambodia and Rwanda, where the result was genocide.

The authors find that in Cambodia, postconflict forms of social capital do not differ markedly from those that existed before hostilities began. Bonding social capital of a familial nature endured during the conflict, providing a basic survival-oriented safety net. In contrast, many associations with professional or developmental objectives, such as rice banks, funeral associations, and water users' groups, withered during wartime but began to increase in number and intensity as the conflict receded.

Analysis of the genocide in Rwanda shows the ambiguous effects that bonding social capital can have in situations of extreme social stress. On the one hand, bonding social capital within families proved critical for survival and led to courageous attempts to save lives or rescue persecuted people. On the other hand, strong and exclusionary social capital emerged within Hutu extremism, resulting in a higher number of killings. The various associations (cooperatives, rotating saving and credit associations, or churches) that existed in Rwanda before the genocide and that could have been a source of bridging social capital proved to be insufficiently inclusive to provide a counterweight to the politics of hate during the conflict. The genocide destroyed these associations; those that have re-emerged since the end of the conflict are very different from those that existed before. For example, the low level of trust remaining after the war negatively affected the re-creation of relationships based on credit or reciprocal gift giving.

In chapter 10, Bates and Yackovlev study the challenges facing states in Sub-Saharan Africa as they try to address the issue of ethnic politics by establishing appropriate governance structures. The challenge they face flows from the double role of ethnicity. On the one hand, ethnicity offers incentives that organize the flow of resources across generations and provides the capital for urban migration and the acquisition of skills for industrial employment. On the other hand, ethnic tensions can lead to costly acts of violence. Using data from Africa, Bates and Yackovlev explore both faces of ethnicity. They find that the presumed link between ethnicity and violence is more complex and less threatening than generally assumed. Specifically, they find that as the size of the largest ethnic group in a country increases, the odds of protest increase initially, but the odds of violence decrease. When the size of that group enters a "danger zone" of 40–50 percent of the population, the opposite pattern occurs. Based on these results, the authors argue that common political prescriptions such as winner-takes-all elections are counterproductive, since they carry with them the risk of permanent exclusion of minority group interests. Similarly, the creation of ethnically homogeneous regional political units can be dangerous if they replicate "danger zones" of ethnic dominance at the local level.

The volume ends with a conclusion that attempts to bring together the main findings from the studies and to distill lessons about measurement issues and policy directions. Based on a brief review of the different empirical tools used by the case studies, the conclusion makes recommendations and raises caveats about the future direction of empirical work on social capital. It is argued that both structural and cognitive concepts of social capital need to be used for successful empirical analysis and that the case studies have identified several useful indicators and measurement instruments that capture both concepts. The case studies clearly demonstrate that both quantitative and qualitative methods of inquiry are useful for understanding how social capital affects development outcomes.

The conclusion also sketches implications for governments and donors eager to invest in – or at least protect – social capital in development projects. Experience suggests that social capital complements other types of capital and can leverage the impact of investments in human, physical, and natural capital. The case studies indicate that governments and donors can have a measurable effect on increasing social capital but that such efforts seem to be successful only in limited and specific circumstances, pertaining mostly to structural social capital and in formal arrangements such as those exemplified by supracommunity organizations. In addition, in view of the potential negative consequences of social capital on welfare and social peace, donors need to fully understand the nature and channels of the target social capital before investing in it. To make such investment successful, development practitioners will want to adapt the concept of social capital to local conditions and manifestations. The case studies presented in this book provide useful lessons on how to start doing so in different settings across the world.

REFERENCES

Becker, G., 1962. "Investment in Human Capital: A Theoretical Analysis." *Journal of Political Economy* 70: 9–49

Coleman, J., 1990. *Foundations of Social Theory.* Cambridge, MA: Harvard University Press

Grootaert, C., 1997. "Social Capital: The Missing Link?" In World Bank, *Expanding the Measure of Wealth: Indicators of Environmentally Sustainable Development,* Washington, DC

Jacobs, J., 1961. *The Life and Death of Great American Cities.* New York: Random House

Judson H. L., 1920. *The Community Center.* Boston: Silver, Burdette

North, D., 1990. *Institutions, Institutional Change, and Economic Performance.* New York: Cambridge University Press

Olson, M., 1982. *The Rise and Decline of Nations: Economic Growth, Stagflation, and Social Rigidities.* New Haven: Yale University Press

Portes, A., 1998. "Social Capital: Its Origins and Applications in Contemporary Sociology." *Annual Review of Sociology* 24: 1–24

Putnam, R., 1993. *Making Democracy Work: Civic Traditions in Modern Italy.* Princeton, NJ: Princeton University Press

Schultz, T. W., 1963. "Investment in Human Capital." *American Economic Review* 51: 1–16

van Bastelaer, T., 1999. "Does Social Capital Facilitate the Poor's Access to Credit? A Review of the Microeconomic Literature." Social Capital Initiative Working Paper 8. World Bank, Social Development Department, Washington, DC

Woolcock, M., 1998. "Social Capital and Economic Development: Toward a Theoretical Synthesis and Policy Framework." *Theory and Society* 27(2): 151–208.

Woolcock, M. and Narayan, D., 2000. "Social Capital: Implications for Development Theory, Research, and Policy." *World Bank Research Observer* 15(2): 225–249

Part 1

Social capital at the micro and macro levels: a conceptual discussion and review

1   Social capital and poverty: a microeconomic perspective

Paul Collier

Social capital is commonly studied from the perspective of sociology or political science. This chapter investigates the concept from a microeconomic perspective. I suggest that from an economic perspective, social capital is "social" because it generates externalities arising from social interaction. It is "capital" only if its effects persist.

The model of social capital that I construct has three building blocks: social interaction, the effects of social interaction, and the mechanisms by which social interaction works. Each of these building blocks is sub-divided based on four types of social interaction: simple one-way relations between an agent and others, networks, clubs, and hierarchical organizations. I distinguish three types of effects, all involving externalities: those relating to knowledge, those relating to opportunistic behavior, and those relating to free-riding. I identify two mechanisms by which social interaction achieves each of these effects. The resulting schema is not the only way of conceptualizing social capital. However, greater simplicity would be achieved at the price of leaving out some aspect of social interaction on which there is empirical evidence of an economic effect. Greater complexity is always possible but would obviously have a price in terms of accessibility.

I begin by defining and classifying types of social capital and then analyzing how social interaction raises output. After extending the analysis by allowing the amount of social interaction to be endogenous, I disaggregate the social capital generated by civil society and that created by government.[1] I then turn to the measurement and empirical application of the analytic concepts. The last three sections of the chapter deal with policy issues, examining the circumstances under which social capital can be damaging, how policy should respond when civil social capital is useful but underprovided, and how social capital affects poverty.

---

[1] The focus of the chapter is on civil social capital. Many people restrict the term "social capital" to civil social capital. As long as clear analytic distinctions are made, the usage of the term is of little consequence.

Defining social capital

To be meaningful, social capital must have features that distinguish it from other forms of capital and social behavior. I first consider what makes social capital social, and then consider what makes it capital.

What is "social" about social capital?

Social capital is "social" because it involves people behaving sociably. There is another potential meaning of more interest to economists: social capital can be social because it arises from a nonmarket interaction of agents that nevertheless has economic effects. The economic effects are not internalized into the decision calculus of each agent by the prices faced in markets. In the language of economists, the effects are "externalities." I argue that social capital is usually characterized by three types of externalities. Two of these are intrinsic and thus defining features of social capital; the third is common, but not essential and thus not a defining feature. First, the initiation of social interaction always involves an externality. Second, the social interaction has an economic effect that is not mediated through the market. Third, this economic effect is usually not the primary purpose of the social interaction but is incidental or even unintended.

The most famous example of social capital is probably Putnam's amateur choirs. Consider how an amateur choir has each of these features. Using Putnam's (1993) classification, an amateur choir is a horizontal association (I use the term "club" for short). Because a choir cannot consist of a single singer, its formation requires surmounting a coordination problem. Thus investment in setting up choirs in a society is subject to an externality in a way that investment in physical capital is not (since physical capital can be purchased by individuals). As a result of this externality, society does not produce enough choirs. Note that this result is obtained before we allow for any externalities of the effects of choirs. If choirs turn out to be unrivalled organizations for the dissemination of information about healthy diets they will be doubly underprovided; if they make such a din that they keep the neighborhood awake, their underprovision may be offset by a countervailing externality.

I now turn to the external effects of the choir. According to Putnam, an amateur choir has economic value because by participating in it people learn to trust one another. The consequent reduction in opportunistic behavior reduces transactions costs. The choir generates an externality: its members learn to trust one another even though this is not the purpose of their interaction. The generation of trust extends beyond the choir's membership. Participants learn to trust not just other choir members but other members of society as well. Putnam's amateur choir thus creates three types of externalities: externalities to people who get to sing in the choir, externalities to choir members who benefit from the mutual trust created among members by repeated social interaction, and externalities conferred on nonmembers by a generalization of the trust created by the choir.

None of these features on its own is sufficient for a sensible definition of social capital. First, consider the externality involved in initiating any social interaction, whether it confers economic benefits or not. Since all social interaction involves externalities, it is always underprovided. However, once we detach the concept of social capital from external economic benefits we encounter problems. Suppose that amateur choirs have no benefit in terms of building trust: they just sing. In this case, choirs are indeed social, but it is hard to conceive of them as capital. We might argue that the amateur singing is unrecorded national income, but such singing does not differ from individuals singing in the shower. Putnam is obviously not arguing for the intrinsic merit of singing but rather for the economic benefits of social interaction.

Second, suppose that social capital covered any social interaction that had economic externalities. The choir is so noisy that people cannot sleep. This does not make the choir (harmful) social capital. However, social capital cannot be defined so widely as to ignore social interaction. Consider what would be implied by defining social capital as the stock of assets in an economy that generates output that would otherwise not be produced by the market. This output that could otherwise not be produced, V, is produced by factors of production, typically labor and capital:

$$V = V(L, K). \tag{1.1}$$

The capital used to produce V might then be the definition of the social capital of the economy. This social capital may take many forms, some of which will be marketable and others not. For example, the "tragedy of the commons" can be overcome by securing individual claims, but the cost is the price of securing the claims. The invention of barbed wire drastically reduced the cost of securing claims to rangeland and transformed the pastoral economy of North America in the nineteenth century. In this sense, barbed wire represented a highly productive form of social capital. However, like most other capital, in equilibrium the value of barbed wire will equal its cost. It will not be underprovided, although like other capital its stock may differ across societies.

It is evident that defining social capital simply in terms of externalities does not generate a concept that is useful in the context of the present literature. Barbed wire is not what people mean by social capital. Moreover, underprovision is intrinsic to the concept of social capital.

These examples suggest that we cannot relax the requirement that social capital involve some externality of social interaction. However, social capital need not be confined to social interactions that have unintended economic effects. Both choirs and tontines are examples of social capital. Putnam chose a form of social interaction in which the economic effects are incidental because in civil society the vast majority of social interactions that have economic effects do so only incidentally. There are three major exceptions: government, the firm, and the household. Government can be regarded as an arrangement for overcoming many of the problems of collective action, most notably through the creation of an agent with the power to tax. Within both the firm and the household, resources are allocated partly by nonmarket processes, permitting externalities to be internalized. However, it is generally sensible to work with a concept of civil social capital that excludes the activities of government, the internal organization of the firm, and the internal organization of the household, partly because we already have a huge corpus of work on them and partly because they are so different from other social interactions. I refer to the social interactions that exclude the organization of government and the internal organization of the firm and the household as "civil society." Civil society thus includes interaction among households, interaction among firms, and interaction between households and firms.

Even with this restriction, which excludes the three main types of organization for internalizing externalities, there remain many instances of social interaction that are designed to generate some externality. However, they face the obvious problem of free-riding. The reason that most of the economic effects achieved by the social interactions of civil society are unintended spin-offs of associations with quite different purposes (such as entertainment or religion) is that these social interactions must be providing something else that makes participation worthwhile in order to overcome the free-rider problem. Few people will bother to found societies for the building of trust; those that do exist will have few members. Such organizations are likely to be boring, and the bulk of the benefits of increased trust will accrue to nonmembers. Members of choirs, in contrast, enjoy participating in them, which is why they are more common. Hence it is not a necessary part of our definition of social capital that the economic benefits are unintended but simply a likely feature of most civil society social interactions.

To summarize, social capital is social if it is a social interaction that generates an externality. It will be underprovided, because the establishment of social interaction involves an externality, because many of the benefits accrue to nonparticipants, and because even the benefits that accrue to participants are likely to be unrecognized.

Why is social capital a form of capital?

For social capital to be capital, its economic effects must persist. If each day the community meets and allocates the commons for the day, there is a flow of social interaction producing a flow of externalities but no meaningful stock. This phenomenon could be called "social labor" rather than "social capital."

Persistence can be intrinsic to the social interaction itself or to the effects of the social interaction. I consider each in turn.

The persistence of social interaction can be defined in terms of either its composition or its structure. For example, a marriage is designed to persist in terms of its composition: the same two people meet day after day. In contrast, a singles bar is a persistent structure of social interaction, although the composition of the interaction is constantly changing. Putnam would confine the concept of social capital to forms of social interaction that have compositional persistence, because he focusses on the benefit of trust building. Because other economic effects of social interaction benefit from at least some compositional rotation, I propose to regard the persistence of social interaction as constituting social capital whether that persistence is compositional or structural. An increase in the stock of social capital occurs if there is a long-term change in the amount of social interaction. An example of structural persistence is location. The villagization program in Tanzania in the 1970s may have permanently increased social interaction by reducing the distance between households, facilitating the formation of social capital.

The most obvious way in which social interaction can have persistent effects even if it is not itself persistent is by inducing investment in physical capital. Suppose that a village community organizes itself collectively to buy a bus or build a school. There is a clear economic benefit as a result of social interaction. How should this be treated? The bus and the school are not social capital – they will already be recorded in the stock of physical capital. Putnam is not arguing that they should be reassigned from the physical capital stock to the social capital stock. However, social interaction has in this case had a clear and persistent economic benefit. The social capital is the value of overcoming the free-rider problem: everyone wants the village to have a bus or a school, but no one wants to help purchase it.

Let us suppose the economic return is higher on the bus or school than on other assets. Collective action enables this higher return to be realized. The value of the collective action – the present value of this incremental stream of benefits – is the social capital of the village community.

More generally,

$$V = V(SI, L, K).   (1.2)$$

The bus uses K; the school uses both L and K. These conventional inputs are not to be counted as social capital. Social capital is the contribution of social interaction (SI) to V. The value of social interaction is the surplus of the return on social interaction once the cost of the other inputs has been met. Whether this stream of returns can be turned into a present value and hence meaningfully valued as social capital depends on whether the stream is intrinsically persistent.

Social interaction can have permanent effects even if it is not itself permanent. Instead of being stored in physical capital, the effects of social interaction can be stored in human capital: if, for example, social interaction leads to an increase in the stock of knowledge, its effect will persist even if the social interaction ceases. Another possibility is for the effects of social interaction to be stored directly in another form of social capital. For example, even if the choir is disbanded, the norm of trust that it has built up may persist. The choir is the social interaction; trust is the output, which is durable.

Classifying social capital

Social capital can be classified by distinguishing the forms of social interaction, the particular type of externality generated, and the mechanisms that induce it to be generated. I briefly set out this classification here, explaining it more fully later in the chapter.

The simplest form of social interaction scarcely deserves the name, since it involves only a one-way relationship. However, since it can have all the other characteristics of social capital it is appropriate to include it. The most primitive form of one-way social interaction is *observation*: one agent watches another and learns from observing (even if the motive for the observation is nosy curiosity rather than economic advancement). One-way interaction can also characterize highly sophisticated forms of social interaction, notably hierarchies: the youth defers to the kin group elder, while the elder ostentatiously ignores the youth.

The other form of social interaction is *reciprocal interaction*, which characterizes both networks and clubs. A network is a spontaneous free association of agents; a club has an organizational form and a defined membership. For example, the grapevine through which a firm picks up gossip on other firms, thereby discovering which are reputable, does not have the capacity to make collective decisions and it lacks a defined network membership; each firm is linked only to some other firms in a chain. Nevertheless, the grapevine generates an externality by reducing opportunism. In contrast, hierarchies and clubs, being organizations, have the capacity for group decisions. This capacity is lacking in observation and networks. The two higher-order forms of social interaction, hierarchies and clubs, generally facilitate lower-order social interaction: a hierarchy facilitates observation, a club facilitates networking. Hierarchies and clubs are equivalent to observation and networking in which the capacity for group decision is added. It is useful to denote these four forms of social interaction as SI_o, SI_n, SI_h, and SI_c.

Three types of externalities are generated by social interaction. Two of these – knowledge about the behavior of other agents and knowledge about the non-behavioral environment – are knowledge externalities, but they are so different that it is worth keeping them distinct. Sharing knowledge about the behavior

Table 1.1   *Classification of forms of social capital*

	Durable social interaction		Durable effects of social interaction	
Externality	One-way interaction	Reciprocal interaction	One-way interaction	Reciprocal interaction
Knowledge	Teaching	Networks	Copying	Pooling
Opportunism	Repeat trade	Networks	Trust	Gossip generating reputation
Free-riding	Hierarchical authority institutions	Clubs	Deference	Norms, rules, coordination

of other agents diminishes the danger of opportunistic behavior and so reduces transactions costs (in table 1.1 this externality is referred to as opportunism). Sharing knowledge about the nonbehavioral world (such as knowledge about prices and technologies) is the very stuff of the new growth economics (in table 1.1 this externality is referred to simply as knowledge). The third externality is the benefits of collective action that overcomes the free-rider problem. For example, collective action might enable groups to impose sanctions against opportunism, establish rules for the management of common pool resources, provide public goods, and reap scale economies through such mechanisms as insurance and rotating savings and credit associations.

Thus social capital is first a sub-set of the processes that generate externalities, namely, those generated by social interaction. It is then the sub-set of social interactions that are durable or the effects of which are durable. The same social interaction might meet both criteria for social capital. That is, it might be a durable form of interaction and have durable effects. Putnam's choirs are durable forms of social interaction that build trust, a durable effect. Even if the choirs were dissolved, the trust would continue.

A good way of testing a definition of social capital is to determine whether trust is on the left-hand or right-hand side of any social capital equation. Fukuyama (1995) treats it as a right-hand-side variable that explains transactions costs; Putnam (1993) and Barr (2000) treat it as a left-hand-side variable that is explained by social interaction. In my classification it is an intermediate variable, produced by social interaction and producing a reduction in transactions costs, but its durability gives it the property of capital. Transactions costs are a function of trust, and trust is a function of social interaction. This is the basic structure when the effects of social interaction are durable: social interaction is a flow that generates stocks of inputs into the production process such as trust, knowledge, and norms.

Generating durable externalities

I now turn to a more detailed analysis of how social interaction raises output. It is useful to distinguish three externalities: learning about the world (V_k), learning about the reliability of other agents (V_a), and enhancing the capacity for coordinated action (V_c). The first two types of externalities correspond to social learning.

Learning about the world

Social interaction can improve the ability to make allocative decisions through two mechanisms, copying and pooling. *Copying* occurs when there is a hierarchy of knowledgeable agents and agents lower down the hierarchy copy those higher up, thereby improving their decisions. When no single best-informed agent exists but different agents instead have different packets of knowledge, pooling enables all agents to improve their decisionmaking. The importance of knowledge sharing through social interaction depends on how much knowledge there is to share and on the availability of substitute mechanisms, such as newspapers and the formal educational system.

Copying can occur through one-way social interaction. Such interaction requires that the agents with the most information be highly observable to those lower down. Copiers also need to ensure that those whom they copy face economic circumstances that are similar to their own. Copying is easy in a village of similar people in which one agent has a knowledge advantage. It is precisely this high incidence of knowledge free-riding in peasant agriculture that inhibits peasant innovation; for this reason, the impetus for research needs to come from outside. There is most to be gained from copying when there is a large difference between the efficiency frontier and the mean producer. We might expect that villages are better for copying than for pooling. Copying is intrinsically subject to ripple effects, because it depends on people being able to see others like themselves, whereas pooling will follow the information highways because it depends upon an interactive exchange of information.

Pooling involves exchanging information that may be put to different uses by different agents, not copying decisions made by others. Pooling requires reciprocal social interaction, which requires meetings and good communications technology, such as telephones. Knowledge pooling is most beneficial when knowledge differs significantly across agents.

Pooling depends on having a diverse network and on the second- and third-hand information from further layers of networks (Barr 2000). Clubs and hierarchical social interactions can contribute to pooling but probably only because each is also a network. The features of clubs and hierarchical social interactions that distinguish them from networks may actually be disadvantageous for information pooling, because clubs tend to admit agents who are similar to one another, thereby reducing diversity relative to open access networks. Hierarchies have problems in reciprocal flows of information, because those lower down the hierarchy have an incentive to mislead those above.

One-way social interaction and reciprocal social interaction require different inputs and face different costs. The costs of copying are the costs of observation; the costs of pooling are the costs of communication. The effects of copying and pooling are intrinsically durable because they add to the stock of knowledge. Memory sustains knowledge even if the flow of copying and pooling ceases. However, since the knowledge frontier keeps advancing, more recent copying is more valuable than less recent copying. The social interactions that give rise to copying and pooling may or may not be durable.

Formally,

$$V_k = V_k(\text{copying}, \text{pooling}). \tag{1.3}$$

$$\text{copying} = c(SI_o, SI_n, SI_c, SI_h). \tag{1.4}$$

$$\text{pooling} = p(SI_n, SI_c). \tag{1.5}$$

Learning about the reliability of other agents

The literature on transactions costs emphasizes the importance of knowledge about whether other agents are reliable. Both one-way and reciprocal social interaction add to information about other agents. The one-way social interaction used by many firms in Africa is repeat transactions (Fafchamps 2000). Repeat transactions enable a promise–trust relationship to build up by providing an incentive for honesty. I describe repeat transactions as a one-way flow of information, because the nature of the transaction may repeatedly place all the risk on one side of the transaction (for example, a purchaser may always receive credit and face no risk exposure with respect to the supplier).

The reciprocal social interaction that provides knowledge about reliability is the network. It does so through gossip that assigns and updates a reputation for each agent known to the network. We can think of reputation as the pooling of information on promise–trust relationships. As Barr (2000) argues, the sort of one-way social interaction suitable for promise–trust relationships is much more restricted than that needed for copying. Similarly, the sort of reciprocal social interaction suitable for reputation is very different from that suitable for learning about the world. Whereas the latter requires diversity, the former requires that agents in the network are sufficiently similar to know the same people (essentially, one another) and to have similar trading relationships.

Formally,

$$V_a = V_a(\text{trust, reputation}). \tag{1.6}$$

$$\text{trust} = t(SI_o, SI_n, SI_c, SI_h). \tag{1.7}$$

$$\text{reputation} = r(SI_n, SI_c). \tag{1.8}$$

How important agent knowledge is depends partly on the substitutes available and partly on the alibis for opportunism. For example, where transport is poor or there is civil war, agents have plausible excuses for default on promises. The benefits of evaluating an agent are thus greater than they are where agents have fewer excuses for defaulting. The substitutes for information through the network are information through the market, notably credit-rating agencies. The value of information depends upon complementary enforcement mechanisms, notably the courts and social sanctions. Social sanctions can be produced by a different type of social capital, namely, collective action.

Posner (1980) argues that traditional social interactions within the village and the kin group provide almost complete information about other agents, so that the problems of asymmetric information are overcome. Collier and Gunning (1999) contrast this traditional environment with the modern African economy, which they argue faces much more severe moral hazard problems.

Enhancing the capacity for collective action

Social interaction produces coordinated action in various ways. It is useful to distinguish between interactions that produce coordination spontaneously and those that produce it as a result of conscious decisions. Spontaneous coordination occurs as a result of norms and related priors. Sociobiology explains how a predisposition toward moral conduct can occur through natural selection. Gambetta (1996) discusses how a norm of distrust persists in Sicily, passed on by one-way social interaction. Tirole (1996) discusses how norms of both trust and distrust can persist through one-way social interaction, because the priors formed about new entrants are influenced by the behavior of the initial stock of agents. Norms of coordination need have no moral content. For example, for everyone to go to a particular location to market or work Monday through Friday may require no centralized decision either to originate or to persist.

Again we have a process in which persistence is achieved through the durability of the effect (the norm, the prior), while development of the norm and the prior is achieved through social interaction (one way and reciprocal). Hence the stock of social capital is represented by the norms and priors, although it is produced by the flow of social interaction:

$$V_c = V_c(\text{norms, priors}) = V_c(SI_n, SI_o, SI_h, SI_c). \tag{1.9}$$

Much other coordinated action requires some process of collective decision, which in turn requires either an accepted hierarchy or a club rather than just a network or one-way social interaction. Although clubs and hierarchical organizations may help form norms and priors, they do so only because they double as networks and forms of one-way social interaction. Their distinctive contribution is establishing rules and making allocative decisions. It is likely that the persistence of these forms of coordination depends on the persistence of the social interaction institutions that generate them. As a club weakens, its social capital probably falls. Formally, this sort of social capital depends on the current rather than the past state of the social interaction that generates it:

$$V_c = V_c(\text{rules, decisions}) = V_c(SI_h, SI_c). \tag{1.10}$$

The capacity for coordinated action raises V in four ways. First, it introduces social sanctions against opportunism, thereby lowering transactions costs. Second, it enables common pool resources to be managed. Third, it enables public goods to be provided. Finally, it enables economies of scale to be reaped in nonmarket activities.

The importance of coordinated action through social interaction depends on the substitutes available. Both governments and firms provide alternative mechanisms for coordination. Furthermore, as transactions costs fall, many activities that depended on nonmarket allocation mechanisms come to depend on market mechanisms (perhaps the most important example is the provision of support in old age). In effect, market institutions gradually solve the problems posed by externalities. In the schema presented here, the need for social capital diminishes as the market becomes capable of performing a wider range of activities. In Africa, for example, where firms and governments are weak and transactions costs high, there is high need for coordination through social interaction.

The building blocks of the analysis are thus the three externalities, the four types of social interaction, and the six mechanisms. The reduced form is:

$$V = V(SI_o, SI_n, SI_h, SI_c) \tag{1.11}$$

Note that opportunism can be tackled by trust, reputation, norms, and social sanction. Imposing social sanctions requires overcoming the free-rider problem of collective action and so requires a different type of social capital from actions that simply facilitate information pooling. Trust is a very slippery concept. I apply it to the very narrow context of the confidence generated by repeat transactions (we can imagine the purchaser making and the seller trusting a promise). I distinguish reputation from this one-on-one relationship as something that circulates in the business community. D learns that A and B both have promise–trust bilateral relations with C. This gives C a reputation with D, who is thereby willing to enter into a deal with C, even though D does not have a promise–trust relationship with C. There can also be a norm of trust

Table 1.2   *Trust regressed on the costs of social interaction*

Variable	Coefficient	t-statistic
Constant	-50.11	-3.27
ELF	-0.14	-1.25
LnTelephones	16.35	6.22
Pop. density	-0.18	3.01
Pop. density sq.	0.00043	2.92

Notes: $n = 23$, adjusted $R^2 = 0.62$, $F = 10.11$. Values for trust range from 6.4 to 66.1. Values for ELF, the level of ethno-linguistic fractionalization, range from 0 to 100. Values for LnTelephones, the natural log of telephones per worker, range from 4.4 to 7.1. Values for Pop. density, the population density as of 1985, range from 2.3 to 412.1.

in society, which itself reduces opportunism. This trust in society is what is measured in the attitudinal surveys.

Endogenizing social capital

Isham, Kaufmann, and Pritchett (1997) show that the return on development projects is higher when civil liberties are greater. The interpretation they give to this finding, with some supporting evidence, is that a free society is more conducive to collective lobbying, which is a type of social capital. This result suggests that it should be possible to endogenize social capital, something that is critical for policy purposes.

It is useful to establish that – and to what extent – social capital is productive, but the key step is to determine how to induce it. Knack and Keefer (1997) find that trust is greater in societies in which incomes are more equal, education levels are higher, and the population is more ethnically homogenous. However, the obvious way of endogenizing social capital is to explain it in terms of the costs of social interaction. The costs of social interaction are the political penalties against its formation and the financial costs of communication.

At a highly aggregate level, we might suppose that the stock of social capital is a function of civil liberties, telephone density, ethno-linguistic fractionalization (ELF), and population density (a proxy for the distance between agents). I illustrate this relation by running a regression in which trust, as measured by comparable attitudinal surveys, is the dependent variable (table 1.2). I exclude civil liberties because of potential endogeneity problems.

The results are encouraging given that the measurement of trust is dependent upon an apparently soft attitudinal question. The telephone network is both highly significant and powerful. However, telephone density is endogenous to social interaction: the more social interaction, the more people need phones. Moreover, the utility of a phone depends not only on its price but also on how many other people have phones. Population density, as a quadratic, is also important: the trust score of the society with a very high population density (412) is 18.5 points higher than that of the society with the least trust-conducive density (202). Very low population density environments are also conducive to trust, perhaps because there is less competition for resources. The effect of ethnic diversity is negative but not quite significant. Overall, these results suggest that it may well be possible empirically to quantify the endogeneity of social capital to the policy environment.

Disaggregating into government and civil social capital

As discussed in the introduction to this book, the broadest definition of social capital includes government. This is consistent with the analysis here, since government allows benefits to be realized that would not be achieved through the market and those benefits will be durable because government is itself durable. Government is a hierarchical nonmarket organization; indeed, in most societies it is the most important such organization (kin groups and families are alternative contenders). Precisely because government is so dominant, however, it is probably best to separate social capital associated with it from that associated with purely civil society.

Government is a system of internally self-enforcing rules, some of which provide for the use of force. Civil society social interaction can be defined as those forms of social interaction that are not directly dependent on this government rule system.

Consider the three externalities identified earlier. Government is an important solution to the problem of free-riding. With the power of coercion, government achieves collective action, most notably through taxation, enabling the delivery of public goods and the management of common pool resources on a far larger scale than would otherwise be possible. Government policies attempt to generate knowledge externalities through education, extension, and training. Government also seeks to reduce opportunism through commercial and criminal law.

Civil society achieves these effects without direct recourse to government powers of coercion (although indirectly, civil institutions depend on government in many ways). Some of these effects are better achieved by civil society than by government. For example, the pooling of business knowledge is a more efficient way for firms to learn than is education by government, which itself often lacks access to pertinent knowledge. Indeed, government-supplied education may be a complement to rather than a substitute for other forms of learning, increasing the returns to information pooling, since education is specialized and provides different people with different knowledge.

Other effects are better achieved by government. Exclusive reliance on networks and clubs for contract enforcement, for example, may limit the scope of transactions.

Civil society social capital and government social capital can thus be both substitutes and complements. Since the efficiency of substitution differs, as the provision of government social capital increases, the composition of civil society social capital will change (to the extent that it is an endogenous response to economic needs). The most important example of this is probably the transition from kin group insurance and intergenerational transfers to government insurance and pensions. More generally, as Barr (2000) suggests, there is probably a transition from morality-supplying civil social capital to information-supplying civil social capital.

In aggregate, the substitution between civil and government social capital can be stated as:

$$V = v(SC_c, SC_g). \tag{1.12}$$

It may be possible to measure these substitutions. The Regional Program on Enterprise Development (RPED) surveys, for example, may provide evidence of links between the quality of the courts (based on international ratings), the proportion of disputes settled through the courts, and the reliance on networks and clubs for contract enforcement.

Measuring civil social capital and its effects at the micro level

In measuring social capital, in principle we should measure each of the four types of social interaction and derive the integral of the two unorganized types (observation and networks). Alternatively, or additionally, we could measure the six mechanisms for raising output through social interaction or the extent to which each of the three types of economic benefit is generated. Micro-level evidence is best suited to measure the mechanisms by which social interaction produces its effects and the stock of each type of social interaction. Macro-level evidence, reviewed in chapter 2, is better suited to measure the effects themselves.

One-way social interaction

Consider first how it might be possible to measure the extent to which one-way social interactions augment knowledge (through copying) and trust. One-way social interaction among rural households can be proxied by the distance between holdings, which in turn can be proxied by population density. Low population density reduces the amount of interaction (by raising its cost, as in Tiffin, Mortimore, and Gichuki 1994). The hypothesis would be that diffusion is faster in areas with higher population density, so that they are, on average, closer to the efficiency frontier.

Copying has been estimated directly. Besley and Case (1993) model it in Indonesian agricultural innovation. Jones (1997) models it in Ethiopian household decisions about primary education. She shows that there are externalities to a household's decision to send a child to school because other households copy its behavior, possibly because they infer that the returns to education are higher than they had originally perceived. Burger, Collier, and Gunning (1996) model copying in Kenyan agriculture, where they find evidence of gender segmentation (women copy women, men copy men). In these studies social interaction is implicit: spatial proximity is the proxy for interaction in the first two studies, gender-based association is implicit in the third.

Narayan and Pritchett (1999) measure the extent of village clubs, finding evidence of a link with agricultural innovation. Recall that a club contains all the social interaction of both a network and one-way social interaction. (Clubs also do much more, but these additional capacities are not important for knowledge diffusion.)

We do not yet have a study that directly measures all the social interaction pertinent for copying and links it to knowledge.

In peasant agriculture the anthropological evidence on one-way social interaction and trust is summarized by Posner (1980). He claims that traditional peasant social structures are efficient responses to the problems of opportunism and free-riding, partly because they create high observability and repeated transactions.

For firms, one-way social interaction can be proxied by the number of repeat transactions. This can be approximated by the turnover of the firm times the proportion of transactions that are repeat transactions. In the face of high opportunism, firms confine themselves to repeat transactions. For example, in Uganda in the early 1980s (when the country was rated the riskiest in the world on the Institutional Investor scale), one of the main banks refrained from taking on any new clients for an entire year: all its business was repeats. The bank was attempting to accumulate social capital in the form of trust because means of contract enforcement by norms and rules, or by non-social capital, were all in radical decline. The RPED surveys pick up a high incidence of repeat transactions among manufacturing firms (Fafchamps 2000). There may be enough data in those surveys to quantify the link from repeat transactions to the reduction in default costs.

Networks and pooling

Networks can be measured, and sometimes have been. Barr (2000) shows how various attributes of the network of the firm affect its productivity and values the network. Barr and Narayan and Pritchett (1999) value at least a component of social capital. Knowledge pooling is the most reasonable interpretation of the mechanism by which the social interactions that they identify generate the observed increase in output. Biggs and Srivastava (1996) report convincing evidence on the use of networks for reputation purposes, but they do not quantify the relationship.

Clubs, hierarchies, and collective action

Clubs, which Putnam (1993) focusses on, are the easiest form of social capital to measure. There is evidence that business clubs have been used to impose social sanctions to lower the cost of transaction enforcement (Greif 1993). In peasant agriculture, Posner (1980) argues that the kin group (sometimes taking the form of a hierarchical organization, sometimes taking the form of a club) is a mechanism for collective action. For example, by having a rule of automatic membership, the kin group avoids the self-selection problems of its central activity, insurance. Widner (1998) attempts to measure rural club-type capital and link it to collective action. Narayan and Pritchett (1996) find that the quality of schools is linked to the stock of club-type social interaction.

Trust is measured directly in international attitudinal surveys, which measure trust as a norm. There is also work showing that trust is associated with growth (La Porta, Lopez-de-Silanes, Schleifer, and Vishny, 1996). However, trust as a norm is an intermediate variable; ideally, it should be treated as a dependent variable of social interaction. This has not yet been done, although there may now be enough measures to proxy social interaction internationally.

Finally, Isham, Kaufmann, and Pritchett (1997) provide indirect evidence that the rate of return on projects is higher in an environment in which civil liberties and public protest exist. Their results suggest that collective action improves public sector performance. Presumably, what is happening is that as the costs of protest are reduced, the amount of protest increases and performance improves.

When is social capital damaging?

One theme in the social capital literature is that not all social capital is good. The control of free-riding by clubs and hierarchies can produce rent-seeking institutions (such as the Mafia) as well as increase the supply of public goods. Copying may spread criminality as well as new agricultural technologies.

There is nothing special here about social capital, for the same is true of all factors of production. Physical capital and labor can also be put to bad uses. However, the fact that income is positive implies that on average factors of production are put to good uses rather than to bad, and there is no reason to expect that the same is not true for social capital. Furthermore, when the effects on income are detrimental, they are not usually attributable to some specific type of social capital (any more than they would be attributable to any specific type of physical capital) but rather to the use to which that capital is put. The same association of manufacturers that pools information and lobbies the government for a more reliable electricity supply also lobbies the government for protection. Where an activity is profitable, resources will be invested. Control of rent seeking should focus on the incentive structure.

There is some rationale to studying the social capital involved in income-reducing activities, because sometimes policy interventions may be more effective in undermining the needed social capital than in changing other aspects of the incentive structure. Tirole (1996) shows how opportunism can be persistent in a group. Because the history of the behavior of each agent is only partially known by other agents, when estimating each agent's honesty, agents make inferences from the behavior of others deemed to be in the same group. If all agents in the group are expected to behave dishonestly, they have little incentive to do otherwise. If a sub-group is provided with a readily distinguishable separate identity, however, a coordinated and publicized change in the incentive regime may tilt the balance of advantage to honesty for the sub-group. Members of the sub-group are no longer automatically contaminated by their association with the larger group. If the sub-group is then gradually expanded by the entry of the rest of the group, each new entrant in effect changes his or her identity. This would be the theory behind the reform of civil services by the creation of ringfenced elite groups with higher pay. Similarly, creation of small professional associations with clear standards of conduct and entry requirements can gradually raise standards in a profession.

Gambetta (1996) analyses how the Mafia works. His thesis is that the Mafia does not depend on mystical norms of distrust, violence, and secrecy embedded deep in the culture of Sicily. Rather, he argues, the core business of the Mafia is the supply of protection and contract enforcement. The Mafia is, paradoxically, a supplier of civil social capital. Unfortunately, in the process it destroys a lot of other social capital, because its method of supply requires both force and a monopoly of information (a byproduct of which is secrecy). Competition within the Mafia for the supply of protection then produces a high level of violence and a high level of contract default leading to distrust. If Gambetta's thesis is correct, the state can undermine the Mafia not only by pursuing its criminal activities but by competing with it to supply less expensive protection and enforcement.

A third example of damaging social capital is the effect of kin groups in the formal sector labor market. In the traditional economy, kin groups are valuable sources of social capital, in effect enforcing bonds of reciprocal obligation that enable the supply of insurance and pension services. In the modern labor market, the same bonds of obligation are used by job seekers and workers to extract patronage from managers. Collier and Garg (1999) show that in Ghana, public sector workers who are members of the locally dominant kin groups earn a 25 percent wage premium, controlling for employee characteristics. (The premium is not found in the private sector, presumably because of the pressures of competition.) Since in the traditional economy kin groups supply valuable economic services, the appropriate policy response is not to weaken the kin groups but rather to adopt rules of hiring and promotion that are transparent, where possible using the same practices of individual wage determination used in the private sector.

A fourth example of dysfunctional social capital is the relation between ethnic diversity and civil war. It is often supposed that ethnic diversity may lead to increased civil strife (Collier 2001). In fact, the actual relation is an inverse-U, with the most ethnically diverse societies safer than ethnically homogenous societies (Collier and Hoeffler 1998). Organization of a rebellion requires a high degree of collective action among those who are disaffected with the government. The coordination of disaffection is aided when there are two ethnic groups in a society rather than one, because if the government is disproportionately identified with one of the ethnic groups, potential rebels can more easily identify as a group distinct from the government. However, as ethnic diversity increases, many ethnic groups make up the disaffected, increasing the difficulties associated with coordinating a response. In effect, for the purposes of rebellion, the (negative) value of social capital peaks when there is a moderate amount of ethnic diversity and falls as diversity increases beyond that level. (In chapter 10, Bates and Yackovlev present very similar results.)

African countries have, on average, a very high degree of ethnic diversity. While this increases the difficulties of collective action, this applies to all activities, good and bad. Since rebellion is intensive in the capacity for collective action, Africa's diversity makes it relatively safe from civil war. That Africa actually has a high incidence of civil war reflects the fact that the major cause of civil war is poverty: Africa has no higher incidence of civil war than expected given its level of poverty (Collier and Hoeffler 2002). A policy implication is that in Africa ethnic cleansing is unlikely to be effective in reducing civil war and is indeed on average more likely to increase it. Ethnic diversity in Africa is such that reductions in diversity are likely to increase the risk of civil war. Conversely, increases in diversity (such as might be produced by federations) are likely to reduce the risk of civil war.

Public action and social capital

By definition, the supply of civil social capital is nonoptimal, since its creation and its effects involve externalities. In the more usual case in which the effects of social capital are beneficial, there will be a problem of undersupply. How should the government respond to this underprovision? There are two types of response. The first is to supply government social capital as a substitute for civil social capital. The second is to promote civil social capital.

The clearest externality in which civil and government social capital are substitutes is in the reduction of opportunism. The weaker civil social capital is, the stronger courts and other substitutes (such as fines) should be. Sometimes the government intervention should be to internalize externalities by creating property rights: land titling and fencing are alternatives to norms for the management of rangeland, secure financial assets are an alternative to intertemporal kinship obligations.

Promotion of civil social capital is largely a matter of lowering its costs. The most obvious cost is the cost of telephones and transport. Relative to other parts of the world, the costs of telephone service are very high in Africa, and the telephone system is almost entirely public and subject to very high implicit taxes. A second cost of civil social capital is political repression. Governments often penalize free association, seeing it as a threat to government control.

Social capital and poverty

I now turn to how social capital affects poverty. There is a reasonable presumption (and evidence) that growth reduces poverty. The poor have a lower opportunity cost of time and a lower stock of financial and physical capital than the rich. Since social interaction is time intensive and social capital can often substitute for private capital, the poor may choose to rely more on social capital than the better-off. Sometimes, however, there are countervailing considerations. To demonstrate these considerations, I return to the three types of externalities.

Consider first the generation of knowledge externalities. The mechanisms are copying and pooling; the key forms of social interaction are one-way informal social interaction and networks. Copying has one obvious feature that tends to make it distributionally progressive: those with the most knowledge will tend to have higher incomes – this is indeed the inducement for others to copy. Copying can thus be expected to be powerfully poverty-reducing. There may, however, be barriers to the poor copying those with higher incomes. Burger, Collier, and Gunning (1996) find that in Kenya, rural households headed by women do not copy households headed by men. Such limits to copying may not indicate the segmentation of information, since if agents are sufficiently different it would be unwise to copy their decisions. However, where the lack of copying corresponds to an obvious segmentation in social interaction, it is reasonable to infer that information is not flowing well. A similar barrier to the flow of information is language or ethnicity. Potentially, these barriers might produce substantial income disparities between social groups that might be socially disruptive. Similarly, the spatial concentration of copying can reinforce spatial differences in incomes.

Pooling has more potential to be regressive, because it is reciprocal. Networks tend to include people with similar quantities of knowledge, because people with a lot of knowledge will find it advantageous to pool with others who also have a lot of knowledge. Treating the quantity of knowledge as a constraint on which networks an agent can join, the incentive to join an information network is greater the greater the amount of information in the network. People with little knowledge to share are thus confined to networking with others with little knowledge, and so have less incentive to join a network than people with large quantities of knowledge. Pooling is therefore regressive in two ways: more knowledgeable people will have larger networks, and they will gain more information from each contact in the network. In effect, pooling introduces an exponent term onto private knowledge. A tendency to exclude the poor is thus built into private incentives to pool knowledge.

The second externality is the reduction in opportunism, which is achieved through repeat transactions and reputation. Repeat transactions have the effect of socially excluding new entrants and so tend to disadvantage the poor. Reputation magnifies the gain from repeat transactions. Repeat transactions produce a promise–trust bilateral relationship; reputation enables those who are in a promise–trust relationship to access many other transactions. Biggs and Srivastava (1996) show how this phenomenon hurts African-owned firms relative to Asian-owned firms in Kenya.

The third effect is collective action, which is achieved through norms and rules. Some of these norms and rules apply across the society. Putnam's choirs, for example, build trust not just among choir members but among the population as a whole. Such social capital is likely to be proportionately more beneficial to the poor, who are less able to invest in substitutes. For example, an agent is protected against crime both by private expenditures on security and by the norms and rules of society. Because the poor are less able to afford private security expenditures, they are more dependent on norms and rules. Generally, the victims of crime are disproportionately drawn from the poor (which probably reflects differences in security expenditures), so that the stronger are norms and rules, the more the poor gain relative to the better-off.

Other norms and rules apply only to the group. Thus the rules of a club may make it an effective agency for increasing the incomes of its members. In general, the poor have more to gain from norms and rules than higher-income groups and so have more incentive to join clubs and authorities. In credit transactions, for example, social sanction and collateral assets are alternative means of reassuring lenders. Wealthy people do not need social sanction, whereas the poor do. Similarly, the economies of scale that collective action facilitates are more likely to be otherwise unreachable by the poor (hence membership in rotating savings and credit associations). Bates and Yackovlev argue in chapter 10 that it is the wealthy who are most tempted to exit from the obligations of kin groups. Finally, if the main cost of membership is time, the poor have an advantage, since they face lower costs. There is, however, an offsetting tendency. The creation of clubs and authorities will generally require some leadership, which is much more likely to come from people in higher-income groups. Members of higher-income groups are respected more than members of lower-income groups and thus face lower costs of initiating collective action; since initiative will tend to produce both leadership and income, the two will be correlated. If the clubs and authorities necessary for the creation of norms and rules are initiated predominantly by people from higher-income groups, they will tend to both address the problems of and attract membership from higher-income groups. This will be especially true where the same social interaction performs the double role of pooling and coordination.

To summarize, the distributional consequences of civil social capital are likely to be mixed. Copying will tend to be progressive, except where barriers of social segmentation are high; pooling, repeat transactions, and reputation will tend to be regressive; and norms and rules will tend to be progressive, except where the concentration of leadership among people from higher-income groups marginalizes the interests and participation of the poor.

What is the implication for a pro-poor public policy? The distributional consequences of different mechanisms suggest that public policy should focus on promoting those mechanisms that are distributionally most progressive and attempt to redress the regressive aspects of the other mechanisms. The mechanism that most warrants public expenditure on distributional grounds is thus probably the promotion of copying. Reduction or elimination of the regressive effects of the other mechanisms may be problematic. The regressive nature of repeat transactions and reputation is probably unavoidable. The most effective public intervention is likely to be to improve the government social capital substitute for opportunism-reducing civil social capital. For example, the creation of more effective courts and the strengthening of penalties for writing bad checks reduce the need for repeat transactions and reputation.

Pooling is unavoidably regressive. Here the best substitute is likely to be to internalize externalities by creating a market in information. For example, where there is a good financial press, the business community is less reliant on network pooling. Policies that lower the cost of producing newspapers will transform information provision into a market activity. Similarly, where credit-rating agencies exist, the value of information obtained through the network is reduced: Africans in Kenya would benefit relative to Asians in Kenya from the introduction of credit-rating agencies. Finally, the formation of clubs and hierarchies requires leadership that is likely to come from higher-income groups. Public action may therefore be useful in supplying the initial leadership that establishes collective action among the poor.

REFERENCES

Alesina, A., Baqir, R., and Easterly, W., 1997. "Public Goods and Ethnic Divisions." *Quarterly Journal of Economics* 94: 1243–1284

Barr, A., 2000. "Social Capital and Technical Information Flows in the Ghanaian Manufacturing Sector." *Oxford Economic Papers* 52(3): 539–559

Besley, T. and Case, A., 1993. "Modelling Technology Adoption in Developing Countries." *American Economic Review* 83(2): 396–402

Biggs, T. and Srivastava, P., 1996. "Structural Aspects of Manufacturing in Sub-Saharan Africa: Findings from a Seven- Country Enterprise Survey." World Bank Discussion Paper 346, Africa Technical Series. World Bank, Washington, DC

Burger, K., Collier, P., and Gunning, J. W., 1996. "Social Learning: An Application to Kenyan Agriculture." Free University, ESI-VU, Amsterdam

Collier, P., 2001. "Ethnic Diversity: An Economic Analysis." *Economic Policy* 32: 129–166

Collier, P. and Garg, A., 1999. "On Kin Groups and Wages in the Ghanaian Labour Market." *Oxford Bulletin of Economics and Statistics* 61(2): 133–151

Collier, P. and Hoeffler, A., 1998. "On Economic Causes of Civil War." *Oxford Economic Papers* 50: 563–573

   2002. 'On the Incidence of Civil War in Africa.' *Journal of Conflict Resolution* 46(1): 13–28

Collier, P. and Gunning, J. W., 1999. "Explaining African Economic Performance." *Journal of Economic Literature* 37: 64–111

Fafchamps, M., 2000. "Ethnicity and Credit in African Manufacturing." *Journal of Development Economics* 61(1): 205–235

Fukuyama, F., 1995. *Trust: The Social Virtues and the Creation of Prosperity.* New York: Free Press

Gambetta, D., 1996. *The Sicilian Mafia: The Business of Private Protection.* Cambridge, MA: Harvard University Press.

Greif, A., 1993. "Contract Enforceability and Economic Institutions in Early Trade: The Maghribi Traders' Coalition." *American Economic Review* 83: 525–548.

Grootaert, C., 1997. "Social Capital: The Missing Link?" In World Bank, *Expanding the Measure of Wealth: Indicators of Environmentally Sustainable Development*, Washington, DC

Isham, J., Kaufmann, D., and Pritchett, L., 1997. "Civil Liberties, Democracy, and the Performance of Government Projects." *World Bank Economic Review* 11(2): 219–242

Jones, P., 1997. "Working It Out in Africa: Empirical Essays on African Wages Productivity and Skill Formation." PhD dissertation, University of Oxford

Knack, S. and Keefer, P., 1997. "Does Social Capital Have an Economic Pay-Off?" *Quarterly Journal of Economics* 112: 1251–1288

La Porta, R., Lopez-de-Silanes, F., Schleifer, A., and Vishny, R.W., 1996. "Trust in Large Organizations." NBER Working Paper 5864. National Bureau of Economic Research, Cambridge, MA

Narayan, D. and Pritchett, L., 1999. "Cents and Sociability: Household Income and Social Capital in Rural Tanzania." *Economic Development and Cultural Change* 47(4): 871–897

Posner, R. A., 1980. "A Theory of Primitive Society, with Special Reference to Law." *Journal of Law and Economics* 23: 1–53

Putnam, R., 1993. *Making Democracy Work: Civic Traditions in Modern Italy.* Princeton, NJ: Princeton University Press

Tiffin, M., Mortimore, M., and Gichuki, F., 1994. *More People, Less Erosion.* Chichester, UK: Wiley

Tirole, J., 1996. "A Theory of Collective Reputation with Application to the Persistence of Corruption." *Review of Economic Studies* 63: 1–22

Widner, J., 1998. "Quantifying Social Capital." *Africa* 68: 1–24

2   Social capital, growth, and poverty: a survey of cross-country evidence

Stephen Knack

This chapter surveys the major contributions to the rapidly growing empirical literature on social capital and economic performance, focusing primarily on cross-country approaches. It first addresses characteristics of governments that fall under broad definitions of the term *social capital*. It then reviews studies of "civil," or nongovernmental, social capital.

Most of this literature explores the determinants of growth in *per capita* income, devoting no attention to distributional effects. This chapter is a preliminary attempt to fill that gap by providing new cross-country evidence on the effects of social capital on poverty and the distribution of income.

This chapter is limited primarily to cross-country studies of social capital and economic performance. It does not attempt to comprehensively review regional-, village-, or individual-level analysis or the expanding literature on social capital's impact on noneconomic outcomes, such as health, education, or crime. Nor does it examine the rapidly growing body of work that explores the determinants of social capital.

Defining social capital

The breadth of the term *social capital* varies from one researcher to another. In keeping with the scope of the World Bank's Social Capital Initiative, the term is defined broadly here to include features of both government and civil society that facilitate collective action for the mutual benefit of a group, where a group may be as small as a household or as large as a country.

In chapter 1, Collier distinguishes between government social capital and civil social capital. Adopting his terminology (if not his precise definitions), I use government social capital to refer to government institutions that influence people's ability to cooperate for mutual benefit. The most commonly analyzed of these institutions in the literature reviewed here include the enforceability of contracts, the rule of law, and the extent of civil liberties permitted by the state. Civil social capital encompasses common values, norms, informal networks, and associational memberships that affect the ability of individuals to work together to achieve common goals.

42

What unifies the two concepts is that both types of social capital help solve the problem of social order by overcoming collective action problems. Social norms and generalized trust are analogous to legally enforced property and contract rights: they reduce uncertainty and transactions costs, enhancing the efficiency of exchange, encouraging specialization, and promoting investment in ideas, human capital, and physical capital.

A theme repeatedly emerging from cross-country empirical studies is that development is largely a function of incentives faced by wealth-maximizing individuals. In some countries, the structure of incentives steers people primarily toward producing new wealth; in other countries it is easier to obtain wealth by diverting it from others. Social capital determines the relative payoffs associated with production ("making") and predation ("taking"). Where social and legal mechanisms for the efficient resolution of prisoners' dilemma and principal–agent games are weak or absent, the private returns to predation increase while the private returns to production fall.

Cooperation at what level, or which groups benefit?

In studying the relation between social capital and economic well-being, the choice of *units of analysis* is crucial. Fundamentally, the social capital question concerns the benefits and costs of cooperation. Within-group collective action often imposes costs on nonmembers. Thus scholars have gradually recognized the potential importance of negative as well as positive effects of social capital. Cooperation within a group will often have multiple effects. Welfare within the group generally will be enhanced, in the sense that the collective gains net of costs to group members are positive – this is the standard hypothesis concerning social capital's impact. However, the welfare of nonmembers may also be affected – and not always for the better.

When the goal of one group is to reduce the well-being of members of some other group, we can hypothesize that successful collective action in the first group will entail welfare losses for members of the second group (gains by the Nazi Party in Germany in the 1930s, for example, came at the expense of European Jews). More often, a group may not directly value a reduction in the welfare of nonmembers, but it may nonetheless be willing to impose costs on nonmembers in pursuit of its own goals. Sugar producers in the United States, for example, are not interested in reducing the welfare of sugar consumers, but they are willing to lobby for import quotas that increase their profits at consumers' expense. The implication is that in general we can predict only that cooperation by members of a group will improve the welfare of a group's own members; the effect on other groups or on the village, ethnic group, or country as a whole is ambiguous. If, for example, the members of each household in a village cooperate in the interests of the household, the village as a whole may be worse off than a neighboring village in which individuals are less willing or able to impose costs on people outside the household.

To see how cooperation can reduce aggregate social welfare, suppose that social ties within a village raise the rate of return to a public project, making all village residents better off. If these same social ties are responsible for the village's success in lobbying for outside funds to finance the project, a second village with weaker social ties that loses out in the competition for funds is made worse off. If the funds would have been more productively spent in the second village (because it was poorer, for example), the first village's high level of social capital can actually reduce social welfare at the aggregate level.

Strong ethnic ties can improve the welfare of members of an ethnic group, but they often do so at the expense of other groups.[1] Depending on how encompassing a group is, the costs it is *willing* to impose on nonmembers in the pursuit of its members' interests may be a large multiple of the group's gains from collective action (Olson 1982). A group's *ability* to impose costs on nonmembers is likely to vary with a society's governance structures. Where the populace has secure civil liberties, and property rights and the rule of law are strong, fewer social resources are up for political grabs and groups have less opportunity to benefit from zero-sum or negative-sum competition against other groups (Rodrik 1999; Lane and Tornell 1996).

Identifying Olson (1982) and Putnam (1993) – with some exaggeration – as either end of a continuum of views about the effects of groups, the Olson perspective suggests that social capital within one group generally has negative effects on other groups and on the country as a whole. The Putnam perspective holds that social capital by one group has positive effects on all groups, because cooperation among members of a group creates habits and attitudes toward serving the greater good that carry over to members' interactions with nonmembers. Which effect dominates is an empirical question that is likely to depend on both cultural and institutional factors (religions, for example, may differ in their emphasis on the desirability of behaving altruistically toward strangers.) Narayan and Pritchett (1999), Grootaert (1999), and others have begun testing hypotheses about the effect of household- and village-level social capital. Varshney (1998) and others are investigating the impact of interethnic and intraethnic ties on the frequency and intensity of ethnic conflict. This chapter reviews evidence from studies in which country-level indicators of well-being are the dependent variables. Most of this evidence bears specifically on the hypothesis that an increase in cooperation within a country as a whole improves national well-being. Most of the evidence provides strong support for the

---

[1] Intraethnic collective action against another ethnic group (such as the violence by the Bosnian Serbs against the Bosnian Muslims) generally strengthens ties within the victimized group, making the net impact of collective action on the welfare of members of the first group ambiguous.

hypothesis that social capital as measured at the national level is associated with improved economic welfare of societies, as measured by growth, investment, and poverty indicators.

Social capital, investment, and growth: a survey of the empirical literature

Indicators of governmental social capital are almost always measured at the national level. Values for the rule of law, for example, are assigned to countries, not to constituent parts of countries, such as provinces, villages, or households. In part, this is a question of data availability; one could conceivably attempt to measure differences in local laws or differences in the ways in which local governments enforce national laws regarding, say, the enforceability of contracts. However, within-country variation in government social capital is likely to be very small relative to cross-country variation, particularly since governments are highly centralized in most of the world.[2]

Measuring civil social capital is more problematic. While the judicial system in most countries is likely to enforce contracts more or less equally well across all regions, cooperative norms, interpersonal trust, and the social ties that generate them are more likely to vary by locality. Because they will vary more than government social capital, they are more likely to play a role in explaining regional differences in economic performance within countries. Measuring regional differences within countries – through surveys or other means – is costly, however, and is not likely to be undertaken in a comparable fashion for a large sample of countries any time soon.

Cooperative norms, trust, and social ties are usually measured by conducting representative surveys of individuals. Important issues arise in aggregating survey-based measures to assign values to countries. A country populated by individuals with strong intrafamily or intraethnic trust or ties, for example, is not what Fukuyama (1995) and others mean by a "high-trust society."

Conceptually, the type of trust that should be unambiguously beneficial to a country's economic performance is trust between strangers – or, more precisely, between two randomly matched residents of a country. Particularly in large and mobile societies, where personal knowledge and reputation effects are limited, a sizable proportion of potentially mutually beneficial transactions will involve parties with no prior personal ties. In societies in which strangers can trust one another to act in the collective interest, not only can people leave their bicycles unattended and unlocked on the street, they can contract with a wide range of parties without drafting lengthy written agreements and run

---

[2] Of course, legal systems often protect the rights of some citizens more effectively than others, based on gender or ethnicity, for example.

businesses without devoting a lot of time to monitoring employees, partners, and suppliers. They may also be more likely than members of low-trust societies to support efficient economic policies, whether or not they increase one's personal income.

It is something like trust in strangers – or the propensity to cooperate in large-numbers prisoners' dilemma settings (whether such trust is created by social or government mechanisms or some combination of the two) – that we must measure to test the hypothesis that social capital at the national level is associated with improved national economic welfare. Within-family trust, intraethnic trust, or other forms of particularized or specific trust may be corrosive to generalized trust (trust in strangers). Strong intraethnic trust in an ethnically heterogeneous society may restrict the scope for transacting and lead to segmented markets, reducing gains from specialization and perhaps from economies of scale (Greif 1994). Because of the importance of these and other measurement issues, the question of measurement is a recurring theme in the empirical literature on social capital and economic performance.

Government social capital

Researchers measure government social capital in a variety of ways. Some look at civil liberties and political freedom. Others measure the frequency of political violence or study subjective ratings of political risk. This section examines these and other ways of measuring government social capital.

Civil liberties and political freedoms.   Kormendi and Meguire (1985) appear to have been the first to explore the relation between government social capital and economic performance using a cross-country statistical approach. Their study is based on *International Financial Statistics* data on the average annual growth in *per capita* income and the investment to GDP ratio for a sample of forty-seven countries between 1950 and 1977. In regressions with growth and investment as the dependent variables, they test hypotheses on income convergence, population growth, government size, trade openness, and inflation and examine the relation between economic performance and "civil liberties." "Civil liberties" is an index constructed by Raymond Gastil (1990) for Freedom House (see the appendix to this chapter, p. 73). Values range from 1 to 7, with lower scores indicating greater civil liberties. Gastil's criteria are primarily political and social rather than economic. Kormendi and Meguire were interested in also testing the impact of "economic rights, such as freedom from expropriation or the enforceability of property rights and private contracts" (p. 154). They acknowledge that the civil liberties index was not intended to measure economic rights but argue that the two are likely correlated.

Kormendi and Meguire dichotomize the Gastil index, classifying countries with scores of 1 and 2 as high civil liberty countries. This dummy variable has a positive and marginally significant impact in their growth regression. Growth rates in the high civil liberties countries average about 1 percentage point higher than in other countries, controlling for income convergence, population growth, government size, trade openness, and inflation. They find evidence that the association between civil liberties and growth is attributable almost entirely to the effect of civil liberties on investment rates: when the investment to GDP ratio is added to the growth regression, civil liberties no longer has any independent effect. In a regression with the investment to GDP ratio as the dependent variable, civil liberties is by far the most powerful explanatory factor. High civil liberties is associated with a 5 percentage point increase in investment's share of GDP (which averages about 20 percent).

The Kormendi and Meguire study is limited to forty-seven countries for which data were available beginning in 1950. Grier and Tullock (1989) explore the relation between a similar set of independent variables and growth with a much larger sample (113 countries). Each observation in their analysis covers a five-year period, so that six observations are available for a country for which data are available from 1950 to 1980 and four observations are available for countries for which data are available only since 1960.

Using an F-test, Grier and Tullock reject the null hypothesis that it is appropriate to pool observations from different continents and they run separate regressions for OECD, Latin American, African, and Asian countries. They construct a dichotomous variable from Gastil's civil liberties indicator in which countries in the two most repressive categories are distinguished from all others, creating what they call "a proxy for the political infrastructure." They find that political repression is associated with a significant reduction in annual growth rates of about 1.5 percentage points in Latin America and Africa but that repression has no effect in Asia (no OECD country was classified as repressive).

The research design employed by Grier and Tullock treats every observation within each continent grouping as independent. It includes no country dummies, or tests or corrections for autocorrelation.[3] Other studies using pooled time-series cross-country data routinely find regression residuals to be strongly correlated within countries. It is doubtful that civil liberties would remain statistically significant using a more appropriate research design, particularly for the Latin America sample (where the t-statistic for civil liberties is only 1.88).

Scully (1988) uses the civil liberties indicator and other indicators provided by Gastil as measures of the "institutional framework." He views Gastil's

---

[3] Because all observations for a country are assigned the same value (from the late 1970s) for the civil liberties index, including country dummies would make it impossible to estimate the impact of civil liberties.

criterion of the "independence of the judiciary" as a proxy for the rule of law. A separate Gastil indicator assigns countries to one of five categories based on their level of "economic freedom," which Scully takes as a proxy for the security of private property rights. A third Gastil variable rates political freedoms on a seven-point scale.

Scully constructs a series of dummy variables from these three measures and tests their effects on income growth over the 1960–80 period for a sample of 115 countries, controlling for changes in the capital–labor ratio. He finds that income growth in countries with greater civil liberties (or political or economic freedom) is about twice that in countries with less freedom. Because civil, political, and economic freedoms are highly correlated, including all three sets of measures in one regression increases these growth differences only slightly: countries that rate high on all three indicators enjoy growth rates three times that of countries that receive low ratings on all three dimensions (2.73 percent versus 0.91 percent annual growth).

Causality is a serious and largely neglected problem in all of these studies. Bilson (1982) shows that civil liberties are strongly associated with *per capita* income (and positively but not significantly related to recent income growth), but his interpretation is that economic performance determines freedoms rather than the other way around. The Gastil ratings were constructed beginning in 1973. Scully uses the average values for the 1973–80 period in his study of 1960–80 growth. Kormendi and Meguire (1985) analyze growth over the 1950–77 period, Grier and Tullock (1989) over the 1950–80 period, each apparently using Gastil's ratings for 1978 or 1979. A potentially serious limitation of this work is that the effect precedes the cause: the key independent variables of the three studies represent conditions prevailing in the late 1970s, while the dependent variables measure economic performance over extended periods ending in 1980 or before. Using Gastil indexes averaged over the years 1974–89 in tests measuring investment and growth over that same period, Knack and Keefer (1995) obtain much weaker effects for civil and political freedoms.

Because of the large number and wide variety of criteria used in Gastil's civil liberties index, it is a questionable proxy for narrower concepts, such as the rule of law, contract enforceability, or security of property rights. While certain criteria incorporated in the index are highly relevant (rights to property, independence of the judiciary, freedom from government corruption), others (the presence of free religious institutions, free trade unions, and freedom from "gross socioeconomic inequality" and "gross government indifference") are not.

Studies conducted in the 1990s on the relation between type of regime and growth interpret Gastil's political freedoms and civil liberties indexes as measures of democracy. Barro (1996) and Helliwell (1994) find that the Gastil indexes are positively related to growth only if variables such as educational attainment and investment rates are omitted as explanatory variables. They conclude that any beneficial effect of democracy on growth may operate through these factor accumulation channels. Barro finds that a curvilinear relation between growth and the Gastil index fits the data better than a linear specification, with the fastest rates of growth exhibited by countries that are only partly free.[4] Barro, Helliwell, and Burkhart and Lewis-Beck (1994) all conclude that the positive relation between income levels and democracy is largely attributable to the effect of income on democracy rather than vice versa. These results are consistent with Lipset's (1959) interpretation of the correlation between income and democracy. (See Przeworski and Limongi 1993 for a critical review of the extensive and inconclusive literature on the relation between regime type and economic performance.)

Isham, Kaufman, and Pritchett (1997) analyze the impact of the "quality of governance" on the performance of hundreds of projects financed by the World Bank in developing countries between 1974 and 1993. They find that rates of return are higher in countries with greater civil liberties, as measured by the Gastil index and other indicators of civil liberties. Controlling for national policy variables, capital–labor ratios, project complexity, and regional dummies, each one-point improvement in the seven-point Gastil scale is associated with improvement of more than 1 percentage point in the rate of return (which averaged about 16 percent over all projects). Gastil's political freedoms index and other indicators of democracy are unrelated to project performance. Civil unrest (frequencies of riots, strikes, and protest demonstrations) is positively associated with performance – in the authors' view because civil unrest is indicative of environments in which mechanisms for expression of discontent with government performance are available and effective. The authors interpret their findings as evidence for the view that increasing public voice and accountability improves government performance.[5]

Frequency of political violence. Barro's (1991) classic empirical study on the determinants of growth tests indicators of political instability, which he interprets as adverse influences on property rights. These instability variables have important advantages over the Gastil indexes as proxies for property rights and other dimensions of the quality of governance. First, they are objective measures, consisting of the number of incidents of various types of political violence. Second, they are constructed for the entire period covered by the Summers–Heston (1991) income data set, not just for recent years, allowing for a fuller empirical treatment of causality issues.

---

[4] Studies of the determinants of deaths from political violence found a similar curvilinear relation, with deaths highest among countries with intermediate Gastil indexes. See, for example, Muller and Weede (1990).

[5] By this interpretation of the Gastil civil liberties indicator, it could represent civil rather than government social capital.

The two violence measures Barro tests are the average annual number of revolutions (or coups) and of political assassinations, using data from Banks (1993). He finds that each of these variables is significantly and negatively related to growth rates and to private investment's share of GDP between 1960 and 1985.[6] Barro reports that once these variables are included, Gastil's indexes (which he tested in earlier unpublished drafts) are no longer significant.

Endogeneity is a potentially serious problem with violence indicators: Barro acknowledges that the relation between violence and growth might reflect the positive effect of growth on political stability rather than the other way around. Investigations of this issue using time-series data provide mixed results. Alesina, Ozler, Roubini, and Swagel (1996) show that political instability and violence are jointly determined: coups lead to worse economic performance, but slow growth increases the likelihood of coups. Londregan and Poole (1990, 1992) also conclude that coups are caused by low growth, but they find that more frequent coups do not reduce growth rates. Using income inequality as an instrument for political instability and the price of investment goods as an instrument for investment, Alesina and Perotti (1996) find that instability lowers investment's share of GDP but that investment rates do not significantly affect political violence.

As with the Gastil measures, it is questionable how well the frequency of political violence captures variations in the underlying country characteristics of interest, such as the security of property rights and the rule of law. Coups, for example, often entail only changes in the identity of the kleptocratic chief executive, with few or no implications for the property rights of anyone outside the ruler's and ex-ruler's circles of key supporters. Conversely, some stable (long-lasting) governments have been known to legislate economic policies erratically through numerous and unpredictable executive decrees.

Subjective ratings of political risk. The deficiencies of violence counts and the Gastil indexes, coupled with the increasing prominence of new institutional explanations for underdevelopment (North 1990), created a demand for more direct measures of the quality of governance. In independent but simultaneous research, Mauro (1995) and Knack and Keefer (1995) turned to subjective ratings marketed to international investors by firms specializing in political risk evaluation. These ratings services include the International Country Risk Guide (ICRG), Business Environmental Risk Intelligence (BERI), and Business International (BI). (For a description of these services, see the appendix to this chapter.)

The ICRG rates the institutional environments of countries on many dimensions. Knack and Keefer (1995) construct an index from the five dimensions

---

[6] Indexes of political instability constructed from several violence indicators have been linked to growth (Gupta 1990) and to investment (Alesina and Perotti 1996).

they view as being of greatest relevance to the security of private property and the enforceability of contracts: corruption in government, the rule of law, risk of expropriation, repudiation of contracts by government, and quality of the bureaucracy. They construct a similar index from the following BERI variables: contract enforceability, nationalization risk, bureaucratic delays, and infrastructure quality.

Adding the ICRG index to a Barro-type growth regression, Knack and Keefer find that a one standard deviation increase in the index (about 12 points on a 50-point scale) increases average growth by 1.2 percentage points. Substituting the BERI index for the ICRG index produces a similar association with growth. These indexes (particularly the BERI index) prove to have strong explanatory power for private investment as well. Moreover, in growth or investment regressions that include the violence counts or Gastil indexes as well as the Knack and Keefer property rights indexes, only the Knack and Keefer indexes prove statistically significant. Because of their much better cross-country coverage relative to the BERI or BI indicators, the ICRG indicators have become widely used in the cross-country empirical literature on economic performance.

In related work, Knack (1996) and Keefer and Knack (1997) show that the rate at which poor countries converge to the richest countries' income levels varies with the quality of governance, as proxied by the ICRG and BERI indexes. Keefer and Knack test interactions between initial *per capita* income and institutional quality. They find that the ability of poor countries to take advantage of the rapid growth opportunities afforded by relative backwardness is a function of property rights and contract enforcement. That is, as predicted by convergence theories, the coefficient on initial income is negative and significant only when the values of ICRG and BERI are sufficiently high.

Mauro (1995) tests three variables constructed from BI indicators: corruption; a bureaucratic efficiency index constructed from corruption, bureaucracy and red tape, and the quality of the legal system and judiciary; and a political stability index constructed from six indicators representing the likelihood of changes in government, terrorist acts, labor unrest, other domestic conflict, or conflict with neighboring countries. These indexes are positively and significantly related to growth and investment in Barro-type regressions. Although the indexes are strongly correlated with one another, the political stability and bureaucratic efficiency indexes are each marginally significant when both are entered in the same regression. When investment is included in the growth regression, the BI coefficients decline somewhat, suggesting that part but not all of the growth effects of political stability and bureaucratic efficiency are attributable to efficiency and innovation channels. This pattern also emerges when the ICRG index is used. Using the BERI index, the institutional environment appears to influence growth primarily through investment rates.

Mauro's BI indicators are averages for the 1980–3 period, while investment and growth are measured over the 1960–85 period, raising the issue of causality. Economic success may improve bureaucratic efficiency and political stability. Moreover, possible biases in coding that are correlated with economic performance are more problematic with these indicators than with the Gastil indexes or political violence counts. An expert might surmise, for example, that corruption must not be too severe in a particular country because it attracts foreign investment or is growing rapidly.

Mauro deals with the reverse causation issue by using an index of ethnic fractionalization and a set of colonial heritage dummies as exogenous instruments for the BI indicators. For the most part, his two-stage least-squares estimates of the association between the BI indicators and economic performance are positive and significant. Although he reports that overidentification tests confirm the validity of the instruments, the use of ethnic fractionalization is questionable because of evidence that it influences growth independently of its effects on bureaucratic efficiency and political stability. Using a variety of ethnicity indicators, Easterly and Levine (1997) show that ethnic heterogeneity is associated with a broad range of inefficient economic policy choices. In the ICRG sample (which is larger than the BI sample), ethnic fractionalization remains significantly related to growth even after controlling for institutional quality.

Knack and Keefer (1995) also acknowledge the potential for reverse causality from economic performance to (real or perceived) institutional quality. Their response is to measure institutions as far back in time as possible and to measure their dependent variables farther forward in time. They focus primarily on growth and investment rates over the 1974–89 period (using data from Levine and Renelt 1992), using the first available observation for each country for their institutional indicators (1982 for ICRG and 1972 for BERI for most countries).

Chong and Calderon (2000) employ a more rigorous approach to causality, using BERI data (the longer time series for BERI makes it preferable to BI or ICRG data for conducting causality tests exploiting time-series variation in the data). They obtain strong evidence for two-way causality: growth increases the BERI measures and higher BERI values increase growth rates.

A potentially important drawback of the political risk indicators used by Mauro and Knack and Keefer is that these measures likely better represent conditions facing foreign investors (the paying clients of risk assessment firms) than conditions confronting domestic investors. Given the crucial importance of foreign technology and capital for successful catch-up growth in poor countries, conditions facing would-be foreign investors are by no means irrelevant. Unless those conditions are perfectly correlated across countries with conditions facing domestic investors, however, subjective political risk evaluations represent only partial indicators.

Surveys of entrepreneurs. A very different approach to measuring property rights, contract enforceability, and bureaucratic integrity and efficiency is to survey foreign and domestic entrepreneurs operating in developing countries. This approach has been implemented most impressively by Borner, Brunetti, and Weder (1995) and in the private sector survey conducted for the 1997 World Development Report (see World Bank 1997, Brunetti, Kisunko, and Weder 1997).

Brunetti, Kisunko, and Weder (1997) construct a country-level credibility of rules index from the survey data, designed to characterize "unclear property rights, constant policy surprises and policy reversals, uncertain contract enforcement, and high corruption." The index is based on country means of survey responses to ten items measuring expectations of the frequency of government changes and policy surprises, protection from criminal actions, unpredictability of the judiciary, and the frequency of "irregular additional payments" necessary to operate a business. Each item has six possible responses. The authors treat the responses as interval-scale variables and compute averages for each question by country. They then average over all ten items, creating an index ranging from a best possible value of 1 to a worst possible value of 6.

For their forty-one-country sample, Brunetti, Kisunko, and Weder find their credibility of rules index to be significantly related to growth and investment during 1983–94, after controlling for initial income and educational attainment. Although they did not report the quantitative impact of their index, their regression coefficients imply extremely large effects: each one level improvement in the 1–6 credibility scale is associated with a 3.7 percentage point increase in investment's share of GDP and a 1.5 percentage point increase in annual average income growth.

Because original surveys can be guided by theory, they produce even more direct and relevant measures of the quality of governance than those provided by political risk evaluators such as the ICRG, BERI, and BI ratings. The questions can also be asked of both domestic and foreign investors. These survey indicators have several major limitations, however. First, the studies have been conducted only in a relatively small number of countries – far smaller than the number covered by ICRG, for example. Second, studies employing these data have not subjected them to adequate reliability testing. Confidence in the accuracy of country estimates produced by the data would be increased if the researchers were able to report that the average variance of responses within countries for any given survey item was small relative to the variance across countries. Third, the data are measured end-of-period, as the surveys used in Brunetti, Kisunko, and Weder (1997) were conducted in 1996. Questions about whether conditions were better, worse, or the same ten years ago are included in the questionnaire, but for many obvious reasons such recall measures are a very crude means of tackling causality issues.

Finally, these surveys may not measure current conditions more accurately than political risk indicators such as ICRG. The sample is drawn from a censored population, which may have a more optimistic view of the investor climate than the true population of interest (namely, all potential investors). The entrepreneurs surveyed in each country include only those who chose to invest; would-be investors scared away by poor governance or other factors are not represented in the sample. The degree of censoring will increase with poor governance, as a larger proportion of potential investors will decline to invest. Cross-country variation would also be reduced if only the most dissatisfied entrepreneurs were sufficiently motivated to respond to the survey (which had a response rate of about 30 percent). One likely effect of this problem is to reduce the cross-country variation in these indicators, making it more difficult, other things equal, to reject null hypotheses. Given these problems – especially the small number of countries surveyed and the small number of entrepreneurs sampled in each country – it is all the more remarkable that Brunetti, Kisunko, and Weder find significant links to investment and growth.

"Contract-intensive money".   In response to the perceived shortcomings of subjective measures, Clague, Keefer, Knack, and Olson (1999) introduced an objective measure called "contract-intensive money," equal to the proportion of M2 not constituted by currency outside banks. Data coverage for contract-intensive money over time and across countries, calculated from standard monetary indicators, is far superior to that of any of the subjective measures. Moreover, because it is objectively measured, contract-intensive money is not subject to contamination by knowledge of recent economic performance by country experts or surveyed entrepreneurs, removing an important potential source of endogeneity.

The logic behind using contract-intensive money is that for various reasons individuals will hold a larger proportion of their financial assets in the form of currency in environments in which third-party enforcement of contracts is unreliable. Bank deposits are less safe in environments in which one cannot rely on contracts. Not only are banks more likely to default on their obligations, but governments unable or unwilling to enforce contracts between private parties are unlikely to respect private property themselves (by refraining from expropriating bank deposits, for example). The contract-intensive money ratio is the outcome of choices by wealth-maximizing firms and individuals: it will increase in countries in which governments better enforce and respect contracts and private property rights. Where property and contract rights are less clearly defined and secure, borrowers will find it more difficult to offer collateral as security against default, inhibiting the development of financial institutions and sophisticated financial instruments and limiting the availability of money other than currency.

Clague, Keefer, Knack, and Olson show that contract-intensive money is significantly and positively correlated with growth rates and (even more strongly) with investment's share of GDP over the 1970–92 period. Each one standard deviation increase in contract-intensive money (about 0.14) is associated with a 0.6 percentage point increase in growth and a 2.5 percentage point increase in investment's share of GDP in Barro-type regressions. Findings are very similar if the initial value for contract-intensive money (from 1969) is substituted for the period (1969–90) average to minimize endogeneity problems. Results are not sensitive to controlling for inflation (which makes holding currency less attractive) or for the ratio of M2 to GDP, the most common measure of financial development.

Despite its virtues as an easily measured, objective indicator with broad coverage over time and across countries, contract-intensive money is an imperfect indicator, because it only partially captures variations in the institutional environment. It measures the tradeoff between holding assets in only one of two forms: currency and bank deposits. Ideally, a broader measure could be constructed that captures holdings of foreign currencies, gold, and other assets (which should constitute a higher proportion of assets in countries with poor contract enforcement). Unfortunately, the data do not permit construction of such indicators for a reasonably sized sample of countries.

All of these studies point to significant and positive relations between good governance and growth, with strong indications that good governance causes higher growth. While any single measure of government social capital is imperfect, the shortcomings of each of the various measures used in the literature are largely independent of one another. The empirical findings generated by this body of work must therefore be taken very seriously.

Civil social capital

Civil social capital can affect economic performance through two major channels: microeconomic and macropolitical. At the microeconomic level, social ties and interpersonal trust can reduce transactions costs, help enforce contracts, and improve access to credit for individual investors. At the macropolitical level, social cohesion and civic engagement can strengthen democratic governance (Almond and Verba 1963), improve the efficiency and honesty of public administration (Putnam 1993), and improve the quality of economic policies (Easterly and Levine 1997). For the most part, formal theory about microeconomic level effects is better developed than is theory about macropolitical channels. (The exception is Alesina and Drazen 1991, which sets forth a theory of macro channels. For microeconomic effects, see Greif 1993, Zak and Knack 2001.) The empirical literature represents a mix of the two channels. In some studies the evidence simply shows that civil social capital matters for economic performance, with no attempt to distinguish microeconomic from macropolitical channels.

Civic community and government performance. Helliwell and Putnam (1995) provide a rigorous test of Putnam's (1993) hypothesis on the role of social capital in accounting for variations in economic performance in different parts of Italy. They test three alternative regional indicators of social capital (borrowed from Putnam), all of which they find to be positively and significantly related to growth over the 1950–90 period, controlling for 1950 *per capita* income. The simplest indicator is based on surveys of citizen satisfaction with the activities of regional governments. This measure aggregates the share of respondents who were "very" or "rather" satisfied by region over all such surveys conducted between 1977 and 1988.

The second indicator measures regional government performance by aggregating twelve variables – some objective, others subjective – into a single index. Variables include the timeliness of budgets, legislative innovation, and the speed and accuracy of responses to requests for information.

The third measure is an index of "civic community," based on four components: newspaper reading, number of sports and cultural organizations, turnout in referendums, and the incidence of preference voting (a proxy for patron–client networks, which Putnam views as antithetical to social capital). Civic community is viewed as a determinant of institutional performance, leading to greater citizen satisfaction with regional government. Putnam (1993) had earlier demonstrated strong relationships among the regions between civic community and government performance and between civic community and citizen satisfaction with government.

Helliwell and Putnam (1995) emphasize the effects of institutional performance on growth, arguing that the civic community and citizen satisfaction indicators are proxies for regional government performance, which is difficult to measure directly. They also note, however, that social capital could influence the efficiency of operations within individual firms, an idea discussed at much greater length in Putnam (1993). Conceivably, then, civic community could be related to growth independently of its effects on government performance. Helliwell and Putnam do not test for the relative importance of microeconomic and macropolitical channels, however, as their regressions never include more than one of the three social capital indicators at a time.

Generalized trust. Fukuyama (1995) appears to have been the first scholar to attribute cross-national differences in economic performance to variations in trust and "spontaneous sociability." Although these dimensions of civil social capital are not perfect substitutes for contract and commercial law, the presence of a high degree of trust as an additional condition of economic relations can increase economic efficiency by reducing ... transactions costs, incurred by activities like finding the appropriate buyer or seller, negotiating a contract, complying with government regulations, and enforcing that contract in the event of dispute or fraud. Each of these transactions is made easier if the parties believe in each other's basic honesty: there is less need to spell things out in lengthy contracts; less need to hedge against unexpected contingencies; fewer disputes, and less need to litigate if disputes arise. (p. 151)

Fukuyama stresses the relation between social capital and industrial organization, arguing that where trust does not extend beyond the family, the supply of capital and of qualified managers is limited, constraining the scale of private firms. More generally, he argues that higher-trust societies are better able to implement efficient organizational innovations when changes in technology or other factors make existing organizational forms obsolete. Trust can influence economic outcomes through macropolitical channels as well, because "sociability is also a vital support for self-governing political institutions" (p. 325), as it is in Putnam (1993).

Fukuyama's empirical evidence is mostly descriptive and qualitative rather than quantitative. Based on impressionistic evidence, he classifies the United States, Japan, and Germany as high-trust societies and France, Italy, China, the Republic of Korea, Hong Kong (China), and Taiwan (China) as low-trust societies,

La Porta, Lopez-de-Silanes, Schleifer, and Vishny (1997) and Knack and Keefer (1997) use data from the World Values Surveys to conduct systematic tests of Putnam's and Fukuyama's hypotheses. These surveys polled roughly 1,000 respondents in each of several dozen countries. The first round of surveys, conducted in the early 1980s, included mostly industrial countries. The second, larger round, conducted in the early 1990s, included more developing countries and transition economies. The surveys were intended to be nationally representative, but urban areas and better-educated people are believed to be somewhat overrepresented, particularly in developing countries (Inglehart 1994).

Trust values for each country are calculated as the percentage of respondents who agree with the statement that "most people can be trusted" rather than with the statement that "you can't be too careful in dealing with people." Values range from about 8 percent for Brazil to about 60 percent for the Nordic countries.

La Porta, Lopez-de-Silanes, Schleifer, and Vishny (1997) and Knack and Keefer (1997) show that trust is associated with better ratings on subjective measures of government efficiency, corruption, and infrastructure quality (from ICRG and other sources).[7] Knack and Keefer also find that trust in people strongly predicts World Values Survey measures of confidence in government

---

[7] La Porta, Lopez-de-Silanes, Schleifer, and Vishny control for *per capita* income, include all countries for which data were available, and use trust values from the second round of surveys.

institutions. These findings are consistent with Putnam's (1993) finding that government performance is higher in Italian regions scoring higher on social capital indicators. La Porta, Lopez-de-Silanes, Schleifer, and Vishny also find that higher-trust societies have lower infant mortality, controlling for income, a result found in the United States by Kawachi, Kennedy, Lochner, and Prothrow-Stith (1997).

La Porta, Lopez-de-Silanes, Schleifer, and Vishny test Fukuyama's firm scale hypothesis, regressing the ratio of the revenues of the twenty largest firms to GDP on *per capita* income, trust in people, and a measure of trust in family members. The scale measure is unrelated to income, strongly and positively related to trust in people, and strongly and negatively related to trust in family, providing striking support for Fukuyama.

Knack and Keefer (1997) and Zak and Knack (2001) provide the most extensive cross-country tests of the relation between trust in people and economic performance. For the twenty-nine market economies included in the World Values Surveys, Knack and Keefer add the survey's trust measure to Barro-type investment and growth regressions. Each 12 percentage point increase in trust is associated with an increase in annual income growth of about 1 percentage point. Each 7 percentage point increase in trust is associated with a 1 percentage point increase in investment's share of GDP. Given the wide range of observed values for trust (54.5 percentage points separate Norway from Brazil), these are very large effects.

Because trust is measured in 1980 or 1981 for most of the sample and in 1990 for the remainder, the dependent variables in Knack and Keefer (1997) are measured for the 1980–92 period. Results for growth but not for investment are weaker when longer periods (1970–92 or 1960–92) are used. As a correction for possible endogeneity of trust, Knack and Keefer also report two-stage least-squares estimates, using ethnic homogeneity and the number of law students as a fraction of all postsecondary students as exogenous instruments. Trust remains a significant predictor of growth for the 1980–92 period. Testing an interaction term comprising *per capita* income and trust, Knack and Keefer find that the impact of trust on growth is significantly higher for poorer countries, suggesting that interpersonal trust is more important where legal systems and financial markets are less well developed.

Zak and Knack (2001) present a general equilibrium growth model in which investors of varying types (defined by ethnicity, class, age, or other differences) are randomly matched each period with brokers of varying types, where trust declines with differences in type. Low trust is predicted to reduce investment and growth. Their empirical work adds twelve countries to the twenty-nine-country sample used by Knack and Keefer (1997), using data from a third

Knack and Keefer control for income and education, exclude countries that were once communist, and use the results of the first round of surveys on trust.

round of World Values Surveys conducted in 1995–6 (see the appendix to this chapter). Their results strengthen earlier findings: trust is significantly related to growth even for longer periods, such as 1970–92, and the estimated impact of trust on growth is less sensitive to model specification than in Knack and Keefer (1997).

Zak and Knack (2001) report that trust is higher in countries with stronger formal institutions for enforcing contracts and reducing corruption and in countries with less-polarized populations (as measured by income or land inequality, ethnic heterogeneity, and a subjective measure of the intensity of economic discrimination). They also show that formal institutions and polarization appear to affect growth rates partly through their effect on trust. Income inequality, land inequality, discrimination, and corruption, for example, are associated with significantly lower growth rates, but the association of these variables with growth dramatically weakens when trust is controlled for.

Several other studies briefly report tests of the relation between trust and growth. La Porta, Lopez-de-Silanes, Schleifer, and Vishny find that trust in people is positively associated with growth (significant at the 10 percent level) over the 1970–93 period, controlling only for 1970 *per capita* income. Granato, Inglehart, and Leblang (1996a) test trust and five other "cultural" variables in growth regressions for the 1980–9 period. Controlling for *per capita* income levels and primary education enrollment in 1980, they find that trust is positively and significantly related to growth.

Helliwell (1996) finds that trust and an index of group membership are each negatively and significantly related to productivity growth for a sample of seventeen OECD members. His sample omits the poor- and middle-income countries for which trust has the largest effects (Knack and Keefer 1997). In examining productivity growth only, Helliwell neglects the possibility that trust influences income growth largely through factor accumulation channels, as Knack and Keefer (1997) show.

In their investment and growth tests, Knack and Keefer (1997) supplement the trust in people measure with an indicator of trustworthiness based on other items in the World Values Surveys. They construct an index of trustworthiness, or of the strength of "civic norms," from responses to five questions about whether various forms of cheating are ever justifiable. The items include cheating on taxes, claiming government benefits to which one is not entitled, failing to report damage one has done accidentally to a parked vehicle, avoiding paying a fare on public transport, and keeping money one finds. As with trust in people, this civic norms index is positively and significantly related to growth over the 1980–92 period and to investment over various periods (1960–92, 1970–92, 1980–92).

Few of these studies devote any attention to measurement issues, neglecting the possibility that translation differences or less than fully random samples could introduce substantial error into country-level estimates of trust derived from the World Values Surveys. An exception is Knack and Keefer (1997), who find that trust is strongly correlated ($r = 0.67$) across countries with the percentage of "lost" wallets returned in experiments conducted by *Reader's Digest*. This result is consistent with the view that nonrandom samples and translation difficulties do not introduce severe measurement error in the cross-country trust data. The high correlation between the trust indicator and returned wallets and the low correlation between the trust indicator and trust in family members also suggest that the trust indicator is capturing generalized trust (trust in strangers) rather than specific or particularized trust in people with whom one has repeated interactions or who belong to the same groups. This is an important finding, as generalized trust is viewed by most social capital theorists as a source of reduced transactions costs and reduced social conflict (Zak and Knack 2001), whereas particularized trust has more ambiguous implications for economic performance. Cooperation and trust within ethnic groups or special interest groups can facilitate their organization for rent-seeking purposes or even violent conflict (Knack and Keefer 1997).

Group membership.   Putnam (1993) views memberships in horizontal (i.e. non-hierarchical) associations as a source of trust and of social ties conducive to economic performance (see chapter 1 in this volume). Olson's (1982) view of associations is much less favorable; he emphasizes their growth-impairing, rent-seeking functions. Knack and Keefer (1997) test these alternative theories using World Values Survey data on group memberships in twenty-six market economies. The surveys asked respondents whether they belonged to any of ten types of organizations. Knack and Keefer calculate the mean number of group memberships per respondent and compute country averages.

In Barro-type regressions, group memberships are found to be unrelated to growth and negatively related to investment rates. These findings offer no support to Putnam (1993) and little support to Olson (1982). Knack and Keefer conjecture that both could be right, however, with the positive effects of groups hypothesized by Putnam canceling out the negative effects stressed by Olson. They attempt to provide a finer test by disaggregating groups into those that seem to have primarily social goals ("Putnam groups") and those that are more likely to engage in lobbying ("Olson groups"). Memberships in Olson groups (trade unions, political parties or groups, professional associations) shows no significant relation to growth or investment rates. Paradoxically, Putnam groups (religious organizations, youth groups, and education, arts, music, or cultural activities) show a strong but negative association with investment and no significant association with growth.

There are several possible explanations for these surprising findings. It could be that the World Values Surveys data on group memberships are faulty. The categories of groups included in the surveys are very broad, making it difficult to confidently distinguish rent-seeking from purely social groups, and the depth of commitment to groups is not measured. However, there are serious theoretical deficiencies in the perspectives on groups advanced by both Putnam (1993) and Olson (1982). Putnam claims that associations "instill in their members habits of cooperation, solidarity, and public-spiritedness" (pp. 89–90). But many (even purely social) groups segregated by class, occupation, or ethnicity may build cooperation and trust only among group members, perhaps even encouraging distrust between members and nonmembers. Olson's predictions on growth and groups overlook the fact that professional or trade associations that engage in special-interest lobbying activities may also enforce ethical codes and standards that build generalized trust (Bergsten 1985) and reduce transactions costs by spreading information about the identity of cheaters (Bernstein 1992).

Social polarization. Several studies focus on ethnic divisions and inequality as sources of slower growth through their effects on trust, social cohesion, economic policymaking, and even violent conflict. Most of these studies posit macropolitical channels through which polarization impairs economic performance. (An exception is the model of Zak and Knack 2001, in which the strength of informal sanctions against cheating weakens with social distance, increasing monitoring costs of contractual agreements between investor–broker pairs.)

Easterly and Levine (1997) show that more ethnically heterogeneous societies grow more slowly than others, controlling for the usual growth regressors. The predicted growth rate for the most homogeneous societies (such as Japan) exceeds the predicted rate for the most heterogeneous societies (such as Tanzania) by more than 2 percentage points. Ethnic heterogeneity is correlated with a range of indicators of inefficient policies, including a high black market currency premium, high levels of corruption, low schooling rates, a lack of financial development, and poor infrastructure.

Easterly and Levine argue that ethnic divisions increase polarization of preferences for public goods, impeding agreement over their provision. (Alesina, Baqir, and Easterly 1999 provide evidence from US city and county data supporting this hypothesis.) Ethnically divided societies will also be prone to competitive rent-seeking, with increased incentives for the group in power to create rents (through overvalued exchange rates and other means) that accrue to their own ethnic group at the expense of others. As Easterly and Levine acknowledge, however, ethnic divisions generally remain a significant predictor of slower growth even when a wide range of policies is controlled for, consistent with the possibility that polarization influences growth through microeconomic channels as well.

Building on models of social choice under polarized preferences, Keefer and Knack (forthcoming) find that property rights are more uncertain in highly polarized societies, as measured not only by ethnic tensions and heterogeneity but by income and land inequality as well. Berg and Sachs (1988) test the effects of income inequality on indebtedness, finding that countries with high income inequality are more likely to default on sovereign debt, as indicated by discounts on country debt in secondary markets. They conclude that the adoption of needed policy changes (including trade liberalization and deficit cutting) on a timely basis is hindered by high income inequality. Using a wider array of polarization indicators and a subjective indicator of the likelihood of default, Keefer and Knack (forthcoming) corroborate the Berg and Sachs findings for a much larger sample of countries.

Keefer and Knack (forthcoming) examine various arguments explaining why inequality is commonly linked empirically with slower growth, as Alesina and Rodrik (1994) and others have shown. They present evidence that inequality's impact on growth occurs at least partly through increasing the uncertainty of property rights. Controlling for the ICRG property rights index, they show that the estimated impacts of income and land inequality on growth diminish substantially but do not disappear. Their results leave open the possibility that polarization may have more direct effects on economic performance – by impairing the social and psychological basis for trust among individual transactors, for example. Consistent with this possibility, Zak and Knack (2001) find that income and land inequality are strongly associated with slower growth in their forty-one-country sample but that the association disappears when the World Values Surveys trust indicator is controlled for.

Rodrik (1999) constructs a simple model of social conflict in which a country's ability to adjust efficiently to exogenous shocks (such as adverse shifts in the terms of trade) is a function of "latent social conflict" and "institutions of conflict management." Efficient adjustment to adverse shocks often has substantial distributional consequences: where deep social cleavages exist along ethnic or other lines, negotiating a new social bargain will take longer, as Alesina and Drazen (1991) show. Strong conflict management institutions essentially provide rules that reduce the share of society's resources that the competing groups can potentially capture. Rodrik hypothesizes that adverse shocks will be more harmful for growth when latent conflicts are more severe and when rules effectively constrain the stakes of the conflict.

Rodrik's dependent variable is the change in the average annual growth rate between 1960–74 and 1975–89. Low values are identified with growth "collapses," in which economies that grew rapidly before the shocks of the 1970s subsequently stagnated or shrank. He finds that changes in the terms of trade during the 1970s are associated with larger declines in growth, although this result is sensitive to changes in the sample and the model specification. Countries with smaller declines in growth have better conflict management institutions, as proxied by Gastil's civil liberties and political freedoms indicators, indexes from ICRG or BI, and social security and welfare expenditures. Smaller declines in growth are also associated with less severe latent social conflict, as measured by income or land inequality, ethnic diversity or tensions, and the World Values Surveys trust indicator.

Rodrik's central hypothesis calls for testing three-way interaction terms: shocks harm growth more when latent conflict is worse and institutions are weaker. He constructs several of these interaction terms, multiplying the change in the terms of trade by a latent conflict proxy and a conflict management proxy (for example, ethnic heterogeneity and the Gastil index). As predicted, higher values of these terms are associated with larger growth collapses. However, none of the components of the interaction terms is allowed to enter the regression independently, because the model specification forces all of the growth effects of any one component (such as ethnic heterogeneity) to be conditional on the levels of the other component. A properly specified test of the basic hypothesis, recognizing the many other theories on how polarization and institutions influence economic performance, would allow the data rather than the researcher to decide whether they influence growth only by conditioning responses to external shocks.

Collier (1998) views the impact of ethnic diversity as being conditional on political institutions. According to him, "an ethnically diverse society [may] gain more from democracy than a homogeneous society because the latter has less need of dispute resolution" (p. 5). Collier finds empirical support for this proposition in a sample of ninety-four countries (1960–90). In his sample the harmful effects of ethnic heterogeneity on growth are significantly stronger among countries with fewer political freedoms, as measured by the Gastil index.

The impact of ethnic diversity on social and political outcomes often turns out to be nonlinear. As Horowitz (1985) notes, polarization can be greatest when there are a small number of groups of roughly equal size. With a proliferation of small groups, no one group will normally have the incentive or opportunity to impose its will on all others. Collier (1998) finds some evidence that the likelihood of civil wars is greatest for countries that rank in the middle in terms of ethnic heterogeneity. (This result is similar to what Bates and Yackovlev report in chapter 10 of this volume.) Interpersonal trust also initially declines as heterogeneity increases before rising again (Zak and Knack 2001). Keefer and Knack (1995) find that the uncertainty of property rights is greatest for countries in the middle of the ethnic heterogeneity rankings.

Cultural explanations: "achievement motivation" and communitarianism. Participants in a symposium in the *American Journal of Political Science* debated the importance of cultural influences on economic performance (Granato, Inglehart, and Leblang 1996a, 1996b; Jackman and Miller 1996; Swank 1996). Building on Weber's Protestant ethic thesis, Granato,

Inglehart, and Leblang (1996b) hypothesize that norms encourage social mobility and the accumulation of human and physical capital in some societies but discourage them in others, with implications for economic development. Using World Values Surveys data from twenty-five countries, they find that an index of "achievement motivation" is positively and significantly related to growth in a Barro-type model.

Granato, Inglehart, and Leblang construct the achievement motivation index from responses about traits children should be encouraged to acquire. Index values equal the percentage of the population in each country that cites "thrift" or "determination" minus the percentage that cites "obedience" or "religious faith." Because growth is measured for 1960–89 and the index is measured from surveys conducted in the early 1990s, their results could easily be driven by reverse causation. The social and geographic mobility induced by rapid growth, for example, could disrupt traditional social ties that encourage obedience and religious faith (Olson 1963).

Achievement motivation is hypothesized to influence economic performance by increasing individuals' willingness to save, invest, work hard, and acquire productive knowledge. Swank (1996) takes a macro political approach, building in part on Olson's (1982) theory of "encompassing interests." He argues that economic policymaking will be less conflictual and more conducive to growth in "communitarian" societies, including "social corporatist" polities such as Austria, Denmark, Finland, Norway, and Sweden and "Confucian statist" polities such as China, Japan, and the Republic of Korea. Adding dummy variables for "corporatist" and "Confucian" to the Granato, Inglehart, and Leblang (1996b) model, Swank shows that growth rates are significantly higher in those societies and that once these additional variables are controlled for, achievement motivation is no longer related to growth. Unexplained is how Confucianist norms, long believed inimical to economic progress, suddenly became conducive to rapid growth in recent decades.

Poverty, income distribution, and social capital

Evidence from household and village studies suggests that civil social capital in the form of trust or social ties can play an important role in alleviating poverty (Grootaert 1999; Narayan and Pritchett 1999). The rich, it can be argued, have much less to gain than the poor from membership in groups that provide mutual aid or health or education services, because they can afford to purchase these services (Grootaert 1999). Similarly, institutions or cultural traditions that broaden participation (as proxied by Gastil's civil liberties index) can be expected to have progressive effects, extending to poor people the kind of political influence and access that the rich tend to have in all societies.

The distributional implications of government social capital are more ambiguous. Secure property rights and effective contract enforcement are often viewed as benefiting primarily the rich at the expense of the poor. This perception is based on the intuition that unlike rich landowners or capitalists, the poor have little property to protect. Similarly, contractual agreements are often perceived as the product of unequal bargaining power, with rich creditors, landowners, or capitalists enforcing contract provisions against poor borrowers, tenants, employees, or consumers.

But institutions for promoting property rights and enforcement of contracts may have powerful egalitarian effects, enabling individuals with little property and no political connections to invest in human capital and small enterprises. Fair and transparent procedures for property, contracts, and government regulation of business facilitate the entry of informal sector entrepreneurs and workers – most of whom belong to low- or middle-income groups – into the formal sector and promote the accumulation of physical and human capital, raising profits and wages (de Soto 1989). Strong and predictable property and contract rights are necessary for the emergence of well-developed financial markets, which are at least as important for poor and middle-income borrowers as for the well off, who can more easily arrange alternative sources of credit. Unlike the rich, the poor may be dependent on credit for acquiring secondary school education, which has a high cost in terms of forgone income in developing countries.

Thus one could argue that the institutions that best ensure property rights and contract enforceability are the very institutions that best improve the welfare of the poor. Olson (1994) goes even farther, arguing that much of the poverty in the developing world is the product of institutions chosen by politically connected individuals and groups in their own interests. Bureaucratic corruption enriches government officials, for example, who supplement their salaries with bribes obtained by imposing burdensome procedures for obtaining licenses and permits.

The rest of this section examines empirically the relation between social capital indicators and measures of poverty and distribution. One way to address this question is by noting that property rights are significantly related to growth (Knack and Keefer 1995) and that growth is associated with reductions in poverty rates (Squire 1993). Thus property rights must make the poor better off. It is conceivable, however, that the source of growth matters. Most episodes of growth are accompanied by reductions in poverty, but the exceptions could be those in which, for example, growth is generated by secure and stable property and contract rights rather than by public investments in primary or secondary education, health, or infrastructure. New and direct evidence on these issues is presented in this section.

Income distribution

To test the effect of social capital on income distribution, we use the Gini coefficients of income inequality and income share by quintile from the "high quality" sub-set of the Deininger and Squire (1996) time-series compilation. The change in Gini coefficients is computed for roughly the 1970–92 period. (Inequality data are not available for every year for every country, so beginning and end years may differ somewhat across countries.)

Average annual growth in *per capita* income was computed for each of the five income quintiles for the same period, using the purchasing power-adjusted income data from Summers and Heston (1991). The initial-year *per capita* income for each country is first multiplied by the initial-year share of each quintile and then multiplied by five to obtain the *per capita* income for each quintile. This procedure is repeated using end-year values; average annual growth in *per capita* income is computed from these initial- and end-year *per capita* income levels (table 2.1).

We calculate standard Barro-type growth regressions for the sample of countries for which data on quintile shares are available, where the dependent variable is average annual income growth over the 1970–92 period (table 2.2). Independent variables are (the log of) 1970 *per capita* income as a share of US income; mean years of completed education for people 25 and older in 1970 (from Barro and Lee 1993); the trade intensity ratio averaged over the growth period (exports plus imports as a share of GDP, from Summers and Heston 1991); and the ICRG index of property rights, as constructed by Knack and Keefer (1995). Most results for this thirty-seven-country sample are consistent with those generated from larger samples: incomes converge conditional on other variables included in the model, and education, trade intensity, and property rights are all associated with higher growth rates. Education and trade intensity are not significant in this sample, however. The ICRG index coefficient implies that each 10-point increase in the 50-point scale is associated with an increase in growth of nearly 1.6 percentage points a year.

Table 2.2 also reports analogous tests in which the dependent variable is the growth of incomes for each quintile, from the poorest (Q1) to the richest (Q5). In addition to the regressors included in tests of growth overall, the quintile growth regressions control for initial quintile share. Where the initial quintile share is already relatively high, that quintile's income growth is less likely to get a boost from further increases in the share, so the expectation is that the sign on this coefficient will be negative. As expected, all coefficients are negative, but they are not statistically significant at conventional levels.

The ICRG coefficients are slightly smaller for the poorer two quintiles than for the richer three, but these differences are not statistically significant. For the regression for the second quintile, which produces the lowest ICRG coefficient

Table 2.1 *Countries included in one or more regressions*

Country	Gini 1990–Gini 1970	ICRG	BERI	CIM	Trust
Australia	9.7				
Bangladesh	2.8		×		
Brazil	1.99				
Canada	−4.65				
Chile	11.88				
Colombia	−0.7				
Costa Rica	1.67		×		×
Denmark	2.20				
Dominican Republic	4.00		×		
Finland	−5.69		×		
France	−11.3				
Germany	−5.47				
Greece	0.08				
Hong King	4.1		×	×	×
Honduras	−9.25		×		×
Hungary	9.44	×	×	×	
India	1.64				
Indonesia	0.99				×
Iran	−2.55				×
Ireland	−4.09				
Italy	−4.11				
Jamaica	−2.79		×		×
Japan	−0.5				
Korea, Rep. of	0.34				
Malaysia	−1.65				
Mexico	−2.72				
Netherlands	0.78				
New Zealand	10.16		×		×
Norway	−2.73				
Pakistan	1.24				×
Panama	−0.53		×	×	×
Philippines	−4.39				
Poland	3.27	×	×	×	
Portugal	−4.95				
Singapore	−2				×
Spain	−11.2				
Sri Lanka	8.99		×		×
Sweden	−0.97				
Taiwan (China)	0.69			×	
Tanzania	−0.9		×		×
Thailand	8.87				×
Tunisia	−2.06		×		×
Turkey	−11.91				
United Kingdom	7.3				
United States	4.3				
Venezuela	6.19				×
Yugoslavia	−0.12		×	×	×

Table 2.2   *Relation between ICRG index and income growth, by quintile,*
1970–1992

Variable	Overall	Q1	Q2	Q3	Q4	Q5
Intercept	5.044	6.397	5.721	5.679	7.182	6.267
	(1.260)	(1.575)	(1.462)	(1.456)	(1.481)	(2.040)
Log (income/US income),	−2.705	−2.366	−2.484	−2.573	−2.615	−2.908
1970	(0.577)	(0.640)	(0.691)	(0.619)	(0.587)	(0.629)
Quintile share, 1970		−0.225	−0.057	−0.057	−0.129	−0.017
		(0.123)	(0.106)	(0.095)	(0.077)	(0.024)
Mean years education 1970	0.068	0.053	−0.048	−0.028	0.070	0.170
	(0.108)	(0.174)	(0.143)	(0.123)	(0.108)	(0.110)
Trade intensity, 1970–90 mean	0.007	0.010	0.009	0.008	0.008	0.006
	(0.006)	(0.006)	(0.007)	(0.006)	(0.006)	(0.007)
ICRG index of property rights	0.157	0.133	0.147	0.165	0.166	0.151
	(0.028)	(0.030)	(0.032)	(0.029)	(0.029)	(0.032)
Adjusted R^2	0.56	0.27	0.39	0.46	0.52	0.56
Standard error of the estimate	1.18	1.86	1.58	1.45	1.34	1.19
Mean, dependent variable	2.22	2.15	2.26	2.27	2.22	2.22

Notes: Number = 37. White-corrected standard errors are shown in parentheses.

(0.133), the null hypothesis that the ICRG coefficient is equal to 0.166 (its highest value, from quintile 4) cannot be rejected. Trade openness generates somewhat larger coefficient estimates for the poorer quintiles, although the differences across quintiles are not significant.

Interestingly, the model better explains growth variations for the richer quintiles than for the poorer ones: adjusted R^2 values steadily increase (from 0.27 for quintile 1 to 0.56 for quintile 5) and standard errors steadily fall (from 1.9 to 1.2). This difference may be caused by greater measurement error in attempting to measure percentage point changes in small numbers (incomes of the poor) than in large numbers (incomes of the rich). There is no evidence in these data of a global trend toward greater or lesser inequality of incomes within countries, as mean growth rates vary little across the quintiles (from 2.15 percent to 2.27 percent).

A similar set of regression results for growth over the shorter (1980–92) period (which also differs slightly for some countries) is shown in table 2.3. Because the ICRG index is measured in 1982, this period is less subject to endogeneity problems than the longer period. The disadvantage of using shorter periods is that growth variations are driven more by shocks and are more difficult to explain with models designed to account for cross-country variations in long-run growth.

The ICRG column in table 2.3 reports the coefficients and standard errors for the ICRG index from a set of six regressions identical to those in table 2.2 (with other independent variables appropriately adjusted to 1980). The coefficient is

Table 2.3 *Relation between social capital and income*
growth, by quintile

Item	ICRG Income growth 1980–92	BERI Income growth 1970–92
Overall	0.196 (0.038)	0.360 (0.110)
Quintile 1 (poorest)	0.331 (0.099)	0.580 (0.158)
Quintile 2	0.209 (0.061)	0.575 (0.118)
Quintile 3	0.214 (0.050)	0.581 (0.090)
Quintile 4	0.217 (0.038)	0.544 (0.079)
Quintile 5 (richest)	0.164 (0.044)	0.256 (0.133)
Number	39	27

Notes: White-corrected standard errors are shown in parentheses. Other independent variables are initial *per capita* income, initial quintile share (except in "overall" growth equation), initial mean years completed education, and period mean of trade intensity ratio.

at its highest (0.331) for the poorest quintile – twice as high as for the richest quintile (0.164). The null hypothesis that the fifth quintile coefficient is 0.331 can be rejected at the 5 percent level.

Regressions were also run using the BERI property rights index. Because the BERI index is measured in 1972, there is less potential for reverse causation than with ICRG, so only the 1970–92 growth period is analyzed. The growth effects of BERI for the four poorest quintiles vary only trivially, with each 2-point increase in the 16-point scale raising growth by more than 1 percentage point for each quintile. This impact declines by more than half for the richest quintile, where an increase in BERI of 4 points is required to raise growth 1 percentage point. The coefficient for the fifth quintile (0.256) is significantly smaller than for the other quintiles.

Similar tests were conducted using contract-intensive money and the World Values Surveys trust indicator as social capital measures. In these small samples, neither proves to be a significant determinant of growth, either for overall growth or for the growth of incomes in any of the five quintiles.

The findings in tables 2.2 and 2.3 strongly indicate that government social capital improves incomes for all groups, not merely those with the most property in need of protection. If anything, incomes of the poor increase more rapidly than those of the rich when the quality of governance is higher, as shown by the pattern of coefficients in table 2.3.

Similar tests were run with changes in the Gini index of income inequality between 1970 and 1992 as the dependent variable (table 2.4). These samples are somewhat larger than in the quintiles regressions, because Deininger and Squire (1996) include more Gini values than quintile share values.

Table 2.4   *Relation between social capital and changes in*
Gini coefficient of income inequality, 1970–1992

Variable	ICRG	BERI	Trust
Intercept	6.276	12.049	11.965
	(3.517)	(4.552)	(5.220)
Gini coefficient	−0.143	−0.139	−0.280
	(0.084)	(0.101)	(0.113)
Mean years	0.773	1.622	0.603
education	(0.392)	(0.402)	(0.449)
Trade intensity	0.008	0.014	−0.030
	(0.011)	(0.008)	(0.024)
ICRG index	−0.148		
	(0.082)		
BERI index		−1.630	
		(0.375)	
Trust			−0.117
			(0.073)
Number	45	32	30
R^2	0.14	0.30	0.18
Adjusted R^2	.05	.20	.05
Standard error of the estimate	5.40	5.04	5.76
Mean, dependent variable	−0.16	−0.55	−0.50

Note: White-corrected standard errors are shown in parentheses.

Gini values converge in this sample (conditional on the other regressors), as higher initial levels of the Gini index are associated with larger (but not always significant) declines over the period. Higher educational attainment is associated, somewhat surprisingly, with increasing inequality, although this effect is not always significant. Trade intensity shows no strong or consistent impact on changes in Gini.

Higher scores for ICRG and BERI are associated with declines in income inequality. For ICRG this relation is only marginally significant at conventional levels: each 7-point increment in the 50-point ICRG scale is associated with a 1-point decline in the Gini coefficient. For BERI the relation with Gini declines is highly significant, with each 1-point rise in the 16-point BERI scale reducing the Gini coefficient by 1.6 points. Inequality also declines in higher-trust societies. Each 8- or 9-point increase in the percentage of people trusting is associated with a 1-point decline in the Gini coefficient. This partial correlation is only marginally significant, however. The results shown in table 2.4, derived using a composite indicator of inequality and a slightly larger sample than the earlier tests used, confirm the findings from the quintile growth regressions. All of these results show that social capital not only improves economic performance, it is progressive, in the sense that it helps the poorer classes more than it helps the richer classes.

Absolute poverty

Bruno, Ravallion, and Squire (1998) find that growth is unrelated to changes in income distribution, implying that absolute poverty should fall with growth. They provide direct evidence on this point, showing that a 10 percent increase in *per capita* income is associated with a 20 percent average decline in the percentage of a country's population living on $1 a day or less. In seventeen of the twenty countries with data on changes in this measure of absolute poverty over time, *per capita* income and the percentage of people living on less than $1 a day move in opposite directions.

Because the social capital indicators analyzed earlier have either neutral or pro-egalitarian effects on income distribution and have elsewhere been linked to more rapid growth, there is a strong presumption that improvements in the rule of law, property and contract rights, and trust in people reduce absolute poverty. Data on changes over time in absolute poverty are available for only a very small number of countries. For this reason, no direct tests are provided here of the impact of social capital variables on changes in absolute poverty. Data on absolute poverty levels are available for enough countries represented in the ICRG data set to conduct tests of the effect of government social capital on absolute poverty. These tests, of course, are more subject to concern about reverse causality than they would be if changes in absolute poverty rates were the dependent variable.

Regressions were run on a sample of 35 countries in which the dependent variables are the percentage of a country's population living on less than $1 a day (equations (1) and (3) of table 2.5) and less than $2 a day (equations (2) and (4). For countries with two or more observations on poverty, the most recent one was used. The earliest observation used is from 1986; the most recent is from 1995. The mean year is 1992, with a standard deviation of two years.

The ICRG index (averaged over 1982–90) is negatively and significantly related to poverty levels in equations (1) and (3). Each 1-point rise in the 50-point ICRG index reduces the percentage in poverty by slightly more than 1 percentage point on average. This relation weakens when *per capita* income is controlled for (equations (2) and (4), indicating that government social capital reduces poverty rates in part by raising incomes generally.

These regressions control for a time trend variable, because poverty is measured in different years for different countries. "Year" is equal to the year in which poverty is measured minus 1985; it thus varies from 1 (poverty measured in 1986) to 10 (poverty measured in 1995). Coefficients for this variable are negative and insignificant. Education is controlled for, using measures of the

Table 2.5 *Relation between government social capital and absolute poverty*

Variable	Equation (1) (percentage of population living on less than $1 a day)	Equation (2) (percentage of population living on less than $2 a day)	Equation (3) (percentage of population living on less than $1 a day)	Equation (4) (percentage of population living on less than $2 a day)
Intercept	77.129	110.220	70.942	99.478
	(17.313)	(14.520)	(18.639)	(15.907)
Year of survey	−0.914	−0.777	−0.869	−0.699
	(1.504)	(1.539)	(1.465)	(1.373)
Primary school completed	1.971	0.101	2.000	0.152
(percent)	(4.184)	(4.392)	(3.958)	(3.784)
Secondary school	−19.432	−20.029	−17.067	−15.922
completed (percent)	(7.211)	(6.798)	(7.367)	(6.594)
Tertiary school completed	−18.791	−10.998	−0.687	20.434
(percent)	(27.808)	(26.684)	(28.762)	(26.797)
ICRG (1982–90 mean)	−1.045	−1.183	−0.671	−0.531
	(0.578)	(0.501)	(0.651)	(0.599)
Per capita income, 1980			−3.890	−6.754
(in thousand $)			(2.204)	(2.801)
R^2	.38	.44	.41	.53
Adjusted R^2	.27	.35	.28	.43
Standard error of the estimate	20.84	20.84	20.69	19.58
Mean, dependent variable	27.57	52.65	27.57	52.65

Notes: Number = 35. White-corrected standard errors are shown in parentheses.

percentage of adults who have completed primary, secondary, and tertiary schooling. Only secondary education is significant. An increase of 5–6 percentage points in secondary schooling is associated with a fall in poverty of 1 percentage point.

All of these results support the view that social capital reduces poverty rates and improves – or at a minimum does not exacerbate – income inequality. Improving government and civil social capital are not the only ways, or necessarily the best ways, of reducing poverty. But there clearly is no equity-based justification in the data for opposing the strengthening of property and contract rights in developing countries.

Conclusion

Most of the research described here examines "big picture" issues concerning social capital and economic performance. It is useful to understand the country-level relations between various dimensions of governance or civil society on the one hand and economic performance on the other. This body of research is also valuable in illuminating issues deserving further study at less aggregated levels or in more detailed ways.

Most of the chapters in this volume explore relations between social capital and economic welfare at much lower levels of aggregation. By and large, the findings of these micro studies are consistent with those of the macro studies reviewed here.

More refined studies at the macro level are needed. Ethnic heterogeneity, for example, appears to be associated with less efficient policies, less social trust, and slower growth. But observation of many successful heterogeneous societies suggests that important qualifications may hide behind these simple relations. Under what conditions does ethnic heterogeneity fuel conflict and distrust, and under what set of conditions or institutions are heterogeneous societies less conflictual? To resolve questions such as these, more studies like that of Bates and Yackovlev in chapter 10 are needed.

Other needed refinements of macro studies include identifying and collecting better and more comprehensive data. Each round of the World Values Surveys adds many new countries, improving our knowledge of cross-country differences in levels of trust, group membership, and other measures of civil social capital. Increases in the sophistication of measurement are equally important, however. The nature of groups' activities and goals, for example, and the composition of their membership may be more important for economic welfare than the simple number of group memberships. Some more detailed measures are already being collected in some countries, for use in World Bank household- or village-level studies on the role of social capital (World Bank 1998).

Although measurement issues remain, a consensus has developed on the importance of government social capital for economic performance; a similar consensus is rapidly developing on civil social capital. For this knowledge to have any practical implications for policy, the next logical focus of both macro and micro research should address the fundamental sources of social capital.

APPENDIX: DATA SOURCES FOR CROSS-COUNTRY SOCIAL CAPITAL INDICATORS

This appendix provides brief descriptions of the most commonly used country-level indicators of social capital. More detailed information can be found at the Internet sites for each source.

Gastil/Freedom House civil liberties and political freedoms indexes

Beginning in the early 1970s, Raymond Gastil constructed cross-country indexes of "civil liberties" and "political freedoms" as part of the Comparative Survey of Freedom, published by Freedom House, a nonprofit organization dedicated to the promotion of democracy, political rights, and civil liberties. Since 1990 the indexes have been published without Gastil's participation.

The index assigns countries scores of 1–7, with lower values assigned to countries with greater liberties. (Many users of the indexes have reversed the scale so that larger numbers indicate greater freedom.) The survey is unusually inclusive, covering about 170 countries and territories.

The Gastil/Freedom House index assigns values based on an overall assessment of each country in terms of fourteen measures of civil liberty and eleven measures of political freedom. (Only one value is assigned to each country based on a collective evaluation of these criteria; numerical values are not assigned for each criterion.) The criteria include such measures as the existence of an independent judiciary, free trade unions and religious institutions, and multiple political parties and the absence of political censorship and military or foreign control. (For a discussion of the methodology used to create the indexes and some of the problems associated with the ratings, see Gastil 1990; Barro 1996; and Burkhart and Lewis-Beck 1994. Also see *<www.freedomhouse.org>*.)

International Country Risk Guide (ICRG)

The International Country Risk Guide (ICRG) has been published monthly since 1982. Produced for sale to international investors, the guide is designed to identify political and other risks to overseas investments. Country experts prepare in-depth country reports; editors assign numerical ratings to each country, based on the country reports and other information. Ratings are based on thirteen indicators of political risk and five measures of financial risk. Most researchers have followed Knack and Keefer (1995) in using an additive index based on five of these variables: law and order tradition, quality of the bureaucracy, corruption in government, risk of expropriation of private investment, and risk of repudiation of contracts by government. (For additional information, see Coplin *et al.* 1991 or *<www.prsgroup.com>*.)

Business Environmental Risk Intelligence (BERI)

Business Environmental Risk Intelligence (BERI) has published an operations risk index and sub-indexes since 1972. Scores for all countries are constructed from surveys of a panel of about 105 experts, including academics, government officials, bankers, and foreign investors, all with extensive international experience. Country ratings are produced by omitting the maximum and minimum values and computing the mean of the remainder. Sub-indexes cover political continuity, attitude toward foreign investors and profits, degree of nationalization risk, monetary inflation, balance of payments, bureaucratic delays, economic growth, currency convertibility, enforcement of contracts, labor cost/productivity, professional services and contracts, communications and transportation, local management and partners, availability of short-term credit in local currency, and availability of long-term credit in local currency. (For additional information, see <*www.beri.com*>.)

Because the BERI ratings go back much farther in time than the ICRG ratings, they are less subject to reverse causation problems in analyses of long-run economic performance. They cover a much smaller number of countries than the ICRG ratings, however (about 50 versus 140 covered by ICRG in 1998). Coverage is determined in part by investor interest (when countries become extremely poor risks, they are dropped from the sample). The resulting reduction in cross-country variation should make it more difficult to find statistically significant links to economic outcomes using these data.

A second disadvantage of the BERI data is that ratings on bureaucratic delays, nationalization risk, and contract enforceability are intercorrelated at about 0.9. The rate of intercorrelation among the ICRG components is just 0.6. Very high correlations between items suggest that ratings by BERI evaluators may reflect their overall sense of a country's investment environment rather than the individual dimensions of that environment.

Business International

Business International (BI) provided numerical ratings on various dimensions of investor risk between 1971 and 1988. The measures and the sample changed substantially in 1980. From 1971 to 1979 Business International rated fifty-seven countries on at least twenty factors, including political stability, probability of nationalization, delays in getting approval, government intervention in business, and quality of infrastructure. From 1980 to 1988 the sample was expanded by about ten countries, and a different and larger set of indicators became available. These include quality of the legal system and judiciary, bureaucracy and red tape, corruption, political stability, labor stability, terrorism, probability of opposition group takeover, and others.

The BI data are less useful than the ICRG or BERI data for time-series analyses because each of its two series was published for only about nine years. In contrast, ICRG data have been available since 1982, and BERI data have been available since 1972, and both continue to be produced.

Humana's World Human Rights Guide

Charles Humana's World Human Rights Guide (1984, 1986, 1992) rates ninety or more countries on forty dimensions of human rights. For each dimension, countries are assigned to one of four categories depending on the level of rights.

Dimensions rated include freedom to travel or disseminate information, equality for women and ethnic minorities, and various legal and personal rights.

Economic freedom indexes

Since 1995 the Heritage Foundation has published an annual index of economic freedom. Ten dimensions of economic freedom are rated on a subjective scale of 1 to 5. Most of these dimensions are related to economic policies, including banking, trade, tax, and monetary policies. Ratings are assigned to more than 100 countries.

A second economic freedom index is produced annually by the Economic Freedom Network, which links dozens of institutes around the world, including the Cato Institute in the United States and the Fraser Institute in Canada. The index is based largely on objective measures, such as government spending, inflation, and tax rates. Because most of these variables are available over long periods of time, indexes have been constructed for the years 1975–95 (Gwartney, Lawson, and Block 1996). Dawson (1998) uses the 1975–90 data from this source to explain cross-country variations in investment and growth over the same period. His positive results are hardly surprising, however: the index incorporates policy variables such as inflation, trade openness, and government consumption that have been linked to economic performance in innumerable previous studies.

Freedom House sponsored one economic freedom index in the early 1980s (Wright 1982) and another in the 1990s (Messick 1996). Both are subjective indexes, based on measures such as freedom to have and control property, freedom of association, freedom of movement, and freedom of information. Spindler (1991) finds that freedom of property and information are each positively related to the level of income *per capita*, while freedom of association is negatively related to income *per capita*.

A fourth economic freedom index is that of Scully (1992). He constructs an index of "economic liberty" from fifteen indicators from Humana (1986), Wright (1982), Gastil, and other sources.

Competitiveness indexes

Two organizations produce cross-country numerical ratings of economic competitiveness. The World Economic Forum (*<www.weforum.org>*), with assistance from the Harvard Institute for International Development, issues an annual *Global Competitiveness Report*. Based on standard economic data and a survey of about 3,000 business executives, it evaluates 155 separate criteria in fifty-three countries. The survey includes items on bribery and corruption, tax evasion, and the reliability of the judicial system. Although the report has been issued annually since 1980, the current methodology dates only to 1996.

The Institute for Management Development (<*www.imd.ch.*>) produces a similar competitiveness index for its annual *World Competitiveness Yearbook.* Ratings are based on a survey of several thousand businesspeople around the world. For the 1996 yearbook 3,162 businesspeople responded to a seventy-two-question survey sent to 21,000 national and expatriate businesspeople. Respondents include both local and international companies, reportedly representing a cross-section of the economy in each country. The *World Competitiveness Yearbook* evaluates forty-six countries, including all OECD members and eighteen other countries chosen on the basis of their economic importance and the availability of data. Hard data are used to supplement the survey, with about 260 total criteria rated. The survey queries respondents about relations between managers and employees, employees' identification with company objectives, managers' sense of social responsibility, confidence in the administration of justice, security of persons and property, government transparency, the adequacy of the legal framework and bureaucracy in the public sector, protection of intellectual property rights, the frequency of tax evasion, and the occurrence of improper practices, such as bribing or corruption.

Transparency International's corruption perceptions index

Transparency International (<*www.transparency.org*>) constructs a "corruption perceptions index" based on ratings by ICRG; the *World Competitiveness Yearbook*; the *Global Competitiveness Report*; Brunetti, Kisunko, and Weder's (1997) credibility of rules index; World Bank-sponsored surveys; and other sources. Each source is weighted equally, on a scale of 0–10.

The index is produced annually, with country coverage varying as available data sources change. Countries are rated only if data are available from at least three of the twelve sources used. Eighty-five countries were rated in 1998. Like the competitiveness ratings, Transparency International's index postdates the cross-country data on economic performance, limiting their usefulness in studying the determinants of investment and growth.

World Values Surveys

The World Values Survey, organized by Ronald Inglehart with collaborators from around the world, have been conducted in sixty-eight countries. The first round of surveys, conducted in 1981, included twenty-four countries, most of them advanced industrial economies. A second round, conducted in 1990–1, added twenty-one new countries, most of them formerly socialist economies and middle-income developing countries. A third round, conducted in 1995–6, covered forty-two countries, including more than twenty not represented in either of the first two rounds. About half of the countries added in this round were formerly socialist economies, the other half developing countries. A fourth round conducted in 2000–2001 is adding several more developing countries. (See <*http://wvs.isr.umich.edu/index.html*> for more detailed information.) The best-known work based on these surveys addresses the emergence of "post-materialist" values in advanced industrialized nations (e.g. Inglehart 1990). Recently numerous items included in the survey have been exploited in cross-country research on social capital. Respondents are asked in the survey about their memberships in various groups, their attitude towards socially cooperative behaviors, their levels of trust in other people, and their tolerance towards alternative values and lifestyles.

REFERENCES

Alesina, A. and Drazen, A., 1991. "Why Are Stabilizations Delayed?" *American Economic Review* 81(5): 1170–1188

Alesina, A. and Perotti, R., 1996. "Income Distribution, Political Instability, and Investment." *European Economic Review* 40(6): 1203–1228

Alesina, and Rodrik, D., 1994. "Distributive Politics and Economic Growth." *Quarterly Journal of Economics* 109(2): 465–490

Alesina, A., Baqir, R., and Easterly, W., 1999. "Public Goods and Ethnic Divisions." *Quarterly Journal of Economics*, 114(4): 1243–1284

Alesina, A., Ozler, S., Roubini, N., and Swagel, P., 1996. "Political Instability and Economic Growth."*Journal of Economic Growth* 1(2): 189–211

Almond, G. A. and Verba, S., 1963. *The Civic Culture: Political Attitudes and Democracy in Five Nations.* Newbury Park, CA: Sage

Banks, A. S., 1993. "Cross-National Time-Series Data Archive." State University of New York at Binghampton, Department of Political Science

Barro, R., 1991. "Economic Growth in a Cross-Section of Countries." *Quarterly Journal of Economics* 106(2): 407–433

1996. "Democracy and Growth." *Journal of Economic Growth* 1(1): 1–27

Barro, R. and Lee, J.-W., 1993. "International Comparisons of Educational Attainment." *Journal of Monetary Economics* 32(3): 363–394

Berg, A. and Sachs, J., 1988. "The Debt Crisis: Structural Explanations of Country Performance." *Journal of Development Economics* 29(3): 271–306

Bergsten, G. S., 1985. "On the Role of Social Norms in a Market Economy." *Public Choice* 45(2): 113–137

Bernstein, L., 1992. "Opting Out of the Legal System: Extralegal Contractual Relations in the Diamond Industry." *Journal of Legal Studies* 21(1): 115–157

Bilson, J. F. O., 1982. "Civil Liberty: An Econometric Investigation." *Kyklos* 35(1): 94–114

Borner, S., Brunetti, A., and Weder, B., 1995. *Political Credibility and Economic Development.* London: Macmillan

Brunetti, A., Kisunko, G., and Weder, B., 1997. "Credibility of Rules and Economic Growth." Policy Research Working Paper 1760. World Bank, Office of the Chief Economist and Senior Vice President, Development Economics, Washington, DC

Bruno, M., Ravallion, M., and Squire, L., 1998. "Equity and Growth in Developing Countries: Old and New Perspectives on the Policy Issues." In V. Tanzi and K. Chu (eds.), *Income Distribution and High-Quality Growth*. Cambridge, MA: MIT Press

Burkhart, R. and Lewis-Beck, M., 1994. "Comparative Democracy: The Economic Development Thesis." *American Political Science Review* 88(4): 903–10

Chong, A. and Calderon, C., 2000. "Causality and Feedback Between Institutional Measures and Economic Growth." *Economics and Politics*, 12(1): 69–81.

Clague, C., Keefer, P., Knack, S., and Olson, M., 1999. "Contract-Intensive Money." *Journal of Economic Growth* 4(2): 185–211

Collier, P., 1998. "The Political Economy of Ethnicity." Centre for the Study of African Economies Working Paper Series WPS/98–8. University of Oxford

Coplin, W., O'Leary, M. N., and Sealy, T., 1991. *Political Risk Services: A Business Guide to Political Risk for International Decisions*. Syracuse, NY: Political Risk Services, Inc.

Dawson, J. W., 1998. "Institutions, Investment and Growth: New Cross-Country and Panel Data Evidence." *Economic Inquiry* 36(4): 603–619

de Soto, H., 1989. *The Other Path: The Invisible Revolution in the Third World*. New York: Harper & Row

Deininger, K. and Squire, L., 1996. "A New Data Set: Measuring Income Inequality." *World Bank Economic Review* 10(3): 565–592

Easterly, W. and Levine, R., 1997. "Africa's Growth Tragedy: Policies and Ethnic Divisions." *Quarterly Journal of Economics* 112(4): 1203–1250

Fukuyama, F., 1995. *Trust: The Social Virtues and the Creation of Prosperity*. New York: Free Press

Gastil, R. D., 1990. "The Comparative Survey of Freedom: Experiences and Suggestions." *Studies in Comparative International Development* 25(1): 25–50

Granato, J., Inglehart, R., and Leblang, D., 1996a. "Cultural Values, Stable Democracy, and Economic Development: A Reply." *American Journal of Political Science* 40(3): 680–696

 1996b. "The Effect of Cultural Values on Economic Development: Theory, Hypotheses, and Some Empirical Tests." *American Journal of Political Science* 40(3): 607–631

Greif, A., 1993. "Contract Enforceability and Economic Institutions in Early Trade: The Maghribi Trader's Coalition." *American Economic Review* 83(3): 525–548

 1994. "Cultural Beliefs and the Organization of Society: A Historical and Theoretical Reflection on Collectivist and Individualist Societies." *Journal of Political Economy* 102(5): 912–950

Grier, K. B. and Tullock, G., 1989. "An Empirical Analysis of Cross-National Economic Growth, 1951–80." *Journal of Monetary Economics* 24(2): 259–276

Grootaert, C., 1999. "Social Capital, Household Welfare and Poverty in Indonesia." World Bank Policy Research Working Paper 2148. Washington, DC

Gupta, D. K., 1990. *The Economics of Political Violence: The Effect of Political Instability on Economic Growth*. New York: Praeger

Gwartney, J., Lawson, R., and Block, W., 1996. *Economic Freedom of the World: 1975–95*. Vancouver, British Columbia: Fraser Institute

Helliwell, J., 1994. "Empirical Linkages Between Democracy and Economic Growth." *British Journal of Political Science* 24(2): 22–48

1996. "Economic Growth and Social Capital in Asia." NBER Working Paper 5470. National Bureau of Economic Research, Cambridge, MA

Helliwell, J. and Putnam, R., 1995. "Economic Growth and Social Capital in Italy." *Eastern Economic Journal* 21(3): 295–307

Horowitz, D. L., 1985. *Ethnic Groups in Conflict.* Berkeley, CA: University of California Press

Humana, C., 1984. *World Human Rights Guide.* New York: PICA Press

1986. *World Human Rights Guide*, 2nd edn. New York: Facts on File Publications

1992. *World Human Rights Guide*, 3rd edn. New York: Oxford University Press

Inglehart, R., 1990. *Culture Shift in Advanced Industrial Society.* Princeton, NJ: Princeton University Press

1994. *Codebook for World Values Surveys.* Ann Arbor, MI: Institute for Social Research

Isham, J., Kaufmann, D., and Pritchett, L., 1997. "Civil Liberties, Democracy, and the Performance of Government Projects." *World Bank Economic Review* 11(2): 219–242

Jackman, R. and Miller, R. A., 1996. "A Renaissance of Political Culture." *American Journal of Political Science* 40(3), 632–659.

Kawachi, I., Kennedy B. P., Lochner, L., and Deborah Prothrow-Stith, D., 1997. "Social Capital, Income Inequality, and Mortality." *American Journal of Public Health* 87(9): 1491–1498

Keefer, P. and Knack, S., forthcoming. "Polarization, Politics and Property Rights: Links between Inequality and Growth." *Public Choice*

1997. "Why Don't Poor Countries Catch Up? A Cross-Country Test of an Institutional Explanation." *Economic Inquiry* 35(3): 590–602

Knack, S., 1996. "Institutions and the Convergence Hypothesis: The Cross-National Evidence." *Public Choice* 87 (June): 207–228.

Knack, S. and Keefer, P., 1995. "Institutions and Economic Performance: Cross-Country Tests Using Alternative Institutional Measures." *Economics and Politics* 7 (November): 207–227

1997a. "Does Inequality Harm Growth Only in Democracies?" *American Journal of Political Science* 41(1): 323–332

1997b. "Does Social Capital Have an Economic Payoff? A Cross-Country Investigation." *Quarterly Journal of Economics* 112(4): 1251–1288.

Kormendi, R. C. and Meguire, P. G., 1985. "Macroeconomic Determinants of Growth." *Journal of Monetary Economics* 16(1): 141–163

Lane, P. R. and Tornell, A., 1996. "Power, Growth, and the Voracity Effect." *Journal of Economic Growth* 1(2): 213–241

La Porta, R., Lopez-de-Silanes, F., Shleifer, A., and Vishny, R. W., 1997. "Trust in Large Organizations." *American Economic Review Papers and Proceedings* 87(2): 333–338

Levine, R. and Renelt, D., 1992. "A Sensitivity Analysis of Cross-Country Growth Regressions." *American Economic Review* 82(4): 942–963

Lipset, S. M., 1959. "Some Social Requisites of Democracy: Economic Development and Political Legitimacy." *American Political Science Review* 53(1): 69–105

Londregan, J. B. and Poole, N. T., 1990. "Poverty, the Coup Trap, and the Seizure of Executive Power." *World Politics* 42(2): 151–183

1992. "The Seizure of Executive Power and Economic Growth: Some Additional Evidence." In Alex Cukierman, Zvi Hercowitz, and Leonardo Leiderman (eds.), *Political Economy, Growth, and Business Cycles*. Cambridge, MA: MIT Press

Mauro, P., 1995. "Corruption and Growth." *Quarterly Journal of Economics* 110(3): 681–712

Messick, R., 1996. *Economic Freedom in the World, 1995–96*. New Brunswick, NJ: Freedom House

Muller, E. N. and Erich Weede, E., 1990. "Cross-National Variation in Political Violence." *Journal of Conflict Resolution* 34(4): 624–651

Narayan, D. and Pritchett, L., 1999. "Cents and Sociability: Household Income and Social Capital in Rural Tanzania." *Economic Development and Cultural Change* 47(4): 871–897

North, D. C., 1990. *Institutions, Institutional Change and Economic Performance*. New York: Cambridge University Press

Olson, M., 1963. "Rapid Growth as a Destabilizing Force." *Journal of Economic History* 23(4): 529–552

1982. *The Rise and Decline of Nations*. New Haven, CT: Yale University Press

1994. "Who Gains From Policies that Increase Poverty?" IRIS Center Working Paper 137. Center for Institutional Reform and the Informal Sector, University of Maryland, College Park

Przeworski, A. and Limongi F., 1993. "Political Regimes and Economic Growth." *Journal of Economic Perspectives* 7(3): 51–69

Putnam, R. D., 1993. *Making Democracy Work: Civic Traditions in Modern Italy*. Princeton, NJ: Princeton University Press

Rodrik, D., 1999. "Where Did All the Growth Go? External Shocks, Social Conflict, and Growth Collapses." *Journal of Economic Growth* 4(4): 385–412

Scully, G., 1988. "The Institutional Framework and Economic Development." *Journal of Political Economy* 96(3): 652–662

1992. *Constitutional Environments and Economic Growth*. Princeton, NJ: Princeton University Press

Spindler, Z., 1991. "Liberty and Development: A Further Empirical Perspective." *Public Choice* 69(2): 197–210

Squire, L., 1993. "Fighting Poverty." *American Economic Review Papers and Proceedings* 83(2): 377–382

Summers, R. and Heston, A., 1991. "The Penn World Tables. Mark V: An Extended Set of International Comparisons, 1950–88." *Quarterly Journal of Economics* 106(2): 327–368

Swank, D., 1996. "Culture, Institutions, and Economic Growth." *American Journal of Political Science* 40(3): 660–679

Varshney, A., 1998. "Ethnic Conflict and the Structure of Civic Life." Paper presented at the annual meetings of the American Political Science Association, September 3–6, Boston, MA

World Bank, 1997. *World Development Report: The State in a Changing World.* New York: Oxford University Press

 1998. "The Local Level Institutions Study: Program Description and Prototype Questionnaires." Local Level Institutions Working Paper 2, Social Development Department, World Bank, Washington, DC

Wright, L. M., 1982. "A Comparative Survey of Economic Freedoms." In Raymond Gastil (ed.), *Freedom in the World: Political Rights and Civil Liberties, 1982.* New York: Freedom House

Zak, P. J. and Knack, S., 2001. "Trust and Growth." *Economic Journal*, 111: 295–321

Part 2

The impact of social capital on development

3   Mapping and measuring social capital through
     assessment of collective action to conserve and
     develop watersheds in Rajasthan, India

Anirudh Krishna and Norman Uphoff

Social capital is a popular current concept in the development literature and
in development agencies. But is it real enough to be measured in the field
and validated by achievement of desired outcomes of development programs?
Is it something that can be purposefully increased? This chapter reports on
the observed relationships between social capital measures and development
outcomes in sixty-four villages in the Indian State of Rajasthan. Since 1991
these villages have participated in a watershed conservation and development
program funded by the Indian government and the World Bank. The villages
provide an empirical basis for evaluating whether social capital can be identified
and measured quantitatively.

The database includes interviews with 2,397 individuals, split about evenly
between men and women; sixty-four focus group sessions with village leaders and elected representatives; and relevant village- and household-level data
obtained from official records. By classifying the villages' performance in
restoring their degraded or vulnerable common lands through collective action
as having been high, medium, or low, we assess whether certain social-structural
or cognitive variables associated with social capital can explain differences
in the measured manifestations of *mutually beneficial collective action* – the
benefit flow we associate with and expect to observe from the asset of social
capital.

We find that an index of social capital variables is positively and consistently
correlated with superior development outcomes, both in watershed conservation
and in cooperative development activities more generally. In addition to social
capital, we find two other variables – political competition and literacy – to

We wish to thank Chris Barrett, Chris Grootaert, Niraja Jayal, Julie Fisher, Jane Mansbridge, Walter
Mebane, Bo Rothstein, Sidney Tarrow, Thierry van Bastelaer, Jonathan Wand, Frank Young, and
seminar participants at Cornell University, the Kennedy School of Government, and the World
Bank for providing helpful comments and advice. We also thank the Social Capital Initiative of
the World Bank for funding this study, and the Government of Rajasthan, especially its Watershed
Development Department, for sharing their data resources. The Cornell International Institute for
Food, Agriculture and Development (CIIFAD) provided administrative support and some complementary funding for this work, and we thank especially Virginia Montopoli and Cynthia Telage for
their assistance.

have some statistically significant associations with measured development performance. Surprisingly, the effects of other factors that were expected, based on theories and hypotheses in the literature, to be associated with superior outcomes are not confirmed by data analysis using correlation, regression, and factor analysis techniques.

Our data indicate that "history" matters but that by itself it does not determine much of the stock of social capital of a household or village. Intradistrict differences are much greater than are the interdistrict differences that could be attributed to socially formative experience in previous generations. Purposive action to enhance social capital can be undertaken, we conclude, by acting on its constituent factors.

Giving substance to the concept of social capital

There is, unfortunately, more demand for rigorous conceptualization of *social capital* than there is supply. Although the term is widely used in both the social science literature and development agency discourse, most references to it have been more descriptive than analytical. We aim here to contribute to an understanding of social capital that is rigorous and theoretically informed, as well as relevant for development work.

We started with the approach known as "subordinate conceptualization," breaking the concept into major components. The study of other forms of capital in economics would be much less advanced today if there had not been some basic distinctions made within what are otherwise large and diverse categories. It has been very important, for example, to distinguish renewable from non-renewable natural resources, skilled from unskilled labor, and physical from financial capital.

If the concept of social capital is to mean anything more than social organization or social values, it needs to share some basic similarities to the familiar concept of capital as this has been elaborated in the discipline of economics. (See the discussion under "Is It Capital?" in the introduction to the book.) The core meaning of capital is that it represents a *stock of assets* that yields a *flow of benefits*, such as income or revenue streams. Although one can identify capital and estimate its value by looking at the flow of benefits that it yields, capital should not be equated with that flow, since stocks and flows are different things.

What is the flow associated with social capital? By what fruits will we know it? We propose that the stream of benefits from social capital – the social income or revenue flow that comes from it – is mutually beneficial collective action. While this is a matter of definition, it reflects mainstream opinion in the literature (Woolcock 1998).

There is no need to invoke an explanation as complex – and still controversial – as social capital for purely individual action. What purely economic analysis and theory have found difficult to explain is behavior that involves cooperation for mutual advantage, i.e., behavior that involves significant transactions costs and that surmounts deterrents such as free-riding. The existence of mutually beneficial collective action is an empirical fact that is difficult to explain solely with individualistic, self-interest-maximizing concepts of people's motivation.

The concept of social capital has been proposed not just to account for people's willingness or predisposition to act cooperatively for mutual benefit but also to deal with more aggregated phenomena – to explain why societies may be more productive than can be explained by evaluating their material resources. There is a growing suspicion, even among orthodox economists, that some factors in the realms of culture, psychology, or social relationships can make for wholes that are more than the sums of their parts, with the observation that nonmaterial causes can have significant material effects.

A central characteristic of mutually beneficial collective action is that it produces *positive-sum* outcomes. People by working together and helping each other can gain greater mutual satisfaction over time – though they do not gain always equally or necessarily at all points in time. Cooperative relationships at the individual or group level can facilitate cooperation at the societal or national level, resulting in productive behavior that differs from behavior motivated solely by individual self-interest. This is the understanding of social capital with which we start, influenced by our reading of the literature, and which we have examined and tested empirically in the study reported here.[1]

We propose that there are two main kinds or categories of social capital: *structural* forms and *cognitive* forms. Both pertain to and affect social relationships and interactions among people, and both affect and are affected by expectations. Structural social capital *facilitates* mutually beneficial collective action through established roles and social networks supplemented by rules, procedures, and precedents. Cognitive social capital, which includes shared norms, values, attitudes, and beliefs, *predisposes* people toward mutually beneficial collective action.

These two kinds of social capital interact and reinforce one another, but they differ in several ways. Structural capital is relatively objective in that it includes

---

[1] The understandings on which this analysis is based have been discussed in chapters 12 and 13 of Uphoff (1996); also in Uphoff (2000) and Krishna (2000a, 2000b). Note that according to our conceptualization, groups such as the Ku Klux Klan or the Aryan Nation, although they can have high levels of solidarity, trust, and other characteristics associated with social capital, do not represent forms of social capital because their purpose is not to enhance the welfare of others through cooperative effort. As such, our concept of social capital may be more restrictive than that used in other chapters of this book.

elements that are visible and that can be devised through group deliberation. Cognitive social capital is essentially subjective, having to do with how people think and feel. Structural social capital is *external*; it can be observed and modified directly. Cognitive social capital is *internal*; it resides within people's heads and cannot be changed easily by outside action.

Both forms of social capital qualify as capital because they both require some investment – of time and effort if not always of money. A variety of resources can be expended to establish roles, rules, procedures, and precedents and to create norms, values, attitudes, and beliefs. These concepts have already been elaborated in Uphoff (2000), so they are presented here only briefly, to introduce the theoretical framework from which this empirical work in Rajasthan proceeded.

The questions that we asked the villagers in our sample were constructed to identify both structural forms of social capital (roles, social networks, rules, procedures, and precedents) and cognitive forms (norms, values, attitudes, and beliefs). We were particularly interested in roles that can facilitate decisionmaking, mobilization and management of resources, communication and coordination, and conflict resolution, as these are crucial for lowering the transaction costs of collective action.

Primary forms of cognitive social capital that we considered included trust, solidarity, cooperation, and generosity; secondary forms included honesty, egalitarianism, fairness, participation, and democratic governance. We examine the importance of such factors in promoting mutual well-being through collective action by comparing them with other factors that have been proposed in the literature as leading to such action.

Watershed development as a focus for assessing the nature and effects of social capital: the Rajasthan case

Watershed development offers an important arena for investigating the empirical correlates and origins of social capital – considered here as a source (capital stock) for mutually beneficially collective action (flow) – and for assessing its levels and impact in participating villages. Protecting and improving soil, water, and plant resources in a catchment area is something that can be done only incompletely at best by individual activities and investments. Indeed, measures to forestall erosion in a single location may actually accelerate it elsewhere. Although there can be some benefits from conservation measures to their implementers in the short run, major benefits accrue to others, to downstream communities and to subsequent generations. Watersheds thus present situations in which one would expect social capital to be significant in explaining successful implementation of improvement programs.

The villages in the database have all been participating in the integrated watershed development program of the Rajasthan state government, funded by the World Bank and the government of India. Program activities were launched in each participating village at about the same time in 1991. The programs have been in effect long enough, we believe, to warrant an investigation of the causes and correlates of community-level performance in watershed programs that will reflect people's cooperation to create public as well as private goods.

More than 70 percent of Rajasthan villagers depend on agriculture and animal husbandry for their livelihoods. Agriculture depends largely on rainfall, as there are no major canal systems in the area. Water drawn from wells and tubewells irrigates less than 20 percent of the crop area of any of the villages studied. Animal husbandry serves both as a source of supplementary income and as insurance against failure of uncertain and risk-prone cropping operations. On average, each household owns eight farm animals, mostly cows, sheep, and goats, with richer households owning more cows and buffaloes than poorer households. Most households own at least some farm animals, and even the poorest households draw support from the small numbers of sheep and goats they own.

All households thus depend to a significant extent on village common lands for obtaining fodder for their animals (Jodha 1990; Brara 1991; Krishna 1997). Nearly half of the land in each village is not privately owned but is instead vested with the state government or with local government units, village panchayats, having jurisdiction over as many as five villages, depending on the size of the villages. In addition to serving as a source of fodder, such common lands are also the most important source of domestic energy in the form of fuelwood.

Many of these common land areas had already become, or were on the verge of becoming, wastelands. Very low growth rates of biomass on these lands had sharply restricted the total offtake of fodder and fuelwood. Development of village common lands, which could increase the yield of fodder and fuelwood, was thus a key component of watershed development efforts, and were in many villages quite successful.[2]

Five to eight residents in each participating village were elected by fellow villagers to a user committee. The program expected this group to organize and manage a variety of soil and water conservation works on common lands on behalf of the village. These works included planting trees and grasses, enforcing rules for protection and extraction, and fencing common lands against stray cattle and human encroachment. With project advice and assistance, these activities were expected to sustainably enhance fodder and fuelwood yields

---

[2] Before program implementation, average yields on common lands were less than 75 kilograms of grass per hectare. After program implementation more than 750 kilograms per hectare was observed being harvested (Rajasthan Agricultural University 1993).

on these lands. Each committee worked with government staff to draw up and implement a development plan for the common lands of its village. Its members, who were unpaid, were wholly responsible for formulating and implementing the local rules that would govern the sharing of costs for the program and the distribution of its benefits.

The need for common land development was keenly felt by village residents. Nearly 90 percent of the more than 2,000 residents whom we interviewed for this study identified "improvement of common lands" as one of the three most important development needs; other important needs included drinking water, schools, and improved roads.

Under the program, villagers had to contribute themselves at least 10 percent of program costs. Benefits were shared among the villagers according to rules devised by their user committees and approved by the village as a whole; 88 percent of all respondents stated that they had participated in decisionmaking, either personally or through their representatives, and 87 percent felt that the program had delivered tangible benefits to the community – a remarkably positive evaluation for any public sector program in India.

Although common land development represents a collectively organized response to a need that is felt acutely by most villagers, program results varied considerably from village to village. Some villages performed much better than others in terms of both objective indicators (survival rates of trees, grass harvested per capita) and subjective evaluations (levels of individual satisfaction).

Sample and database

Sixty-four villages were selected, sixteen in each of four districts in Rajasthan – Ajmer, Bhilwara, Rajsamand, and Udaipur. These districts were chosen to include two different approaches to watershed development in the state, those supported by the World Bank and those of the Indian government. (We did not, however, undertake to compare and evaluate the two approaches separately.) To ensure sufficient spread and range for the dependent variable, the villages were selected to reflect different levels of prior program performance – high, medium, and low – judged on the basis of information available from project field reports. The numbers of high-, medium-, and low-performing villages were distributed as evenly as possible across the four districts.

The database consisted of interviews with individuals, focus group interviews with village leaders, and data obtained from official sources. Interviews were conducted with a total of 2,397 individuals. Households were selected on the basis of simple random sampling in each village, using the most current voter lists for each village. To ensure a gender-balanced sample, one man was selected at random from all odd-numbered households and one woman from all even-numbered households in the sample.

The sample reflects the largely poor, uneducated, agriculture-dependent nature of the region's population. A standard instrument was used to interview user committee members in each village. Field investigators also measured average fodder yields and plant survival rates in each village after drawing a sample from the areas planted under program auspices. Official data included statistics from the Census of India and from the state government departments of agriculture on watershed development, elections, local self-government, land holdings, cooperatives, and animal husbandry.

Our methodology thus yielded two parallel data sets: household data ($n = 2,397$) and village data ($n = 64$). This enabled us to evaluate and cross-check social capital and institutional achievements at both levels.

In the next several sections, we consider relationships at the village level because the village has been and continues to be a fundamental unit of local community in India (Srinivas 1987; Schomer, Erdman, Oldrick, and Rudolph 1994). This makes it relevant to focus our examination of social capital at this level. We supplement data collected at the village level with analysis of the village means and standard deviations of the household data that were collected in each village. Analysis of social capital also at the household level is presented on p. 120.

Constructing the first dependent variable: the Common Land Development Index

A measure of common land development, the Common Land Development Index, was constructed based on six criteria, all highly correlated with one another and loading commonly on a single factor when examined using the methodology of factor analysis. The six criteria of measured performance in watershed development that constitute the Common Land Development Index are:

- *Quantity of work.* Percentage of a village's common land developed under the program.
- *Quality of protection.* Survival rates for trees and shrubs planted under program auspices.
- *Productivity.* Quantity of fodder and fuelwood harvested the previous year, measured in headloads per family.
- *Voluntary action.* Number of times in the previous five years that the user committee voluntarily replanted and filled gaps in its forested areas.
- *Diversification of activities.* Number of times in the previous five years that the user committee engaged in community development activities not directly related to watershed development.
- *Support for local contributions.* Percentage of total costs of watershed development that villagers would be willing to bear. This measure, more subjective

Table 3.1   *Common land development: factor loadings
for components*

Component	Factor
Quantity of work	0.59601
Quality of protection	0.69309
Productivity	0.82895
Voluntary action	0.81953
Diversification of activities	0.85734
Support for local contributions	0.65181

than the other measures, reflects villagers' willingness to mobilize local resources.[3]

These six measures are highly correlated with one another, with coefficients all significant at the 0.05 level or better. Not surprisingly, factor analysis points to one common factor on which all six of these elements load highly (table 3.1). This single common factor has a communality of 3.514, which would account for almost 60 percent of the combined variance of the six variables. Also, the scree plot drawn for these variables shows a sharp discontinuity, or "elbow," between factors 1 and 2, which reinforces the conclusion that these variables together represent a single common factor.[4] The index was constructed by first standardizing each item with the values rescaled so that each had a maximum value of 1.0; each variable was given an equal weight within the index as the six scores were then summed.[5] The maximum index score was thus 6.0. In table 3.2, we show the average component scores for villages categorized

[3] Support for making local contributions reflects respondents' satisfaction levels with the performance of the common land development activity in their village. This interpretation was verified by comparing the contribution levels reported here for future common land development with the contributions that the same set of respondents were willing to make for other development activities – such as drinking water, schools, and approach roads – regarded as at least as important as common land development. In villages in which the other five elements of the Common Land Development Index are high, contribution levels reported for future common land development are much higher than those reported for other important development needs. This suggests that support for local contributions is more closely related to satisfaction levels with common land development than to some general willingness on the part of villagers to contribute to common development needs.

[4] The conclusion that a single common factor exists is given added weight by the fact that the root mean square of off-diagonal residuals equals 0.107 – well within the acceptable limit of 0.126 suggested by Harman's criterion for a sample size of 64. Kaiser's measure of sampling adequacy was 0.81.

[5] An alternative index, which weighted the individual items by their factor scores, was highly correlated with the Common Land Development Index (correlation coefficient = 0.97), indicating that the index is robust against alternative weighting schemes.

Table 3.2 *Component scores for villages grouped by Common Land Development Index category*

Component	Low Common Land Development Index (less than 1.5) $n = 15$	Medium Common Land Development Index (1.5–3.0) $n = 23$	High Common Land Development Index (3.0 or more) $n = 26$
Quantity of work	1.23	2.43	2.93
Quality of protection	0.50	0.78	1.80
Productivity	1.00	1.65	3.00
Voluntary action	0.23	0.61	2.00
Diversification of activities	0.12	0.70	2.00
Support for local contributions	0.31	0.65	1.40

according to whether their Common Land Development Index score was low, medium, or high. The Common Land Development Index correlates highly with each of its six components (Cronbach's alpha coefficient = 0.89). Each of the individual correlations among the index components is statistically significant and positive at the 0.0001 level, with a value of 0.60 or higher.

Testing alternative hypotheses for variations in watershed performance

To explain variations in collective action outcomes, we first consider several hypotheses other than that of social capital. Each of these corresponds to a theoretical argument prominent in the social science literature on development. As we see, however, none of these hypotheses can explain the variations in performance across a large and diverse set of communities. To begin, we examine the effects of possible explanatory variables separately; then we consider whether any better explanation can be constructed by examining the effects of multiple independent variables in combination. A set of regression models, reported later in this chapter, makes use simultaneously of all the variables examined in this section. Significance results from regression analysis are not different from those reported here for correlation analysis.

The hypotheses we test represent complex bundles of factors. Each is operationalized by looking at specific, quantifiable measures that reflect the determinants proposed in the literature. Our study was not originally designed to examine these hypotheses in detail, so we have to consider them using the best available measures of factors that could influence mutually beneficial collective action outcomes.

Relative need of communities

Cooperative behavior is sometimes explained by the extent to which people will benefit materially from working together. As reported already, all villages in the sample faced shortages of fodder and fuelwood, but some have more severe shortages than do others. A rational-actor explanation of collective action would predict that those communities in which members have a greater objective need for fodder and fuelwood would be more able and likely to establish and operate effective user committees than other communities (Wade 1994).

Two sets of variables were analyzed to assess relative need. The first variable measures the pressure of the village's animal population on available grazing land. Where such pressure is great, the rewards from increasing the production of fodder from common lands will be greater. Since animals of different sizes (or ages) have different feed requirements, we standardized for size, and thus for grazing pressure, by converting the village's number of animals into "Cow Units," using formulae widely used by animal husbandry experts. The total number of Cow Units in a village was divided by the area of available grazing land to get a measure of Cow Units for each village. According to the relative-need hypothesis, the greater the population pressure on grazing lands, the more readily villagers should combine to undertake communal land development. This hypothesis predicts that Cow Units will be significantly and positively related to the Common Land Development Index.

The second variable, Rainfed Land Ratio, is the ratio of rainfed (unirrigated) cropped area to irrigated cropped area. This variable measures how important common lands are to villagers. Villages with relatively more irrigated land would have less dependence on common land. The relative-need hypothesis holds that villagers more dependent on rainfall for crop production will participate more actively in watershed development. High values of Rainfed Land Ratio should therefore coincide with high values of the Common Land Development Index.

The relative need of communities hypothesis is not supported by the data, however, at least in simple monocausal form. The correlation coefficient between the Common Land Development Index and the Cow Units variable has a small negative value (-0.136), while the correlation between the Common Land Development Index and Rainfed Land Ratio has a value of 0.06, with neither coefficient significant at even the 0.1 level.

Relative need of powerholders

A refinement of this hypothesis should be considered. According to Knight (1992), collective action is most likely to occur when the powerholders in a society are most in need of the rewards likely to result from such action. According to this hypothesis, the Common Land Development Index should be higher when the persons with power and wealth in the village are themselves most in need of fodder or fuelwood.

We examined the validity of this hypothesis for explaining watershed development efforts by looking at the distribution of animal ownership by households. The higher the standard deviation of animal ownership in a community, the more likely it is that richer households control a disproportionately large number of animals. A larger standard deviation of animal ownership should, according to this hypothesis, be associated with a higher Common Land Development Index. But in fact, a small and statistically insignificant negative correlation is found between these two variables. The hypothesis that collective action is undertaken to serve the interests of more powerful villagers is not supported by our data.

Government staff support

The Rajasthan Watershed Development Program was initiated by a government department. Although planning, implementing, and managing local plans were the responsibility of elected user committees, the bulk of program funds was provided by the government, and government staff were expected to provide technical support to user committees.

Differences in the motivation and competence of government staff assigned to work with different villages and in the extent to which they participated in the community's activities could possibly account for differences in program performance. Indeed, senior government officials with whom we discussed this study expected this variable to account for much of the observed differences in the Common Land Development Index.

It is difficult to measure the caliber and activity of government staff directly. Given the difficulty that officials had in visiting these villages, many of which are remote and poorly served by infrastructure, we believe that a measure of government staff interaction with user committees reflects staff motivation and provides a good indication of the amount and quality of external support for communities' watershed development efforts. To assess this level of interaction, we included two questions in the focus group questionnaires:

- How frequently did staff of the government's Watershed Development Department visit your village?
- Suppose that 100 percent of all villagers recognize the person who is the headmaster of the village school. On such a scale, what percentage of village residents do you think would recognize the local staff of the Watershed Department?

Responses to these two questions were averaged to calculate the variable Government Staff Support (range 0.5–4.0). According to the hypothesis that government staff support makes a difference for village collective action, a higher Government Staff Support score should correspond with higher values of the Common Land Development Index. In fact, the observed correlation coefficient is small (0.062) and not significantly different from zero. Correlating the Common Land Development Index separately with responses to each of the two questions does not change the results (neither coefficient is significantly different from zero). By itself, then, staff input does not really account for intervillage differences in program performance. In combination with social capital measures, we find a positive association between government staff input and program performance, though not a very strong one. Without sufficient levels of social capital, this variable appears to have no significant effect.

Modernization

According to the modernization hypothesis, communities that are in some sense more modern than others – more closely linked to external markets, more advanced in terms of mechanization of production, better served with infrastructure facilities – should be more progress-oriented and willing to engage in mutual efforts that improve living conditions further. According to this hypothesis, changes in material conditions are associated with the emergence of values and attitudes that facilitate reciprocity, cooperation, and a preference for bargaining and accommodation in everyday dealings. Modernization is also expected to go together with the development of associations, including market, political, and social organizations, that help knit people together in networks of mutual support (Lipset 1960, 1994).

There is in the literature a converse hypothesis that associates greater cooperation with more "traditional" communities and societies, expecting these to have more collective action. If this alternative explanation is correct, we would see a significant negative relationship from our data between degree of modernization and the Common Land Development Index. Our methodology tests both hypotheses at the same time.

Three different sets of variables – measuring commercialization, mechanization of agriculture, and infrastructure – were used to determine whether there is any association between attributes of modernization and the dependent variable, Common Land Development Index.

Villages that are more closely connected to the market economy, it is suggested, will more quickly seize upon any opportunities that become available for development. This hypothesis is tested by analyzing two variables: Distance to Market, the distance to the nearest market town, measured in kilometers, and

Fare to Market, the cost of traveling to that market town, denominated in rupees. However, neither variable has any significant correlation with the Common Land Development Index, and neither coefficient is significantly different from zero (the coefficient for Distance to Market is actually slightly negative).

The variable Mechanization represents the number of tractors and mechanical threshers in the village. It reflects the degree to which agriculture, the main economic activity in these villages, has progressed beyond manual labor. This variable also has no significant correlation with the Common Land Development Index.

Villages with more modern infrastructure facilities might be expected to be more disposed to undertake development activities. To test this hypothesis, we looked at five types of facilities: educational facilities, health care facilities, communication facilities, transport facilities, and electricity. Villages were each given scores ranging from 1 to 5, depending upon the level to which they are served by each type of infrastructure. In the case of educational facilities, for example, a village served by only a primary school received a 1, one with a middle school received a 2, one with a secondary school received a 3, one with a high school received a 4, and one with a junior college received a 5. Other infrastructure facilities were scored similarly, based on the highest level of service provided in the village.

Scores for various types of facilities are highly correlated with each other. They are also highly correlated with the size of a village's population. Not surprisingly, larger villages tend to have more and better infrastructure than smaller villages. Given the high correlations among the various scores, it was appropriate to combine the various measures into a single score. A composite variable, Infrastructure, represents the sum of the scores for each type of infrastructure. The correlation coefficient of the Infrastructure variable with the Common Land Development Index is low (0.004) and not significantly different from zero. Taken individually, none of the five types of infrastructure is significantly correlated with the Common Land Development Index. Villages that are more commercial, more highly mechanized, or better served by infra-structure facilities are not found to have higher levels of collective action than others. Neither the modernization hypothesis nor the counterhypothesis is thus supported by the data.

Heterogeneity and stratification

It has been proposed that having a homogenous population may facilitate col-lective action, whereas a population that is divided by caste, class, and faction may deter it (e.g., Johnston and Clark 1982). We focus here on caste because it is regarded as the most divisive influence in Indian villages and one that creates large economic differences.

Two variables were constructed to assess the influence of caste on collective action. Number of Castes counts the castes residing in a village. This variable ranges from 2 to 21. If villages with more castes face more impediments to collective action, we should find a negative correlation between the number of castes and the Common Land Development Index.

Caste Dominance represents the number of households in a village from the numerically largest caste as a percentage of the total number of village households. The higher this proportion, the easier it should be to mobilize collective action because there is a dominant group to take leadership. Higher values of the Common Land Development Index should thus be associated with higher values for Caste Dominance.

Correlations between the Common Land Development Index and both of these variables are not statistically significant. Nor is there a significant correlation between the Common Land Development Index and a third variable reflecting social homogeneity or heterogeneity, measuring the combined proportion of scheduled caste and scheduled tribe populations in a village. Correlation with a fourth variable measuring inequality of land ownership in the community in terms of the standard deviations of landholding is also statistically insignificant.

We thus find that socially and economically heterogeneous villages are not less likely to act collectively than more homogeneous populations. This result is consistent with previous cross-national analysis that found no statistically significant association between local organization and rural development performance and social homogeneity (Esman and Uphoff 1984, see pp. 116–118, 160–162).

Literacy

It has been argued that in developing countries, especially India, education is the single most important factor explaining economic growth and civic growth (Almond and Verba 1989; Drèze and Sen 1995). If this hypothesis is true, differences in literacy levels should correlate positively with the Common Land Development Index.

Of the various hypotheses examined, this is the only one that appears to have some validity as a single independent variable. The correlation between literacy – measured as a percentage of the total population – and the Common Land Development Index is positive (0.282) and significant at the 0.05 level. However, correlations between the Common Land Development Index and measures of female literacy and the proportion of the population with high school or higher education are not statistically significant.

Table 3.3   *Ordinary least squares regression results
for alternative hypotheses*

Item	Independent variable	Coefficient	Standard error
Intercept		−0.0238	1.96
Hypothesis			
Relative need	Rainfed Land Ratio	0.004	0.014
	Cow Units	−0.16	0.13
Staff quality	Government Staff Support	0.415	0.278
Modernization	Distance to Market	−0.019	0.04
	Mechanization	−0.046	0.034
	Infrastructure	−0.117	0.08
Literacy	Literacy	0.097**	0.03
Heterogeneity	Number of Castes	0.08	0.07
	Caste Dominance	0.468	1.19

Note: $**p \leq 0.05$. $n = 64$, $R^2 = 0.342$, adjusted $R^2 = 0.177$.
F-ratio $= 2.076$, F-probability $= 0.058$.

Combining independent variables

As we have just seen, only one of the alternative hypotheses considered by itself holds up with this sample of sixty-four villages from which detailed data were collected and analyzed. Only literacy had a demonstrably significant correlation with the dependent variable, the Common Land Development Index, though not a very strong one.

It may be that these variables have some significant effects when combined with other variables. Since theory provides no guidance about which causes should be combined, we consider a simple linear model, taking independent variables from each of the alternative hypotheses (table 3.3).[6]

In multivariate analysis, literacy is still the only variable exhibiting a significant coefficient, with none of the other variables having a coefficient significantly different from zero. The results do not change significantly when alternative specifications of the model are introduced. Literacy is significant within any alternative specification, while none of the other variables is significant under any alternative specification (at the 0.1 level or better). Moreover, although it is statistically significant, literacy by itself can account for no more than 8 percent of the variance in the dependent variable ($R^2 = 0.079$ in a bivariate regression, after removing all variables found to have nonsignificant coefficients). To account for the differences observed in the Common Land Development Index, we

[6] Since skewness is between −1 and 1 for each variable, there is no empirical indication of a need for making nonlinear transformations.

must examine other variables that were measured in our field studies. We return to literacy as a factor affecting development cooperation and performance later in the chapter, when we deal with social capital and institutional supports.

Developing a broader measure of collective action for development

Social capital represents cognitive and structural assets that create propensities and capacities for mutually beneficial collective action. These assets arise from roles, networks, and other social relationships that facilitate cooperative behavior and from norms, values and other cognitive commitments that predispose people to work together for mutual benefit.

Specific empirical correlates of social capital may vary across cultures. Norms and forms of association that promote collective action in one cultural milieu may fail to do so in another. Some kinds of networks may facilitate collective action in a given environment, while other kinds of networks may inhibit such action. It is not the networks *per se* that are important but the meanings these networks hold for their members and the possibilities for collective action and personal benefit that they open up.

The association between mutually beneficial collective action and particular norms and networks must be validated empirically in specific cultural, social, economic, and political environments; but the phenomena of norms and networks will be found, to varying extents, everywhere. Exactly how one assesses trust, for example, will vary across cultures and social settings, but the phenomenon of trust is important everywhere for encouraging people to work together for their mutual benefit.

Before looking for norms, organizations, and other phenomena associated empirically with development-oriented collective action within a particular setting, we first assess the robustness and breadth of the dependent variable. Does the Common Land Development Index affect only one set of actions that translate into good performance within a certain sector (watershed conservation and development)? Or does the Common Land Development Index correspond more broadly to a general propensity for collective action at the village level?

We address these questions by looking at three other outcome variables in addition to the Common Land Development Index. These variables reflect collective action in other areas that are related to development at the village level (table 3.4):

- Community Projects measures the number of community development projects implemented and carried to completion in each village within the previous five years. Such projects typically include school buildings, access

Table 3.4 *Measures of collective action beside watershed activity*

Variable	Mean	Standard deviation	Minimum value	Maximum value
Community Projects	2.84	1.56	0	6.0
Collective Representation	1.09	1.31	0	5.0
Service Satisfaction	2.32	0.87	0.75	4.25

Table 3.5 *Relationship between the Common Land Development Index and other measures of collective action*

Variable	Low Common Land Development Index (less than 1.5)	Medium Common Land Development Index (1.5–3.0)	High Common Land Development Index (more than 3.0)
Community Projects	2.04	2.64	5.53
Collective Representation	0.42	1.00	2.40
Service Satisfaction	1.81	2.36	3.17

roads, and similar projects proposed and implemented by the villagers. Significant among these were projects undertaken under a state government scheme announced in 1992 for which villagers needed to put up 25 percent of the funds to be eligible for support.

- Collective Representation measures the number of times within the previous five years when villagers organized themselves and collectively represented some grievance or demand to a high-ranking administrative official or politician from the ruling party.
- Service Satisfaction measures villagers' satisfaction with four services commonly provided by the government in all villages. Satisfaction levels – rated from 1 (lowest) to 5 (highest) – were measured for basic health services, the village primary school, the local land revenue official, and the agriculture cooperative. Scores for the four measures were averaged to produce a combined index of satisfaction with services. A high level of satisfaction across all four measures indicates not just that government agencies are performing well but that people in the village are working together both to demand good service and to help achieve it.

If these separate measures of collective action in four separate spheres correlate well with each other, a case can be made that there is a single underlying propensity that supports mutually beneficial collective action across diverse areas of development activity. Our results show that villages with high Common Land Development Indexes also have high scores on each of the other three indices (table 3.5).

Table 3.6 *Correlation coefficients between the Development-Oriented Collective Action Index and its components*

Variable	Correlation coefficient
Common Land	
Development Index	0.87914
Service Satisfaction	0.76473
Community Projects	0.83386
Collective Representation	0.81446

Note: Cronbach's alpha coefficient $= 0.881$.

High and significant correlations are found among all pairs formed by these variables, indicating an apparent common propensity at work in diverse areas for collective enterprise, particularly as it relates to development. All of the correlations are high and significant at the 0.001 level.

Combining the four separate indices into a single index provides us with a single composite measure that reflects development-oriented collective action more broadly than any individual measure (table 3.6). The resulting Development-Oriented Collective Action Index is a composite measure, scaled between 0 and 100.

Because of the high correlations between the Common Land Development Index and three other independent indicators of development-oriented collective action, we believe it reasonable to infer that the Common Land Development Index is closely associated with a general propensity for collective action at the village level. Villages with a high propensity for mutually beneficial collective action have not only done better for themselves in the watershed development program; they have also outperformed other villages in other aspects of development in which collective action was required.

Residents of villages that have performed relatively poorly in the watershed development programs have not been able to attract or undertake as many government projects as other villages. They have not been as active in making representations to higher-ups, and they appear less able to enforce accountability and performance from local-level government functionaries. The level of services that they obtain leaves them feeling less satisfied than residents in villages that are better able to take collective action.

Villages that display high levels of collective action in one sphere of development activity also exhibit high levels of collective action in other spheres. It is probable that a single underlying cause or combination of causes accounts for this phenomenon. The leading candidate is social capital, although this conclusion is best deferred until we have some independent measures of social capital.

Table 3.7   *Voter turnout, newspaper readership, and number of associations*

Variable	Mean	Standard deviation	Minimum value	Maximum value
Voter turnout	66.1	11.55	41.0	94.3
Newspaper readership	1.5	0.38	1.0	2.6
Number of associations	0.5	0.68	0	3.0

Measuring social capital in Rajasthan

Our search for independent measures of social capital relevant to the cultural and historical context in Rajasthan is necessarily exploratory in nature. Following the analysis and reasoning of Putnam (1993) we first constructed an index of social capital based on measures that operationalize the following variables: number of formal associations in each village, voter turnout (the proportion of eligible voters casting ballots in the most recent general election), and newspaper readership. Respondents were asked how often they read a newspaper. Responses were coded 1 for "never" through 4 for "every day." The number of associations and percentage of eligible persons voting in a village were obtained from the village-level database; newspaper readership was averaged from household data from the same villages (table 3.7).

Regressing the three variables against the first dependent variable, the Common Land Development Index, yields no coefficients that are significantly different from zero. The regression model as a whole also lacks significance, as indicated by the F-statistics (table 3.8).

Perhaps more important than the fact that none of the three variables is statistically significant in regression analysis is the fact that the variables do not co-vary in the same direction. In contrast to the findings of Putnam (1993), we find no single factor on which all the variables load in common. Instead, we find three separate factors corresponding to each of the three variables accounting for 39 percent, 35 percent, and 26 percent of the total variance. Further regression of these variables on the other, broader dependent variable, the Development-Oriented Collective Action Index, did not provide significantly different results. These independent variables were also used in other regression models, alongside a larger set of control and independent variables. None of them achieves any level of significance, even after the other variables are included in the analysis.

The measures that Putnam (1993) employed in his study of social capital in northern Italy tell us little about social capital in Rajasthan. Other measures that are better suited to the region must be developed. Newspaper readership, for example, is not a useful measure for our sample of villages, because 73 percent of respondents never read a newspaper and another 17 percent read newspapers

Table 3.8   *Ordinary least squares regression results for correlation between selected variables and the Common Land Development Index*

Item	Coefficient	Standard error
Intercept	1.286	1.152
Independent variables		
Voter turnout	0.001	0.015
Newspaper readership	0.399	0.440
Number of associations	0.286	0.252

Notes: $n = 64$, $R^2 = 0.045$, adjusted $R^2 = -0.0074$, F-ratio $= 0.858$, F-probability $= 0.469$.

once a week or less. Measures of the number of formal associations are also not very relevant to villages in northern India. More than half (thirty-six) of the sixty-four villages we studied have no formally registered voluntary associations in operation; another twenty-three have only one. Of the remaining five villages, four have two formal associations and one has three. With very few exceptions, the associations that do exist are government-sponsored youth clubs or *mahila mandals* (women's groups). These groups were set up at the direction of the government to foster social and economic development; they do not have a voluntary grassroots origin. Interviews with village leaders in eight of the twenty-eight villages in which such groups existed indicate that most of the groups are moribund anyway. Nearly all have very small memberships (fewer than twenty members), and members rarely have close ties with other members. The measures Putnam employed thus do not capture levels of social capital in Rajasthani society.

Informal networks, which are far more common than formal networks in northern India – and in many developing countries – are more relevant here.[7] We concluded that it would be more appropriate to ask people about their cognitive maps of social relations. These maps represent the beliefs people hold about how they will act toward and with different people in given situations. Sentiments toward other people create bonds that enable people to work together to perform specific tasks or respond to particular contingencies. The predisposition for such networking is, we believe, a better indication of the capacity for collective

[7] Informal networks may be important in other settings as well. In his work on social capital in contemporary Russia, Richard Rose (1999) indicates that far more people there rely on informal networks and everyday mutual support groups that do not keep any formal membership records than rely on formal networks.

action in this setting than is membership in formal groups. We studied informal networking by examining people's responses to questions about their social relationships.

To be relevant to development efforts in Rajasthan, indicators of social capital need to correspond with the patterns of life in this largely agrarian setting. Measures of the structural or network aspects of social capital have to relate to the types of networks or mutual support organizations found in this region. We started by considering the types of activities in which people in this area are commonly engaged. Not all activities observed in this area can automatically be considered as appropriate measures of social capital. We agree with Coleman (1988, 1990) that social capital exists in the relations among persons. Only activities that are not mostly or usually undertaken in isolation from other people can be considered valid structural or cognitive components of social capital.

Our questionnaires included questions about a variety of locally relevant activities. The responses indicated that some of these activities are mostly performed individually. Activities for which more than 80 percent of respondents reported that they performed the activity individually were excluded from further inquiry.

Responses to six questions were combined to construct an index of social capital (box 3.1). This index, which integrates the structural and cognitive dimensions of social capital, appears to be conceptually and empirically valid for this region. Questions 1–3 are concerned with social relationships, networks, or the structure of social interaction. Given that formal associations are virtually absent in these villages, informal networks and established roles were assessed. Questions 4–6 address cognitive phenomena regarding social relationships, specifically norms, values, or attitudes that reflect a sense of solidarity and mutual trust.

Question 6 operationalizes the factor of trust, which is included in most treatments of social capital. The second alternative would give each person access to more land (12.5 *bighas* instead of 10 *bighas*), but it would require working with another person and sharing the output with that person.[8] More than 70 percent of respondents preferred to receive less land in order to avoid having to depend on cooperative relations with others. This preference was especially pronounced in villages that scored low on the preceding five questions.

Like other questions, this question was worded so that the respondent was indicating how he or she thinks *others* in the village would assess the tradeoff. This item thus reflects evaluations of a village-level characteristic rather than just individual attitudes. This made it easier to respond, allowing respondents to attribute their reply to others rather than to themselves.

---

[8] One *bigha* equals approximately 0.25 hectare.

Box 3.1 Activities or attitudes reflecting social capital in Rajasthan villages

1. If a crop disease were to affect the entire standing crop of this village, who do you think would come forward to deal with this situation?
[1] Every person would deal with the problem individually   1,084
[2] Neighbors among themselves   347
[3] The dominant political faction   298
[4] All village leaders acting together   230
[5] The entire village   378
2. Who in this village has historically looked after the common pasture lands?
[1] No one does anything for protecting these lands   391
[2] There are old customs that are followed here   283
[3] Our leaders take decisions that we all follow   509
[4] A village committee exists that makes these decisions jointly   666
[5] We all discuss and jointly decide what is to be done   442
3. Suppose two people in this village had a dispute with each other, who do you think would resolve this dispute?
[1] No one   49
[2] Some political leaders   667
[3] Their neighbors   421
[4] Their caste fellows   493
[5] The entire village collectively   715
4. Suppose some children of the village tend to stray from the correct path – for example, they are disrespectful to elders, they disobey their parents, are mischievous, etc. – who in this village feels it right to correct other people's children?
[1] No one   85
[2] Only close relatives   1,566
[3] Relatives and also neighbors   202
[4] Anyone from the village   493
5. Which among the following is the most important reason why people in this village plant and protect grasses and trees?
[1] Because fodder and fuelwood are in short supply   973
[2] Because this way there is less need to protect our crops from cattle   396
[3] Because this is the right thing to do and earns us religious merit   357
[4] Because this activity keeps the villagers united   283
6. Suppose a friend of yours in this village faced the following alternatives, which one would he or she prefer most?
[1] Own and farm 10 *bighas* of land entirely by themselves   1,674
[2] Own and farm 25 *bighas* of land jointly with one other person   670

Table 3.9 *Factor loadings for the social capital index*

Component	Factor
Dealing with crop disease	0.73052
Dealing with common pastures	0.64826
Settling disputes	0.73272
Dealing with errant children	0.72029
Value placed on unity	0.78680
Trust placed in others	0.66859

Responses to the six questions were highly correlated, and they loaded commonly on a single factor (table 3.9). The single common factor accounts for about 55 percent of the combined variance.

The six variables were combined into a social capital index, in which each variable has equal weight. The index score for each village was obtained by summing the six scores after first dividing each variable by its range so that each variable had a maximum score of 1.0. The index was rescaled so that values range from 0 to 100 in order to facilitate interpretation of regression results.[9]

On the 0–100 scale, about a quarter of villages scored below 50; the highest quarter scored above 62. The combined index is highly correlated with its constituent parts (Cronbach's coefficient alpha = 0.855; individual correlations with the index are all 0.75 or higher). The index also correlates well with other measures of norms and networks, indicating that it is a reasonably robust measure of social capital for this cultural setting.

The theoretical justification for the social capital index is that it combines structural and cognitive aspects of what is understood as social capital, reflecting how predisposed and able people are to act cooperatively in support of each other. Villages that have high social capital index scores also score well in terms of other measures of trust and propensity to participate in associations, both of which are emphasized in the literature on social capital. The significant and high correlations found between this index and these other variables support the notion of a generalized measure of social capital (table 3.10). Moreover, the results do not depend on the particular items used to construct the index.[10]

[9] An alternative index was constructed that weighted the individual items by their factor scores. The two indices were highly correlated (0.967).

[10] To test how sensitive our results are to the items used to construct the index, we constructed three alternative indices of social capital, combining different sets of variables. These alternative constructions are highly correlated with one another, as would be expected. Moreover, changing the index does not change the statistical significance of the variables in the regression results reported later in this chapter. We are grateful to the editors of this volume for suggesting this method of considering and testing alternative formulations.

Table 3.10   *Correlations between the social capital index and other aspects of social capital*

Indicator	Survey question	Correlation
Informal networking and mutual support	If an epidemic were to occur among cattle or humans in this village, what do you think the people of this village would do? Will they act in a united manner?	0.771
Trust	Suppose some person from this village had to go away for a while with his family. In whose charge would this person leave his fields? Can only close relatives or a larger group of villagers be trusted?	0.645
Reciprocity	"People here look out mainly for the welfare of their own families, and they are not much concerned with society's welfare." How strongly do you agree or disagree with this statement? (Strongly agree = 1, strongly disagree = 4.)	0.492
Solidarity	Is it possible to conceive of a village leader who puts aside his own welfare and that of his family to concern himself mainly with the welfare of village society? (Impossible = 1, possible = 2.)	0.420
Expectations about future cooperation	What do you feel is likely to happen once government funding for the watershed program comes to an end? How likely is it that villagers will come forward to protect these investments and undertake further developments of their own accord? (Will not be able to protect by themselves = 1; some protection is possible, but not as much as before = 2; villagers will protect these areas but not plant afresh or develop any new areas = 3; villagers will carry on and develop more areas by themselves = 4.)	0.612
Concern for future generations	Which of the following statements would you agree with: "When people have urgent economic needs, they should be expected to exploit natural resources as much as needed," or "Natural resources belong to future as well as present generations, so people should never exploit them so as to diminish them for the future. "(Should exploit for present need = 1, should preserve for future = 3.)	0.392

Note: All coefficients significant at the 0.01 level or better.

Testing the association between social capital and development outcomes

We next try to determine what relationship our index has, if any, with the two dependent variables, the Common Land Development Index (village-level performance in the watershed development program) and the Development-Oriented

Collective Action Index (development-oriented collective action more generally). To facilitate comparison and interpretation, each of these indices has been adjusted so that it ranges from 0 to 100.

Our measure of social capital in Rajasthan has a significant and positive association with development-oriented collective action at the village level. Villages with high levels of development performance usually also have high social capital index scores (although such scores are not the sole determinant of performance).

In bivariate regression on the Development-Oriented Collective Action Index, social capital has a coefficient of 0.821, significant at the 0.01 level ($R^2 = 0.125$). A similar result holds for the other dependent variable, the Common Land Development Index. In regressions with this index, social capital has a significant and positive coefficient (0.879), although the fit is imperfect – see table 3.12, p. 113, for R^2s for multiple regression analysis.

Although social capital has, on the whole, a strongly positive relationship with the two dependent variables, the association is not sufficient to account for a major part of the variation in these variables. Other variables need to be considered as well.

With the exception of literacy, none of the variables suggested from the literature was associated with the two dependent variables in a statistically significant manner. We therefore looked at other variables that, in association with social capital, might help account for variation in the levels of development-oriented collective action.

Our database enables us to construct three other indexes representing characteristics of village social life that might correlate with collective action and development performance. The first measures the number and depth of divisions, often described as factions, that exist within the village. The second measures the attitudes and beliefs villagers have about the honesty or dishonesty of fellow villagers. The third represents the level of political competition in the village.

Divisions and factions

To assess the separate and combined influence of various divisive factors at the village level, we asked respondents a series of five questions. To what extent, we asked, do differences in education, wealth, caste, age, and length of residency in the village divide people in your community?

Responses to each question were scored as follows: "Not at all" was scored as 1, "somewhat" as 2, and "very much" as 3. In factor analysis, responses to the five questions loaded together very clearly on a unique common factor, which accounts for more than 70 percent of the combined variance of the five variables. The scores on all five variables were summed to form a single composite variable, Divisive Factors, reflecting the combined divisive influences of these five constituent variables in any particular village. The variable was constructed so that it ranged from 0 to 100.

Attitudes and beliefs about honesty

Respondents were asked three questions to determine their tolerance for dishonesty, a factor that reduces social capital:

- "Whenever it is to their advantage, people will tell lies." To what extent do you agree with this statement?
- "It is not necessary for a leader to be exactly honest in public dealings if he knows this will interfere with getting his work done." To what extent do you agree with this statement?
- "If a leader in local government is highly skilled, one should overlook minor instances of dishonesty." Do you agree or disagree with this statement?

Responses were scored along a range from 1 (strongly agree) to 4 (strongly disagree). High scores on the combined index reflect attitudes and expectations that honesty should and will prevail in the village. The variable Tolerance of Dishonesty was constructed by summing across the three scores and rescaling the results so that the variable has a range of 0–100. High scores on the combined index reflect attitudes and expectations that honesty should and will prevail in the village.

Political competition

An index of political competition was constructed by analyzing the number of votes polled by different candidates in the most recent elections for the village panchayat.[11] This unit of local government usually encompasses between two and five villages, although large villages may constitute a single panchayat. The jurisdiction of each panchayat is divided into wards, with residents of each ward electing their own representative to the panchayat council. A ward may comprise a whole village, a hamlet, or part of a village. Since the ward is the unit of action for panchayat election purposes, we computed the index at this level and then averaged the figures for all the wards in that village to obtain a village-level index.

We used the Herfindahl–Hirschman concentration index, which is based on the inverse of the sum of the squares of vote shares obtained by each candidate. For each ward we took the share of total votes cast for each candidate,

---

[11] For a discussion of the effectiveness of panchayats as units of governance or units of development planning and implementation, see Baviskar and Attwood (1995), Kaviraj (1997).

next squared these shares, and then summed the figures across candidates. The inverse of this sum represents the index of political competition.[12]

Villages in which a single candidate obtained all of the votes score a 1. Villages in which two candidates divide the vote equally score a 2; those in which the vote is divided equally among three candidates score a 3. The scores for the sixty-four villages range from 1 to 2.11. The variable Political Competition is obtained by adjusting the index so that it ranges from 0 to 100.

Political competition was included in our analysis following a round of field visits by Krishna between May and August 1997. Visits to some of the villages suggested that measures of solidarity, reciprocity, and community would not be sufficient by themselves to account for strong development performance.

Somewhat surprisingly, collective action appears to work best when accompanied by political competition at the local level. From attending meetings of panchayats and user committees and speaking with leaders and other villagers, Krishna observed that debate and competition coexist alongside high levels of solidarity in high-performing villages. This observation warranted statistical testing.

Data on political competition were collected for all sixty-four villages. Analysis of these data revealed no correlation coefficients significant at the 0.05 level. At the 0.10 level, there is a weak positive correlation between the Tolerance of Dishonesty and Divisive Factors and a weak negative correlation between the social capital index and Tolerance of Dishonesty. Since Tolerance of Dishonesty is thought to reduce social capital, it is not surprising that this is higher where there is more divisiveness, and lower where indicators of social capital are stronger.

Significantly, there is no correlation between the Social Capital Index and the Divisive Factors variables, indicating that even where divisions do exist – between rich and poor, young and old, high and low caste, educated and illiterate, long-time residents and new settlers – levels of social capital are not necessarily affected by these differences. Further, the absence of any significant correlation between the Divisive Factors and Political Competition variables indicates that factionalism at the local level does not necessarily translate into more active competition for political power.

The three possible explanatory variables and the social capital index, relatively independent of each other, were used in multiple regression analysis. In this analysis we reconsidered the independent variables that correspond to the alternative hypotheses examined earlier, looking at them now in association with social capital and other variables.

We first considered broad development performance (the Development-Oriented Collective Action Index) as the dependent variable (table 3.11) and then performance in the watershed development program (the Common Land

[12] We thank Walter Mebane for suggesting this procedure, described in detail in Taagepera and Shugart (1989).

Table 3.11 *Ordinary least squares regressions on development performance (rescaled Development-Oriented Collective Action Index)*

Item	Model 1	Model 2	Model 3	Model 4
Intercept	−18.90	−34.3*	−44.239**	−40.93**
	(24.68)	(18.04)	(17.627)	(16.89)
Independent variables				
Social capital index	0.689**	0.691**	0.721**	0.703**
	(0.276)	(0.272)	(0.288)	(0.261)
Divisive factors	−0.001			
	(0.041)			
Tolerance for dishonesty	−0.051			
	(0.064)			
Political competition	0.42***	0.38**	0.376**	0.391***
	(0.121)	(0.118)	(0.120)	(0.117)
Mechanization			0.205	
			(0.337)	
Infrastructure		−1.31		
		(0.884)		
Literacy		0.732*	0.471	0.596*
		(0.355)	(0.321)	(0.298)
Number of castes		0.123		
		(0.690)		
Population size		0.005	0.002	
		(0.003)	(0.003)	
N	64	64	62	64
R^2	0.277	0.354	0.331	0.315
Adjusted R^2	0.226	0.283	0.271	0.286
F-ratio	5.453	5.018	5.536	8.91
F-probability	0.0009	0.0004	0.0003	0.0001
Durbin–Watson statistic	1.973	2.02	1.946	1.959

*$p \leq 0.1$. **$p \leq 0.05$. ***$p \leq 0.001$.
Notes: Standard errors are in parentheses.

Development Index) (table 3.12). To facilitate interpretation of the results, each of these variables was rescaled to range from 0 to 100.

Model 1 includes four variables: social capital, divisiveness, tolerance of dishonesty, and political competition. Only the coefficients of social capital and political competition are significant. Models 2 and 3 test the alternative hypotheses that were rejected using bivariate regression. To determine whether village size has any impact on development performance, we also include village population as another variable for analysis. In theory, village size could have either a positive or negative effect on development performance. On the one hand, following Olson (1965), smaller villages should be better at engaging in

Table 3.12 *Ordinary least squares regressions on watershed performance (rescaled Common Land Development Index)*

Item	Model 1	Model 2	Model 3	Model 4
Intercept	−48.81*	−60.56**	−69.536**	−68.84**
	(25.64)	(21.92)	(21.71)	(21.48)
Independent variables				
Social capital index	0.728**	0.762**	0.748**	0.781**
	(0.286)	(0.262)	(0.268)	(0.263)
Divisive factors	0.026			
	(0.041)			
Tolerance for dishonesty	−0.001			
	(0.068)			
Political competition	0.513***	0.496***	0.472***	0.470***
	(0.128)	(0.124)	(0.125)	(0.124)
Rainfed land ratio[a]		0.029		
		(0.164)		
Government Staff			0.216*	0.210*
Support			(0.124)	(0.122)
Infrastructure		−1.43		
		(0.97)		
Literacy		0.549*	0.566*	0.539*
		(0.306)	(0.332)	(0.309)
Population			−0.001	
			(0.004)	
n	64	62	62	64
R^2	0.320	0.406	0.370	0.368
Adjusted R^2	0.274	0.342	0.315	0.325
F-ratio	6.948	6.370	6.703	8.462
F-probability	0.0001	0.0001	0.0001	0.0001
Durbin–Watson statistic	1.66	1.792	1.576	1.572

*$p \leq 0.1$. **$p \leq 0.05$. ***$p \leq 0.001$.
Notes: Standard errors are in parentheses.
[a] Neither this variable nor the other variable related to the relative need hypothesis, Cow Units, results in a significant coefficient under any alternative specification of the model. Similarly, none of the modernization variables is significantly associated with the dependent variable. Neither are variables related to social heterogeneity statistically significant.

collective action than larger ones. On the other hand, larger villages are more likely to have an effective *k*-group, which can initiate and lead the collective development effort itself (Hardin 1982).

Coefficients are not significant for any of the modernization variables (mechanization, infrastructure, distance to market), regardless of the specification of the model. None of the stratification variables shows any significant impact on development performance, as neither the Number of Castes nor Divisive Factors variable has a significant coefficient.

We included the three variables from Putnam's analysis to test whether these variables attain any significance in multivariate regression. All three variables (voter turnout, newspaper readership, and number of associations) again fail to produce statistically significant coefficients.

Only two variables are consistently significant. The coefficient for the social capital index is robust and substantial, regardless of which other variables are considered simultaneously. The size of the coefficient remains within a range of 0.69–0.72, indicating that an increase of 1 percentage point in social capital is associated on average with an increase of 0.7 percentage points in collective action for development.

The coefficient for the political competition index is also consistently significant and robust, regardless of how the model is specified. This coefficient remains within a range of 0.38–0.42, indicating that a change of 1 percentage point in political competition would be associated with a 0.4 percentage point change in collective action. This variable was not initially included in our analysis of social capital. It was added on the basis of observations of and conversations with village residents. The result is surprising. Whether political competition would loom this large (or larger) in other settings remains to be investigated elsewhere.

Literacy is the third variable found to be significant. A change of 1 percentage point in literacy is associated with a change in development performance of 0.47–0.73 percentage points.[13]

Results for the other, narrower dependent variable, the rescaled Common Land Development Index, reveal that variations in levels of program performance are associated with the same factors that affect the broader development variable – social capital, political competition, and literacy (table 3.12, p. 113). In addition, staff input is moderately significant at the 0.1 level. When this variable is standardized on a 0–100 scale, it produces a coefficient of about 0.25. This means that controlling for differences in social capital and political competition, a 1 percentage point change in staff input would thus be associated with a 0.25 percentage point change in program performance. The coefficient for this variable is less robust than those of the other three variables. The effect of staff input is evident only when it is combined with high levels of social capital and political competition.

---

[13] Despite the low R^2 for these regressions, the variables may be significant. The t-ratios and F-statistics in Model 4 imply that although social capital, political competition, and literacy are significantly associated with the dependent variable, some other variables (or some other functional forms) may remain to be considered. Multicollinearity is low to moderate in each of the four models investigated, so this is somewhat reassuring. The highest value of the condition index (for Model 4), for instance, is 9.61. White's general test reveals no significant heteroskedasticity in the model. Inferences regarding statistical significance and relative magnitude of coefficients do not change even if nonlinear forms are specified.

Identifying factors that affect the formation of social capital

Social capital is manifested in the relations among people, as Coleman (1988) has suggested, but it resides in people's minds. The roles that people recognize, accept, and perform and the norms, values, attitudes, and beliefs they hold structure people's relationships with each other. Coming into play when people interact with one another or plan to interact, social capital is an attribute that exists and operates within and between individuals. However, norms, values, attitudes, and beliefs acquire efficacy to the extent that they are shared. Roles, networks, rules, procedures, and precedents can operate only if sets of individuals agree on them. Social capital is, then, a product of collective thinking and activities that represents more than the sum of individual actions and cognition.

What goes into the formation of social capital? According to Putnam (1993), social capital is largely determined by historical factors; it can thus not be enhanced in the short term. This view has been challenged in the literature (Schneider *et al.* 1997; Jackman and Miller 1998). We explored these relationships by constructing social capital index scores for individuals based on their responses to survey questions. These scores mirror but disaggregate the scores calculated for villages. Looking at both indexes allows us to identify what other individual-level attributes correlate with variations in the social capital index. Inferring causation (or at least influence) from these correlations, we can thus account for differences in individuals' propensities for collective action.

Ostrom (1990) maintains that collective action becomes more likely and successful when individuals in a community abide by rules that have been constructed through joint consultation rather than by force or outside coercion. There is an internalization of rules among community members that is conducive to compliance. According to this view, acceptance of and compliance with rules is enhanced when community members have participated in the process of rule formation.

Comparative studies of local institutional development have affirmed that participatory action is an important factor in successful development at local levels (Esman and Uphoff 1984). How local organizations are structured and the relationships that their leadership and membership roles establish affect how people learn and think about their social responsibilities and social activity. In our surveys, we explored the effects of how decisions are made at local levels to see whether greater participation had any effect on those attributes associated with social capital.

Though not dependent upon particular alignments arising from the distant past, once cooperation is achieved, it can provide powerful cognitive and emotional scaffolding for cooperation in the future, according to Hirschman (1984). On the basis of his study of local development in Latin America, he concludes that prior experience with collective action can help energize new common endeavors. People who have worked together in the past, fashioning suitable roles and appropriate attitudes, can bring the skills they learned to bear on the problems they might face together in the future.

These are interesting issues, so we tested various hypotheses relating to the formation of individual-level social capital, which aggregates into higher levels of this social-structural and psychological asset. Respondents' social capital levels were taken as the dependent variable for analysis, and various possible explanations are examined for their bearing on the extent of social capital among individuals. The most interesting findings, considering some current debates in the literature, concerned the explanatory power of "history," with which we conclude our analysis. We begin by considering the standard demographic factors that might affect individuals' respective endowments of social capital.

Demographics

Correlation coefficients of age, gender, and family size with social capital endowments are not significant. (Women scored 0.41 points higher than men on a 100-point scale, but this difference is not statistically significant.) The correlation between length of residence in the village and social capital is also statistically insignificant. Alternative formulations of the regression model do not change these results.

Wealth and status

Some previous studies of social capital have found that wealth and income are positively correlated with households' levels of social capital (Grootaert 1999, Narayan and Pritchett 1997). This positive association could be explained by the fact that members of richer households have more leisure time to devote to membership organizations. Higher levels of activity in associations are in turn correlated with higher levels of social capital.

Our data from rural Rajasthan fail to reveal a relationship between wealth and individual levels of social capital. Measuring wealth in terms of landholding or number of farm animals owned – the two most relevant measures of wealth and income-generating assets in these communities – produces no statistically significant coefficients. Poorer households are as likely to share norms and attitudes associated with higher social capital as are their richer, better-endowed counterparts in the same village. Similarly, we find no relationship between caste and social capital, as higher-caste villagers did not have higher social capital index scores, an interesting finding.[14]

---

[14] We took account of the correlation between caste and landholding by using one or the other of these variables in alternative formulations of the regression model. Multicollinearity is mild,

Education

To our surprise, given previous findings in this analysis, education has no statistically significant correlation with social capital at the household level. Indeed, the regression coefficient has a small negative value, made insignificant by a high standard error.

In our earlier analysis, in which we examined development-oriented collective action as the dependent variable, literacy proved to be a significant variable. Literacy is thus important for explaining variations in villages' level of development activity. It is not similarly salient, however, for explaining differences in individual households' levels of social capital. Whether education is positively correlated with household levels of social capital in other parts of the world is worth investigating.

Participation

Several measures of participation appear to help account for observed differences among households' levels of social capital. Regard for locally formulated rules and experience with collective action variables have also consistently significant correlations, even in alternative formulations of the model.

Households that had worked with others in the village to help solve a community problem even once within the previous twelve months have average social capital indexes more than five points higher than households that had not engaged even once in collective action activities. It could be argued that the direction of causation works the other way around, from social capital to collective action. One could argue that people with higher social capital engage more readily in such activities, as indeed they do. This is not a simple relationship. However, Hirschman's analysis (1984) offers a social–psychological explanation of why collective learning and reinforcement would build up the stock of social capital, which he discusses in terms of resulting "social energy" flows, and why prior experience would produce subsequent flows of cooperation.

Decisionmaking processes

The value of participation in decisionmaking is supported as well by other results, suggesting that institutional processes can contribute to social capital formation. Here the direction of causation is clearer. Where local decisions are made in an inclusive manner rather than exclusively or even primarily by

even for the formulation in which both variables are retained. As measured by the highest-level condition index, multicollinearity is scaled at 17.7 – not very high for a model with 18 variables and 1,500 observations (missing variables reduced the number of cases that could be analyzed from the larger sample).

traditional leaders or technical specialists, individuals show more of the characteristics associated with social capital. Households reporting a preference for participatory decisionmaking on issues relating to village development have average social capital ratings that are one to two points higher than other households.

Information

Information has a statistically significant correlation with social capital. Adding one more source of information to those already used by a household appears to enhance its social capital by 0.8 points on average, all other things remaining constant. Increases in information are often associated with modernization processes, suggesting that modernization may have some effect on social capital at the individual level, even if we did not find such an effect at the village level.

Rulemaking and enforcement

The greatest increases in social capital are seen where beliefs about participation are reinforced by the existence of clear and fairly implemented rules. Controlling for other attributes and beliefs of households, people who perceive the existence of clear and fair rules in their village have average social capital scores that are 4.85 points higher than people who do not.

The combined effect of attitudes about participation, rules that facilitate participation, and experience of participating in a collective enterprise adds as much as 14 points to the social capital index – a difference of more than 1 standard deviation in the household distribution of social capital. Accumulated among a large number of households in a village, such an increase in social capital could augment development activity by 10 percentage points, a substantial achievement.

History

Where does history come in? History is not some abstract force but rather a legacy, maintained in people's minds and memories, of past social relationships and outcomes associated with different ways of acting by individuals and groups. From our data, we can make the case that "history matters." But close analysis shows that history is not a very strong determinant of social capital, because local factors produce substantial variations.

Looking back into Rajasthan's past, there are marked differences between the northern districts of Ajmer and Bhilwara and the southern districts of Rajsamand and Udaipur, in terms of the degree of outside interference in local affairs and the level of community self-management.

Table 3.13   *Social capital indexes, by district*

District	Average score	Minimum score	Maximum score
Ajmer	54	30	97
Bhilwara	53	27	88
Rajsamand	63	38	93
Udaipur	62	33	97

Until 1947, when India became independent from British colonial rule, Udaipur and Rajsamand had experienced continuous rule by a single dynastic ruling house (Mewar) for at least ten and as many as fourteen centuries by some accounts. Arrangements worked out by local rulers with the colonial power in the eighteenth century perpetuated princely rule, provided that they paid tribute to the British monarch. While local rulers' independence of action was curtailed to some extent by this agreement, with British oversight exercised by a Resident assigned to the Mewar court, much local autonomy was sustained.

In contrast, Ajmer and Bhilwara shared a more turbulent history. In the twenty centuries preceding British rule for which records are available, no single king or dynasty was able to assert control over the region for more than two generations. Because of its strategic position in the Aravalli range of mountains, for most of its history Ajmer was a battlefield in which competing claimants fought. Ruled by the Mughals for sporadic intervals during their imperial history, Ajmer was annexed by the British and ruled directly by a British Chief Commissioner. Bhilwara, located directly south of Ajmer and directly north of Rajsamand, was established as a separate administrative district after independence by combining some areas from Ajmer with more turbulent northern parts of Mewar.

Two differences in historical background are quite evident. First, villages in Udaipur and Rajsamand have experienced relatively stable rule over much longer periods than did those in Ajmer and Bhilwara. Second, in Udaipur and Rajsamand, the rules that villagers lived by had continuities with local tradition, in contrast with Ajmer and Bhilwara, where local residents experienced continuous change and had less local control over events.

On average, we find that the social capital index scores for households in Ajmer and Bhilwara are eight points lower than those of households in Udaipur and Rajsamand (table 3.13). This difference can be attributed to the erosion of village-level structures compared to Udaipur and Rajsamand and perhaps to the history of unstable rule. These differences are consistent with the view of social capital offered by Putnam (1993).

These indexes conceal vast differences among villages within each district, however – differences that are several times larger than the observed variations

Table 3.14   *Ordinary least squares regressions of social capital on household attributes, with household-level social capital as the dependent variable*

Item	Coefficient	Standard error
Intercept	27.38***	2.49
Hypotheses and independent variables		
Demographic variables		
Gender (male = 1, female = 2)	0.41	0.56
Family size	0.08	0.12
Length of residence in the village (years)	−0.25	0.20
Wealth/status		
Landholding	0.04	0.02
Caste	−0.16	0.27
Education (years)	−0.59	0.45
Prior experience with collective action[a]		
Experience of collective action within past twelve months	5.27***	0.27
Experience with collective management of common lands	0.74*	0.30
Rulemaking[b]		
Clear and fair rules regarding common land development	4.85***	0.66
Information		
Number of sources of information	0.80***	0.15
Decisionmaking[c]		
Participative decisionmaking versus decisionmaking by group head alone	1.09*	0.58
Decisionmaking by all versus decisionmaking by technical specialists	2.09***	0.57
History (district dummy variables)[d]		
Bhilwara	−1.69*	0.81
Rajsamand	8.60***	0.83
Udaipur	8.03***	0.84

Notes: *p ≤ 0.1. ***p ≤ 0.001. $n = 1{,}451$, $R^2 = 0.453$, adjusted $R^2 = 0.447$.
F-ratio $= 79.24$, F-probability $= 0.0001$, Durbin–Watson statistic $= 1.690$.
[a] See Hirschman (1984).
[b] See Ostrom (1990).
[c] See Esman and Uphoff (1984).
[d] Ajmer was the baseline against which the other three districts were compared. There is, therefore, no separate dummy variable for Ajmer. Coefficients for the district dummy variables should be interpreted as the additional points on the social capital scale scored by villages in these districts relative to villages in Ajmer.

between districts. History cannot begin to explain these large intradistrict variations. To account for such substantial interhousehold differences within districts, we need to consider other variables, such as wealth and status, education, and participation. At the individual household level we see again that standard demographic, wealth and other variables are not reliable explanatory factors (table 3.14). However, factor like experience, information and participation do show significant relationships.

Conclusion

We examined social capital in a very specific context – rural Rajasthan – for two reasons. First, we wanted to have some concrete and rigorous measures of development performance against which to test and validate the phenomenon of social capital. Studying village-level performance in the watershed program allowed us to obtain these measures. Second, we believed that the manifestations of social capital would be conditioned by a host of biophysical, social, cultural, institutional, economic, political, historical, and other factors. To do such analysis, we could get access in Rajasthan to extensive and detailed data on development-oriented collective action against which we could examine a variety of hypothesized causal factors, including ones identified with social capital.

To operationalize and measure social capital we needed to have some systematic conception of it. Simply stipulating an "operational definition" would not suffice. The literature is already too full of ad hoc specifications that are more descriptive than analytical. The distinction made here between structural and cognitive forms of social capital provides a way to study social capital meaningfully in different contexts. At the same time, the distinction allows us to understand social capital as a universal phenomenon existing to varying extents in virtually all contexts, even if what constitutes social capital is not always the same. We believe, based upon data and analysis, that there is a common factor underlying social as well as economic and political production that can meaningfully be called "social capital." This enables communities and even countries to get more benefit from existing material resources through various mechanisms and mentalities favoring mutual cooperation.

Our analysis, though extensive and detailed, cannot be considered definitive. This is still a relatively new area of inquiry, and we have analyzed social capital relationships in one institutional and cultural setting. Our theoretical formulation enjoins us and others to take different settings into account. We think that analysis that first distinguishes between structural and cognitive forms of social capital and then combines them will enable researchers to deal with the phenomenon more concretely and more conclusively than has been done in the past. Factors that facilitate mutually beneficial collective action are not the same as those that predispose people toward such activity, but they clearly interact to produce certain results.

This conceptualization and method of analysis has the further advantage of linking levels at which collective action can occur. Social capital is produced in the minds of individuals, but roles and networks, rules, procedures, and precedents are social, i.e., collective creations, as are the norms, values, attitudes, and beliefs associated with and supporting them. Social capital can be understood as aggregated at the village, regional level, or even national level, in terms of the amounts (and effectiveness) of rules, roles, procedures, precedents, networks, norms, attitudes, values, and beliefs conducive to collective action.

Individual action is in no way derogated by the existence of social capital. Indeed, it is usually made more effective and productive by a social context of cooperation within which individual endeavors and even competition are conducted.

Our work here was motivated in the first instance by concern with whether social capital, if shown to have some empirical foundation, can be purposefully created to accelerate development, especially for poor and marginalized populations. If Putnam's (1993) formulation of social capital as historically derived is correct, there is little or no scope for increasing it in the short run, as a contributing factor to economic and social development. Fortunately, from our perspective, we did not find such a constraint in the villages we studied. Despite similar historical and cultural legacies, there is wide variation in local endowments of social capital, as there is in villages' initiative and effectiveness in producing common benefits.

We had hoped in the course of our study to obtain a better understanding of how external agencies and actors could invest resources to increase social capital in order to improve local-level development performance. While our inquiry – focussed on whether variations in and effects of social capital can be empirically demonstrated – has provided some leads, it has produced no prescriptions. Such normative analysis (in the economic rather than the philosophical sense) remains to be done.

We have observed the benefits of social capital not only in watershed conservation and development in Rajasthan but also in the Gal Oya irrigation scheme in Sri Lanka, the largest and previously most deteriorated and disorganized system in that country (Uphoff 1996). The investment of personnel in "catalyst" roles produced a system of local organization with normative reorientations that fifteen years after creation continues to produce remarkable economic as well as social and political benefits, with rates of return several times greater than those normally expected from development investments. There is evidence of a four-fold increase in the productivity of water as well as interethnic cooperation that is quite remarkable (Uphoff and Wijayaratna 1997, 2000).

Social capital is a matter of more than academic concern. Examinations of social capital deserve all of the rigor that academic analysis can bring to them, but this analysis must also contribute to an understanding of social capital that can be applied to real-world settings. After all, we make as well as inherit history.

REFERENCES

Almond, G. and Verba, S., 1989. *The Civic Culture: Political Attitudes and Democracy in Five Nations.* London: Sage

Baviskar, B. S. and Attwood, D. W., 1995. *Finding the Middle Path: The Political Economy of Cooperation in Rural India.* New Delhi: Vistaar Publications

Brara, R., 1991. "Are Grazing Lands 'Wastelands'? Some Evidence from Rajasthan." *Economic and Political Weekly,* February 22. Bombay

Coleman, J. S., 1988. "Social Capital in the Creation of Human Capital." *American Journal of Sociology* 94: S95–S120

1990. *Foundations of Social Theory.* Cambridge, MA: Harvard University Press

Drèze, J. and Sen, A., 1995. *India: Economic Development and Social Opportunity.* Oxford: Oxford University Press

Esman, M. J. and Uphoff, N., 1984. *Local Organizations: Intermediaries in Rural Development.* Ithaca, NY: Cornell University Press

Grootaert, C., 1999. "Social Capital, Household Welfare, and Poverty in Indonesia." Local Level Institutions Working Paper 6. World Bank, Social Development Department, Washington, DC

Hardin, R., 1982. *Collective Action.* Baltimore: Johns Hopkins University Press

Hirschman, A. O., 1984. *Getting Ahead Collectively: Grassroots Experiences in Latin America.* New York: Pergamon Press

Jackman, R. W. and Miller, R. A., 1998. "Social Capital and Politics." *Annual Review of Political Science* 1, 47–73

Jodha, N. S., 1990. "Common Property Resources: Contributions and Crisis." *Economic and Political Weekly,* June 30. Bombay

Johnston, B. F. and Clark, W. C., 1982. *Redesigning Rural Development: A Strategic Perspective.* Baltimore: Johns Hopkins University Press

Kaviraj, S. (ed.), 1997. *Politics in India.* Delhi: Oxford University Press

Knight, J., 1992. *Institutions and Social Conflict.* Cambridge: Cambridge University Press

Krishna, A., 1997. "Participatory Watershed Development and Soil Conservation in Rajasthan, India." In A. Krishna, N. T. Uphoff, and M. J. Esman (eds.), *Reasons for Hope: Instructive Experiences in Rural Development,* 255–272. West Hartford, CT: Kumarian Press

2000a. "Creating and Harnessing Social Capital." In P. Dasgupta and I. Serageldin (eds.), *Social Capital: A Multifaceted Perspective,* 71–93. Washington, DC: World Bank

2000b. "Social Capital, Collective Action, and the State: Understanding Economic Development and Democratic Governance in Rural North India." PhD dissertation, Cornell University, Department of Government, Ithaca, NY

Krishna, A., Uphoff, N. T. and Esman, M. J. (eds.), 1997. *Reasons for Hope: Instructive Experiences in Rural Development.* West Hartford, CT: Kumarian Press

Lipset, S. M., 1960. *Political Man: The Social Bases of Politics.* New York: Doubleday

1994. "The Social Requisites of Democracy Revisited." *American Sociological Review* 59: 1–22

Narayan, D. and Pritchett, L., 1997. "Cents and Sociability: Household Income and Social Capital in Rural Tanzania." Policy Research Working Paper 1796. World Bank, Social Development Department and Development Research Group, Washington, DC

Olson, M., 1965. *The Logic of Collective Action: Public Goods and the Theory of Groups.* Cambridge, MA: Harvard University Press

Ostrom, E., 1990. *Governing the Commons: The Evolution of Institutions for Collective Action.* Cambridge: Cambridge University Press

Putnam, R. D., 1993. *Making Democracy Work: Civic Traditions in Modern Italy.* Princeton, NJ: Princeton University Press

Rajasthan Agricultural University, 1993. *Baseline Survey Report.* Udaipur: College of Technology and Agricultural Engineering, Rajasthan Agricultural University

Rose, R., 1999. "What Does Social Capital Add to Individual Welfare?" Social Capital Initiative Working Paper 15. World Bank, Social Development Department, Washington, DC

Schneider, M., Teske, P., Marschall, M., Mintrom, M., and Roch, C., 1997. "Institutional Arrangements and the Creation of Social Capital: The Effects of Public School Choice." *American Political Science Review* 91: 82–93

Schomer, K., Erdman, J. L., Oldrick, D. O., and Rudolph, L. I., 1994. *The Idea of Rajasthan: Explorations in Regional Identity*, vol. II: *Institutions.* Delhi: Manohar Publishers

Srinivas, M. N., 1987. "The Indian Village: Myth and Reality." In M. N. Srinivas, *The Dominant Caste and Other Essays*, 20–59. Delhi: Oxford University Press

Taagepera, R. and Shugart, M. S., 1989. *Seats and Votes: The Effects and Determinants of Electoral Systems.* New Haven, CT: Yale University Press

Uphoff, N., 1996. *Learning from Gal Oya: Possibilities for Participatory Development and Post-Newtonian Social Science.* London: Intermediate Technology Publications

2000. "Understanding Social Capital: Learning from the Analysis and Experience of Participation." In P. Dasgupta and I. Serageldin (eds.), *Social Capital: A Multifaceted Perspective*, 215–249. Washington, DC: World Bank.

Uphoff, N. and Wijayaratna, C. M., 1997. "Farmer Organization in Sri Lanka: Improving Irrigation Management in Sri Lanka." In A. Krishna, N. T. Uphoff, and M. J. Esman (eds.), *Reasons for Hope: Instructive Experiences in Rural Development*, 166–183. West Hartford, CT: Kumarian Press.

2000. "Demonstrated Benefits from Social Capital: The Productivity of Farmer Organizations in Gal Oya, Sri Lanka." *World Development* 28

Wade, R., 1994. *Village Republics: Economic Conditions for Collective Action in South India.* San Francisco: Institute for Contemporary Studies

Woolcock, M., 1998. "Social Capital and Economic Development: Toward a Theoretical Synthesis and Policy Framework." *Theory and Society* 27, 151–208

4 Social capital and the firm: evidence from agricultural traders in Madagascar

Marcel Fafchamps and Bart Minten

Economists typically use physical capital and labor as inputs in the description of production processes as it is believed that these inputs are essential to production. The same reasoning could be applied to other inputs. In particular, anybody involved in purchases and sales activities knows that contacts and relationships are also essential inputs for a firm's survival. However, while the importance of this "social" capital has long been recognized in other social sciences (see, for example, Granovetter 1985, 1995; Coleman 1988; Putnam 1993; Helliwell and Putnam 1995), this view has only recently received attention in the economics literature (Narayan and Pritchett 1997; Barr 1998; Fafchamps 1998; Fafchamps and Lund 1998; Grootaert 1999).

The definition of social capital in different economic and social studies has not been uniform. Some researchers have defined it in terms of trust and norms of civic cooperation (Knack and Keefer 1997; Temple and Johnson 1998) or in terms of cultural values, such as degrees of compassion, altruism, and tolerance (Fukuyama 1995). Others have emphasized institutions and the quality and quantity of "associational" life (Coleman 1988; Putnam 1993; Narayan and Pritchett 1997; Grootaert 1999). While those definitions share common elements, their exact meaning is imprecise and thus difficult to measure. The vagueness of the concept may be one reason why economists have been wary of using it.

Social capital in its broadest sense can influence economic exchange in two ways. Trust and emotional attachment to a group, society, or association may improve public sector efficiency or facilitate greater cooperation for services benefiting that group, society, or association, as Coleman (1988), Gambetta (1988), Putnam (1993), Greif (1993, 1994), and Platteau (1994a, 1994b) show. Benefits can also accrue directly to an individual or firm as a result of knowing people with whom it forms networks of interconnected agents. These networks may facilitate screening in labor and credit markets (Montgomery 1991;

We benefited greatly from conversations and comments from Jean-Claude Randrianarisoa, Eliane Ralison, Chris Grootaert and Thierry van Bastelaer. Special thanks go to Ousmane Badiane for obtaining funding for this research. We acknowledge financial support from the World Bank's Social Capital Initiative and the United States Agency for International Development.

Cornell and Welch 1996), reduce the search costs for market opportunities (Kranton 1996), improve the diffusion of information on innovations (Barr 1998) or bad payers or cheaters (Kandori 1992; Fafchamps 1998), and reduce risk (Fafchamps 1992; Fafchamps and Lund 1998). Much of the work on individual effects of social capital in the economics literature has been in markets in which moral hazard issues are severe, such as credit and labor markets.

Most of the recent analysis in agricultural markets has focused on price variability, price transmission, and margins. Studies of the behavior of agricultural traders have been less common. Most studies that have examined behavior have paid little attention to social capital (Palaskas and Harriss-White 1993; Badiane *et al.* 1997). Exceptions include Klitgaard (1991), Crow and Murshid (1994), and Staal, Delgado, and Nicholson (1997). However, none of these studies quantifies the effects of social interactions.

This chapter contributes to the literature on social capital by illustrating its economic effect on the functioning and performance of agricultural trade. The similarities between social capital and other types of capital are indicated. After describing the survey methodology and the structure of agricultural trade in Madagascar, the chapter examines the role of high transactions costs in imperfect markets and the potential benefits of social capital in such environments. It then uses regression analysis to identify the determinants of social capital and measure the quantitative impact of social capital on performance.

Survey methodology and the structure of agricultural trade in Madagascar

A survey of agricultural traders in Madagascar was conducted in 1997 as part of a joint project between the International Food Policy Research Institute and Madagascar's Ministry of Scientific Research. The survey consisted of two rounds. The first round, conducted between May 1997 and August 1997 (the main trading season), focussed on individual characteristics of traders and the structure, conduct, and performance of the agricultural trading sector. The second round, conducted between September 1997 and November 1997, focussed on the nature of traders' relationships with other traders, customers, and suppliers. The sample design was constructed to be as representative as possible of all traders involved in the food marketing chain, from producer to consumer.

Three main agricultural regions – Fianarantsoa, Majunga, and Antananarivo[1] – were included in the study, with traders from each region representing roughly

---

[1] Each region was additionally divided in different agro-ecological zones, i.e. Hauts Plateaux and Côte et Falaise in the Fianarantsoa region, Plaines et Hauts Plateaux in the Majunga region, and Vakinankaratra and Antananarivo (city) in the Antananarivo region.

a third of the sample. Traders in three types of location were surveyed: large and small urban markets in the main town of every province and district, areas outside the regular markets, and rural markets in rural counties. The survey focussed on traders who market locally consumed staples, such as rice, cassava, potatoes, beans, and peanuts. Traders involved primarily in export crops, fruits, vegetables, and minor crops were excluded. Two-thirds of surveyed traders report that the agricultural product they trade most intensively is rice, the main staple food in Madagascar.[2] Other actively traded products are beans and lentils (18 percent), cassava (5 percent), potatoes (5 percent), peanuts (4 percent), and maize (2 percent).

Eight hundred and fifty traders were surveyed in the first round; 729 of them were surveyed again in the second round. The results presented here are based on responses from traders who completed both rounds of surveying. Retailers constitute the bulk of the sample. They are divided into retailers with a semiper-manent selling point (usually a table or stall in the market) and retailers without a fixed selling point (those that sell from the roadside). Roadside sellers are typically smaller and less formal than retailers with stalls. The largest traders are assemblers (traders who collect large quantities from the country-side and assemble them for shipment) and wholesalers (traders who operate in bulk). (For a more detailed description of the survey and of agricultural trading in Madagascar, see Fafchamps and Minten 1998a, Badiane et al. 1998, and Mendoza and Randrianarisoa 1998.)

On average, Malagasy traders are thirty-seven years old, male, and married with three children (table 4.1). For most traders, trading in agricultural crops is the main activity. Most traders deal in various crops and have spent an aver-age of six years trading agricultural products. Two-thirds of traders (68 percent) started their business in the 1990s, some time after agricultural trade liberaliza-tion had begun. New entry seems to have come to a halt more recently, however (Mendoza and Randrianarisoa 1998). The lack of new entry seems to be driven by changes in the overall economic situation rather than by entry requirements, as market licenses are easy and inexpensive to obtain, according to the majority of traders interviewed.

Malagasy traders have very few employees, with family members and own labor accounting for half the total number of person-months used by traders. Two-thirds of total labor used by wholesalers and assemblers is hired non-family labor. In contrast, retailers rely heavily on own and family labor. Non-family hired labor represents only 5–20 percent of total labor employed by retailers.

---

[2] Rice is estimated to make up half of the calorie intake of the population in rural areas (Secaline 1996). The percentage is significantly higher in the regions included in the survey because the province of Tulear, which has a much drier climate – and therefore different agricultural production and consumption habits from the rest of the country – was not included in the sample.

Table 4.1   *Characteristics of Malagasy agricultural traders*

	Wholesaler	Retailer with fixed selling point	Retailer without fixed selling point	Assembler	Total
Sample distribution					
Total sample (percent)	30	44	15	11	100
Total sample (number)	226	328	91	80	725
Antananarivo	83	36	0	11	130
Vakinankaratra	40	75	7	24	146
Fianarantsoa (Hauts Plateaux)	48	99	13	19	179
Fianarantsoa (Côte et Falaise)	22	60	2	0	84
Majunga (Plaines)	24	31	26	18	89
Majunga (Hauts Plateaux)	9	27	43	80	97
Human capital					
Average age (years)	38	37	33	40	37
Male (percent)	68	48	30	69	54
Married (percent)	83	77	59	87	79
Highest educational attainment					
Primary to secondary I schooling (percent)	53	65	66	46	60
Secondary II to higher schooling (percent)	47	35	34	54	40
Average number of years in business	8	6	3	7	6
Number of languages spoken	1.5	1.5	1.2	1.7	1.5
Labor					
Total number of person-months	66.9	26.7	12.2	57.3	40.2
Owner	10.9	11.4	9.7	9.4	10.8
Family	13.2	10.1	1.9	11.3	10.0
Permanent workers	26.6	3.9	0.6	26.5	12.9
Temporary workers	16.2	1.2	0.1	10.1	6.6
In business on a full-time basis (percent)	93	95	74	69	89
In business all-year-round (percent)	85	94	68	47	83
Characteristics of operation					
Working capital (dollars)	3,656	566	209	6,366	2,109
Vehicles	0.19	0.05	0.01	0.47	0.14
Storage capacity (metric tons)	37	8	3	94	26

Table 4.1   (*cont.*)

	Wholesaler	Retailer with fixed selling point	Retailer without fixed selling point	Assembler	Total
Equipment value (dollars)	651	53	11	1,308	372
Monthly value of sales (dollars)	5,545	1,310	390	8,713	3,294
Monthly value of purchases (dollars)	4,349	1,259	320	7,560	2,815
Gross margin per month (dollars)	813	130	75	1,872	489

The surveyed businesses are fairly small and unsophisticated. Average working capital is about $2,100 – large compared with Madagascar's 1997 GDP of $230 but very small compared with the turnover of grain trading companies in Europe or the United States. Few traders possess their own means of transport, and investment in equipment is low relative to working capital. Most working capital seems to be tied up in agricultural products.

Traders vary greatly in size. Assemblers have the highest monthly gross margins – more than $1,800 – while retailers without fixed selling points earn just $75 a month. Traders in the top third of the firm size distribution use 15 times as much working capital and twice as much labor as smaller firms, and their gross margins are almost 50 times as high as traders in the bottom tercile (Fafchamps and Minten 1998a). Large traders thus have much higher total factor productivity (TFP) than smaller ones. We examine possible explanations for these differences and investigate the role of social capital. The next section illustrates how traders do business in markets with high transactions costs and how social capital might be useful in this type of environment.

Imperfect markets and social capital

Different factors account for success in business, according to Malagasy traders (table 4.2). Relationships are by far the most important factor, with 71 percent of traders regarding reputation and relationships as "very important." Relationships are considered much more important than other factors, including access to credit, granting credit, the level of purchase or sales price, and access to transport equipment. Relationships and social capital can have multiple advantages for traders, helping them overcome three obstacles in imperfect markets that are typical in commodity markets in developing countries: poor market institutions, high search costs, and imperfect and asymmetric information.

Table 4.2   *Traders' perceptions of factors important for success*

Factor	Very important	Important	A little bit important	Not important
Personal reputation and relationships	71	14	10	5
Access to credit	11	19	31	39
Granting credit	3	15	32	50
Purchase price	30	44	21	5
Sales price	35	48	15	2
Transport equipment	27	24	17	32

Poor market institutions

Social capital matters when market institutions fail. It can be a source of trade credit in environments in which formal credit is rare, it can be used for insurance through risk sharing, and it can substitute for contract enforcement where formal institutions are not effective.

Lack of formal credit.   The use of trade credit by traders is extremely limited. The vast majority of traders (89 percent) report that they use only their own funds to finance their business operations (table 4.3). A mere 4 percent of traders have ever asked for credit from a formal institution (Fafchamps and Minten 1998a), and just 0.3 percent of traders use formal credit. The major reasons given for not applying for credit are lack of understanding of credit procedures or availability, high interest rates, complicated application procedures, and lack of collateral.

Traders who do borrow do so on the informal market. One reason why traders might value social capital is that it increases access to informal trader credit. Informal credit does not substitute for the lack of formal credit, however, with only one of ten traders receiving some part of working capital from informal credit sources.

The minor role of formal institutions in traders' operations is illustrated by the fact that only 15 percent of the surveyed traders have bank accounts, 10 percent have savings account, and 1 percent have bank lines of credit. Less than 0.5 percent of traders use checks. Most agricultural trade – sales as well as purchases – takes place without the placing of orders and without credit: 82 percent of purchases and 86 percent of sales are cash-and-carry transactions, and only 2 percent of purchases are ordered ahead of time. Therefore, search and supervision costs are high, and massive amounts of currency circulate in the countryside, where they are vulnerable to theft and inflation tax.[3]

---

[3] Rural insecurity and cattle theft are serious problems in Madagascar, with some areas resembling the Wild West of the United States. Rural insecurity increased significantly after the impeachment

Table 4.3 *Use of and access to credit*

Item	Percent of traders
Main source of funding	
Own funds	89.0
Formal credit	0.3
Informal credit	2.2
Own funds and formal credit	1.2
Own funds and informal credit	7.3
Use of bank or financial institution	
Traders with bank account	15.5
Traders with line of credit	1.2
Traders with savings account	10.4
Traders member of rotating savings group ("tontine")	1.0
Use checks for purchases	0.4
Use checks for sales	0.4
Use of credit	
Credit purchases	15.9
Cash purchases	82.0
Purchases involving ordering	1.8
Credit sales	13.7
Cash sales	85.6
Sales involving a deposit	0.6

Note: n = 729.

Inadequate contract enforcement. The use of formal institutions for contract enforcement is also extremely rare among Malagasy traders. Only 5 percent of traders report ever having used the police, lawyers, or courts since they started their businesses (table 4.4). The dominant means of resolving conflict is negotiation with the other party or (less often) use of a third party as mediator. The lack of use of legal institutions does not imply that contracts are not enforced: most disputes are resolved and trade continues. Contractual disputes are resolved through negotiation, apparently because traders want to maintain their relationships. These relationships are valued because most traders report that they would find it fairly or very difficult to find a new supplier if they lost their current one. Conflicts thus have to be solved. They are resolved more often when traders have longer-term relationships with their suppliers (Fafchamps and Minten 1999).

Lack of formal insurance. Commodity trade is characterized by high variability and is subject to many kinds of risks. Covariate risks and idiosyncratic

of President Ratsiraka in 1991. In 1997 an average rural village reported two thefts of cattle, twelve thefts of agricultural products, and thirty thefts of small animals (Minten, Randrianarisoa, and Zeller 1998).

Table 4.4   *Use of institutions to resolve problems*

Item	Percent of traders
Types of institution used to resolve conflicts ($n = 729$)	
Third person or mediator	14.0
Police	4.0
Lawyer	0.6
Court	0.1
Conflict resolution technique used to resolve most recent conflict	
Theft ($n = 56$)	
Went to the police after theft	37.5
Went to court after theft	10.7
Contractual problem with supplier ($n = 178$)	
Negotiate directly with supplier	86.0
Seek help of mediator	3.4
Seek help of lawyer	0
Go to the police	0
Go to court	0.6
Contractual problem with customer ($n = 220$)	
Negotiate directly with customer	93.6
Seek help of mediator	9.1
Seek help of lawyer	0.5
Go to the police	3.6
Go to court	0.9

risks hinder agricultural trade and may cause financial stress for small trading companies. Covariate risks include inadequate road infrastructure, high levels of insecurity, climatic disasters, and large price fluctuations.

Idiosyncratic risks include nonpayment and late payment and the inability to detect poor quality. A system of insurance and risk sharing might mitigate the consequences of adverse outcomes or even allow traders to obtain higher returns by pursuing riskier activities. In the absence of formal institutions, social capital may play this role.

The overwhelming majority of traders are involved in some kind of informal insurance mechanism. Three-quarters of traders report having been helped by others, and 77 percent report having helped others (table 4.5). Larger traders are more likely to be involved in solidarity networks than smaller traders. They also perceive relationships differently. Large traders are more likely to believe that they will be helped by family and others when they need it, and they are more likely to help others if needed. They are also less likely than smaller traders to perceive family and friends as a burden. Not surprisingly, smaller traders are prouder than larger traders of what they achieved without help from others.

Table 4.5 *Risk sharing and access to financial assistance*

Item	Small	Medium	Large	Total
		Firm size		
Has ever helped others (percent of all traders)	71	79	80	77
Has ever been helped by others (percent of all traders)	75	77	74	75
Number of people who can help	1.76	2.46	2.73	2.32
Beliefs (index values)[a]				
"The rich have more friends than the poor."	4.75	4.55	4.44	4.58
"The poor are poor because they have nobody to assist them."	3.10	3.06	3.02	3.06
"I am only proud of what I accomplish without others' help."	4.61	4.18	4.25	4.35
"I solve my financial problems by myself."	4.32	4.47	4.52	4.44
"I help others when they are in need."	3.53	3.90	3.93	3.79
"I can count on my friends and family when in trouble."	3.40	3.60	3.95	3.65
"If my business failed, I would have to sell my possessions to survive."	2.18	2.58	2.44	2.40
"If I became poor, my family and friends would help me."	3.26	3.31	3.53	3.37
"If my business prospers, my family and friends will live at my expenses."	3.57	3.07	2.94	3.19
Number of observations	227	254	243	724

Note: [a] Values range from 1 (quite false) to 5 (quite true).

The results presented here are consistent with results on the mild impact of breaches of contract (Kandori 1992; Greif 1993, 1994; Fafchamps 1998) and the low reliance on legal institutions (Fafchamps 1996; Bigsten *et al.* 1998). They contradict findings that show that successful traders or market development are associated with more anonymous exchange and individualistic behavior (Greif 1993, 1994; Platteau 1994a, 1994b).

High search costs

A significant percentage of traders indicate that they face occasional problems finding potential buyers or sellers. Given that most agricultural goods are perishable and that storage conditions are often poor, high search costs can be disastrous for traders. The findings suggest that the establishment of regular relationships upstream and downstream may be in the interest of traders, customers, and suppliers alike. These findings are consistent with theoretical

Table 4.6   *Choice and regularity of supply (percent of traders, except where indicated)*

Item		Small	Medium	Large	Total
			Firm size		
Trader does not find suppliers					
	Yes, often	15.3	9.5	9.8	11.5
	Sometimes	26.9	37.2	35.1	33.1
	No, never	57.9	53.3	55.1	55.4
Possibility of choice between suppliers					
	Always	47.1	41.3	48.6	45.7
	Often	35.5	26.9	27.8	30.0
	Seldom	17.4	31.8	23.7	24.3
Trader buys from regular suppliers		37.2	65.7	71.0	58.0
Relation between main supplier and trader is only commercial		80.0	85.5	85.6	84.4
Trader faces an unlimited number of suppliers		20.2	8.7	26.1	18.4
Number of suppliers if number is limited		14.4	17.4	18.6	16.8
Number of regular suppliers		1.5	3.5	5.2	3.4
Number of years regular suppliers exist		1.2	2.8	3.3	2.4
Percent of purchases coming from regular suppliers		24.1	45.4	47.7	39.1
Solutions when the quality of the product of supplier is bad					
	"It is my problem."	69.0	48.8	45.7	54.5
	"The supplier partly refunds me."	11.2	23.6	24.5	19.8
	"The supplier gives me other products."	7.0	7.0	11.0	8.4
	Other	12.8	20.7	18.8	17.4
Buy from unknown suppliers					
	Yes, often	71.9	71.1	76.3	73.1
	Sometimes	6.6	6.6	6.9	6.7
	No, never	21.5	22.3	16.7	20.2

models on cooperation among individuals in an environment in which search costs are high (Ghosh and Ray 1996; Fafchamps 1998).

Supply.   Search costs for supply are high in Madagascar, with 45 percent of traders reporting that they encounter problems finding suppliers at least some of the time (table 4.6). This result is consistent with the fact that 55 percent of traders have not always a choice between suppliers. Given these high search costs, there is an incentive for traders to try to ensure regularity in supply. Traders who have the largest number of regular suppliers are also the ones who have the fewest problems ensuring regular supply (Fafchamps and Minten 1998a). Overall, almost 60 percent of traders report buying from regular suppliers, who account for almost 40 percent of their purchases. The likelihood of having a regular supplier increases significantly with the size of the firm (71 percent of large traders have regular suppliers, while only 37 percent for small traders do). In most cases, the long-term relationship between traders and regular suppliers is based exclusively on commercial and not on family, religious, or ethnical ties.

Regular relationships with suppliers also allow traders to engage in forward ordering. The practice is more common among larger traders: almost 19 percent of large traders place orders, while only 7 percent of small traders do so. Steady relationships between suppliers and traders also help prevent losses that result from low quality products. Large traders are better able to have their products replaced or to obtain refunds when problems occur. Small traders are more likely to have to solve quality problems on their own. Uncertainty over quality may be one of the reasons why 20 percent of traders refuse to buy from unknown suppliers.

Demand.   The cost of finding customers appears to be lower than the cost of finding suppliers: only 16 percent of traders often fail to find customers, and 56 percent report always being able to choose between customers (table 4.7). Incentives to develop a regular customer base are thus lower than incentives for developing regular suppliers.

Almost three-quarters of larger traders sell to regular customers, while less than a third of smaller traders do so. Overall, 54 percent of traders sell to regular customers, who represent 27 percent of the value of sales. Traders seem to be more willing to refund purchases to regular customers when quality problems are noted. Smaller traders' regular customers are more likely than those of larger traders to be people with whom they share kinship, religious, or ethnic ties. Few traders have a problem selling to strangers, however.

Imperfect and asymmetric information

Agricultural traders in Madagascar face imperfect and asymmetric information on the market situation, on the credibility of suppliers and customers, and on products. In the absence of efficient information services, the development of social capital might help share relevant information. Given weak market institutions, traders might become more efficient by developing a reliable supplier and customer network that allows them to grant and receive credit, order in advance, and spend less time checking quality.

Table 4.7   *Choice and regularity of customers (percent of all traders, except where indicated)*

		Firm size			
Item		Small	Medium	Large	Total
Trader does not find customers					
	Yes, often	17.4	16.1	14.3	15.9
	Sometimes	18.2	23.1	25.3	22.2
	No, never	64.5	60.7	60.4	61.9
Possibility of choice between customers					
	Always	61.6	48.8	57.1	55.8
	Often	22.7	18.6	15.5	18.9
	Seldom	15.7	32.6	27.3	25.2
Traders who sell to regular customers		31.4	58.7	73.1	54.5
Relationship between customers and trader is only commercial		88.2	93.0	97.2	94.0
Traders face an unlimited number of customers		70.2	70.7	63.3	68.0
Number of customers if number is limited		34.9	47.5	41.3	41.2
Average number of regular customers		2.1	4.6	11.3	6.0
Number of years that regular customers exist		0.8	2.3	3.3	2.1
Percent of sales to regular customers		15.1	25.7	40.7	27.2
Solutions when the quality of product for the customer is poor					
	"It is his problem."	76.9	58.3	51.8	62.3
	"I partly refund him."	8.7	19.4	21.2	16.5
	"The supplier gives me other products."	4.5	5.4	4.5	4.8
	Other	9.9	16.9	22.4	16.5
Sell to unknown customers					
	Yes, often	96.3	96.7	95.5	96.2
	Sometimes	0.4	1.2	0.8	0.8
	No, never	3.3	2.1	3.7	3.0

Information on the market situation.   Access to modern means of communication is limited in Madagascar. Ninety-five percent of traders do not have a telephone or fax for their business (table 4.8). Although more than half report having access to a phone, 84 percent report never using one to conduct business. Traders obtain information on the market situation through personal

Table 4.8 *Access to and sources of market intelligence and market news*

Item		Percent of traders
Owns phone		5.1
Has access to phone		56.5
Never uses a phone for business		83.8
Owns a fax		0.5
Has access to a fax		21.8
Never uses a fax for business		99.2
Main sources of information		
About prices		
	Suppliers	24.1
	Other traders	59.9
	Customers	4.1
	Messengers	8.9
About demand		
	Customers	75.9
	Other traders	16.5
About supply		
	Suppliers	65.6
	Other traders	23.2

Note: n = 729.

contacts with other traders, suppliers, customers, and messengers. The role of public sources of information, such as newspapers, radio, and public services is extremely marginal.

Different types of information are obtained from different sources. Sixty percent of traders obtain information about price changes from fellow traders. In contrast, only 17 percent use other traders to obtain information about market demand and only 23 percent use other traders to find out about market supply information. Most traders obtain information about supply directly from suppliers and customers.

Information on the credibility of suppliers and customers.   If traders want to engage in more sophisticated types of trading, they need to establish a system of exchanging information on the credibility of customers and suppliers in order to improve contract enforcement. Traders in Madagascar rarely use forms or recommendations in writing, recommendations by other traders, or bank information to verify credibility (table 4.9). Instead, credibility appears to be established on the basis of long-term relationships. Most traders report that they will not grant or receive credit or order supplies before having dealt

Table 4.9   *Trust in customers and suppliers (percent of all traders, except where indicated)*

Item	Obtaining credit from supplier	Ordering from supplier	Extending credit to customer
Would never use this mode on first transaction	92.3	83.7	94.7
Would require the following conditions			
Form (in writing)	0.5	2.0	1.8
Recommendation	11.3	22.4	17.1
Collateral	1.5	2.0	2.4
Frequent number of transactions	79.9	65.3	71.1
Number of transactions required if frequent number is required	8.9	11.3	12.7
Other	18.9	44.9	39.5
Conditions of deal			
Discount if paid in cash	1.5	n.a.	2.0
Delay offered (in days)	6.1	6.9	12.7
Trader settles deal later than agreed			
Never	17.0	28.6	18.9
Seldom	24.2	53.1	35.3
Sometimes	38.7	12.2	33.5
Often	20.1	6.1	12.2
Trader has to settle previous deal before obtaining new one	77.8	77.6	63.1
Supplies cut off after predetermined limit	60.4	100.0	87.2
Responses to problems			
Threatens to go to the police	2.1	6.1	4.7
Threatens to go to court	0.5	0.0	1.8
If traders have problems with a customer or supplier, other traders will refuse to deal with him			
No other traders	11.3	38.8	21.2
Some other traders	40.2	36.7	58.4
Most other traders	31.4	10.2	15.3
All other traders	17.0	14.3	5.0
Ability to find new supplier if trader loses current one			
Very easy	8.2	n.a.	25.3
Rather easy	16.0	n.a.	49.8
Rather difficult	44.3	n.a.	18.9
Very difficult	31.4	n.a.	6.0
Number of observations	194	49	339

Note: n.a. Not applicable.

with a trading partner repeatedly (nine–thirteen transactions on average). There seems to be little reward for immediate payment of a transaction, as prices are reduced on average only by 1.5 percent. However, given that the delay for payment is only six–thirteen days, this still constitutes an extremely high annual interest rate (compounded between 150 percent and 250 percent).

The more sophisticated the transaction, the higher the incidence of problems (Fafchamps and Minten 1999). Eighteen percent of traders who place orders, more than half (59 percent) of the traders who obtain credit from suppliers, and almost half (46 percent) of the traders granting occasional credit to customers are regularly unable to settle their accounts in the time required. Breaches of contract appear to carry few consequences, however: if traders are not able to honor their agreements, they are simply unable to obtain new supplies. Threatening to call the police or to sue (let alone actually doing so) is almost unheard of. Moreover, nonpayment of one supplier does not seem to affect the likelihood of the trader receiving credit or ordering from other suppliers.[4] However, the majority of traders believe that it is hard to find suppliers willing to extend credit. It seems that once traders are on good terms with a supplier, they have an incentive to preserve that relationship.

Information on products.   Most traders weigh products to determine quantities (Mendoza and Randrianarisoa 1998). Determining quality is more difficult. Quality varies significantly across as well as within regions: only 6 percent of traders report that quality across regions never varies, and only 7 percent report that quality within regions never varies (table 4.10). Because the Green Revolution did not occur in Madagascar, many local unimproved varieties are found in local markets (Badiane *et al.* 1998). Verification of quality is thus important: 85 percent of traders and customers report that they always inspect quality before making a purchase. Determining quality is particularly important because prices are based on it, according to 94 percent of traders.

Given the multilayered nature of agricultural trade and the large number of transactions, checking for quality can be assumed to account for a substantial part of the spread between producer and consumer prices. The vast majority (93 percent) of traders report checking quality themselves, suggesting that quality control is perceived to be critical to firm performance. To ensure quality, traders make frequent trips to supply areas, searching for buyers and sellers at each location. Some of these trips are in vain as traders do not use telephones, cannot or will not place orders. In such an environment of high search costs the development of social capital clearly reduces the costs of doing business.

---

[4] Elsewhere the circulation of information among traders is much faster (Hayami and Kawagoe 1993). This issue deserves more research.

Table 4.10   *Quality variation and verification*

Item	Percent of all traders
Quality variation	
Quality of products varies systematically by geographical origin	
A lot	36.7
A little bit	57.4
Not at all	5.9
Quality of products within region varies	
Never	6.8
Seldom	36.7
Sometimes	37.1
Often	14.2
Always	5.2
Price of product varies with quality	
A lot	33.1
A little bit	60.8
Not at all	6.1
Quality verification	
Trader always verifies quality before purchase	84.3
Customer always verifies quality before purchase	85.8
Person responsible for verification of quality	
Owner/manager	93.2
Family aide	4.4
Employee	1.1
Agent collector	0.6
Nobody	0.7

Note: n = 729.

Determinants of and returns to social capital

Regression analysis is used to determine the quantitative impact of social capital and to identify the channels through which social capital affects performance. First, the different measures of social capital that are used in the analysis are discussed and their determinants analyzed. Second, returns to social capital are estimated.

The following production function is used:

$$Q = f(L, K, H, S) \tag{4.1}$$

where Q stands for output, L for labor, and K for physical capital, H for human capital, and S for social capital. If S has any effect on performance, its inclusion in the production function should lead to reduced regression coefficients of the other variables.

After evaluating the effects of social capital, we run a second specification to identify the channels through which social capital might work:

$$Q = f(L, K, H, S; C) \tag{4.2}$$

where C stands for different channels (reduction in imperfect information and search costs, substitution for market institutions). If S affects Q only because it reduces C, including C in the regression should result in a nonsignificant coefficient for S. If, however, S has an effect on output beyond its effect on C, then both C and S should be significant. The effect of the accumulation process of inputs on firm performance is further unraveled as the channels through which business experience influences performance are tested through different specifications.

Four potential problems may distort the regression results (these problems are discussed extensively and dealt with through robustness testing in Fafchamps and Minten 1998b). First, the dependent variable and some of the independent variables may be simultaneously determined. It is possible, for instance, that traders respond to good market opportunities by raising more working capital and hiring more workers. To prevent this problem, we construct instrumental variables – including variables on family background, business start-up experience, personal wealth and financial assets, and access to telecommunication equipment – based on an extensive data set of exogenous variables (for details see Fafchamps and Minten 1998b).

Second, there may be bias resulting from past covariate and idiosyncratic shocks. To minimize these problems, we include measures of location and firm-specific sales shocks.

Third, the specification might be prone to omitted variable bias. If, for instance, traders who are more efficient are more sociable, then S will capture differences in entrepreneurial quality and the coefficient of S will be biased.[5] Fafchamps and Minten (1998b) run alternative specifications in which they include variables that capture entrepreneurs' propensity to socialize and accumulate wealth, as well as their capacity to monitor their workers. The results obtained are similar to those reported here.

Fourth, it could be argued that social capital is just a byproduct of economic success. Discussions with respondents suggest that maintaining an extensive and up-to-date network of business contacts is not costless, however: socializing is time consuming and can even involve out-of-pocket expenses. Even if socializing were costless, overaccumulation of social capital would only bias the estimated coefficient toward zero.[6] Consequently, a significant coefficient

---

[5] The possible correlation between entrepreneurial characteristics and the factors of production is a general problem, not one peculiar to social capital.

[6] Firms might also accumulate financial assets and real estate that are not required for their business. One could argue that such assets should be omitted from production function analysis. In practice, it is not always possible to disentangle nonessential from essential factors of production in a firm's accounts, in which case the coefficient of capital would also be underestimated.

Table 4.11 *Determinants of social capital, labor, and physical capital*

| | Social capital | | | | | | | | | | Labor | | Physical capital | |
| | Number of relatives in trade | | Number of people who can help | | Number of traders known | | Number of customers known personally | | Number of suppliers known personally | | Manpower (ln in man-months) | | Equipment (ln in local currency) | |
Variable	Coefficient	t-statistic	Coefficient	t-statistic	Coefficient	t-statistic	Coefficient	t-statistic	Coefficient	t-statistic	Coefficient	t-statistic	Coefficient	t-statistic
Years of schooling of owner/manager	0.0079	1.352	0.0075	1.205	0.0029	0.347	0.0116	1.098	0.0369	3.925	0.0387	5.403	0.1517	6.421
Age of owner/manager	0.0078	0.718	0.0135	1.153	0.0330	2.089	0.0279	1.418	0.0427	2.438	0.0226	1.690	0.0601	1.364
(Age of owner/manager)^2	-0.0001	-0.965	-0.0002	-1.325	-0.0004	-2.019	-0.0003	-1.083	-0.0004	-1.954	-0.0001	-0.490	-0.0003	-0.521
Gender (1 = male)	-0.0198	-0.514	-0.0012	-0.028	-0.1315	-2.352	-0.0522	-0.749	-0.0844	-1.362	-0.1618	-3.418	-0.5267	-3.375
Years of experience in agricultural trade	0.0409	1.345	0.0785	2.405	0.3286	7.445	0.2299	4.176	0.1884	3.847	0.1238	3.312	0.5767	4.680
Dummy if full-time trader	0.0080	0.123	0.0436	0.628	0.0017	0.018	-0.0023	-0.020	0.0440	0.423	0.0469	0.590	-0.7342	-2.802
Dummy if trader all-year-round	-0.0984	-1.691	-0.0445	-0.712	0.1250	1.480	0.1355	1.286	-0.1797	-1.917	0.1360	1.900	-0.2846	-1.206
In capital city	-0.3420	-2.341	0.1575	1.004	0.3152	1.486	0.5625	2.126	-0.6174	-2.623	-0.0986	-0.549	-1.3378	-2.259
In another city	0.1608	3.234	0.0241	0.452	-0.1695	-2.349	-0.2780	-3.088	-0.2753	-3.437	-0.0575	-0.941	-0.1803	-0.895
In Vakinankaratra region	-0.3816	-2.647	-0.1924	-1.243	0.3125	1.493	0.2212	0.848	-0.5748	-2.475	-0.1196	-0.675	-0.1443	-0.247
In Fianarantsoa (Hauts Plateaux)	-0.4611	-3.194	-0.1881	-1.214	0.0081	0.039	-0.2882	-1.102	-1.1810	-5.078	0.0143	0.081	-2.5406	-4.341
In Fianarantsoa (Côte et Falaise)	-0.4546	-3.030	-0.0623	-0.387	-0.0665	-0.305	-0.3443	-1.267	-1.1604	-4.800	-0.1211	-0.656	-3.0002	-4.932
In Majunga (Plaines)	-0.6612	-4.456	-0.2832	-1.777	-0.0262	-0.122	-0.7347	-2.734	-1.6255	-6.800	-0.6186	-3.390	-4.0686	-6.764
In Majunga (Plateau)	-0.6078	-4.254	-0.2862	-1.866	-0.2301	-1.109	-0.6517	-2.519	-1.6372	-7.112	-0.5777	-3.287	-5.0498	-8.718
Intercept	0.6358	2.542	0.7666	2.854	0.6857	1.888	0.7378	1.629	0.9240	2.293	2.0824	6.770	3.7861	3.734
R^2	0.088		0.094		0.192		0.265		0.317		0.349		0.495	

Note: n = 704.

on social capital should be interpreted as a good indication that social capital matters even if the accumulation of network capital is costless or if it is used for purposes other than business.

Output is measured through the value of sales and total value added the previous year. Value added is computed by subtracting purchases from sales. Since both are subject to measurement error and the average difference between the two is small, estimates of value added are much less precise than estimates of total sales or total purchases. In addition, respondents are often reluctant to divulge their profit margins for fear that survey data will be used to assess taxes. Labor is measured in person-months. Physical capital is measured in terms of the value of business equipment. Human capital variables, entrepreneurial characteristics, and family background are included because they potentially increase the efficiency of labor and capital. The five measures of social capital (number of relatives in agricultural trade, number of traders known, number of people who can help financially, number of suppliers known personally, and number of customers known personally) are entered in log form to account for the possibility that marginal returns to social capital are decreasing. Experience in trade is also entered in log form. To avoid losing observations when a respondent has no storage capacity while remaining consistent in the use of logged gross margin as dependent variables, storage capacity is added as log(storage+1). Other nonessential variables are treated the same way. Two measures of shocks are included: whether the firm was the victim of a theft in the preceding year and a measure of aggregate sales shock, computed as the growth in total annual sales enjoyed by traders in the same location. Location dummies are added to control for differences in competition and business environment across space. Before we turn to the results on the returns to social capital, we first look at determinants of the five measures of social capital used in the analysis.

Accumulation of social capital

We assume that just as entrepreneurs need to accumulate machinery and equipment to be successful, they need to accumulate most forms of social capital. Entrepreneurs have to use valuable resources, including time, to invest in social capital. Regression results illustrate the process by which social capital, labor, and physical capital are accumulated (table 4.11).

For all variables except relatives in trade, social capital increases with the number of years in trade. Elasticities range from 8 percent for the number of people who can help to 33 percent for the number of traders known. These results seems intuitive, as it takes more time and effort to develop a relationship with someone willing to help in time of financial trouble than to develop relationships with traders, suppliers, and customers. The number of relatives in trade seems to be difficult to influence by one's own actions. Although successful traders may employ more family employees over time, thereby increasing the number of relatives in agricultural trade, doing so does not seem to be a major determinant of this measure of social capital (the coefficient on experience is small and insignificant).

When the same type of regression is run with labor and physical capital (the inputs used in a typical production function) as dependent variables, the variables exhibit the same kind of behavior in response to business experience. The elasticity of labor with respect to business experience is 0.12. The elasticity of the value of equipment is very high (0.57). Given that most physical capital represents a long-term investment, traders often need access to credit to finance it. Because social capital might improves this access, it might indirectly improve performance.

Other variables have little effect on the development of social capital. The level of education shows a positive sign in all regressions, but the coefficient is significant in only one case. The gender of the trader shows a negative sign in all regressions, but it is significant in only one. Women may be less successful than men in developing social capital in Madagascar because they have to spend more time on household chores and childrearing. The age of the trader shows the expected positive sign for the different measures of social capital as well as a decreasing marginal effect, as the quadratic term is always negative. The coefficients are significant in two of five cases. In short, the findings suggest that traders accumulate social capital – as well as other inputs – over time.

Returns to social capital

Three sets of variables are used to explain traders' performance: human capital variables only; human capital variables plus labor and physical capital; and human capital, labor, physical capital, and social capital. The purpose of the different specifications is to illustrate the effect of business experience. Because relatives in agricultural trade are not accumulated over time (as shown in table 4.11), this form of social capital is included in all the specifications.

The results show that experience is highly significant in the specification in which social capital, human capital, and labor are included (table 4.12). In that specification, a doubling of the years of experience in trade increases sales by 50 percent and value added by 60 percent. Evaluated at the mean and controlling for other inputs, one additional year in business increases sales and value added by about 10 percent.[7] In the specification that controls for physical capital and labor, the magnitude – as well as the significance – of the experience coefficient drops to 19 percent for total sales and 25 percent for value added.

---

[7] As we have no panel data on traders, this result does not reflect growth in the agricultural marketing sector. Only successful traders remain in trade; unsuccessful traders move on to other activities.

Finally, after controlling for social capital, the significance of the effect of experience in trade disappears for both sales and value added, while elasticity declines another 10 percent. Hence we conclude that a large part of the effect of business experience on performance comes from the accumulation of social capital over time rather than from the development of other types of expertise. In Madagascar the effect of "learning by doing" over time is almost completely explained through "learning by knowing." The major difference between other production inputs and social capital seems to be a well-identified opportunity cost. Unlike the cost of overaccumulation of labor and physical capital, which shows up in lower profits, there appears to be no direct cost associated with overaccumulation of social capital.

Most measures of social capital increase gross margins or value added significantly, even after controlling for working capital and equipment, labor, human capital, and management skills. A joint F-test for the significance of the coefficients on nonfamily social capital is significant in both specifications. The two most important dimensions of social capital appear to be the number of traders known and the number of people a trader can count on in times of trouble. The estimated coefficients indicate that a doubling of the number of known traders increases value added 27 percent and total sales 19 percent, while the number of people who can help in times of trouble increases value added 18 percent and total sales 29 percent.

The number of close relatives in trade does not have the expected sign but is highly significant in all specifications. The coefficient is no longer significant when the subsidiary dummy (= having another sales/purchase outlet) is omitted from the regression, however, and it declines in absolute value when close interaction with businesses held by relatives is controlled for. (Neither specification is reported.) This result is consistent with the idea that traders who have close relatives in trade confuse their businesses with those of their relatives and, as a result, tend to overreport the working capital and the equipment that is truly theirs. Another possibility is that unclear business boundaries dilute incentives and result in lower unobserved efforts.[8] In either case, it is clear from these results that family relationships do not constitute the only – or even the major – component of social capital, contrary to what is often assumed (see, for example, Granovetter 1995). If anything, nonfamily networks are more important than family networks in business. This finding is consistent with Bigsten *et al.* (1998) and Minten and Kyle (1999), who report that family links account for only a minute percentage of relationships in manufacturing in Africa and agricultural trade in the Republic of Congo.

Working capital and labor have the expected signs and are highly significant. Traders with a subsidiary create twice the value added of traders who do not. For

---

[8] Fafchamps and Minten (1999) show that more relatives in agricultural trade leads to more unresolved conflicts between traders and suppliers and traders and customers.

Table 4.12 *Determinants of value added and total sales*

Variable	ln (value added)						ln (total sales)					
	Coefficient	t-statistic	Coefficient	t-statistic	Coefficient	t-statistic	Coefficient	t-statistic	Coefficient	t-statistic	Coefficient	t-statistic
Capital and equipment												
Working capital[a]			0.4445	4.668	0.3990	4.438			0.3984	4.878	0.3519	4.649
Dummy if subsidiary			0.9873	3.486	0.9541	3.507			0.9438	4.021	0.9538	4.290
Value of equipment			−0.0113	−0.301	−0.0057	−0.157			0.0304	1.027	0.0313	1.114
Storage capacity			−0.0167	−0.210	0.0518	0.668			−0.0153	−0.255	0.0438	0.767
Number of vehicles			−0.3080	−1.032	−0.3482	−1.191			−0.4928	−2.134	−0.4861	−2.191
Utilization of telephone[a]			−0.1173	−0.330	0.0075	0.022			0.4947	1.701	0.5986	2.186
Labor and management												
Manpower (in months/year) (ln)[a]	0.1294	0.471	1.1143	3.832	0.8345	2.879	0.1699	0.828	0.9868	4.326	0.7236	3.234
Dummy if full time trader (1 = yes)	−0.1308	−0.588	0.0243	0.106	0.0671	0.304	0.0290	0.160	0.1630	0.978	0.1340	0.854
Dummy if trader all year round (1 = yes)			0.1338	0.609	0.1889	0.896			0.3219	1.921	0.3834	2.412
Years of schooling of owner/manager	0.1191	4.985	0.0370	1.709	0.0294	1.422	0.1138	5.582	0.0280	1.577	0.0218	1.299
Years of experience in agricultural trade (ln)	0.6087	5.654	0.2545	2.596	0.1456	1.521	0.5034	5.479	0.1954	2.483	0.0913	1.199
Speak another language (1 = yes)	−0.3235	−1.883	−0.2951	−1.941	−0.2055	−1.399	−0.2325	−1.572	−0.3147	−2.525	−0.2227	−1.876
Social capital												
Number of relatives in agricultural trade (ln)	−0.4093	−2.421	−0.6390	−4.341	−0.2714	−2.208	−0.4032	−2.762	−0.6292	−5.195	−0.2737	−2.794
Number of traders known (ln)					0.2737	3.124					0.1924	2.837
Number of people who can help (ln)					0.1874	1.682					0.2875	3.270

	(1)		(2)		(3)		(4)		(5)		(6)	
Number of suppliers known personally (ln)					0.1230	1.567					0.0721	1.149
Number of customers known personally (ln)					0.0649	0.797					0.1103	1.704
Shocks												
Aggregate sales shock	−0.1079	−0.781	0.2589	2.138	0.1721	1.471	−0.0173	−0.156	0.2422	2.664	0.1926	2.235
Theft in the last 12 months (1 = yes)	0.1954	0.720	−0.2797	−1.214	−0.4126	−1.861	0.4170	1.915	−0.1250	−0.703	−0.2560	−1.518
Location												
In capital city (1 = yes)	−0.8216	−1.059	−0.6809	−1.045	−0.9366	−1.496	−0.8866	−1.966	−0.3714	−0.995	−0.5231	−1.482
In another city (1 = yes)	0.1715	0.947	0.2367	1.420	0.2521	1.571	0.2144	1.370	0.1798	1.316	0.1792	1.386
In Vakinankaratra region (1 = yes)	−0.2206	−0.285	−0.6385	−0.968	−0.8061	−1.265	−0.5145	−1.159	−0.4561	−1.296	−0.4315	−1.292
In Fianarantsoa (Hauts Plateaux) (1 = yes)	−0.3222	−0.417	−1.0887	−1.650	−0.9559	−1.504	−1.1145	−2.482	−1.4706	−3.959	−1.2057	−3.403
In Fianarantsoa (Côte et Falaise) (1 = yes)	−0.3625	−0.464	−0.8636	−1.282	−0.6929	−1.070	−1.3415	−2.884	−1.3968	−3.634	−1.1150	−3.038
In Majunga (Plaines) (1 = yes)	−0.7281	−0.914	−0.2488	−0.365	−0.0116	−0.018	−1.7595	−3.702	−0.7898	−2.023	−0.4667	−1.250
In Majunga (Plateau) (1 = yes)	−0.7726	−0.970	−0.5884	−0.858	−0.2611	−0.395	−2.1073	−4.478	−1.3310	−3.394	−0.9785	−2.610
Intercept	7.1695	8.477	1.4736	1.626	1.6147	1.846	10.0980	20.203	4.4555	6.945	4.5114	7.447
Number of observations	637		627		627		694		681		681	
F-value	7.17		19.70		19.62		12.51		32.19		32.47	
R^2	0.146		0.416		0.470		0.215		0.509		0.568	
Joint test of nonfamily social capital					0.0107						0.0012	

Note: [a]Regarded as endogenous.

Table 4.13 *Determinants of value added and total sales, controlling for modes of transaction*

	In (value added)				In (total sales)			
	Ordinary least squares		Instrumental variable specification		Ordinary least squares		Instrumental variable specification	
Variable	Coefficient	t-statistic	Coefficient	t-statistic	Coefficient	t-statistic	Coefficient	t-statistic
Capital and equipment								
Working capital (ln)	0.247	6.843	0.387	4.110[a]	0.218	7.264	0.383	4.691[a]
Dummy if subsidiary (yes = 1)	0.639	2.540	−0.099	−0.307	0.881	4.319	−0.287	−1.163
Value of equipment (ln)	0.008	0.264	0.246	0.668	0.046	1.885	0.878	2.767
Storage capacity (ln)	0.121	2.255	0.415	1.231	0.150	3.564	0.344	1.282
Number of vehicles (ln)	−0.031	−0.126	−0.007	−0.182	−0.134	−0.691	0.019	0.625
Utilization of telephone (yes = 1)	0.239	1.434	0.076	0.923[a]	0.285	2.093	0.057	0.905[a]
Labor and management								
Manpower (in months/years) (ln)	0.466	4.062	0.517	2.149[a]	0.442	5.049	0.606	3.131[a]
Dummy if full-time trader (yes = 1)	0.037	0.185	0.575	1.893[a]	0.124	0.833	0.816	3.186[a]
Dummy if trader all-year-round (yes = 1)	0.436	2.528	−0.004	−0.017	0.493	3.675	0.004	0.025
Years of schooling of owner/manager	0.025	1.343	−0.001	−0.039	0.020	1.326	−0.001	−0.071
Years of experience in agricultural trade (ln)	0.053	0.612	−0.012	−0.120	0.026	0.362	−0.011	−0.132
Speaks another language (yes = 1)	−0.226	−1.664	−0.022	−0.138	−0.198	−1.772	−0.094	−0.696
Social capital								
Number of relatives in agricultural trade (ln)	−0.193	−1.692	−0.107	−0.801	−0.259	−2.790	−0.206	−1.831
Number of traders known (ln)	0.193	2.374	0.194	2.031	0.121	1.851	0.155	1.945
Number of people who can help (ln)	0.189	1.847	0.204	1.804	0.300	3.645	0.304	3.315

	(1)		(2)		(3)		(4)	
Number of suppliers known personally (ln)	0.209	2.656	0.121	1.111	0.070	1.101	−0.011	−0.117
Number of customers known personally (ln)	−0.059	−0.808	−0.081	−0.934	0.084	1.433	0.036	0.510
Shocks								
Aggregate sales shock (ratio)	0.061	0.585	0.056	0.463	0.148	1.859	0.153	1.680
Theft in the past months (yes = 1)	−0.459	−2.252	−0.482	−2.093	−0.272	−1.729	−0.280	−1.566
Location								
In capital city (yes = 1)	−1.337	−2.194	−2.035	−2.485	−0.688	−1.917	−1.079	−1.946
In another city (yes = 1)	0.336	2.423	0.292	1.734	0.335	2.943	0.189	1.343
In Vakinankaratra region (yes = 1)	−1.014	−1.724	−1.364	−2.016	−0.402	−1.238	−0.327	−0.825
In Fianarantsoa (Hauts Plateaux) (yes = 1)	−0.951	−1.633	−1.329	−2.032	−0.832	−2.513	−1.054	−2.614
In Fianarantsoa (Côte et Falaise) (yes = 1)	−0.600	−1.014	−1.181	−1.732	−0.755	−2.189	−1.078	−2.529
In Majunga (Plaines) (yes = 1)	0.119	0.197	−0.063	−0.093	−0.199	−0.558	−0.154	−0.372
In Majunga (Plateau) (yes = 1)	−0.057	−0.094	−0.104	−0.155	−0.672	−1.870	−0.508	−1.207
Mode of transaction to reduce imperfect information								
Info on prices from customers and suppliers (yes = 1)	0.631	4.690	0.552	1.710^a	0.436	4.011	0.299	1.086^a
Info on prices from messengers (yes = 1)	1.006	5.716	0.772	1.675^a	0.575	3.953	0.207	0.530^a
Firm always inspects quality of supplies (no = 1)	0.400	2.370	1.022	2.192^a	0.288	2.081	0.630	1.645^a
Customers always inspect quality of supplies (no = 1)	−0.304	−1.709	−0.096	−0.197^a	−0.174	−1.228	0.179	0.435^a
Mode of transaction to deal with poor market institutions								
Share of purchases with supplier credit	0.448	1.821	1.522	2.098^a	0.354	1.741	1.394	2.225^a
Share of sales with credit to customer	0.914	2.796	0.667	1.001^a	0.460	1.731	0.475	0.817^a
Mode of transaction to reduce high search costs								
Share of purchases from regular suppliers	0.111	0.723	0.594	1.552^a	0.206	1.654	0.575	1.741^a
Share of sales to regular customers	0.855	3.730	1.288	2.261^a	0.569	3.037	0.669	1.330^a
Firm always places orders form suppliers (no = 1)	−0.561	−3.772	−0.957	−2.649^a	−0.137	−1.129	0.054	0.174^a
Intercept	3.435	4.931	2.967	3.094	5.686	12.894	5.054	7.707
Number of observations	640		626		692		677	
R^2	0.555		0.489		0.621		0.552	
Joint test of nonfamily social capital								
F-statistic	6.10		2.95		9.27		5.31	
P-value	0.0001		0.0197		0.0000		0.0003	

Note: ^{a} Regarded as endogenous.

the most part, equipment, storage capacity, and telephone use have the expected signs, but none is significant. In contrast, ownership of transport vehicles appears to have a negative effect on value added, possibly because traders are engaged in transport as well as trade.[9] Being a part-time trader does not appear to have an effect on value added, but year-round traders tend to create more of it. Schooling of the owner increases value added, but the coefficient is not significant. Paradoxically, traders who speak Malagasy and at least one other language earn less than those who speak only Malagasy. It might be that these traders engage in import–export activities that divert their attention from domestic agricultural trading activities, something that is not captured in the measure of performance. Past growth rates are positively associated with performance, indicating that sales shocks are correlated over time. The presence of these long-lasting shocks is consistent with Barrett's (1997) observation that in spite of massive entry Madagascar grain markets remain uncompetitive.

In another experiment (not shown here), we instrumented social capital variables in an effort to control for possible self-selection bias. The instruments included various determinants of traders' propensity to form business relationships, such as previous experience with solidarity, the presence of friends among grain traders, competition they face on the buying and selling side of their business, and their views on the role of relationships in trade and their attitudes about solidarity. Results show that nonfamily network variables remain jointly significant and that the instrumented number of known traders captures most of the beneficial effect of social capital on trader productivity.

Social capital and modes of transaction

How do different modes of reducing transactions costs affect the efficiency of traders? Two sets of regressions are presented (table 4.13). The first regression presents ordinary least squares estimates. The second regression corrects for possible simultaneity bias in working capital, labor, and modes of transaction. Multicollinearity is likely, because we do not have good instruments for distinguishing among the propensities of traders to rely on each mode of transaction.

For transactions costs due to imperfect information, the source of price information seems to be crucial. Estimated ordinary least squares (OLS) coefficients indicate that traders able to rely on customers, suppliers, or messengers to gather information about prices perform significantly better than those who must rely on the information provided by other traders. The effects are large: using customers and suppliers as the main source of price information is associated with a 60 percent increase in gross margin; using messengers leads to an increase of more than 100 percent. Not having to inspect the quality of supplies at each

---

[9] No data are available on the benefits of transport.

purchase is also associated with higher margins. Quality checks by the customer may lead to less rent for the trader, as shown by the negative sign. However, the coefficient is significant only for the value added OLS specification.

A reduction in search costs (proxied by the size of traders' regular customer base) is associated with higher sales and margins. However, contrary to expectations, firms that place orders with suppliers earn significantly lower margins, in the OLS as well as the instrumental variable specification. One possible interpretation is that Malagasy traders place orders only when they cannot find ready supplies. This interpretation is consistent with the fact that orders are often fulfilled late (Fafchamps and Minten 1999). In this context, placing orders is a sign of firm weakness and is associated with smaller margins.

Traders' ability to sell on credit is also an important determinant of performance. Since granting credit is a highly risky proposition, firms that are better able to identify reliable customers appear to be at an advantage, even after controlling for working capital, labor, education, and other variables. The coefficients are strongly significant in both specifications, but the significance disappears when the specification is corrected for endogeneity.

The results provide important insights into the role of different dimensions of social capital: once modes of transactions in imperfect markets are controlled for, only the dimensions that increase efficiency in ways other than by facilitating transactions should remain significant. These effects can be seen by comparing the coefficients on the social capital variables shown in table 4.12. Controlling for modes of transactions in imperfect markets reduces the coefficient on the number of traders known. Having relationships with more traders facilitates transactions in ways that are largely captured by the mode of transaction variables. In contrast, the coefficient on the number of people that can help in a financial emergency remains constant and in some specifications even increases in magnitude. This result indicates that better insurance increases efficiency in ways other than by reducing transactions costs. The reason is likely to be that traders able to deal with liquidity risk are better able to take advantage of arbitrage opportunities without fear of becoming illiquid. The number of close relatives continues to have a negative and significant coefficient, and its size decreases only slightly. Having relatives in trade thus seems to have little to do with transactions costs. Its effect may be linked to the fact that traders overstate their own resources because of failure to distinguish adequately between their resources and those of their relatives.

Conclusion

This chapter uses an extensive data set on agricultural traders in Madagascar to study the effect of social capital, measured by the number and type of relationships, on the performance of firms. It shows that traders with better relationships with other traders, suppliers, and customers earn higher margins. Social capital is shown to have the same characteristics as other types of inputs, such as physical capital and labor. Like other types of capital, social capital is accumulated over time and significantly improves economic performance.

Firms benefit from social capital mainly through a reduction in the high transactions costs typical in agricultural commodity markets. We find evidence that social capital enables traders to deal with one another in a more trusting manner, allowing them to grant and receive credit, exchange price information, and economize on quality inspection. The evidence indicates that three dimensions of social capital should be distinguished: relationships with other traders, which help firms economize on transactions costs; relationships with individuals who can help in time of financial difficulties, which insure traders against liquidity risk; and family relationships, which are found to reduce efficiency, possibly because of measurement error.

These results have important policy implications. Social capital can be increased and transactions costs reduced by encouraging interaction among traders (through a Chamber of Commerce, for example); by refraining from victimizing business communities regardless of their ethnic origin; and by facilitating the flow of information. Laws and a reliable legal system court are often insufficient for enabling efficient markets to arise, because the threat of court action to punish breach of contract is seldom credible for small transactions and because relationships are too valuable to risk losing.

REFERENCES

Badiane, O., Goletti, F., Kherallah, M., Berry, P., Govindan, K., Gruhn, P., and Mendoza, M., 1997. "Agricultural Input and Output: Marketing Reform in African Countries." Report submitted to the Bundesministerium für Wirtschaftsliche Zusammenarbeit (BMZ), International Food Policy Research Institute, Washington, DC

Badiane, O., Goletti, F., Lapenu, C., Mendoza, M., Minten, B., Ralison, E., Randrianiroa, C., Rich, K., and Zeller, M., 1998. "Main Results and Policy Implications of the IFPRI–FOFIFA Research Project on Structure and Conduct of Major Agricultural Input and Output Markets and Response to Reforms by Rural Households in Madagascar." International Food Policy Research Institute, Washington, DC

Barr, A. M., 1998. "Social Capital and Technical Information Flows in the Ghanaian Manufacturing Sector." Oxford University, Centre for the Study of African Economies, Oxford

Barrett, C. B., 1997. "Food Marketing Liberalization and Trader Entry: Evidence from Madagascar." *World Development* 25(5): 763–777

Bigsten, A., Collier, P., Dercon, S., Fafchamps, M., Gauthier, B., Gunning, J. W., Isaksson, A., Oduro, A., Oostendorp, R., Patillo, C., Soderbom, M., Teal, F., and Zeufack, A., 1998. "Contract Flexibility and Contract Resolution: Evidence from African Manufacturing." Stanford University, Department of Economics, Stanford, CA

Coleman, J. S., 1988. "Social Capital in the Creation of Human Capital."*American Journal of Sociology* 94 (supplement): S95–S120

Cornell, B. and Welch, I., 1996. "Culture, Information, and Screening Discrimination." *Journal of Political Economy* 104(3): 542–571

Crow, B. and Murshid, K. A. S., 1994. "Economic Returns to Social Power: Merchants' Finance and Interlinkage in the Grain Markets of Bangladesh." *World Development* 22(7): 1011–1030

Fafchamps, M., 1992. "Solidarity Networks in Pre-Industrial Societies: Rational Peasants with a Moral Economy." *Economic Development and Cultural Change* 41(1): 147–174

　1996. "The Enforcement of Commercial Contracts in Ghana." *World Development* 24(3): 427–448

　1998. "Market Emergence, Trust and Reputation." Stanford University, Department of Economics, Stanford, CA

Fafchamps, M. and Lund, S., 1998. "Risk Sharing Networks in Rural Philippines." Stanford University, Department of Economics, Stanford, CA

Fafchamps, M. and Minten, B., 1998a. "Relationships and Traders in Madagascar." International Food Policy Research Institute – Markets and Structural Studies Division Discussion Paper 24, International Food Policy Research Institute, Washington, DC

　1998b. "Returns to Social Capital among Traders." International Food Policy Research Institute – Markets and Structural Studies Division Discussion Paper 23, International Food Policy Research Institute, Washington, DC

　1999. "Property Rights in a Flea Market Economy." Stanford University, Department of Economics, Stanford, CA

Fukuyama, F., 1995. *Trust: The Social Virtues and the Creation of Prosperity*. New York: The Free Press Paperbacks

Gambetta, D., 1988. *Trust: Making and Breaking Cooperative Relations*. New York: Basil Blackwell

Ghosh, P. and Ray, D., 1996. "Cooperation in Community Interaction without Information Flows." *Review of Economic Studies* 63(3): 491–519

Granovetter, M., 1985. "Economic Action and Social Structure: The Problem of Embeddedness." *American Journal of Sociology* 91(3): 481–510

　1995. "The Economic Sociology of Firms and Entrepreneurs." In A. Portes (ed.), *The Economic Sociology of Immigration: Essays on Networks, Ethnicity, and Entrepreneurship*. New York: Russell Sage Foundation

Greif, A., 1993. "Contract Enforceability and Economic Institutions in Early Trade: The Maghribi Traders' Coalition." *American Economic Review* 83(3): 525–548

　1994. "Cultural Beliefs and the Organization of Society: A Historical and Theoretical Reflection on Collectivist and Individualist Societies." *Journal of Political Economy* 102(5): 912–950

Grootaert, C., 1999. "Social Capital, Household Welfare and Poverty in Indonesia." Local Level Institutions Working Paper 6, World Bank, Social Development Department, Washington, DC

Hayami, Y. and Kawagoe, T., 1993. *The Agrarian Origins of Commerce and Industry – A Study of Peasant Marketing in Indonesia*. London: Macmillan

Helliwell, J. F. and Putnam, R. D., 1995. "Economic Growth and Social Capital in Italy." *Eastern Economic Journal* 21(3): 295–307

Kandori, M., 1992. "Social Norms and Community Enforcement." *Review of Economic Studies* 59(3): 63–80

Klitgaard, R., 1991. "Adjusting to Reality: Beyond 'State versus Market' in Economic Development." Economic Center for Economic Growth. San Francisco: ICS Press

Knack, S. and Keefer, P., 1997. "Does Social Capital have an Economic Pay-Off? A Cross-Country Investigation." *Quarterly Journal of Economics* 112(4): 1251–1288

Kranton, R. E., 1996. "Reciprocal Exchange: A Self-Sustaining System." *American Economic Review* 86(4): 830–851

Mendoza, M. S. and Randrianarisoa, C., 1998. "Structure and Behavior of Traders and Market Performance." International Food Policy Research Institute, Washington DC

Minten, B. and Kyle, S., 1999. "The Impact of Distance and Road Quality on Food Collection, Marketing Margins, and Traders' Wages: Evidence from the Former Zaire." *Journal of Development Economics* 60(2): 467–495

Minten, B., Randrianarisoa, C., and Zeller, M., 1998. "Niveau, Evolution et Déterminants des Rendements du Riz." Cahier de la Recherche sur les Politiques Alimentaires 8, International Food Policy Research Institute, Antananarivo

Montgomery, J. D., 1991. "Social Networks and Labor-Market Outcomes: Toward an Economic Analysis." *American Economic Review* 81(5): 1408–1418

Narayan, D. and Pritchett, L., 1997. "Cents and Sociability: Household Income and Social Capital in Rural Tanzania." World Bank, Policy Research Department, Washington, DC

Palaskas, T. B. and Harriss-White, B., 1993. "Testing Market Integration: New Approaches with Case Material from the West Bengal Food Economy." *Journal of Development Studies* 30(1): 1–57

Platteau, J., 1994a. "Behind the Market Stage Where Real Societies Exist – Part I: The Role of Public and Private Order Institutions." *Journal of Development Studies* 30(3): 533–577

1994b. "Behind the Market Stage Where Real Societies Exist – Part II: The Role of Moral Norms." *Journal of Development Studies* 30(4): 753–817

Putnam, R. D., 1993. *Making Democracy Work: Civic Institutions in Modern Italy.* Princeton, NJ: Princeton University Press

Secaline, 1996. "Evaluation de la situation alimentaire et nutritionelle à Madagascar," Ministry of Health, Antananarivo

Staal, S., Delgado, C., and Nicholson, C., 1997. "Smallholder Dairying under Transaction Costs in East Africa." *World Development* 25(5): 779–794

Temple, J. and Johnson, P. A., 1998. "Social Capability and Economic Growth." *Quarterly Journal of Economics* 113(3): 965–990

5 How do participation and social capital affect community-based water projects? Evidence from Central Java, Indonesia

Jonathan Isham and Satu Kähkönen

Most rural villages in the Indonesian province of Central Java lack regular access to clean drinking water, and many face severe water shortages, particularly during the dry season.[1] The lack of clean water increases rates of sickness and death and reduces the time and resources available for productive activity, thereby diminishing well-being. Household incomes in these villages are low, and access to other types of infrastructure, such as roads, is limited. More than half of rural villages in Central Java are classified as poor, based on infrastructure, housing, and environmental and population characteristics (World Bank 1995).

To improve access to safe drinking water in Central Java, several governmental and nongovernmental organizations (NGOs) initiated rural water projects in the late 1980s and early 1990s. The government of Indonesia implemented two projects that were partially financed by the World Bank, the Water Supply and Sanitation Project for Low Income Communities (WSSLIC) and the Village Infrastructure Project (VIP). WSSLIC serves about 2,000 villages in five Indonesian provinces (Central Java, Southeast Sulawesi, North Sulawesi, Maluku, and Nusa Tenggara Timur). VIP consists of two separate projects, Village Infrastructure Project for Java (VIP I) and its extension, Second Village

This chapter was prepared under the overall supervision of Mike Garn for the Transportation, Water, and Urban Development Department and the Social Capital Initiative at the World Bank. We would like to thank Gregory Ingram and his colleagues at the World Bank Research Committee and Gloria Davis and her colleagues at the Social Capital Initiative for approving the funding for this research. This research would not have been possible without the collaboration of many colleagues. In Indonesia, Bill Collier, Herty Permana, the staff of P.T. Intersys Kelola Maju, and the team at Satya Wacana University implemented the surveys, carried out the participatory exercises and technical assessments, and provided the material for the case studies. Richard Pollard, Ratna Josodipoero, Pam Minnigh, Richard Gnagey, Anton Soedjarwo, and Rizal Malik helped gather information about water projects in Central Java. Jeremy Highsmith provided research assistance, and Diana Rutherford and Elena Vinogradova coded the case studies using the systematic case review method. Finally, we want to thank Christiaan Grootaert, Thierry van Bastelaer, Jennifer Sara, Lee Travers, and, in particular, Mike Garn for their comments on the draft of this chapter.

[1] The province of Central Java is in the heart of the island of Java. It was the center of much of the island's early culture; today it is often considered the most Indonesian part of Indonesia. Central Java is densely populated (867 people per square kilometer) and has a varying terrain with mountains, volcanoes, and flatland. The main source of living in Central Java is agriculture: about 67 percent of household heads are farmers. The population is dominantly (99 percent) Muslim.

Infrastructure Project (VIP II). VIP I serves 1,200 villages in Java; VIP II serves 2,600 villages in Java and Sumatra.

The objectives of WSSLIC are to provide safe, adequate, and easily accessible water supply and to support hygiene education through community-based arrangements. The objectives of VIP – a multisector project in which villages are given a menu of five infrastructure options (roads, bridges, water supply, public toilets, and piers) – are to build small infrastructure projects in poor villages, provide employment, and increase decentralization and village participation. We studied villages served by VIP I or VIP II that spent the grant primarily on water supply.

In addition, NGOs in Central Java have implemented water projects that were partially funded by bilateral donors. Dian Desa, a local NGO, provides technical assistance to villagers on the design and construction of water services. Oxfam, in coordination with other local NGOs, has funded construction of a small number of water services. Since only one Oxfam village was surveyed and the project rules of Dian Desa and Oxfam projects are similar, these projects were merged into one classification (NGO).

All of these projects adopted a decentralized, community-based approach to water delivery. Development organizations and NGOs have advocated this approach for the past decade in response to the systemic failures of supply-oriented water projects in the 1970s and 1980s.[2] The community-based approach focusses on what users want and how much they are willing to pay to obtain it. It is based on the premise that water is an economic good and should be managed accordingly. Services should be provided according to users' preferences and willingness to pay, and they should be managed at the lowest appropriate level, with users involved in planning and implementing projects. In water projects that use the community-based approach, government and NGO officials are typically expected to design and construct water systems in conjunction with users. The government and villagers coproduce the service (Isham and Kähkönen 1998), with users typically expected to be responsible for the operation and maintenance (O&M) of the services built.

The impact of community-based projects in Central Java has varied widely, with projects funded by VIP and NGOs tending to achieve better health outcomes than projects funded by WSSLIC (table 5.1). The percentage of people who were "very satisfied" with service was also higher in villages with VIP or NGO projects than in villages with services funded by WSSLIC.

Why have some water projects performed well and others performed poorly? To answer this question, this chapter reviews how closely these water projects followed the community-based approach. It examines whether services provided

---

[2] Garn (1995, 1998) and Briscoe and Garn (1995) review the poor performance of the supply-oriented approach and the economic underpinnings of the community-based approach. Sara and Katz (1998) provide cross-country empirical evidence on sustainability and demand responsiveness.

Table 5.1 *Outcomes of and level of satisfaction with community-based projects in Central Java (percent of respondents)*

Project	Improvement in health	Decrease in diarrhea	"Very satisfied" with service	"Unsatisfied" with service
WSSLIC	33	25	24	16
VIP	54	42	38	7
NGO	62	36	32	19

were demand-responsive and whether rules governing the design, construction, and O&M of services provided incentives for user participation. In particular, the chapter examines the effect of different rules promoting and coordinating user participation in service design, construction, and O&M on the performance and impact of these services.

The content and enforcement of the rules governing user participation and service delivery may be influenced by social capital, as measured by the prevalence of social networks and patterns of social interactions among users. Social capital may affect how successfully users act collectively to craft and implement rules and whether they comply with the rules.

Collective action among users is not automatic, as the village described in box 5.1 indicates. Low levels of user participation in service delivery and users' inability to form water committees to manage the service – and the subsequent poor performance of the water service – can be partially attributed to low levels of social capital.

The chapter also analyzes the effect of social capital on the content and enforcement of rules that govern service delivery and on the performance and impact of water services. This emphasis on service rules and social capital is motivated by an emerging body of evidence that documents the positive effect of institutions and social capital on the performance and impact of water services (Isham, Narayan, and Pritchett 1995; Sara and Katz 1998; Isham and Kähkönen 1999a, 1999b).

To determine how closely each of these projects followed the community-based paradigm and to analyze the projects' impact and performance, we collected quantitative and qualitative data from forty-four villages in Central Java. Data on household demographics, the impact and performance of water services, rules governing service delivery, and social capital were collected by surveying 1,100 households and forty-four water committees.[3] In addition, a water engineer carried out technical assessments of the performance of each water service, and qualitative data were gathered by interviewing men

---

[3] The province of Central Java consists of twenty-nine districts. For budgetary reasons the survey focused on the eight districts that had the largest number of villages served by the three types

Box 5.1   Lack of collective action reduces service quality

In 1992 Dian Desa, a local NGO, helped households in Tlogo design and construct a gravity-fed piped water service with public standposts. For the most part, village leaders rather than households participated in service design: only 32 percent of households reported that they participated in the selection of the type of service, and 76 percent of households reported that leaders made the final decision about the service technology. By these measures, this project was the least community-based of the seven projects funded by NGOs included in the survey.

Initially, the service functioned well. In 1997, however, several village officials illegally tapped the pipeline to build private connections. These illegal connections diverted water to private households, severely hampering the functioning of the service and reducing the flow of water to public standposts.

In the absence of a formal water committee or a group to manage water services in Tlogo, households have been unable to act collectively and take up the issue with village leaders. One reason for this inability to act collectively is that households in Tlogo are not accustomed to working together or interacting socially. Tlogo has been involved in very few village activities, such as maintaining roads, and relatively few households report that they regularly spend time with their neighbors or even invite them over for special occasions.

Instead of attempting to organize themselves, households report that they are hoping for outside intervention to rectify the situation. In the meantime, only 12 percent of households report that they are very satisfied with the service, and the village has the lowest share of households with improved health (40 percent) of any of the seven villages with NGO-financed projects surveyed.

and women and conducting participatory exercises in focus groups in each village.

The chapter proceeds as follows. After analyzing how rules about demand responsiveness and user participation affect the design of community-based water services, we examine how rules about monitoring and accountability affect the construction and O&M of these services. We then study how the outcomes of design, construction, and O&M affect the impact of these

of projects studied. Villages were randomly selected from the list of all villages served by these projects in the eight districts. The number of villages served by WSSLIC, VIP, or NGOs selected for the sample reflects the overall share of villages served by each project in the eight districts. Since the eight districts contained most of the villages served by these projects in Central Java, these shares also reflect the share of villages served by each project in Central Java.

services and analyze how social capital affects outcomes and impacts. The last section of the chapter summarizes the findings and includes some policy implications.

Effect of demand responsiveness and user participation on design outcomes

To what extent did community-based water projects in Central Java adhere to the demand-responsive approach by providing services that matched households' preferences? How did user participation in service design affect design outcomes? This section will answer these questions.

The planned design of water services

In community-based water projects, government and NGO officials are expected to design and construct the services with users. During the design stage, government officials usually provide a menu of options for water systems to potential service users, with information about the cost and maintenance of each option. Users are expected to collectively choose the type and level of service they want from the provided menu, based on their willingness to pay.

The water services built by WSSLIC, VIP, and NGOs were supposed to have been designed based on what households wanted and were willing to pay for. In projects funded by WSSLIC, villagers were supposed to express their preferences through village water committees established at the start of the project. These water committees were then supposed to prepare village action plans, which included villagers' preferences for the type of technology and the level of service as well as their commitments to contribute a minimum share of the project costs and bear the full cost of O&M. The government was to help villages in this task by hiring consultants to provide technical advice about which options are technically and financially feasible. The final decision on the type of service to be provided for each village was, however, reserved for the government. This decision was to be made based on the overall project budget as well as village preferences.

In villages served by VIP, village development councils were supposed to decide how to spend the infrastructure grant and what type and level of service to provide. These councils, which are headed by the village leader, are established and sponsored by the government to involve residents in local government. Their main task is to assist the village government in planning and implementing development projects.

In NGO projects villagers were to make the final decision about the service design jointly with NGO representatives. (For a detailed description of project rules, see Isham and Kähkönen 1999b.)

Table 5.2   *Household participation in selecting type and level of service (percent of households)*

Project	Household participated in selecting type of service	Household participated in selecting level of service	Primary water collector participated in selection of technology	Household made final decision about water service built
WSSLIC	13	15	8	5
VIP	28	29	19	34
NGO	30	21	16	66

The actual design of water services

How closely were these rules followed in practice? Participation and informed decisionmaking by target households was not consistently high, and the design rules established by projects were not always adhered to. Household participation in service design, information sharing, and final decisionmaking was fairly low in all projects, particularly in villages served by WSSLIC.

To measure household participation in service design and the demand responsiveness of the design process, we created several indicators (for summary statistics of these variables, see Isham and Kähkönen 1999b):

- "Participation in type and level of service" are household-level dichotomous variables that indicate whether households participated in the selection of the type of service (a well versus a piped system) and the level of service to build (a shared versus a private service). Participation was highest in NGO and VIP projects and lowest in WSSLIC projects (table 5.2). A variable on participation in choosing the site of the service (not shown) was highly correlated with these variables.
- "Participation by water collector" is a household-level dichotomous variable that indicates whether a household's primary water collector (usually female) participated in the selection of the technology. Participation was highest in VIP and NGO projects and lowest in WSSLIC projects.
- "Final decision made by households, leaders, or outsiders" are household-level dichotomous variables that indicate who (according to households) made the final decision about the water service that was built. Sixty-six percent of households in villages served by NGO projects reported that they made the final decision; only 2 percent of households reported that the decision was made by outsiders. In contrast, only 5 percent of households served by WSSLIC reported making the final decision; 66 percent reported that outsiders made the final decision.

Table 5.3   *Choice of technology and satisfaction with service design*

Project	Communal well	Public standpost	Private connection	Very satisfied with service design (percent)
WSSLIC	177	227	71	20
VIP	181	139	105	33
NGO	n.a.	127	73	30

Note: n. a. Not applicable.

These results indicate that the level of household participation and decision-making in service design was low in all projects, with nonusers often making design decisions, suggesting that vestiges of the supply-driven approach to water delivery remain in Central Java. That approach was particularly evident in projects financed by WSSLIC. Unlike NGO and VIP projects, WSSLIC reserved to the government the right to make the final decision. The lack of community participation was thus consistent with the project rules, albeit not with the community-based approach.

Design outcomes

The types of water service technologies that were chosen and the level of household satisfaction with service designs varied across projects and villages. In WSSLIC and VIP projects, villages in Central Java could typically choose between communal wells and piped water systems. (NGO projects did not provide wells). In all three projects, either public standposts or household connections could be built in villages with piped water systems.

We used four indicators to measure design outcomes (table 5.3) (for summary statistics of these variables, see Isham and Kähkönen 1999b):

- "Communal well" indicates the choice of a public well that is available to all villagers, usually at no or little cost.
- "Public standpost" indicates the choice of a piped water system with a public standpost that is available to all villagers, usually at some cost. With the exception of seventy households in three villages served by WSSLIC with pump technology, all households use gravity-fed technologies.[4]

---

[4] The choice of a pumped versus a gravity-fed system is typically dictated by the location of a village and the water source: villages at higher elevations than the water source require pumped systems. The results in this and subsequent sections are not altered by sub-categorizing the choice of technologies (gravity-fed, pumped, or well) or by including dummy variables for a pump-driven system.

- "Private connection" indicates the choice of a piped water system with household connections available to each household, usually at some cost. With the exception of fifty-four households in three villages served by WSSLIC with pump technology, all of the connections use gravity-fed technologies.
- "Very satisfied with service design" is a household-level dichotomous variable that indicates whether the household is very satisfied with the way the water system was designed and selected (as opposed to somewhat satisfied or unsatisfied).

These indicators reveal that piped water systems with public standposts are the most common type of system used, except in VIP villages. They also reveal the low level of household satisfaction with service design.

Design outcomes (types of services provided and household satisfaction with them) and household participation in service design and decisionmaking varied widely across projects and villages. This variance allows us to examine a critical assumption about the community-based water paradigm – namely, that more informed participation and decisionmaking by households lead to different technology choices.

Effect of participation on design outcomes

Did informed participation and decisionmaking by households lead to different technology choices in Central Java? As this section shows, household participation in service design and decisionmaking led to both different types of water services and different levels of service.

Effect on the type of service selected.   Villages served by WSSLIC and VIP first decided whether to build a communal well or a piped water system. (NGO projects supported only piped systems.) The decision, which affected all households in the village, was a collective, village-level choice.

Under what circumstances did villages select piped water systems? Did household participation influence the selection? Specification 1 in table 5.4 shows that the probability of choosing a piped system increased when more households participated in the decision on the type of service. Specification 2 shows a similar result when households made the final decision about the service type; specification 3 includes household participation in both the type of service and final decisionmaking. A 1 standard deviation increase in each of these variables leads to a 0.63 increase in the probability of choosing a piped system. These (and subsequent) specifications control for other possible village-level determinants, including average agricultural land holdings; average years of schooling; average household size; the share of households that previously relied on a river, stream, or pond for drinking water; and a dummy variable

Table 5.4 *Factors affecting type of water service selected*

Variable	Specification			
	1	2	3	4
Participation in type of service	2.06* (0.72)		1.15* (0.46)	1.90** (0.68)
Final decision made by households		1.59*** (0.50)	1.12** (0.49)	
Final decision made by leaders				−.39*** (0.25)
Agricultural land	0.03 (0.03)	0.03 (0.02)	0.03 (0.02)	0.04 (0.02)
Years of schooling	0.18** (0.09)	0.28*** (0.09)	0.20** (0.10)	0.18** (0.10)
Household size	−0.16 (0.20)	0.10 (0.14)	−0.15 (0.16)	−0.14 (0.16)
Previous use of river or pond	0.61** (0.36)	0.97*** (0.32)	0.64***(0.35)	0.62*** (0.35)
WSSLIC	0.21 (0.22)	0.40* (0.21)	0.28 (0.20)	0.24 (0.22)

Notes: $*p \leq 0.1$. $**p \leq 0.05$. $***p \leq 0.001$.
$n = 36$ villages served by WSSLIC and VIP. Coefficients estimated from a probit model. Estimates are marginal changes in probability. Huber-adjusted standard errors are shown in parentheses.

for WSSLIC. The results indicate that villages with higher levels of education and villages whose prior source of drinking water was a river, stream, or pond were, *ceteris paribus*, more likely to choose a piped water system than a well. Substituting other income, wealth, or demographic variables does not alter the main results.

In specification 4, when the variable "final decision of the service type made by leaders" is included with "participation in type of service" as a possible determinant of the choice of a piped system, its sign is negative and significant. Village leaders do not seem to represent the technology preferences of households any better than outsiders.[5]

These results show that informed participation and decisionmaking by households (as opposed to village leaders and outsiders) did affect the type of service selected. Village leaders and outsiders did not necessarily represent the preferences of households. Given the opportunity to choose their own type of service, households were likely to choose piped water systems.[6] In contrast, village leaders and outsiders tended to select communal wells.

[5] In specification 4 the test for significance is actually a test of whether "final decision made by leaders" differs from the omitted "final decision made by households" and "final decision made by outsiders." When both the "leaders" and "outsiders" variables are included as regressors, the coefficients are both negative and significant.

[6] Isham and Kähkönen (1999b) studied the willingness of households to pay for more expensive water services. They found that when households were provided with information on the payment required for each service, they were more likely to choose a piped system. When households

"Participation by water collector," tested in specifications equivalent to those in table 5.4, was not found to be a significant determinant of the type of service. This result could not confirm that of other studies of water projects in Indonesia, which show that it is important to give primary water collectors a voice in decisionmaking (Brown and Pollard 1998).

Effect on the level of service selected.   If a piped water system was selected for the village, each household (in most cases) then had to decide whether to pay for a private connection. How did household participation in service design and decisionmaking affect the choice of the level of service?[7]

Evidence on the household-level determinants of selection of private connections in twenty-four villages with piped connections reveals that private connections were built more often when households participated in service design or made the final decision of the service type and level.[8] Specification 1 in table 5.5 shows that when a household served by VIP or WSSLIC participated in decisionmaking on the service type, the probability of choosing a private connection increased by 0.15. Specification 2 shows that when a household made the final decision about a service type, the probability of private connections increased by 0.36. Specification 3 shows that with both household participation and the final decision, the probability of selecting private connections increased by 0.51. Specification 4 shows that when village leaders made the final decision, the probability of receiving a private connection was reduced by 0.25. Similar results were found for households served by NGO projects (specifications 6, 7, and 8 in table 5.5).

Levels of satisfaction were higher among households with private connections. Thirty-eight percent of these households indicated that they were very satisfied with the design process. In contrast, only 18 percent of households

were given the choice of a free water system, they were likely to take it, whether it was a piped system or a well.

[7] An alternative to the methodology used here would be to evaluate the determinants of a simultaneous village- and household-level decision on the type and level of service. Results from multivariate logit estimation (not reported here), in which the three outcome variables are communal well, standpost, and standpost with the option of a household connection, are consistent with the results reported here.

[8] The specifications control for other possible household-level determinants, including agricultural land holdings; years of schooling; household size; whether the household previously relied on a river, stream, or pond; and a dummy variable for WSSLIC. Results from these independent variables (not shown) indicate that for households served by WSSLIC and VIP, years of schooling is positively correlated and previous reliance on a river, stream, or pond negatively correlated with the probability of selecting a private connection. Among households in which water projects were supported by NGOs, landholdings are positively correlated with the probability of selecting a private connection. The fundamental results of interest on technology choices are not altered by exclusion or inclusion of these variables.

Table 5.5 *Factors affecting households' choice of private water connection*

Variable	Specification			
Specifications for WSSLIC and VIP ($n = 407$ households in 20 villages)	1	2	3	4
Participation in level of service	0.15 ***(0.06)		0.15 *** (0.06)	0.18 *** (0.06)
Final decision made by households		0.36 *** (0.06)	0.36 *** (0.07)	
Final decision made by leaders				−0.25 *** (0.06)
WSSLIC	−0.28*** (0.05)	−0.17 *** (0.06)	−0.15 ** (0.06)	−0.27 *** (0.06)
Specifications for NGO projects ($n = 92$ households in 4 villages)	5	6	7	8
Participation in level of service	−0.08 (0.10)		−0.09 (0.10)	−0.10 (0.10)
Final decision made by households		0.25 ** (0.08)	0.24 *** (0.08)	
Final decision made by leaders				−0.22 * (0.10)

Notes: $*p \leq 0.1$. $**p \leq 0.05$. $***p \leq 0.001$.
Coefficients estimated from a probit model. Estimates are marginal changes in probability. Results from other independent variables not reported.
Six villages that had piped connections but charged no fee for the use of public standposts or private connections were not included in this analysis. It is easy to show that households in these villages preferred the free private connection.

served by public wells and 30 percent of households served by public stand-posts indicated high levels of satisfaction.

The fact that village leaders and households made different decisions about the type of service may reflect the fact that village leaders may be financially risk averse. A more plausible explanation is that unlike most households, many village leaders already had adequate access to safe water and thus presumably had less interest in the new water service. The case of the village of Kalibening illustrates how preferences of village leaders and villagers may differ and how decentralizing service delivery to accountable community leaders can improve performance (box 5.2).

These results reveal the importance of involving households in service design and decisionmaking. Informed participation in service design and

---

Box 5.2   Differences between preferences of village leaders and households may reduce village welfare

Village leaders may not necessarily represent the preferences of households or act in their best interest – as experience in the village of Kalibening illustrates. In 1995 VIP agreed to support the construction of a piped water service with public standposts in one of the many hamlets of Kalibening. Implementation of the project and project funds were quickly taken over by the village head. Instead of hiring households to construct the service, as required by VIP rules, the village head hired a private contractor. The contractor turned out to be incompetent, and the service he built did not function. According to households, the village head and contractor overcharged for materials, presumably pocketing the difference. Only after the contractor had finished the work did households discover that, according to VIP rules, the village development council – not just the village head – should have implemented the project and controlled the funds and that villagers – not a contractor – should have been used for the work.

At that point, the head of the hamlet took over. He organized a collective effort by households to fix and modify the water service to match the preferences of users. In addition to improving the distribution tanks, pipes, and water intake, households decided to build private connections from distribution tanks. Households covered all construction costs of this collective effort, contributing both cash and unpaid labor.

Currently, the service is performing well. Minor problems have been quickly repaired by households, which collectively operate and maintain the service. Fifty-two percent of households report that they are very satisfied with the service, and almost two-thirds report that their health has improved.

---

decisionmaking by households led to different technology choices, with households more likely than village leaders or outsiders to choose more expensive technologies.[9] This result implies that if households are not involved in service design and decisionmaking, services provided are not likely to correspond to demand.

---

[9] Brown and Pollard (1998) examine the performance of water services provided by two World Bank–financed water projects in other Indonesian provinces. They emphasize that user participation alone does not ensure that services respond to demand. According to their results, from surveys of households and water committees as well as technical assessments of water services in 31 Indonesian villages, user preferences are often ignored when the final decisions about services are made. Thus, as the quantitative and qualitative evidence presented here also suggest, user participation in final decisionmaking is critical.

Effect of service rules on construction and operation and maintenance outcomes

To what extent have households in Central Java participated in service construction? How effectively have they operated and maintained water services? How have rules governing construction and O&M affected the performance of water services? This section explores these questions.

Planned construction and operation and maintenance of water services

The community-based approach to water delivery usually calls for user participation in service construction and O&M. Villagers are usually expected to construct the service jointly with the government, contributing labor, cash, or materials to the effort. Villagers are also expected to take over responsibility for O&M.

The community-based water projects in Central Java called for household participation in service construction and O&M. In all projects villagers were responsible for O&M. In villages served by WSSLIC, the water service was to be built either by a contractor hired by the government or jointly by villagers and a contractor; the government was supposed to supervise construction. Households were to contribute 20 percent of total construction costs, 4 percent in cash and 16 percent in materials or unpaid labor.

In villages served by VIP, services were to be built by village labor, unless villagers decided to hire a contractor. The government was supposed to supervise the work jointly with villagers. No household contributions were required. Unlike other projects, VIP paid villagers who worked on the project.

In villages served by NGOs, services were to be built by village labor, unless villagers decided to hire a contractor. The local NGO and villagers were to supervise construction. All households – even the poorest – were to contribute at least unpaid labor to construction.

Actual construction and operation and maintenance of water services

In practice, household participation in construction and O&M in Central Java has been modest. While some households have contributed to the construction and O&M of services in all projects, not all households using the services have contributed their required share. Only about half of households using WSSLIC services, for example, contributed cash, labor, or materials to construction as required.

Several indicators of participation in the construction and O&M were developed (table 5.6). These indicators reflect the underlying rules that were supposed

Table 5.6   *Household participation in construction and operation and maintenance of water services*

Variable	WSSLIC	VIP	NGO
Any contribution to water project (percent of households)	55	73	96
Average labor contribution per household (days)	1.8	6.6	19.6
Median cash and in-kind contributions per household (rupees)[a]	2,000	2,500	0
Percent of households reporting contributions were monitored	50	28[b]	54
Percent of households reporting contribution to O&M required	23	63	48
Percent of households reporting water committee was operating	22	3	7

Notes: [a] At the time these surveys were conducted (September–November 1998), the exchange rate was about 10,000 Rs./$.
[b] No household contributions to construction were required.

to govern construction and O&M of services in practice (Isham and Kähkönen 1999b provide summary statistics of these indicators):

- "Any contribution" is a household-level dichotomous variable that indicates whether the household made any labor, cash, or in-kind contribution to the construction of the service.
- "Labor contribution" and "cash and in-kind contributions" are household-level variables that indicate average labor contributions and the sum of cash and kind contributions.
- "Monitoring of contributions" is a household-level dichotomous variable that indicates whether the household reported that construction contributions by households were monitored (usually by village leaders or the water committee).
- "Household O&M required" is a household-level dichotomous variable that indicates whether the household reported that it and other users were required to contribute to O&M.
- "Water committee operation" is a household-level dichotomous variable that indicates whether a household reported that a water committee (as opposed to households themselves, a caretaker, village leaders, or a government agent) is responsible for O&M.

These indicators reveal that household contributions to construction varied substantially across projects. NGO projects were most successful in soliciting household contributions to construction: almost all households in villages served by these projects (96 percent) contributed cash, labor, or materials to construction as required. In contrast, in projects funded by WSSLIC, which also required household contributions to construction, almost half of households made no contributions but chose to free-ride at others' expense. These findings suggest that mechanisms to monitor household contributions were not always in place. Indeed, only 50 percent of households in villages

Table 5.7   *Quality of service reported by households
(percent of households)*

Variable	WSSLIC	VIP	NGO
Water every day	48	80	84
All water from service	49	89	92
Sufficient flow of water	46	79	75
Noncolored water	71	71	63
No failure	43	58	40
Not dried up	42	76	69
Very well maintained	22	27	25

served by WSSLIC reported that household contributions to construction were monitored.

Requirements for household contributions to O&M were low in all projects. Median cash and in-kind contributions were highest in projects financed by VIP. In villages served by WSSLIC, water committees were to have been established to coordinate O&M. Only 22 percent of households served by WSSLIC indicated that a water committee was responsible for O&M, however, and only 23 percent of households indicated that they were expected to perform O&M.

Construction and operation and maintenance outcomes

What were the outcomes of these practices? The quality of construction and performance of water services varied significantly across projects. To measure service performance, several indicators were developed based on the results of household surveys, technical evaluations, and participatory exercises carried out in female and male focus groups. (Summary statistics of these indicators are presented in Isham and Kähkönen 1999b.)

"Water every day" and "all water from service," two household dichotomous variables, are important performance indicators because irregular water systems often force households to turn to unclean sources (table 5.7). Of the 439 households that reported not receiving reliable daily service from their water system, 158 (36 percent) obtained water from rivers, ponds, springs, or rainwater collection tanks. Of the 275 households that indicated that they did not get all of their drinking and cooking water from their system because it often did not work, eighty-four (31 percent) used rivers, ponds, springs, or collected rainwater.

"Sufficient flow of water," "noncolored water," "no failure," and "not dried up" are household dichotomous variables that indicate problems households have encountered during the past year. The results show that less than half of households served by WSSLIC but the vast majority of households served by VIP and NGOs reported having sufficient flow of water.

"Very well maintained" is a household-level dichotomous variable that indicates whether the household considered its service to be very well maintained. Only a minority of households reported that their service was very well maintained.

These indicators reveal that water services provided by the VIP and NGO projects performed better, on average, than WSSLIC – supported projects. Services supported by WSSLIC have had significant problems.

These results were confirmed by technical assessments of water services carried out by water engineers in each village. Engineers assessed each village's service with respect to its functioning; water availability during the wet and dry seasons; sufficiency of water for drinking, cooking, and bathing during the wet and dry seasons; construction faults; design faults; possibility for water contamination; frequency of water testing; water quality; land and facility ownership; evidence of modification and extension of the service; and service management. Following preassigned evaluation criteria, the engineer rated each aspect of service functioning. The sum of the individual performance ratings yielded a total performance score. Possible scores ranged from 0 (nonfunctioning) to 47 (perfect functioning). The average total performance score was 25.2 for the services supported by WSSLIC, 37.4 for VIP, and 35.6 for NGO projects. These averages belie large variances across villages, with scores ranging from 11 to 44.

Related results from the participatory exercises suggest that the quantity of water tends to decrease during the dry season, when many households have to use other sources of water. During the wet season, the quantity of water tends to be adequate, but its quality suffers.

Effect of household contributions and community monitoring on outcomes

Are rules governing the construction and O&M of services associated with the performance of water services? In particular, do some rules, such as rules governing household participation in construction and O&M, lead to better outcomes? Does the effectiveness of these rules depend on the type of service? This section shows that household participation in construction and O&M is indeed associated with better performance of water services.

We tested rules and practices governing construction and O&M as possible determinants of "water every day," a critical performance indicator among households served by public wells, public standposts, and private connections.[10]

---

[10] "Water every day" is used in these specifications because it is highly correlated with most of the other variables and with "improved health," the most critical impact variable. Substantially similar results can be shown with other outcome variables.

We use village means of these indicators (as opposed to household responses), because the regressors of interest are village-level indicators of the strengths of these institutions (table 5.8). For example, for the test of the determinants of "water every day" of household i in village j, "any contribution" is the share of households in village j that reported having made any contribution to service construction. The other independent variables used in all of these specifications are project dummies and the household- and village-level indicators from tables 5.4 and 5.5 (agricultural land, years of schooling, household size, previous use of river, stream, or pond).

Four noteworthy results emerge from these specifications. First, when households contributed to service construction and household contributions to construction were monitored, communal wells (specifications 1 and 2) and public standposts (specifications 5 and 6) were more likely to perform well and provide water every day. The implied magnitudes for "any contribution" (using the technique of multiplying the standard deviation of the independent variable by the corresponding coefficient) are an increase in the probability of having water every day of 0.11 for communal wells and 0.27 for public standposts. The implied magnitudes for "monitoring of contributions" are 0.19 for communal wells and 0.15 for public standposts.

Second, "household contributions to construction" or "monitoring of contributions" are not associated with the performance of private connections. As specifications 11 and 12 in table 5.8 show, neither "any contribution" nor "monitoring of contributions" has a significant effect on the availability of water from private connections on a daily basis.

Third, when households are required to contribute to O&M and these contributions are monitored, communal wells, public standposts, and private connections are more likely to provide water every day. Specifications 3, 7, and 13 indicate that village averages of "household O&M required" are positive and significant determinants of performance. The implied magnitudes are a 0.31 increase in the probability that communal wells provide water every day and a 0.13 increase in the probability that both public standposts and private connections do so. These results hold when "monitoring of contributions" is included in the regression, as specifications 4, 8, and 14 show.

Fourth, the existence of water committees has either no effect or a negative effect on service performance. Specifications 9, 10, 15, and 16 show that "water committee operation" is a negative and insignificant determinant of the performance of public standposts and a negative and significant determinant of the performance of private connections. (Because there is virtually no water committee activity in villages with public wells, they were omitted from the analysis.) These results suggest that water committees in these projects seem to be having an insignificant or even detrimental effect on outcomes.

Table 5.8 *Determinants of performance of water services*

Item	Specification					
Communal well specification (n = 301 households)	1	2	3	4		
Any contribution	0.33*** (0.10)					
Monitoring of contributions		0.64*** (0.21)		1.17*** (0.28)		
Household O&M required			0.94*** (0.15)	1.19*** (0.14)		
Standpost specification (n = 421 households)	5	6	7	8	9	10
Any contribution	0.78*** (0.15)					
Monitoring of contributions		0.53*** (0.12)		0.56*** (0.12)		0.43*** (0.16)
Household O&M required			0.41*** (0.16)	0.46*** (0.15)		
Water committee operation					−0.35 (0.28)	−0.44 (0.29)
Private connection specification (n = 208 households)	11	12	13	14	15	16
Any contribution	−0.01 (0.08)					
Monitoring of contributions		−0.14 (0.11)		0.00 (0.11)		0.45** (0.16)
Household O&M required			0.40* (0.17)	0.39* (0.10)		
Water committee operation					−0.28** (0.14)	−0.28** (0.13)

Note: * $p \leq 0.1$. ** $p \leq 0.05$. *** $p \leq 0.001$.

Coefficients estimated from a probit model. Estimates are marginal changes in probability. Results from other independent variables not reported.

Box 5.3   Lack of a water committee can impede rule enforcement

In the village of Cluwuk, lack of clear rules about the use of the water service and lack of a water committee to implement and enforce those rules has led to problems. Some households have built private household connections from public standposts provided by VIP. Because these households let water run continuously, the flow of water to public standposts has severely diminished, and standposts at the end of the pipeline are often dry. As a result, many households have stopped paying for water. Only two of the twenty-five surveyed household reported still paying for water.

Less than 7 percent of households report being very satisfied with the service, and 20 percent report being dissatisfied. Only 8 percent report that their health has improved. Users are unhappy with the situation and recognize the need to regulate the construction and use of private connections. Cultural reluctance to disrupt harmony, however, has prevented them from taking action.

This result does not imply that the principle of using a water committee is ill founded. Instead, it may suggest that these projects did not put mechanisms into place to properly train and supervise water committees. Indeed, the qualitative evidence suggests that a well-trained water committee does serve a useful role in coordinating O&M of the service – and that the lack of a water committee can be detrimental. The water committee provides a formal mechanism and arena in which users can voice and address problems with the service they might otherwise find difficult or impossible to raise. This is particularly true in Central Java, where communal harmony is highly valued and any kind of open criticism is shunned. Where water committees do not exist, service effectiveness has suffered (box 5.3).

These results indicate that the performance of communal wells and public standposts, unlike the performance of private connections, depends on rules that promote and ensure user involvement in service construction.[11] Communal wells and public standposts are used and maintained by several households as a group. Contribution to construction by each user household is likely to promote the sense of common ownership of the service, thereby increasing households' willingness to maintain it. This leads to improved performance. Working together to construct the service also brings households together, which is likely to facilitate the organization of collective effort to maintain the system. Household contributions to O&M and monitoring of these contributions promote the performance of all types of water services.

---

[11] This result is similar to the conclusions of Watson and Jagannathan (1995), who found that construction of complex systems by beneficiaries is not always necessary or desirable.

Effect of design, construction, and operation and maintenance outcomes on impact

How do the design, construction, and O&M of water services influence the impact of community-based water projects? The previous two sections presented evidence on how rules and practices governing design, construction, and O&M (in particular, rules about user participation in design, decisionmaking, construction, and O&M) affected outcomes – the type of the service constructed and its performance. This section explores how these outcomes in turn affect the impact of community-based water projects. Selected determinants of improved household health are examined, where the dependent variable is a self-reported indicator of improved household health since using the new water service. The analysis focusses on health because it is the most important (though not the only) impact of water projects. Indicators of design, construction, and O&M outcomes are in turn used as possible determinants.

The results indicate that access to a piped water service that provides water every day is associated with dramatic improvements in household health (table 5.9). Controlling for other household- and village-level variables (agricultural land, years of schooling, household size, previous use of a river, stream, or pond) and project dummies, access to a piped service increases the probability of improved health by 0.29. Access to a private connection does not have a significant additional positive effect, but the availability of "water every day" increases the probability of improved health by 0.20. The probability of improved health thus increases by 0.49 among households served by public standposts or private connections with a daily water flow. Similar results can be shown with alternative specifications (sub-dividing service types, for example).

The results also suggest that educating users about the health benefits of safe water handling, hygiene practices, and protection of water sources is likely to increase the health impact of water projects. Participation in a hygiene class increases the probability of improved health by 0.21. Similar results are found in Sara and Katz's (1998) study of the sustainability of community-based water services in six countries and Isham and Kähkönen's (1999a) study of the impact of community-based water projects in India and Sri Lanka.

Combined with the results presented earlier, these results suggest the following chain of causality from design, construction, and O&M participation to improved household health. First, when given the opportunity for informed participation and decisionmaking, households in Central Java express a preference for a piped service. Second, rules that promote and ensure user involvement in service construction and O&M lead to better performance of these services, including the availability of water every day. Finally, both outcomes – the selection of a piped service and the availability of water every day – lead to improved health.

Table 5.9 *Factors affecting the health impact of water services*

Variable	Result
Piped service	0.29***(0.05)
Private connection	0.00 (0.05)
Water every day	0.20*** (0.04)
Hygiene class	0.21*** (0.04)
WSSLIC	−0.25*** (0.06)
VIP	0.04 (0.06)

Notes: *** $p \leq 0.001$.
$n = 873$ households. Coefficients estimated from a probit model. Estimates are marginal changes in probability of independent variable. Huber-adjusted standard errors are shown in parentheses. Results from other independent variables not reported.

Household participation in design, construction, and O&M is not automatic, however; households have an incentive to free ride on others' efforts. Rules about monitoring help, but nothing guarantees that rules are always obeyed.

Effect of social capital on outcomes and impacts

This section examines the effects of social capital on the impact and performance of community-based water services. The ability of households to work together to design, construct, and operate and maintain water services may depend on social capital (box 5.4). This social capital can be measured by the existence of active civic associations and networks, patterns of social interaction, and norms of trust and reciprocity among households.[12]

Social capital is likely to facilitate collective action among households and voluntary compliance with rules.[13] During the design phase, the collective demand for the type and level of service is more likely to be clearly expressed in villages in which households are accustomed to working together, leaders are accountable, and all stakeholders have a voice. During the construction and O&M phases, households in villages with cohesive village groups and traditions of civic activities are more likely to function as a group and construct and maintain the service as planned. In such villages formal and informal ties among people may deter households from free-riding and village leaders from shirking and expropriating funds.

[12] There are several definitions and interpretations of social capital in the literature (Coleman 1988; Putnam 1993; Grootaert 1998). Woolcock (1998) presents a multidisciplinary synthesis of social capital in economic development.

[13] In some cases, social capital may have a detrimental effect on collective action and water service performance. As box 5.3 illustrates, social and cultural norms may prevent potentially beneficial action.

Box 5.4   Social capital can facilitate collective action and improve health

Closeness and familiarity characterize the social relationships among households in Wonorojo. According to the men and women who participated in the focus groups, neighbors help one another in various tasks (such as building houses) and usually participate actively in village groups and associations, including those established by the government.

This social cohesion has affected the performance of the water service provided by VIP. Once a week households get together to clean the water tanks. They also clean the drains (a task they handle while they maintain the village's roads). Sixty-four percent of households interviewed reported that they contributed to the O&M of the service, and all 25 households surveyed said that the service functioned every day without any major problems. Overall, 82 percent of households report that their health has improved.

Indicators of social capital

Several indicators – related to village groups and associations, village activities and norms, and village trust – were developed to measure social capital (table 5.10). These indicators, created from the household surveys, are based partly on indicators used in other recent empirical studies on the effect of the social structure on development outcomes, in particular, Grootaert (1999), Isham and Kähkönen (1999a), and Narayan and Pritchett (1999). The measures included the following variables:

- "Social capital index" is a household-level composite index of the quantity and quality of local groups, based on the social capital index in Narayan and Pritchett (1999). The index is the product of "density of membership" and an additive sub-index of group characteristics of each household's most important group, including heterogeneity of members and leaders by religion and ethnicity, and the participatory nature of decisionmaking mechanisms.[14] The average value of the index among households surveyed was 9.94.
- "Density of membership" is the number of local groups or associations to which a household reports belonging. The average number of memberships among households surveyed was 3.84.
- "Meeting attendance" is a household-level dichotomous variable that indicates whether the household reported frequently (as opposed to occasionally

---

[14] For a detailed presentation of how this index is constructed, see Isham and Kähkönen (1999a). Multiplying the density of membership by this set of group characteristics creates a composite indicator of social capital that attempts to capture the underlying behavior of interest, namely, the household's pattern of working cooperatively with other households and village leaders. Like the Putnam index, this type of index attempts to identify, from microeconomic data, characteristics

Table 5.10   *Indicators of social capital*

		Correlation with service-level institutions	
Variable	Mean	Design participation	Construction monitoring
Social capital index	9.94 (5.25)	0.28***	0.25***
Density of membership	3.84 (1.62)	0.21***	0.31***
Meeting attendance	0.57 (0.26)	0.03	0.40***
Participation index	1.22 (0.42)	0.16***	0.07**
Community orientation	0.67 (0.26)	0.30***	0.36***
Number of joint activities	2.69 (0.95)	−0.22***	−0.13***
Social interaction	2.49 (0.49)	0.14***	0.27***
Neighborhood trust	2.30 (0.56)	−0.13***	0.38***

Notes: ** $p \le 0.05$. *** $p \le 0.001$.
Standard deviations are shown in parentheses.

or not at all) taking part in the activities of its favorite group. Fifty-seven percent of households reported being active participants in their favorite groups.

- "Participation index" is an additive household-level index (with values ranging from 0 to 2) based on the responses to two dichotomous variables: whether households reported that group members (as opposed to leaders) typically make decisions as a group and whether group leaders are elected by group members (as opposed to being appointed by or made up of village leaders). The average value of the index among households surveyed was 1.22.
- "Community orientation" is a household-level dichotomous variable that indicates whether the household reported that its favorite group was formed by villagers (as opposed to externally imposed). Two-thirds (67 percent) of households stated that villagers had formed their favorite group.
- "Number of joint village activities" is the number of joint village activities (building houses for neighbors, constructing and maintaining roads) in which each household reported participating in the past year. On average, surveyed households reported engaging in 2.69 joint village activities.
- "Social interaction" is an additive household-level index (with values ranging from 0 to 4) based on the responses to four dichotomous social interaction variables: whether households reported regularly chatting with, visiting, playing games with, or inviting neighbors to special events. The average value of the index among households surveyed was 2.49.
- "Neighborhood trust" is an additive household-level index (with values ranging from 0 to 3) based on the responses to three dichotomous variables about trust in neighbors: whether households know their neighbors well, whether

of social capital that have been shown to be important elsewhere (Esman and Uphoff 1984; Putnam 1993). For a discussion of the pros and cons of using such an index of social capital, see Grootaert (1999) and Narayan and Pritchett (1999).

Table 5.11   *Effect of social capital on the impact of community-based water projects (based on survey data)*

Variable	Public well		Piped connection	
	Specification	Result	Specification	Result
Social capital index	1	−0.008 (0.011)	9	0.021*** (0.005)
Density of membership	2	0.033 (0.041)	10	0.061*** (0.016)
Meeting attendance	3	0.078 (0.157)	11	0.106 (0.117)
Participation index	4	−0.120 (0.119)	12	0.159*** (0.056)
Community orientation	5	−0.077 (0.127)	13	0.031 (0.136)
Number of joint activities	6	0.062 (0.067)	14	0.093*** (0.025)
Social interaction	7	−0.081 (0.074)	15	0.157*** (0.057)
Neighborhood trust	8	0.004 (0.049)	16	−0.094 (0.071)

Notes: *** $p \leq 0.001$.
$n = 289$ households for public wells and 588 households for piped connections. Coefficients estimated from a probit model. Estimates are marginal changes in probability of independent variable. Huber-adjusted standard errors are shown in parentheses. Results from other independent variables not reported.

they would leave their young child with their neighbors, and whether they would trust their neighbor to look after their house. The average value of the index among households surveyed was 2.3.

Following Dasgupta (1990), we constructed Borda rankings for each village based on these eight indicators in order to get a sense of the relative amounts of social capital in each village. The village of Pragu ranked highest (44), and the village of Jetak Wanger ranked lowest (1). Tlogo, the village examined in box 5.1, received a rank of 14.[15] These indicators reveal that the level of social capital varied significantly across villages. This variance allows the impact of social capital on service performance and impact to be tested.

Evidence from survey data

What evidence is there that social capital affects the outcomes – and impact – of community-based water projects by influencing rules governing design, construction, O&M, and compliance with rules? In most cases, the social capital indicators are positively and significantly correlated (at the 0.01 level) with rules governing design and construction. The exceptions are a positive but insignificant correlation between design participation and meeting attendance, a negative and significant correlation between design participation and social

---

[15] When used as the independent variable in specifications equivalent to those in table 5.11, these rankings have a positive and significant effect on health.

interaction and neighborhood trust, and a negative and significant correlation between construction monitoring and social interaction (table 5.10). With one exception, all of the village-level social capital indicators are positively and significantly correlated with each other (not shown).

These results suggest an additional possible link in the chain of causality – from village-level social capital to participation in design, construction, and O&M to improved household health. Put another way, participation in design, construction monitoring, and other rules that positively affect outcomes and impacts may be (partially) endogenous, determined by extant social networks and norms.[16]

To fully test the reduced-form model, all eight social capital indicators are tested in different specifications as possible determinants of the effect of communal wells and piped water services on health (table 5.11).The other independent variables used in this specification (not reported) are agricultural land, years of schooling, household size, and previous use of a river, stream, or pond.

For public wells no social capital indicator is positively associated with improved household health (specifications 1–8). For piped connections the social capital index, density of membership, participation index, number of joint activities, and social interaction are positive and significant determinants of improved household health (specifications 9–16). The magnitudes of the implied effects for piped connections are large: a 1 standard deviation increase in the social capital index is associated with a 0.11 increase in the probability of improved health, after controlling for household- and village-level indicators of agricultural land, years of schooling, household size, previous use of a river, stream, or pond for drinking water, and project dummies. The magnitudes for the other four significant indicators range from 0.07 to 0.10. These magnitudes are also 'comparable' to the other significant determinants of improved health. For example, similar calculations (averaged over the five significant specifications) show that household years of schooling is associated with a 0.04 increase in the probability of improved health, and previous village-level use of a river, stream, or pond for drinking water is associated with a 0.12 increase.

Supporting evidence from village case studies

To verify and extend these quantitative results on the importance of social capital, we created another data set from the village case studies. These data were used to refine the test of the effect of social capital on the impact of community-based water projects.

[16] Using data from community-based water projects in India and Sri Lanka, Isham and Kähkönen (1999a) present evidence that social capital affects the performance of water service through its effect on service rules.

The procedure for generating these data on social capital was as follows. For each of the forty-four villages studied, local consultants prepared case studies of the history of water delivery. The case studies were intended to provide qualitative evidence to support the quantitative evidence generated from the household and water committee surveys and the village technical assessments. These case studies included qualitative information on the history of villagers' water use before the design and construction of the new community-based water service; the role government agents and representatives of NGOs played in developing the new service; the roles different village stakeholders played in the design, construction, and O&M of the system; and overall household satisfaction with the system.

The systematic case review method was used to transform qualitative evaluations from a set of case studies into data suitable for empirical analysis. The method consists of the following steps. First, a conceptual framework for a system of related phenomena is established, specifying the causal relationships of different sub-sets of the system. Next, a questionnaire is developed to delineate relevant elements of each of these sub-sets and to measure their magnitudes. After the procedure has been tested, two coders independently rate the relevant qualitative information for each question on a numerical scale.[17] This procedure produces a new set of data that can be used to cross-check and enhance the results from other quantitative and qualitative analyses.

There was enough qualitative information in thirty-six of the forty-four case studies to address the following questions:

- What is the extent of tension between different social or economic groups in the village?
- What is the level of everyday social interaction among households?
- To what extent are there joint community activities to develop the village (for example, cleaning or maintaining roads)?
- To what extent do villagers participate in these joint community activities to develop the village?

The results indicate that social cohesion is relatively high in the villages surveyed. The numerical code for each response ranged from 0 (nonexistent) to 7 (very high or very great). The results show that the level of village tension is relatively low (a mean of 0.53 and a maximum of 5.0) and the level of both

---

[17] Following the procedure in Isham, Narayan, and Pritchett (1995), the data from each of the coders were averaged into a single data set. In most cases, the values assigned by independent coders to each question were identical or within one unit of each other. Following Finsterbusch (1990), each coder also generated confidence scores for each question. These scores measure how confident the coders were of the value they assigned to each question. Using these confidence scores as weights in the analysis does not significantly change the overall results reported. This procedure was used to evaluate the determinants of projects outcomes in Finsterbusch and Van Wicklin (1987) and Isham, Narayan, and Pritchett (1995). For a detailed description of the systematic case review method, see Finsterbusch (1990).

Table 5.12   *Levels of tension, interaction, activities, and participation*

Variable	Number of villages	Mean	Minimum	Maximum
Village tension	36	0.53	0.0	5.0
Social interaction	43	6.02	4.0	7.0
Community activities	43	5.72	2.5	7.0
Household participation	38	5.45	2.0	7.0

social interaction and community activities and related household participation relatively high (table 5.12).

The single-stage reduced-form estimates presented in table 5.11 are consistent if two conditions are met: the indicators of social capital accurately measure the patterns of social interaction and norms of trust and reciprocity among water users and their neighbors, and these patterns are mostly exogenous to the delivery of water. If these conditions do not hold, two-stage (instrumental variable) reduced-form estimates are needed and a proper set of instrumental variables needs to be identified. Community variables are "good" instruments if they are positively correlated with the different indicators of social capital index and are not strongly correlated with the error term in the reduced-form equation.

The social capital data generated from the case studies were used as instruments in instrumental variable estimation. The *a priori* case for using these variables as instruments for the social capital index is that these assessments of village tension, social interaction, community activities, and household participation are derived independently of the household surveys. One would expect them to be positively associated with the social capital indicators generated from the survey data but not to have an independent effect on improved health as measured in the household surveys. (See Isham and Kähkönen 1999a for a similar use of this two-stage approach.)

All eight social capital indicators were tested using linear probability and instrumental variable estimation in different specifications (table 5.13). Other independent variables used in these specifications (not reported) were household and village indicators of agricultural land, years of schooling, household size, and previous use of river, stream, or pond.

Specifications 1–8 in table 5.13 show the linear probability equivalents of the probit models presented for piped connections (specifications 9–16 in table 5.11). As in the earlier specifications, the social capital index, density of membership, participation index, number of joint activities, and social interaction are positive and significant determinants of improved household health. The magnitudes of the implied effects for piped connections in table 5.13 are similar to those in table 5.11. For public wells the results from the linear probability

Table 5.13   *Effect of social capital on the impact of community-based water projects with piped connections (based on case study data)*

Variable	Linear probability estimation procedure		Instrumental variable estimation procedure	
	Specification	Result	Specification	Result
Social capital index	1	0.012** (0.005)	9	0.025*** (0.009)
Density of membership	2	0.028* (0.015)	10	0.100*** (0.032)
Meeting attendance	3	0.101 (0.110)	11	0.728** (0.239)
Participation index	4	0.116* (0.061)	12	0.140 (0.110)
Community orientation	5	0.078 (0.129)	13	0.230 (0.179)
Number of activities	6	0.097*** (0.024)	14	0.150** (0.063)
Social interaction	7	0.160*** (0.056)	15	0.180** (0.091)
Neighborhood trust	8	−0.043 (0.085)	16	−0.06 (0.128)

Notes: $^*p \leq 0.1$. $^{**}p \leq 0.05$. $^{***}p \leq 0.001$.
$n = 414$ households. Huber-adjusted standard errors are shown in parentheses. Estimates are marginal changes in probability of independent variable. Results from other independent variables not reported.

and instrumental variable procedures (not shown) are similar to those derived from the survey data. In both cases, social capital does not significantly affect the impact of community-based water projects.

These linear probability results can be compared with the results from the instrumental variable estimation (specifications 9–16 in table 5.13). The instruments for each of the social capital indicators were the data generated from the questions about village tension, social interaction, community activities, and household participation. Comparison of these results shows that for the four social capital indicators that were significant in the linear probability models (the social capital index, density of membership, number of activities, and social interaction), the use of instrumental variables increases the value of the coefficients (and either increases or does not dramatically decrease the significance level). In the case of the participation index, the use of instruments increases the value of the respective coefficients but decreases the significance level. For meeting attendance – which was not significant in either the probit or the linear probability estimation – the use of instruments increases the value of the coefficients and dramatically raises the significance level.

Interpreting the quantitative and qualitative results on social capital and performance

The case study data lend support to the conclusion that by reducing the cost of collective action and promoting cooperation among users, social capital

---

**Box 5.5   Piped systems require more coordination
among stakeholders**

Lack of cooperation has reduced the effectiveness of two WSSLIC projects
in Central Java. WSSLIC partially financed the construction of a gravity-fed
piped water service in Mriyan in 1997. The project paid for construction of
a transmission pipeline from a spring 17 kilometers away; households paid
for the construction of water tanks and the pipe network within the village.
In addition to Mriyan, the transmission pipeline served two other villages
farther down the line. Initially, everything proceeded smoothly. After two
months, however, the flow of water in the pipeline ceased in all but two
hamlets. Households in three villages not served by the WSSLIC project
(through which the transmission pipeline ran) illegally tapped the pipeline
and diverted water for their own use. Heads of affected villages have not
been able to solve the dispute. The case is still open, and villagers are calling
for governmental intervention.

In Sriombo, WSSLIC provided households with two service options:
wells or a gravity-fed piped water service with public standposts. Households
collectively chose the piped service, the level of service, and the locations
of the public standposts. In the first five months of operation, the water service has functioned only partially. The reason for poor performance is that
Sriombo shares the water source (a stream) with another village, located near
the water source. Although the second village initially agreed to the sharing
arrangement and was compensated for it, households there have deliberately
damaged the transmission pipeline going to Sriombo, illegally tapping the
pipeline and diverting water to their own use. As a result, the service in
Sriombo is partially functioning. Forty-eight percent of households report
that they are unsatisfied with the service, and only 8 percent report that their
health has improved.

---

can improve the design, construction, and O&M of community-based water projects, improving the impact of piped water services. What explains
the result that social capital seems to have a positive and significant effect
only for piped water systems? Designing and constructing piped systems require more skills and more joint effort than designing and constructing wells.
A piped network for a village is likely to cross many households' property
within the village; the pipeline from the water source may also cross other
villages. Operating and maintaining piped systems is also more demanding
than operating and maintaining wells and requires more collective effort and
cooperation (box 5.5). Pipes may break and get clogged; overuse of water or
leakage in one part of the piped network affects users in other parts of the
network.

Box 5.6   Corruption can disable community-based water services

By depleting the project budget, corruption can derail the construction of community-based water services. In Kembang Kuning, WSSLIC funded an extension and improvement of the existing gravity-fed piped water service. The project financed the addition of another water intake and the replacement of PVC transmission pipes with steel pipes. Because the transmission pipe the government bought was 500 meters too short, the service constructed was inoperable.

Government officials turned down villagers' request for more piping materials on the grounds that there was no money left in the project budget. Villagers contended that the budget should have permitted the needed purchase: adequate funds had been allocated in the budget for material purchases, but government officials, who controlled project funds, had embezzled part of them before construction commenced. The government considered the project closed, however, and households were forced to complete the pipeline on their own.

In several villages with capital-intensive piped systems, households complain about corruption among government officials and, in particular, private contractors who shirked and cut corners to increase profits. As the experience in the village of Kembang Kuning reveals, corruption thrives when social capital is low (box 5.6).

Conclusion

This chapter examines the determinants of performance and impact of three types of community-based water projects in Central Java. In theory, all of the projects adopted a demand-responsive approach to service delivery that calls for user participation in design, construction, and O&M of the service. In practice, the traditional supply-driven approach to water delivery has not disappeared: user participation in service design was relatively low in all projects, and final decisions of service design were in many cases still made by nonusers.

Where demand-responsive features were introduced, they produced desirable results. Making water services demand responsive improves performance and increases impact, as households are more likely to maintain services that correspond to their needs.

Our results indicate that demand responsiveness of water services can be promoted by involving households in the design process and letting households, not outsiders or village leaders, make the final decision about the type and level of service. Village leaders and outsiders do not necessarily represent households' preferences: household participation in service design and decisionmaking lead to different – usually more expensive and convenient – water technology choices. To ensure that household choice is informed, adequate information needs to be provided to users about the cost and maintenance requirements of different service options during the design process.

Ensuring that villages have effective mechanisms for monitoring household contributions to construction and O&M is shown to be an effective way to improve the performance and strengthen the impact of community-based water services. Without monitoring arrangements, households have an incentive not to contribute their share but to free ride on others' efforts – a phenomenon apparent in many villages.

The evidence on the impact of water committees on service performance is mixed. The qualitative evidence suggests that water committees can play a valuable role in coordinating the management of the service and providing a formal channel through which households can discuss problems they otherwise might find impossible to discuss openly. In some Central Javanese villages that did not have water committees, households were afraid of disrupting communal harmony by openly criticizing and voicing dissatisfaction. As a result, these communities have been unable to address problems caused by some villagers' misuse of the service. The quantitative evidence indicates, however, that the presence of a water committee is no guarantee of improved performance. Why the water committees in Central Java seem to have been ineffective requires further inquiry.

Our results indicate that in villages with high levels of social capital – particularly in villages with active village groups and associations – household participation in design is likely to be high and monitoring mechanisms are more likely to be in place. In these villages, households are used to working together, and social ties deter free riding. In villages with piped water systems, higher levels of social capital are associated with stronger household-level impact.

Not all villages appear to have the necessary social capital to respond effectively to the introduction of demand-responsive elements, particularly when they choose a more complex piped system. Designers of community-based water projects need to take account of the level of social capital as one of the factors that will influence service performance.[18] The allocation of investment resources for water services may need to be adjusted to take account of the fact that water projects are less likely to be effective in villages in which the level of social capital is low. Donors may want to avoid investing in community-based piped water systems in villages with low levels of social capital.

---

[18] Other factors, such as access to spare parts, appropriateness of technology, and incentives faced by government and NGO officials, also affect the performance of community-based water projects (Isham and Kähkönen 1999b, Kähkönen 1999).

REFERENCES

Briscoe, J. and Garn, H. A., 1995. "Financing Water Supply and Sanitation under Agenda 21." *Natural Resources Forum* 19(1): 59–70.

Brown, G. and Pollard, R., 1998. "Responding to Demand: Two Approaches from Indonesia." World Bank, Washington, DC

Coleman, J., 1988. "Social Capital in the Creation of Human Capital." *American Journal of Sociology* 94 (supplement): S95–S120

Dasgupta, P., 1990. "Well-Being and the Extent of Its Realization in Poor Countries." *Economic Journal* 100 (supplement): 132

Esman, M. and Uphoff, N. T., 1984. *Local Organizations: Intermediaries in Rural Development.* Ithaca, NY: Cornell University Press

Finsterbusch, K., 1990. "Studying Success Factors in Multiple Cases: Using Low-Cost Methods." University of Maryland, Department of Sociology, College Park, MD.

Finsterbusch, K. and Van Wicklin III, W., 1987. "Contributions of Beneficiary Participation to Development Project Effectiveness." *Public Administration and Development* 7 (January/March): 1–23

Garn, H. A., 1995. "An Institutional Framework for Community Water Supply and Sanitation Services." World Bank, Washington, DC

1998. "Managing Water as an Economic Good." *Proceedings of the Community Water Supply and Sanitation Conference.* World Bank, Washington, D.C.

Grootaert, C., 1998. "Social Capital: The Missing Link?" Social Capital Initiative Working Paper 3. Social Development Department, World Bank, Washington, DC

1999. "Social Capital, Household Welfare, and Poverty in Indonesia." Local Level Institutions Working Paper 6. Social Development Department, World Bank, Washington, DC

Isham, J. and Kähkönen, S., 1998. "Improving the Delivery of Water and Sanitation: A Model of Coproduction of Infrastructure Services." IRIS Working Paper 210. University of Maryland, Center for Institutional Reform and the Informal Sector, College Park

1999a. "Institutional Determinants of the Impact of Community-Based Water Services: Evidence from Sri Lanka and Indonesia." IRIS Working Paper 236. University of Maryland, Center for Institutional Reform and the Informal Sector, College Park

1999b. "What Determines the Effectiveness of Community-Based Water Projects? Evidence from Central Java, Indonesia, on Demand Responsiveness, Service Rules, and Social Capital." Social Capital Initiative Working Paper 14. Social Development Department, World Bank, Washington, DC

Isham, J., Narayan, D., and Pritchett, L., 1995. "Does Participation Improve Performance?: Establishing Causality with Subjective Data." *World Bank Economic Review* 9(2): 175–200

Kähkönen, S., 1999. "Does Social Capital Matter in Water and Sanitation Delivery? A Review of Literature." Social Capital Initiative Working Paper 9. Social Development Department, World Bank, Washington, DC

Narayan, D. and Pritchett, L., 1999. "Cents and Sociability: Income and Social Capital in Rural Tanzania." *Economic Development and Cultural Change* 47(4): 871–898

Putnam, R. D., 1993. *Making Democracy Work: Civic Traditions in Modern Italy.* Princeton, NJ: Princeton University Press

Sara, J. and Katz, T., 1998. "Making Rural Water Supply Sustainable: Report on the Impact of Project Rules." United Nations Development Programme/World Bank Water Program, Washington, DC

Watson, G. and Jagannathan, N. V., 1995. "Participation in Water." Environment Department Papers Participation Series. World Bank, Washington, DC

Woolcock, M., 1998. "Social Capital and Economic Development: Toward a Theoretical Synthesis and Policy Framework." *Theory and Society* 27(2): 151–208

World Bank, 1995. "Staff Appraisal Report: Indonesia: Village Infrastructure Project for Java." World Bank, Infrastructure Operations Division, Country Department III, East Asia and Pacific Region, Washington, DC

6 Does social capital increase participation in voluntary solid waste management? Evidence from Dhaka, Bangladesh

Sheoli Pargal, Daniel O. Gilligan, and Mainul Huq

This chapter seeks to identify the role of social capital in the private, community-based provision of a public good, in this case, trash collection. The community aspect is vitally important because trash collection involves positive externalities that lead to limited incentives for individual action. Trash collection is also an activity in which collective action is warranted because individual action does not have much impact. Why are some communities better able to organize themselves for the collective good than others? Given the same impetus, what community characteristics lead to activism in some neighborhoods and not in others?

The garbage collection system in Dhaka, Bangladesh, involves municipal pick-up from large dumpsters placed in central areas, with municipal workers responsible for collecting trash from smaller dumpsters located in alleys and side streets and transporting it to the main dumpsters. However, municipal employees are unreliable and frequently fail to collect the trash on a regular basis. In response, some communities, funded by voluntary contributions from community members, have hired private contractors to undertake local trash collection. Other, apparently similar, neighborhoods have not managed to successfully organize an alternative to the municipal service. Why have some communities or neighborhoods displayed such initiative while others have not?

We conjecture that "social capital," which we equate with community cohesiveness, is a critical determinant of such collective action. The cohesiveness of the community is, in turn, a function of factors such as customary or traditional interactions and institutions, a common heritage, values, and ethnic or religious background. Using data obtained from a survey of neighborhoods in Dhaka, we examine the contribution of these factors to neighborhood social capital and, in turn, the effect of social capital on the formation of trash disposal committees.

We use measures of trust and the strength of norms of reciprocity and sharing among neighborhood residents as proxies for social capital. We find that social

We thank Thierry van Bastelaer and Christiaan Grootaert for their help and comments and thank Jyotsna Jalan for very useful suggestions.

capital is, indeed, an important determinant of whether voluntary solid waste management systems are established in Dhaka. The effects of norms of reciprocity and sharing on the probability that a voluntary solid waste management system is created are large and significant; the role of trust is not identified as a significant factor. Measures of homogeneity of interests and, interestingly, the nature of associational activity are also important. Finally, as would be expected, education levels are strongly and robustly associated with the existence of collective action for trash disposal.

This chapter is structured as follows. After briefly describing the literature on social capital relevant to this study, we describe our modeling and empirical estimation strategy, our survey, and our data. We then present and analyze our empirical results and draw some conclusions and policy implications.

Social capital

The term *social capital* has been applied to a variety of ideas about economic returns from networks of social relationships. While there has been limited work in economics on providing a theoretical context for social capital, there is a growing empirical literature that identifies considerable economic returns to networks of social relationships, to trust and norms of reciprocity, and to institutions that foster civic engagement.

Social capital first gained popularity and analytical teeth in James Coleman's works (1988, 1990). Coleman sees social capital as the "social relationships which come into existence when individuals attempt to make best use of their individual resources" (1990, p. 300). While Coleman stresses social capital as resources that accrue to individuals, Putnam (1993) defines social capital in terms of resources that characterize societies: "Social capital here refers to features of social organization, such as trust, norms, and networks, that can improve the efficiency of society by facilitating coordinated actions" (1993, p. 167). Putnam is concerned not only with the role of social capital in economic development but also with its role in forming democratic societies. Thus he equates social capital with the intensity of "civic engagement."[1]

Social networks can be characterized as primarily "horizontal," with individuals sharing equal status and power, or primarily "vertical," with asymmetric

---

[1] Several studies – both theoretical and empirical – consider the economic benefits of trust (Fukuyama 1995; Knack and Keefer 1997; Narayan and Pritchett 1999), norms of reciprocity (Sugden 1984, 1986), culture (Harrison 1992; Greif 1994), and ethnicity (Borjas 1992, 1995) either as (sometimes implicit) determinants of or proxies for social capital. Putnam (1993) argued that the quality and intensity of individual membership in social and professional associations is a good indicator of social capital. This indicator of social capital has been used by many researchers to test the benefits of social capital (see Boxman, De Graaf, and Flap 1991; Meyerson 1994; Helliwell and Putnam 1995; Knack and Keefer 1997; and Narayan and Pritchett 1999, for example).

relationships based on hierarchy and dependence. Putnam argues that horizontal networks, such as "neighborhood associations, choral societies, cooperatives, sports clubs, mass-based parties, and the like" (1993, p. 173), are the building blocks of "networks of civic engagement." These networks are "an essential form of social capital: the denser such networks in a community, the more likely that its citizens will be able to cooperate for mutual benefit" (1993, p. 173). The trust and reciprocity that sustain civic networks (that is, social capital) are self-reinforcing because as these networks become denser the costs of opportunistic or selfish behavior increase. This implies endogeneity in regressions that attempt to explain a product of social capital with a measure of trust or reciprocity.

There are several mechanisms through which social capital might affect economic outcomes. Repeated interaction by economic actors through social networks strengthens trust, lowers transaction costs, improves the flow of information (by reducing information asymmetries), and increases the enforceability of contracts. As a result, social capital can increase welfare by increasing the likelihood of cooperative behavior in prisoner's dilemma-type problems, in the private provision of public goods, and in the management of common property resources (Ostrom 1990, 1996; White and Runge 1994; Baland and Platteau 1996).

There is a growing empirical literature on the contribution of social capital to various measures of welfare. Narayan and Pritchett (1999) use micro-level data to test for an empirical link between social capital and income. Following Putnam, they measure social capital using involvement in civic and professional associations and show that at both the household and village level, social capital is a significant determinant of income for a sample of households in Tanzania.[2] In order to remove the potential endogeneity of social capital due to simultaneous effects of income on associational activity (which would result if social capital were a consumption good), the authors instrument for social capital using indicators of trust from survey questions.[3]

In a cross-country empirical study using indicators of trust and civic cooperation as direct measures of social capital, Knack and Keefer (1997) show that social capital matters for economic growth. They deal with the potential endogeneity of social capital in their regressions of economic performance by using

---

[2] Household social capital is measured by the number of associations to which respondents belong, with membership weighted by the quality of the association. Quality is measured by characteristics of the associations and the respondents' assessment of the trust and social cohesion in the group (based on kin heterogeneity, income heterogeneity, group functioning, group decisionmaking, and voluntary membership). Village-level social capital is defined as the product of the average number of groups per household and the average group characteristics.

[3] This is consistent with Fukuyama's (1995) notion that trust, in part, determines the effectiveness of social capital.

performance data that are subsequent to the measures of trust and civic cooperation. Testing the importance of Putnam's horizontal networks, they find no relationship between associational life and trust, civic cooperation, or economic growth.

There has been little work on the role of social capital in solid waste management. In one contribution, Beall (1997) presents case studies of cooperative action for the provision of solid waste management. In Bangalore, India, she found that free-riding and caste considerations undermined the efforts of horizontal associations sponsored by NGOs to organize neighborhood-based solid waste management. In Faisalabad, Pakistan, she found that richer neighborhoods often had sufficient political clout to guarantee government services while much of the rest of the city went without. Poorer communities were sometimes able to gain access to public services by offering their neighborhoods as vote banks, guaranteeing support at the polls in exchange for electricity, sewerage, and the like. In Pakistan it was vertical rather than horizontal networks between neighborhood leaders and politicians that facilitated the provision of public goods by the government.

Modeling the development of voluntary solid waste management systems

We use a threshold model of public good provision, following Black, Levi, and de Meza (1993). We assume that initiators propose the creation of a voluntary solid waste management system to neighborhood residents for their consideration. Initiators form a neighborhood system only if a large enough number of households decide to participate.[4] Individual households perform cost-benefit analysis to decide whether to join the proposed system, recognizing the impact of their decision on the probability of the system coming into being. Our field work indicates that this analytical context for voluntary solid waste management system formation is a good representation of the actual process occurring in the neighborhoods of Dhaka.

Let N be the number of households in the neighborhood and n the threshold number of participating households necessary for a voluntary solid waste management system to be formed. Let the cost per household of participation, c, be declining in the level of neighborhood social capital ($c'(k) < 0$) as a result of the increased ease of coordination and the improved flow of knowledge as social capital increases. The private benefits to household i of trash disposal, b_i, are augmented by the household's social capital, k_i, so that total private benefits from joining the voluntary solid waste management system are

---

[4] In order for the proposed project to be viable, a minimum number of households is required in order to cover the fixed costs associated with operating the system (such as the purchase of a cart to transport the trash).

$B(k_i, b_i)$.[5] The effect of household social capital on total private benefits from joining the voluntary waste management system depends on the nature of social norms in the neighborhood. If norms of reciprocity are strong, we expect that households with stronger ties in the community (higher k_i) earn greater (net) rewards for their cooperation by reinforcing their standing and by participating in a community initiative ($B_1(k_i, b_i) > 0$). We can assume that these benefits are additive in k_i and b_i, so that if, for example, reciprocity norms are well developed, a household with strong ties in the neighborhood but low concern for public cleanliness may earn as much direct benefit from joining the system as an environmentally conscious household that lacks close neighborhood ties. We also assume that $B(k_i, b_i) < c(k)$ for all $i = 1, \ldots, N$ so that no household is willing to act alone.

The benefits of trash removal as a public good are assumed to be linear in the number of households that enroll in the system, so that the ith household receives an additional benefit equal to b_i for each additional household that joins. Thus if r other households join, the ith household's benefits are augmented by $b_i r$. The probability that r other households will join the system is given by $\Pr(r|\,N\text{-}1, k)$, which is a function of the number of other households in the neighborhood, N-1, and k, the level of neighborhood social capital. If the ith household joins (does not join), the voluntary solid waste management system will come into being only if $r \geq n - 1 (r \geq n)$. We assume the threshold number of participants, n, is determined by the initiators that proposed the scheme and is, therefore, exogenous in the household's decision to join. The ith household will commit to participating if the expected benefits from taking part exceed the expected costs:

$$b_i \sum_{r=n-1}^{N-1} r \Pr(r|N - 1, k) + [B(k_i, b_i) - c(k)]$$

$$\times \sum_{r=n-1}^{N-1} \Pr(r|N - 1, k) > b_i \sum_{r=n}^{N-1} r \Pr(r|N - 1, k). \tag{6.1}$$

The first term in expression (6.1) represents the expected benefits to the ith household of at least $n - 1$ other households agreeing to join the system when the ith household joins, so that the system is formed and trash is collected (the public good element). The second term represents the direct expected net

[5] Household social capital, k_i, is restricted to the social capital that exists in the household's relationships with other households in its neighborhood; neighborhood social capital, k, is a measure of the average social capital of all households in the neighborhood.

benefits to the ith household of its own contribution. The term to the right of the inequality is the expected (nonexcludable) benefits to the ith household assuming it decides not to join but the voluntary solid waste management system is formed anyway.

The probability of a voluntary solid waste management system being formed in neighborhood j is the probability that at least n households agree to participate. Let $\tilde{r}$ be the number of households that agree to join. Defining $y_j = 1$ if a voluntary solid waste management system is formed in neighborhood j and $y_j = 0$ otherwise,

$$\Pr\left(y_j = 1\right) = \Pr\left(\tilde{r} \geq n\right)$$

$$= \sum_{\tilde{r}=n}^{N} \Pr\left(\tilde{r} \mid N, p_1\left(k_1\right), \ldots, p_N\left(k_N\right)\right) \tag{6.2}$$

where $p_i(k_i)$ is the probability of the ith household joining the voluntary solid waste management system – that is, the probability that the participation constraint in expression (6.1) is satisfied for the ith household. This suggests a probit model of neighborhood cooperation in which the latent variable, y_j^*, measures the intensity of cooperation for organizing trash collection in the jth neighborhood. In the next section, we describe the empirical implementation of this model.

Equations (6.1) and (6.2) can be used to identify how a number of other variables affect the probability of such systems coming into being. If, for example, coordinated action is simply more difficult as the number of actors increases, the probability of voluntary solid waste management system formation will be decreasing in the number of households in the neighborhood. On the other hand, a larger neighborhood implies a larger potential set of participants, so that a given threshold, n, may be easier to reach. Education could increase the probability of cooperation if it increases the perceived benefits from environmental improvements. The degree of homogeneity of ethnic or regional origin of neighborhood residents may also affect cooperation, although here again there are arguments in favor of both positive and negative impacts. One might expect that people from the same ethnic group or hometown will have stronger social ties and be more likely to work together. However, these same ties can reinforce inertia and a reluctance to change old ways of doing things. Income may have little direct effect on the probability of cooperation, but it may proxy for other variables that can affect the costs and benefits of joining a voluntary solid waste management system. At higher income levels, the actual cost of joining a voluntary system may represent a very small share of total expenditure, suggesting that it would be easier for these households to join. However, we suspect that higher-income neighborhoods have better municipal trash removal services because of greater influence with local politicians (a form of social capital not captured in our survey), so that the benefits from a voluntary solid waste management system will be lower in these neighborhoods than elsewhere. Variables for each of these determinants of cooperation are included in the neighborhood probit below.

From (6.1) and (6.2), it is not possible to determine the effect of social capital on the probability that a voluntary solid waste management system will form. However, the effect of individual and neighborhood social capital on the private costs and benefits of joining the voluntary solid waste management system are clearer. As noted above, an increase in neighborhood social capital reduces the costs $c(k)$ of participating in collective activity. In addition, we expect household social capital increases the direct benefits $B(k_i, b_i)$ of participation if norms of reciprocity are strong.[6] Both of these effects lower the expected net private costs of participation in (6.1), thereby increasing the probability that the household will join. Our hypothesis is that these cost savings are large enough so that the probability of a voluntary solid waste management system being formed is increasing in household and neighborhood social capital.

Estimation strategy

We implement a probit model of neighborhood cooperation in which the latent variable, y_i^*, measures the intensity of cooperation for organizing trash collection in the ith neighborhood. Cooperation is a function of the past and present level of neighborhood social capital, the number of households, income and education levels, and ethnic homogeneity. However, there is a simultaneous relationship between social capital and the establishment of a voluntary solid waste management system, because the process of developing such a system can strengthen social networks, build trust, reinforce norms of reciprocity, and possibly encourage participation in other civic and social organizations. As a result, any contemporaneous measures of social capital used as regressors in the cooperation equation will be correlated with the error term. To account for this source of endogeneity, we employ the two-stage conditional maximum likelihood (2SCML) estimation procedure developed by Rivers and Vuong (1988) for the probit regression.

We estimate a discrete choice simultaneous equations system that includes three equations that determine continuous measures of social capital (trust, reciprocity, and sharing) plus the probit regression for cooperation with endogenous social capital. Under the Rivers and Vuong approach, the three social capital regressions are estimated first and residuals from these regressions are used as

---

[6] Norms of reciprocity are quite strong in the neighborhoods included in our sample. As a result, we expect any measure of social capital that incorporates norms of reciprocity to have a positive effect on the probability of voluntary solid waste management formation through its effect on the benefits of cooperation ($B_1(k_i, b_i) > 0$).

regressors in the probit equation. This procedure leads to consistent parameter estimates for the social capital variables in the cooperation equation.[7]

Hausman tests for exogeneity did not allow us to reject (at the 5 percent significance level) the exogeneity of voluntary solid waste management systems in the social capital equations. In order to capture the effects of cooperation on social capital, we estimate a modified version of the social capital equations, including the dummy variable for the presence of a voluntary solid waste management system as a regressor as well as the sub-set of exogenous variables that we believe are determinants of our measures of social capital. These variables include measures of previous neighborhood participation in civic associations (past social capital), tenure of neighborhood residents, regional origin of neighborhood residents, employment status, the share of residents that own their home, and the availability of infrastructure to facilitate community meetings.

The survey and some background

To understand voluntary solid waste management practices in Dhaka, we interviewed households and local authorities in sixty-five lower- to upper–middle–class neighborhoods in the city between November 1997 and January 1998. The purpose of the survey was to collect household- and neighborhood-level information that would allow us to construct measures of associational activity, trust, reciprocity, and sharing, as well as learn about neighborhood characteristics that might explain the establishment of voluntary waste management systems in some of these neighborhoods.

The survey was confined to the service area of the Dhaka City Corporation in Dhaka City, which covers about 360 square kilometers. Rich neighborhoods were not included in the sample, as the corporation-run system seems to work well in such areas. The poorest neighborhoods (slum areas) were also excluded, as no voluntary solid waste management systems exist there.

The sample is stratified on whether or not the neighborhood has a voluntary solid waste management system. A total of fifty-five neighborhoods were identified that had such a system in place. An additional forty-four neighborhoods without the systems were selected to form a subpopulation of ninety-nine neighborhoods (out of roughly 1,058 neighborhoods in Dhaka). Within this subpopulation, a sample of thirty-five neighborhoods were randomly chosen from within the stratum that had a voluntary waste management system and thirty were chosen from the stratum without a system. The effect of this *choice-based sampling* approach on the estimation method is discussed below. Within each neighborhood, an average of ten households was chosen for interviews.

---

[7] For a more detailed discussion of the estimation procedure, see Pargal, Gilligan, and Huq (2000).

The structured questionnaire had three modules. The first module captured neighborhood-level variables, such as the number of residents, their districts of origin, the mix of homeowners and tenants, and the age of the neighborhood. It also recorded the number of associations, frequency of meetings, and number of members. Questions in this module were asked of a knowledgeable neighborhood authority. The second module was the household survey from which household heads were asked questions about household income and expenditures, as well as the education, age, and profession of household members. It also included questions on trust, reciprocity, and sharing, which formed the bases of our proxies for social capital. In the third module, questions were asked of the initiators of the voluntary solid waste management systems (in areas with functioning systems) in order to understand the motivation and characteristics of system initiators and of the systems themselves.

The two earliest voluntary solid waste management systems in Dhaka were initiated by individuals who had lived overseas, where they had been exposed to sanitary conditions that were better than those in Dhaka. They invested considerable time and money in an effort to organize trash disposal in their neighborhoods and involve their neighbors in the effort. Many of the later systems were inspired by these pioneer systems, which had been publicized on television.

In neighborhoods with voluntary solid waste management systems, households pay a fixed amount per month, regardless of household size. The monthly charge varies from $0.20 to $0.60 (with a median fee of $0.30 a month); higher charges apply when the collected garbage needs to be removed from the neighborhood altogether. The initial investment required to start such a system appears to be low ($50–$600, with a median of $280). Although nearly all the initiators agreed that the main problem in operating the systems was getting people to pay for a service that is the city's responsibility, some voluntary solid waste management systems have been able to run on a commercial basis (that is, to make a profit). The minimum scale required is about 250 households, according to the initiators we interviewed.

The data and variable selection

Our data set covers sixty-five neighborhoods and 652 households. The basic unit of analysis is the neighborhood. Neighborhood variables, such as median education, median *per capita* income, median tenure in the neighborhood, and residents' professions, were calculated based on household information collected in the survey. Information on the number of households in the neighborhoods, the proportion of homeowners and tenants among the residents and residents' district of origin were gathered from local authorities in the first survey module. Information on the district of origin of residents was used as a dimension of community homogeneity, which proxies the commonality of values and priorities in the neighborhood. We also collected information on the proportion of resident homeowners as well as the percentage of adults in the neighborhood working in business, service, or professional work. We presume that older neighborhoods might be more likely to have stronger community ties and thus greater cooperative activity than other neighborhoods and use the time when the first residents moved in and the average length of tenure to measure neighborhood age.

Summary statistics of the variables used in our analysis are shown in table 6.1. Correlations between the variables are shown in table 6A.1 of the appendix (p. 206). Table 6.2 provides a snapshot of the median levels of these variables in neighborhoods with and without voluntary solid waste management systems.

The survey provides several measures of social capital, allowing us to test the applicability of the theories of Coleman (1900) and Putnam (1993) to the provision of public goods and to identify the differential effects of various types of social capital on cooperation. Following Knack and Keefer (1997) and others, we use a measure of trust plus two unique measures of norms of reciprocity and sharing (based on our questionnaire) as proxies for social capital. Our measures for trust, reciprocity, and sharing are based on the mean of households' scores on the following questions:

Trust: 1. Would you hire someone based on your neighbors' recommendations?

2. In an emergency would you leave your young children with your neighbors?

Reciprocity: 1. Do you or your neighbors help arrange funerals for someone who dies in the neighborhood?

2. Do you or your neighbors send food to the family after a death in the family of your neighbors?

3. Do you or your neighbors help each other in taking sick neighbors to doctors or hospitals?

Sharing: 1. Do you or your neighbors send each other cooked food or sweets during religious and social festivals or on any happy occasion?

2. Do you or your neighbors share fruits or vegetables grown on your own premises or village home?

Household responses of "Never," "Occasionally," or "Frequently" were recorded and converted into an increasing frequency index from 1 to 3 for each question. Household scores for trust, reciprocity and sharing are the average of

Table 6.1 *Summary statistics and variable definitions*

Variable	Description	Mean	Standard deviation	Minimum	Maximum
Trust score	Average trust score in observed households	1.49	0.32	1.00	2.43
Reciprocity score	Average reciprocity score in observed households	2.46	0.23	2.00	2.90
Sharing score	Average sharing score in observed households	2.39	0.27	1.72	2.94
Years of residence	1998 minus year when first resident moved into neighborhood	55.78	27.60	18.00	98.00
Median tenure	Median number of years respondents lived in neighborhood	20.28	13.51	1.50	67.00
Origin = Chittagong	1 if Chittagong is most common district of origin	0.57	0.50	0	1.00
Homogeneity (%)	% of residents from district with highest representation in neighborhood	51.62	14.84	30.00	95.00
Homeowners (%)	Share of residents that own their home	25.64	6.35	16.00	40.00
Business jobs (%)	Share of neighborhood jobs in business	23.03	11.30	0.00	50.00
Median income	Median monthly *per capita* income of respondents (Taka)	3394.97	1283.13	1200.00	8267.86
Number of households	Number of households in neighborhood	605.63	352.63	63	1500
Number of meeting places	Number of centers, clubs, fields, and meeting places in neighborhood	0.631	0.977	0	4.00
Number of private organizations	Number of sports and women's organizations in neighborhood before voluntary solid waste management	0.385	0.490	0	1.00
Number of public organizations	Number of religious, welfare, neighborhood watch, and library organizations in neighborhood before voluntary solid waste management	0.754	0.771	0	3.00
Median education	Neighborhood median of mean years of education of adults in observed households	11.59	1.72	6.50	14.45

Note: $N = 65$, except for Homogeneity, where $N = 59$.

Table 6.2 *Comparison of medians of variables in neighborhoods with and without voluntary solid waste management systems (VSWMS)*

Variable	With VSWMS	Without VSWMS
Trust score	1.60	1.33
Reciprocity score	2.55	2.37
Sharing score	2.41	2.30
Homogeneity (%)	45.0	60.0
Number of Households	650	502
Homeowners (%)	27.8	22.0
Median education	12.0	11.2
Median tenure	15.5	24.3
Median income	3,167	3,238
Business jobs (%)	20.0	26.8
Number of private organizations	0.00	1.00
Number of public organizations	1.00	0.50

the indices for the relevant questions. Neighborhood variables are the means of the household scores for each neighborhood.

In addition, we develop measures of activity in civic and social associations, which Putnam (1993) argues can be an important source of social ties that build social capital. Information on associations and the existence of various community facilities was derived from the nonhousehold interview part of the survey.

We use two variables to proxy associational depth. In order to ensure exogeneity, both are based on the number of associations or organizations that existed before the establishment of the voluntary solid waste management system. The first variable is the number of associations providing a "private" good or service, in this case sports and women's associations, which provide services that are typically available only to association members. The second variable is the number of organizations providing a "public" good or service. Such associations included welfare associations, neighborhood watches, library associations, and religious associations.

Some measurement error is present, because we measure the age of an organization by the date the earliest household joined. We thus know the age of an organization only if one of our respondents is a member. If the organization exists but no member of our sample belongs to it, we do not include it, because we cannot posit an age for it. In addition, the data do not allow us to distinguish between more than one organization of the same type in a neighborhood; only the oldest is thus likely to be counted. This said, we think the errors are unlikely to lead to a serious undercount and thus use these variables as measures of associational activity.

Finally, we include the number of meeting places, playing fields, and similar public venues. This variable is included because this type of physical infrastructure may encourage interaction among residents and thus build social capital in the neighborhood.

Results

Estimation results are presented and discussed below.

Social capital

In Hausman tests of exogeneity of the variable indicating the existence of a voluntary solid waste management system in the social capital regressions, we are unable to reject the null hypothesis of exogeneity at the 5 percent level in any of the three social capital regressions. As a result, we estimated the regressions explaining the measures of trust, reciprocity, and sharing using ordinary least squares (table 6.3). We regress each proxy for social capital against the dummy variable for the presence of a voluntary solid waste management system, previous participation in private and public good-oriented civic associations, median tenure of residents in the neighborhood, predominance of residents from Chittagong district (who have a reputation for strong norms of reciprocity and sharing), share of residents that are homeowners, share of business among neighborhood occupations, and the number of community social facilities.

Both the share of adults working in business and the share of residents that own their home are positively and significantly associated with all three measures of social capital. The business community in Dhaka tends to be close-knit, which may account for the positive effect of business. It is not possible to determine whether this effect is derived from the strength of social networks *within* the business community or whether members of the business community foster greater trust and norms of reciprocity in their relationships with *other* community members, including those not involved in business. Not surprisingly, homeowners appear to have a stronger effect on community social ties than tenants, who may be more temporary residents of the neighborhood and who may have less invested there. Neighborhoods in which a majority of residents come from the Chittagong district also have stronger norms of reciprocity and sharing, although trust among residents is not significantly greater in these neighborhoods. Surprisingly, the number of community social facilities and meeting places builds norms of reciprocity but is negatively associated with trust. This variable, which measures physical infrastructure, may act as a proxy for the level of development of the neighborhoods. Less-developed neighborhoods are likely to have more informal types of social ties that do not depend on

Table 6.3 *Determinants of social capital*

Variable	Trust score	Reciprocity score	Sharing score
	OLS	OLS	OLS
Intercept	0.8427**	1.8705**	1.4387**
	(0.1966)	(0.1398)	(0.1523)
Presence of voluntary solid waste	0.1348	0.0916	0.1022
management system	(0.0839)	(0.0596)	(0.0650)
Median tenure	0.0041	0.0040*	0.0024
	(0.0029)	(0.0021)	(0.0023)
Origin = Chittagong	0.1388	0.1641**	0.2580**
	(0.0889)	(0.0632)	(0.0688)
Homeowners (%)	0.0104*	0.0074*	0.0167**
	(0.0061)	(0.0043)	(0.0047)
Business jobs (%)	0.0076**	0.0070**	0.0111**
	(0.0037)	(0.0027)	(0.0029)
Number of meeting places	−0.1318**	0.0702**	0.0138
	(0.0378)	(0.0269)	(0.0293)
Number of private organizations	0.0736	0.0274	0.0915
	(0.0841)	(0.0598)	(0.0652)
Number of public organizations	0.0286	−0.0499	−0.0376
	(0.0492)	(0.0350)	(0.0381)
Adjusted R^2	0.2626	0.2611	0.3819
N	65	65	65
t-statistic for exogeneity test	0.6050	1.4345	1.8791

Notes: $^*p \leq 0.1$. $^{**}p \leq 0.05$. Standard errors in parenthesis.

structured meeting places but that rely on, and perhaps engender, higher levels of trust.

It is interesting to note that participation in civic associations is not associated here with increased trust or stronger norms of reciprocity and sharing. It is likely that formal membership in groups, which Putnam has demonstrated to be a significant determinant of social capital in the United States and Italy, is less important than other, more casual, forms of associational activity in Dhaka. Hence social capital formation in Dhaka is not dependent on participation in civic associations.

Finally, the presence of a voluntary solid waste management system is not an important determinant of social capital as measured by trust and norms of reciprocity and sharing. This may not be surprising given that the majority of the trash disposal schemes were developed recently, in most cases less than three years before the survey was conducted. It may be that the positive effect of the creation of such a system on social ties develops over time or is otherwise too small to have a discernable effect on our proxies for social capital.

Existence of a voluntary solid waste management system

We estimate the two-stage conditional maximum likelihood probit regression for the formation of a voluntary solid waste management system in the neighborhood using each of the three contemporaneous measures of social capital as regressors in separate equations (table 6.4). We then estimate the probit again including all three measures in the same regression. The first-stage reduced-form regressions are presented in appendix table 6A.2.[8]

The Wald statistics show that the exogeneity of the social capital variables is rejected for each of the regressions estimated, implying that the use of the two-stage conditional maximum likelihood technique to obtain consistent parameter estimates is justified. The estimation results for the cooperation regressions show that the largest and most significant effect from a single social capital variable on the probability that a voluntary solid waste management system will be formed is due to the strength of norms of reciprocity.

We calculate the marginal effect of an increase in the reciprocity score on the probability that a voluntary solid waste management system will form. Fixing all the other independent variables at their sample means, we obtain a marginal effect of 2.69 (standard error of 0.834). This suggests that an increase in the reciprocity score index of 0.1 units will lead to a 27 percent increase in the probability that a voluntary solid waste management system will be formed. Social capital indeed appears to have a major effect on cooperation for public good provision. The fact that, of the three measures of social capital tested, reciprocity has the greatest impact, is consistent with the idea that reciprocity best represents the relationship underlying the phenomenon of organizing for solid waste management in the neighborhood.

Norms of sharing also have a significant positive effect on the probability of a voluntary solid waste management system being formed. The effect of the sharing variable is nearly as large as that of reciprocity, with a marginal effect of 2.25 (standard error of 0.736). In contrast, trust is not an important determinant of voluntary solid waste management system formation. The marginal effect of trust is only 0.600, and this statistic is not significant, with a standard error of 0.485. We conjecture that the relatively low stakes involved and the transactional nature of coordinated action for solid waste disposal may mean that trust between neighbors is not particularly important for setting up such systems. After all, the decision to participate does not imply a long-term binding commitment. Commonality of interests, as captured by reciprocity, may well be all that is required.

---

[8]   We also estimated each of the regressions in table 6.4 using weights to correct for the inconsistency introduced by the choice based sampling technique, following Manski and Lerman (1977). Parameter estimates were changed very little by this reweighting, so these results were omitted. See Pargal, Gilligan, and Huq (2000) for details.

Table 6.4 *Two-stage conditional maximum likelihood estimates for the existence probit regression*

Independent variables	Model I	Model II	Model III	Model IV
Trust score	1.5045			0.1918
	(1.216)			(2.737)
Reciprocity score		6.7371**		8.3312
		(2.092)		(7.636)
Sharing score			5.6696**	0.5002
			(1.854)	(6.567)
Intercept	−2.7586	−19.4028**	−12.56**	−24.7185**
	(2.637)	(6.466)	(4.875)	(12.01)
Homogeneity (%)	−0.0489**	−0.0622**	−0.089**	−0.0828*
	(0.0193)	(0.0247)	(0.0285)	(0.0429)
Median income	−0.0001	−0.0002	0.0000	−0.0002
	(0.0002)	(0.0003)	(0.0002)	(0.0004)
Median education	0.2902*	0.6199**	0.3542	0.7397*
	(0.1727)	(0.247)	(0.217)	(0.4086)
Number of households	−0.0001	−0.0007	0.0001	−0.0009
	(0.0006)	(0.0007)	(0.0007)	(0.0014)
Number of private organizations	−0.818*	−1.691**	−1.9872**	−2.5353**
	(0.4448)	(0.6286)	(0.7968)	(1.007)
Number of public organizations	0.5082	0.9086**	0.6837	1.2124*
	(0.3064)	(0.3708)	(0.4209)	(0.6813)
Modified Wald statistic for exogeneity of social capital	7.6762**	65.316**	144.9**	2.08e+005**

Notes: $N = 59$. $*p \leq 0.1$. $**p \leq 0.05$. Standard errors in parenthesis. Residuals from the relevant social capital regressions were also included as regressors, as required for consistency in the Rivers and Vuong 2SCML procedure. Parameter estimates for these residual variables are omitted.

When the social capital variables are included together as regressors, the strength of the effect of social capital on the probability that a voluntary solid waste management system will exist disappears. This may be caused by multi-collinearity among these measures.

The median level of average household education in the neighborhood is also strongly associated with the likelihood of a voluntary solid waste management system coming into being, except when social capital is measured by the sharing score alone. The relationship between regional concentration in the origin of households in the neighborhood and the existence of a voluntary solid waste management system is strong and negative. This may reflect lack of openness to new ways of doing things or new initiatives in a group that is very homogeneous. Median *per capita* income is not significantly associated with the existence of voluntary solid waste management systems, although the sign on income is negative in three of the four regressions.[9] There are no significant effects of neighborhood size on the probability that a voluntary solid waste management system will form. These results suggest that smaller neighborhoods do not have strong coordination advantages and that there are no benefits to having a larger pool of potential participants. Alternatively, the two effects may offset each other, making it difficult to identify the relationship between neighborhood size and the prospects for coordinated action for public good provision.

Most intriguing was the fact that the number of existing private good-oriented organizations has a strong negative effect on the existence of voluntary solid waste management systems, and the effect of the number of existing public good-oriented associations is insignificant, except in the reciprocity score equation. This result may imply a sort of displacement, or crowding out, effect in which the orientation of the "private" group militates against more publicly oriented activity. It is worth repeating that these variables count the number of groups or associations that existed before the voluntary solid waste management system was formed, making them truly exogenous. Clearly not only associational activity but the type of activity matters.

Conclusion

This chapter presents the results of a survey-based study of households in sixty-five neighborhoods of Dhaka. Our results indicate that the organization of voluntary solid waste management systems is a function of our proxy for social capital and of measures of associational activity and the nature of such activity. The proxies we used for social capital – trust, reciprocity, and sharing – do indeed capture different aspects of social capital, with quite different impacts on community outcomes. Reciprocity among neighbors is far more important than trust, for example, when it comes to cooperating for solid waste management.

A clear policy implication of the analysis is that investments in education are likely to have spillover effects in terms of the ability to organize for solid waste management. We cannot, however, say whether the promotion of associational activity has a positive net impact on the provision of a public good or service by a neighborhood committee, either directly or through the creation of social capital. We also need to keep in mind that, as Beall's (1997) case studies

---

[9] Because the wealthiest and poorest neighborhoods were selected out of the sample, this measure of *per capita* income does not fully control for the effects of income on the presence of a voluntary solid waste management system. Therefore, we do not assign a strong interpretive role to this variable.

demonstrate, the nature of the good or service and the circumstances accounting for its underprovision should not be forgotten.

The different aspects of social capital do not appear to be determined by the existence of a voluntary solid waste management system, although they are in part explained by some of the other structural and associational variables in our data set. Homogeneity of interests and points of view appear paramount in explaining levels of social capital. Thus from a policy viewpoint, social capital may well be a primal variable that resides in the inherent ability of different individuals to relate to one another. While it can be channeled to different uses, our analysis does not indicate that it is something policymakers can easily affect.

This work demonstrates the feasibility of privatizing the collection of solid waste in urban middle-class neighborhoods. It also indicates that the government can play a useful role in publicizing success stories and providing information on how some neighborhoods were able to organize themselves for solid waste management. However, more analysis is needed before one can conclude that the city is ready for wholesale privatization of solid waste collection.

The most important policy implication of our work is that the introduction of public–private partnerships or self-help schemes is more likely to be successful in neighborhoods in which the level of social capital is high. Social capital proxies or determinants can thus be used as predictors of success when targeting neighborhoods for different social or public good-oriented interventions.

Table 6A.1 *Matrix of Pearson correlation coefficients*

Variable	Trust score	Reciprocity score	Sharing score	Years of residence	Median tenure	Homogeneity (%)	Homeowners (%)	Business jobs (%)	Median income	Number of households	Number of meeting places	Number of private organizations	Number of public organizations	Median education
Trust score	1.00													
Reciprocity score	0.37	1.00												
Sharing score	0.44	0.62	1.00											
Years of Residence	-0.11	0.06	-0.05	1.00										
Median tenure	0.12	0.22	0.12	0.58	1.00									
Homogeneity (%)	0.02	0.06	0.15	0.52	0.53	1.00								
Homeowners (%)	0.25	0.22	0.39	-0.10	0.04	0.29	1.00							
Business jobs (%)	0.13	0.17	0.18	0.38	0.30	0.32	-0.18	1.00						
Median income	-0.15	-0.03	-0.13	0.17	0.10	0.01	-0.31	0.06	1.00					
Number of households	0.01	0.08	-0.04	0.00	0.02	-0.09	-0.28	0.09	0.34	1.00				
Number of meeting places	-0.35	0.31	0.06	0.14	0.15	0.00	-0.03	0.10	-0.06	0.13	1.00			
Number of private organizations	0.00	0.11	0.09	0.23	0.32	0.17	-0.27	0.27	0.16	0.22	0.27	1.00		
Number of public organizations	0.21	0.06	0.16	-0.12	0.17	-0.01	0.15	0.20	-0.15	0.23	0.08	0.21	1.00	
Median education	-0.01	-0.09	-0.01	-0.22	-0.39	-0.35	-0.10	-0.38	0.46	0.29	-0.16	0.03	-0.24	1.00

Table 6A.2 *First-stage reduced-form social capital regressions*

	Dependent variable	Trust score			Dependent variable	Reciprocity score			Dependent variable	Sharing score		
Variable	Estimate	Standard error	t-statistic	Probability	Estimate	Standard error	t-statistic	Probability	Estimate	Standard error	t-statistic	Probability
Intercept	0.8027	0.4412	1.8193	0.07524	1.6953	0.3319	5.1083	5.83E-06	0.8329	0.3571	2.3324	0.02402
Median tenure	0.0061	0.003449	1.7594	0.08501	0.0039	0.002595	1.5039	0.1393	0.0027	0.002792	0.9821	0.3311
Origin = Chittagong	0.0672	0.09457	0.7101	0.4812	0.1722	0.07114	2.4205	0.01942	0.2954	0.07654	3.8597	0.000345
Homeowners (%)	0.0169	0.007547	2.2438	0.02959	0.0129	0.005677	2.279	0.02725	0.0151	0.006109	2.4796	0.0168
Business jobs (%)	0.0082	0.004055	2.0103	0.05015	0.0077	0.00305	2.5394	0.01447	0.0124	0.003282	3.7865	0.000433
Number of meeting places	-0.1401	0.03984	-3.5175	0.000978	0.0695	0.02997	2.3204	0.02471	0.0348	0.03225	1.0803	0.2855
Homogeneity (%)	-0.0042	0.003542	-1.1981	0.2369	-0.0012	0.002664	-0.4322	0.6676	0.0032	0.002867	1.1076	0.2737
Median income	-0.0001	3.70E-05	-1.8834	0.06584	0	2.78E-05	-0.5053	0.6157	0	3.00E-05	-1.2592	0.2142
Median education	0.0275	0.03295	0.8342	0.4084	0.009	0.02479	0.3633	0.718	0.0504	0.02667	1.89	0.06493
Number of households	0.0001	0.00012	0.9837	0.3303	0.0001	9.03E-05	1.3767	0.1751	0	9.71E-05	0.2229	0.8246
Number of private organizations	0.0258	0.09096	0.2836	0.7779	0.0085	0.06842	0.1248	0.9012	0.0083	0.07362	0.1133	0.9103
Number of public organizations	0.0311	0.05578	0.5577	0.5797	-0.0584	0.04196	-1.3928	0.1702	-0.0068	0.04515	-0.1507	0.8809
R^2	0.40993				0.36562				0.47116			
Adjusted R^2	0.27183				0.21715				0.34738			

REFERENCES

Baland, J.-M. and Platteau, J.-P., 1996. *Halting Degradation of Natural Resources: Is There a Role for Rural Communities?* New York: Oxford University Press

Beall, J, 1997. "Social Capital in Waste – A Solid Investment?" *Journal of International Development* 9(7): 951–961

Black, J., Levi, M. D., and de Meza, D., 1993. "Creating a Good Atmosphere: Minimum Participation for Tackling the 'Greenhouse Effect.'" *Economica* 60(239): 281–293

Borjas, G. J., 1992. "Ethnic Capital and Intergenerational Mobility." *Quarterly Journal of Economics* 107(1): 123–150

——— 1995. "Ethnicity, Neighborhoods, and Human Capital Externalities." *American Economic Review* 85(3): 365–390

Boxman, E. A. W., De Graaf, P. M., and Flap, H. D., 1991. "The Impact of Social and Human Capital on the Income Attainment of Dutch Managers." *Social Networks* 13(1): 51–73

Coleman, J. S., 1988. "Social Capital in the Creation of Human Capital." *American Journal of Sociology* 94: S95–S120

——— 1990. *Foundations of Social Theory.* Cambridge, MA: Harvard University Press

Fukuyama, F., 1995. *Trust: The Social Virtues and the Creation of Prosperity.* New York: Free Press

Greif, A., 1994. "Cultural Beliefs and the Organization of Society: A Historical and Theoretical Reflection on Collectivist and Individualist Societies." *Journal of Political Economy* 102(5): 912–950

Harrison, L. E., 1992. *Who Prospers? How Cultural Values Shape Economic and Political Success.* New York: Basic Books

Helliwell, J. F. and Putnam, R. D., 1995. "Economic Growth and Social Capital." *Eastern Economic Journal* 21(3): 295–307

Knack, S. and Keefer, P., 1997. "Does Social Capital Have an Economic Payoff? A Cross-Country Investigation." *Quarterly Journal of Economics* 112(4): 1251–1288

Meyerson, E. M., 1994. "Human Capital, Social Capital and Compensation: The Relative Contribution of Social Contacts to Managers' Income." *Acta Sociologica* 37(4): 383–399

Manski, C. F. and Lerman, S. R., 1997. "The Estimation of Choice Probabilities from Choice Based Samples." *Econometrica* 45(8): 1977–1988

Narayan, D. and Pritchett, L., 1999. "Cents and Sociability: Household Income and Social Capital in Rural Tanzania." *Economic Development and Cultural Change* 47(4): 871–898

Ostrom, E., 1990. *Governing the Commons: The Evolution of Institutions for Collective Action.* New York: Cambridge University Press

——— 1996. "Crossing the Great Divide: Coproduction, Synergy, and Development." *World Development* 24(6): 1073–1087

Pargal, S., Gilligan, D. O., and Huq, M., 2000. "Private Provision of a Public Good: Social Capital and Solid Waste Management in Dhaka, Bangladesh." Policy Research Working Paper 2422. World Bank, Washington, DC

Putnam, R. D., 1993. *Making Democracy Work: Civic Traditions in Modern Italy.* Princeton, NJ: Princeton University Press

Rivers, D. and Vuong, Q. H., 1988. "Limited Information Estimators and Exogeneity Tests for Simultaneous Probit Models." *Journal of Econometrics* 39(3): 347–366

Sugden, R., 1984. "Reciprocity: The Supply of Public Goods Through Voluntary Contributions." *Economic Journal* 94(376): 772–787

1986. *Economics of Rights, Cooperation and Welfare*. New York: Blackwell

White, T. A. and Runge, C. F., 1994. "Common Property and Collective Action: Lessons from Cooperative Watershed Management in Haiti." *Economic Development and Cultural Change* 43(1): 1–41

Part 3

The creation and transformation of social capital

7   The impact of development assistance on social capital: evidence from Kenya

Mary Kay Gugerty and Michael Kremer

A large body of literature suggests that social capital is important for development (see Coleman 1990; Putnam 1993; Woolcock 1998, among others). Perhaps in response, many donors are actively trying to support the development of civil society and social capital in developing countries. Donors are funding local NGOs, structuring development projects in ways that allow for participation, and providing organizational training for community groups and NGOs. Yet the effectiveness of these efforts to build social capital is largely unknown.

While considerable effort has gone into elucidating the effects of social capital, the determinants of social capital are less well understood. Is social capital determined exclusively by long-run historical, cultural, and economic forces? Or can it be influenced in the short run by policy? If so, how? One reading of Putnam's work on Italy (1993) is that social capital is the result of long-term institutional development and may be very difficult to produce. Other literature suggests that organizational social capital can be eroded by economic restructuring (Heying 1997; Schulman and Anderson 1998) and may also be created in a relatively short period through either national organizations (Minkoff 1997) or community organizing in face-to-face interactions (Wood 1997).

One problem plaguing many studies of social capital is the difficulty of inferring causation from correlation in retrospective data. For example, a correlation between social capital and outside funding could arise if funding promoted social capital, if groups with more social capital attracted more funding, or if some third factor affected both funding and social capital. Correlations between organizational training and social capital could reflect either the effect of training or donors' judgments that training was badly needed.

To estimate causal impacts, we employ a randomized, prospective evaluation. We examine three projects undertaken by Internationaal Christelijk Steunfonds

The authors would like to thank the Social Capital Initiative at the World Bank for supporting this work. In addition, the efforts of numerous individuals in both the United States and Kenya made this work possible. The authors thank the staff of Internationaal Christelijk Steunfonds (ICS), in Busia, Nairobi, and the Netherlands for their efforts in support of this project. Ted Miguel, Robert Namunyu, Ashok Rai, Sylvie Moulin, Stacey Nemeroff, and Maureen Wechuli all provided helpful advice and comments. Any errors are our own.

(ICS), a Dutch NGO. Since ICS had limited financial and administrative resources, the projects were phased in gradually. The order of phase-in was essentially determined randomly. This provides natural treatment and comparison groups, allowing us to attribute differences between the groups to the effects of the program.

The three projects varied in the extent to which they explicitly attempted to build social capital and in the nature of the assistance provided. One project involved no participation, one involved considerable community participation, and one involved organizational and management training for indigenous community organizations. The first project provided textbooks to primary schools in 1996 and 1997. Parents and school officials had no role in deciding what textbooks their schools would receive. The second project, which provided block grants to school committees in 1997, was more participatory. Parent-elected school committees proposed plans for the use of funds and final decisions were made in an open meeting of parents. The NGO then purchased and delivered the requested inputs. The third project was designed explicitly to build organizational capacity among women's groups, and included training for group leaders in organizational management and group-building techniques, as well as agricultural training and the provision of agricultural inputs.

We find little relationship between the extent to which the programs sought to encourage development of social capital and social capital outcomes. The top-down textbook program and the more participatory program of grants to school committees had similar effects. Neither substantially affected school committee and parent attendance, but both improved teacher attendance and effort. The women's group program, with its explicit focus on social capital and organizational training, did not improve indicators of social capital. In fact, it led to the entry into group membership and leadership of men and younger, more educated women with formal employment, thus changing the very characteristics and composition of these groups that made them attractive to donors. Our results suggest caution about deliberate attempts to "build" social capital. For example, the substantial share of project funds that were spent bringing women's groups' leaders to seminars and meetings and hiring experts to train them might have been better spent elsewhere.

While participatory design and organizational training were not correlated with social capital outcomes in our data, the form of assistance may nonetheless influence social capital. The provision of training and agricultural implements for leaders of women's groups offered substantial rents for group leaders, and this may have stimulated rent seeking. In contrast, the provision of textbooks to schools offered fewer such opportunities. Encouraging collective activity in areas that are more naturally conducted individually, such as agricultural production, may create opportunities for rent seeking, thereby weakening social capital rather than creating it.

The chapter proceeds as follows. The next section examines the effect of textbook provision and grants to school committees on social capital in schools. The following section analyzes how provision of organizational training and agricultural inputs affected social capital in women's self-help groups. The final section concludes.

The textbook and school grant programs

This section examines the impact of a program that provided a predetermined set of textbooks to schools in 1996 and 1997 and a more participatory program of grants to school committees that began in 1997. We first provide background on the primary school projects and describe the educational outcomes. We then discuss the project impacts on parental participation and teacher effort.

School governance in Kenya

In Kenya the national government hires and pays teachers, while parents pay a variety of fees to finance routine nonteacher inputs, such as chalk, books for teachers, and maintenance of school buildings. Parents are also collectively responsible for raising funds for school development projects, such as classroom construction. Total parent financing is roughly $7 per student per year.

Each school has a governing school committee composed of fourteen members. Nine of these members are parent representatives for each grade level (including preprimary classes) who are elected by the parents of children in that grade. Three members represent the school's sponsor (usually a church) and are appointed by the sponsor; two of these members represent and are appointed by the district education board. Most appointed committee members also have a child in the school. The average member in our sample is forty-nine years old, has three children in the school, and has served on the committee for three years. The school committee elects a chair and a treasurer from among its members and the head teacher of the school serves as the secretary of the committee.

The school committee sets activity and development fees at the beginning of the year, but many parents often fail to pay the full fee. Students who have not paid the mandatory fees may be sent home from school, but they often return with only a fraction of the required fee and are nonetheless readmitted. School committee decisions are in principle ratified by an open assembly of parents and teachers known as the parent-teacher association (PTA).[1] Once the

---

[1] The PTA in Kenyan primary schools is not a distinct organization with separate officials and functions, but the name given to open school meetings of parents and teachers.

school committee has set policy (such as the school's fees) for the year and set a fundraising and construction budget for the school, a PTA meeting is called. Both the PTA and the school committee are officially supposed to meet once each term, or three times a year.

In practice, the quality of school committees varies considerably. Some schools have active, well-functioning committees; others are riven by factionalism; and others are inactive, with the school head teacher in fact making most decisions. The quality of the school committee has an important effect on school organization, funding, and morale. A motivated, cooperative committee is clearly visible to the community and tends to encourage more support from parents. In some cases in which head teachers have proved ineffective or corrupt, school committees have intervened with Ministry of Education officials to remove the teacher from the school. A divided committee can stall projects, frustrate parents, and lead to poor school performance and declining enrollments, as it is relatively easy for students to switch to other primary schools.

The education projects

The projects we evaluate are located in Busia and Teso districts, two rural districts in western Kenya. Both are densely populated rural districts that are relatively poor for Kenya. The economy is based primarily on small-scale farming for subsistence and local market trade. There is some limited cash crop production of cotton, tobacco, and sugarcane. The average daily agricultural wage is approximately $0.85 (Gugerty 2000).

In late 1995, the Ministry of Education district office selected 100 schools of the 333 in Busia and Teso districts to participate in the ICS School Assistance Program. These schools were chosen because they were considered to be particularly in need of assistance, yet had not been assisted by an earlier World Bank textbook assistance program that was supposed to target the 100 neediest schools. The 100 schools were randomly divided into four groups to determine which groups would receive funding and when. Schools were first grouped according to their geographic division within each district. From this list, every fourth school, beginning with the first, was assigned to Group One. Every fourth school beginning with the second school was assigned to Group Two, and so on. Group One schools received textbooks at the beginning of 1996 and again in 1997. Group Two schools received a grant at the beginning of 1997. Group Three and Four schools form the comparison group for this evaluation. Both program and comparison schools received chalk as compensation for their involvement in the project. Group Three schools received grants in 1998 and Group Four schools received them in 2000.

Schools participating in the textbook program did not have any choice regarding the number or types of textbooks received. This was decided by ICS.[2] In contrast, schools in the grant program could spend funds on a range of inputs, including books, classroom construction materials, furniture, or other supplies. The school committee, formed of parent representatives and the head teacher, proposed how the grant was to be used and the final decision was made in an open meeting of parents and teachers.[3] The grant program, therefore, was more decentralized and participatory than the textbook program.

To ensure that resources given to the schools were used by the schools and not diverted to individual students or school staff, textbooks were delivered directly to the schools and identified with an ICS stamp to make them more difficult to resell. Schools were subsequently visited to ensure that textbooks were still present. In grant schools, ICS itself purchased the inputs chosen by the schools and delivered them directly to the school compound, rather than providing school committees with money and allowing them to make the purchases directly.

Our data come from surveys administered at the schools by ICS field officers in early 1998 and from unscheduled classroom visits. The survey respondent was generally the head teacher or deputy head teacher. The data therefore reflect two years of program participation for textbook schools and one year for grant schools. We provide summary statistics on the primary schools (table 7.1). School enrollment and test scores were similar across textbook, grant, and comparison schools before the program began (Glewwe, Kremer, and Moulin 1999).[4]

Educational outcomes

Although our focus in this chapter is on social capital outcomes, it is helpful to briefly note the educational outcomes of the projects. Among students with

---

[2] The twenty-five schools in Group One initially received English textbooks for grades 3–7 and math textbooks for grades 3, 5, and 7. Since almost half of grade 8 students already had math and English textbooks, ICS provided science textbooks in grade 8. In January 1997 grades 4 and 6 received math textbooks and grade 8 received agriculture texts. ICS also provided one copy of the accompanying teacher's guide for each set of books provided. The books used are the official government textbooks, which follow the national curriculum. A 60 percent textbook per pupil ratio was provided in English and science; a 50 percent textbook ratio was provided in math.

[3] A block grant was given to each school, based on the student enrollment of the previous year. The schools received $2.70 per student, or an average of $730 per school. On average, 43 percent of the funds were spent on building materials, 47 percent on learning materials (generally books), 10 percent on furniture, and 1 percent on supplies.

[4] Data on attendance rates at school committee meetings prior to the program is available for only half the schools in the sample, but in this group, attendance is higher for both textbook and grant schools than for comparison schools.

Table 7.1   *Summary statistics on primary schools, 1997*

	Mean	Standard deviation	Number of observations
School characteristics			
Average age of school committee member	48.87	3.95	96
Number of years average school committee member has been on committee	2.57	1.98	96
PTA meetings			
Number of PTA meetings held	3.45	1.79	94
School committee members' attendance rate at PTA meetings	0.62	0.23	67
Average annual number of PTA meetings attended per school committee member	0.99	0.94	93
School committee meetings			
Number of school committee meetings held during the school year	3.96	2.17	91
School committee members' attendance rate	0.58	0.11	86
School committee officials' attendance rate	0.92	0.11	86
Average annual number of meetings attended per school committee member	2.00	1.35	92
Teacher outcomes			
Proportion of the time teachers were in the classroom in random spot checks	0.69	0.22	92
Proportion of schools that hold extra instruction for students during the holidays	0.30	0.16	97
Proportion of schools that hold extra instruction for students during the term	0.53	0.34	95

pretest scores in the top quintile of the distribution, students in the textbook schools scored 0.20 standard deviations higher on a posttest than students in comparison schools after one year of program participation. The program had a somewhat smaller effect on students in the second quintile of pretest scores, but did not raise scores for students in the bottom 60 percent of the distribution. Students in the textbook schools were more likely to go on to secondary school. Since only the best students finish primary school and take the examination that governs entrance to secondary school, this finding is consistent with the hypothesis that the strongest students benefited from the textbook program.

The grant program had similar impacts. Among students in the top quintile of pretest scores, those in grant schools had posttest scores 0.23 standard deviations higher than those in comparison schools after one year. The grant program improved test scores by 0.17 standard deviations for students in the 4th quintile of pretest scores in 1997. However, there was no evidence of similar impacts for lower quintiles.

Parental participation in school activities

Social capital and parental and community participation have long been seen as key determinants of educational quality (Coleman 1988, 1990). Research on school performance suggests that the involvement of parents and community in school decisionmaking can improve teacher attendance and effort (Colletta and Perkins 1995). In poor, rural schools such as those we study, teacher attendance and morale are major problems. On average in 1997, teachers in our data were absent from the classroom 31 percent of the time. Most primary school teachers in this area are members of the local school community and thus at least potentially subject to community influence through informal channels, as well as through formal communication between school committees and the Ministry of Education or political leaders. Nearly 80 percent of teachers at the schools in this sample reported that they were living in their "home" area (Gugerty and Miguel 2000).

We measure parental participation through attendance at PTA and school committee meetings and by parental contributions to school projects. Participation in the textbook and grant programs had an ambiguous impact on parental participation at school meetings. The number of PTA meetings held at textbook schools went down, but attendance rates of key figures at these meetings increased. We take this as a slight positive development. The main role of the PTA is to ratify recommendations put forward by the school committee and to agree on fundraising targets for parents. Schools experiencing a great deal of discord over policy often call more PTA meetings to develop consensus among parents or to pressure parents to pay fees. Fewer meetings may therefore be a sign of more efficient decisionmaking, less disagreement among parents over school policy, or less acrimony over fee payment. On the other hand, fewer PTA meetings could also be interpreted as lower levels of parental participation in school decisionmaking.

To test for the impacts of each form of assistance, we regress the dependent variable of interest on an indicator variable that takes the value of one if a school or group is participating in the program. The OLS coefficients on the program indicator can be interpreted as the average value of the dependent variable for the program groups minus the average value of the dependent variable for the treatment groups. Each regression also includes controls for the geographic divisions in which the schools or groups are located.

Textbook schools had fewer PTA meetings than comparison schools (table 7.2,

Table 7.2   *PTA meetings, 1997*

	Number of meetings		All school committee members		School committee officers	
	Number of meetings in 1997	Change in number of meetings 1995–7[a]	Attendance rate[b]	Average number of meetings attended per member	Attendance rate[b]	Average number of meetings attended per officer
Dependent variable	(1)	(2)	(3)	(4)	(5)	(6)
Textbook schools	−1.03**	−1.65**	0.08	−0.16	0.07*	−0.21
	(0.43)	(0.70)	(0.07)	(0.24)	(0.04)	(0.44)
Grant schools	−0.66	−1.37**	−0.01	0.34	0.03	0.54
	(0.41)	(0.58)	(0.06)	(0.22)	(0.04)	(0.36)
Observations	94	77	66	93	67	93
R^2	0.18	0.15	0.21	0.14	0.13	0.10
Mean value of dependent variable in comparison schools	3.89	1.78	0.59	0.98	0.88	1.58

Notes: $*p \leq 0.1$. $**p \leq 0.05$. $***p \leq 0.001$.
OLS regressions with robust standard errors in parentheses. All regressions include indicator variables for the geographic regions in which schools are located.
[a] Missing records for 1995 are evenly distributed between program schools and comparison schools.
[b] Missing records for 1997 are evenly distributed between program schools and comparison schools.

column (1)). Overall attendance rates of school committee members at PTA meetings were not significantly different than at comparison schools, although data on attendance is missing for a number of schools (column (3)). Overall, the average number of PTA meetings attended per school committee member was not significantly different in textbook schools than in comparison schools (column (4)). Conditional on a meeting being called, attendance rates for school committee officers were 7 percent higher than comparison schools (column (5)). The textbook program did not significantly affect the average number of meetings attended per officer.

The grant program, with its explicit parental participation component, did not lead to many statistically significant changes relative to comparison schools. The number of PTA meetings held at grant schools in 1997 is no different than comparison schools (table 7.2, column (1)). The change in the number of annual meetings held from 1995 to 1997 is negative and significant (column (2)), though data on 1995 meetings is missing for a number of schools. While point estimates for the number of PTA meetings attended per school committee member are positive for grant schools (column (4)), it is impossible to reject the hypothesis that the two programs had similar effects on parent committee meetings and attendance rates at meetings.

Table 7.3 *School committee meetings, 1997*

	Number of meetings		All school committee members		School committee officers	
	Number of meetings	Change in number of meetings 1995–7[a]	Attendance rate	Average number of meetings attended per member	Attendance rate	Average number of meetings attended per officer
Dependent variable	(1)	(2)	(3)	(4)	(5)	(6)
Textbook schools	−0.70	−0.89	0.04	−0.23	0.03	−0.36
	(0.55)	(0.82)	(0.03)	(0.34)	(0.03)	(0.51)
Grant schools	−0.41	−0.83	0.02	0.07	0.01	0.06
	(0.56)	(0.76)	(0.03)	(0.35)	(0.03)	(0.48)
Observations	91	73	87	92	96	92
R^2	0.18	0.17	0.12	0.14	0.11	0.17
Mean of dependent variable in comparison schools	4.19	0.98	0.56	2.01	0.91	3.18

Notes: $^*p \leq 0.1.$ $^{**}p \leq 0.05.$ $^{***}p \leq 0.001.$
OLS regressions with robust standard errors in parentheses. All regressions include indicator variables for the geographic regions in which schools are located.
[a] Missing data for 1995 is evenly distributed between program and comparison schools.

Neither program significantly affected participation of school committee members at school committee meetings, as opposed to meetings of the entire PTA (table 7.3). Neither textbook nor grant schools differed significantly from comparison schools in the average number of meetings attended per committee member, attendance rates, or in the number of school committee meetings held. Parents in textbook and grant schools did not contribute higher levels of labor or in-kind project inputs than did parents in comparison schools (not reported).

Teacher effort

Both programs increased teachers' participation in school. NGO field officers conducted random, unannounced classroom visits to learn how the programs affected pedagogy. As part of these visits, they recorded whether teachers were present in the classroom. Surveys also recorded the number of times that teachers held extra classes for students in grades 4 through 8. The surveys recorded the number of times these supplemental coaching sessions were held out of 20 potential sessions during four school terms. These sessions were held to prepare students for district and national exams; we measured the number of extra coaching sessions held during the school term and during school holidays.

Table 7.4   *Teacher outcomes*

Dependent variable	Teacher present in the classroom[a] (1)	Holiday coaching 1997[b] (2)	Term-time coaching 1997[b] (3)
Textbook schools	0.11**	0.09**	0.18**
	(0.05)	(0.04)	(0.09)
Grant schools	0.10**	0.04	0.16**
	(0.05)	(0.04)	(0.08)
Observations	92	97	97
R^2	0.13	0.16	0.10
Mean of dependent variable in comparison schools	0.64	0.26	0.46

Notes: $^*p \leq 0.1$. $^{**}p \leq 0.05$. $^{***}p \leq 0.001$.
OLS Estimates, robust standard errors in parentheses. All regressions include indicator variables for the geographic regions in which schools are located.
[a] Percentage of times teacher present in the classroom. Based on random field checks by NGO field officers, 1997.
[b] Defined as the percentage of times extra coaching was held out of twenty times (for grades 4–8 during four school terms), normalized to be between 0 and 1.

Our results suggest that teachers in program schools are more likely to be in the classroom during school hours and to provide extra instruction for students than teachers in comparison schools. Both the textbook program and the more participatory grant program improved teacher effort significantly, at least in the short run. In comparison groups, teachers were present in the classroom 64 percent of the time (table 7.4, column (1)). Teachers in textbook schools were present in the classroom 75 percent of the time, 11 percent more of the time than in comparison schools (column (1)). In addition, teachers in textbook schools held supplementary holiday coaching sessions for students in 35 percent of the periods we asked about, as compared to 26 percent in comparison schools (column (2)). During the school term, teachers in textbook schools held extra coaching in 64 percent of the periods we asked about, while comparison schools did so 46 percent of the time (column (3)).

Teachers in grant schools were 10 percent more likely to be present in the classroom than teachers in comparison schools (table 7.4, column (1)). Teachers in grant schools were no more likely than comparison school teachers to hold holiday coaching sessions (column (2)), but were 16 percent more likely to run extra coaching sessions for students during the term than were teachers in comparison schools (column (3)).

Both programs induced significantly higher teacher effort, but since neither had substantial effects on parental participation, it seems unlikely that parental participation was the channel through which the programs improved teacher effort. Program impact on teacher effort seems to be direct, rather than mediated through the influence of parents. Provision of textbooks and other inputs may have raised teacher morale or simply made teaching more enjoyable. Either hypothesis could help explain why the degree of participation incorporated into project design appears to have little additional effect on teacher effort.

The women's group program

We find little evidence that a project providing women's groups with agricultural inputs and organizational and agricultural training improved social capital. In fact, the project seems to have spurred rent seeking.

Women's groups in Kenya

In 1997 ICS began funding women's community self-help groups in Busia and Teso districts. The goal of the program was to strengthen community organizations and improve agricultural practices and nutrition in the area.

The activities of the women's groups in the sample are diverse. To be eligible for the project, groups had to be engaged in agricultural activities for income generation. Many groups also provide emergency assistance to members in the face of adverse financial shocks. In the case of illness or death, groups often take up collections and visit members' homes to provide extra labor. Many groups also undertake income-generating projects, such as fish farming, beekeeping, or handicraft production. Women's groups also participate in community projects by contributing to community fundraising events at local schools, clinics, or churches. Most of the groups also run rotating savings and credit associations (ROSCAs), known in Kenya as "merry-go-rounds" (for an analysis of these organizations, see Gugerty 2000). In addition to merry-go-rounds, many groups also operate rotating labor groups during the peak agricultural seasons. In these groups, members visit one another's farms, usually to help with weeding or harvesting. As in the merry-go-rounds, these rotating labor groups rely on the trust and cooperation of members to ensure the continued functioning of the club.

Women's groups in Kenya have their roots in a long tradition of community self-help groups, such as funeral and rotating labor clubs. While women's groups are locally initiated and formed, they are also supposed to be supported by the government through the Ministry of Culture and Social Services. Each administrative district has a community development assistant, whose job is to visit the various groups and provide them with organizational support.

The average women's group in the sample has about twenty members and has been in operation for eight years (table 7.5). While more than 80 percent

Table 7.5   *Summary statistics on women's groups, 1998*

	Mean	Standard deviation	Observations
Number of years average group has been in operation	7.81	5.30	80
Number of members	19.43	7.20	80
Age of average group member	40.70	5.20	80
Years of education of average member	5.39	2.26	80
Proportion of members who are women	0.80	0.16	80
Proportion of members who report no regular off-farm source of income	0.57	0.24	80
Proportion of members who are over 50 years of age in 1998	0.26	0.18	80
Proportion of members who are married	0.98	0.04	80
Average number of individuals entering the groups during the project period	2.44	2.88	80
Average number of individuals leaving the group during the project period	4.33	3.52	80
Proportion of groups who elected new officials[a]	0.51	0.50	80
Attendance rates at group meetings	0.84	0.19	78
Average number of community fundraisings to which groups contributed	3.18	9.14	80
Average annual amount contributed at community fundraisings in US dollars	12.50	38.8	80
Average annual number of times that groups gave members assistance/emergency help to members	12.00	2.26	80

Note: [a] This excludes elections held only to elect a member to the post of farm manager.

of members are women, most groups do have some male members. These are often, but not always, the husbands of members. Some serve as the "patron" of the club or as the club advisor. The average member is 41 years old and has five years of formal education. Fifty-seven percent of group members report no source of income other than their farm.

The women's group project

Several hundred groups operating in the area were identified through lists provided by the Ministry of Culture and Social Services and through the local Community Development Assistants. Eighty of these groups were selected as eligible to participate in the project. The main criteria for eligibility in the project were that the groups met regularly and were engaged in a group-based agricultural activity.

Once the eighty groups were selected and a baseline survey was conducted, the groups were stratified by administrative division, ordered alphabetically, and every second group was selected to receive funding and training in 1998. The composition of the training and agricultural assistance was determined by ICS agricultural officers working in conjunction with extension officers in the Ministry of Agriculture. The program consisted of two components. The first involved two days of group management and leadership training for three group leaders. Funds for travel to Busia town and for food were given to the leaders. A Kenyan trainer specializing in community organizations conducted training which emphasized leadership skills, group management techniques, bookkeeping, and project administration.

The second component was agricultural and included both training and agricultural inputs. Three group leaders and one additional member were brought to Busia town for five days of practical and experiential training on agricultural practices and husbandry. In addition, each group received a set of agricultural inputs that included hoes and other implements, certified seeds for six crops, fertilizer, and pesticide/herbicide sprayers. These were intended for use on collective group farms, but were stored at the homes of individual members. The value of assistance was about $737 per group (an average of $28 per member).[5] For the average person in this area, this represents roughly 1.5 months of income. The value of agricultural inputs represented half the value of total assistance. The organizational and group management training comprised 16 percent of the value of total assistance. The remaining 34 percent of funds were spent on agricultural training.

Three sets of surveys were administered to the groups. A baseline survey was conducted in July and August of 1997, before the randomization was done or funding provided. At the end of the project, in September and October 1998, a second survey was administered to assess the impact of the assistance. Follow-up surveys were also administered in early 1999.[6]

Preprogram comparison

At the start of the project, the groups do not differ from one another on outcome variables in any systematic way (table 7.6). Program groups have lower levels of debts to the group at the start of the project in 1997. Otherwise, there are no statistically significant differences between the two sets of groups.

---

[5] The value of inputs is calculated at the 1998 exchange rate of Ksh 58 to US$1.

[6] Because of the detail and complexity of the surveys, completion of the survey often took almost a whole day. During the major survey rounds, therefore, both the assisted and the comparison groups were given a small set of tools to compensate them for their time. The impacts of assistance should therefore be thought of as the impact conditional on the groups having received farm implements worth about $63 a group (about $3 per group member).

Table 7.6   *Women's groups, 1997, preprogram comparison*

	Program group mean (standard deviation)	Comparison groups mean (standard deviation)	Program-comparison (standard error)
Group composition			
Proportion of members who are female	0.79	0.83	−0.04
	(0.17)	(0.17)	(0.04)
Average age of members	41.50	40.00	0.60
	(6.20)	(4.20)	(1.17)
Proportion of members who are over 50 years of age	0.30	0.25	0.05
	(0.23)	(0.15)	(0.04)
Proportion of members with no formal education	0.36	0.32	0.03
	(0.24)	(0.16)	(0.05)
Proportion of members with salaried job	0.16	0.11	0.05
	(0.17)	(0.11)	(0.03)
Fines and debts			
Proportion of members who report receiving a fine in 1997	0.14	0.21	−0.07
	(0.16)	(0.21)	(0.04)
Average amount of fines members owe to the group	10.20	29.00	−18.40
	(26.20)	(60.10)	(10.37)
Proportion of members who report having an outstanding debt to group in 1997	0.36	0.51	−0.14**
	(0.24)	(0.29)	(0.06)
Average amount members owe to the group (Ksh)	184	155	29.30
	(442)	(214)	(77.60)
Attendance rates at meetings			
Attendance rates at all meetings[a]	0.90	0.92	0.02
	(0.12)	(0.12)	(0.03)
Attendance rates at group farmwork meetings	0.88	0.90	0.02
	(0.17)	(0.17)	(0.04)

Notes: *$p \leq 0.1$. **$p \leq 0.05$. ***$p \leq 0.001$.
[a] Based on the records of individual attendance of eight randomly selected members in each group.

Agriculture project outcomes

In spite of receiving more than $700 worth of inputs, program and comparison groups showed no statistically significant difference in the value of harvest per acre.[7] Although exploring these agricultural outcomes is not the subject of this chapter, it is worth noting that some groups reported conflict within the group

[7] In the first planting season, some groups experienced poor germination with some of the government-certified seeds provided by ICS. However, we do not think that this is the primary explanation for the failure of agricultural output to grow in program groups. These seeds were replaced by ICS. Moreover, yields were no higher in program groups than in comparison groups in the subsequent agricultural season, when there were no germination problems.

Table 7.7   *Group self-evaluation of performance*

Dependent Variable	Average proportion of members reporting:				
	Better leadership in 1998 (1)	More effective meetings in 1998 (2)	Group has changed for the worse in 1998 (3)	Group discourages participatory decision making, 1997 (4)	Change in proportion saying decisions NOT made by consensus, 1997–8 (5)
Program group	0.23***	0.14**	−0.07**	−0.02	0.01
	(0.05)	(0.06)	(0.03)	(0.03)	(0.04)
R^2	0.25	0.09	0.09	0.10	0.09
Observations	80	80	80	80	80
Mean of dependent variable for comparison groups	0.60	0.64	0.15	0.08	−0.02

Notes: $^*p \leq 0.1$. $^{**}p \leq 0.05$. $^{***}p \leq 0.001$.
OLS Regressions with robust standard errors in parentheses. Based on individual interviews with group members. OLS estimates weighted by average number of individuals interviewed per group. All regressions include indicator variables for the geographic division in which a group is located.

over the use of program seeds and tools, and there is some evidence that inputs were diverted to individual farms. This may have negatively affected yields on the group plots.

Although agricultural outcomes were poor, members of treatment groups do report more positive subjective evaluations of group performance in terms of leadership and the effectiveness of meetings (table 7.7). Members in program groups are more likely to report that their leadership had improved and that meetings were conducted more effectively (columns (1) and (2)). It seems quite possible, however, that this positive evaluation stems from a desire to report positively to donors, as we see no objective indictors of better group performance.

Funding does not appear to have a significant impact on group finances as measured by group assets (table 7.8). This is surprising given the very high value of inputs supplied to the groups. Project groups have somewhat higher levels of project assets, including animal stock, project inputs, capital, and so forth, but the difference is not significant, even at the 10 percent level (column (1)). There is no sign that these inputs were converted to cash, since group cash assets are no higher in program groups (not reported). This suggests that some implements may have been diverted to individual members, and indeed more than half the

Table 7.8   *Value of group assets in US dollars, 1998*

Dependent variable	Value of project assets at end 1998[a] (1)	Overall group financial position at end 1998[b] (2)
Program groups	76.2	80.9
	(96.0)	(103)
R^2	0.06	0.03
Observations	77	77
Mean of dependent variable in comparison groups	169	243

Notes: $^*p \leq 0.1$. $^{**}p \leq 0.05$. $^{***}p \leq 0.001$.

OLS Regressions with robust standard errors in parentheses. All regressions include indicator variables for the geographic division in which a group is located.

[a] Does not include value of crops still in the ground, though the survey was undertaken after the end of the agricultural season. One program group with exceptionally high assets is excluded from this regression. The results are not significant even when this group is included.

[b] Calculated as total cash assets + credit − oustanding debts to group + value of project assets. One program group with exceptionally high assets is excluded from this regression. The results are not significant even when this group is included.

groups reported a problem with a member or leader misusing funds or reported conflict over the allocation of group resources, though these reported problems are relatively evenly split between program and comparison groups (Gugerty and Kremer 2000).

Data from the agricultural harvest do not indicate that program groups allocated the proceeds from the harvest differently than comparison groups (not reported). Program groups did not report higher sales of agricultural produce than comparison groups in 1998 and were no more likely to distribute the proceeds from agricultural production to members – either in cash or in kind – than comparison groups. Program groups did not purchase more agricultural inputs with harvest proceeds and were no more likely to keep seeds for future use or to store harvest sale money with the group than were comparison groups.

Labor input and participation rates

Groups that received training and agricultural inputs report that members contributed approximately two more days of agricultural labor in 1998 than comparison groups (table 7.9, column (1)). This is a relatively small additional

Table 7.9 *Labor input and participation rates*[a]

	Hours of agricultural labor per member in 1998 (1)	Average number of weekly agriculture meetings[b] (2)	1998 Attendance rates at farmwork meetings (3)	Change in attendance from 1997 to 1998 (4)	1998 Attendance at general meetings (5)	Change in attendance from 1997 to 1998 (6)
Program groups	13.8**	0.45***	−0.09**	−0.07	−0.04	−0.02
	(6.67)	(0.09)	(0.05)	(0.06)	(0.04)	(0.05)
Observations	76	78	79	72	78	77
R^2	0.12	0.26	0.08	0.04	0.08	0.11
Mean of dependent variable in comparison groups	49.30	0.70	0.86	−0.04	0.86	−0.08

Notes: $^*p \leq 0.1$. $^{**}p \leq 0.05$. $^{***}p \leq 0.001$.
OLS Regressions with robust standard errors in parentheses. All regressions include indicator variables for the geographic division in which a group is located.
[a] Group rates are based on group attendance records for six randomly selected individuals for each group. Average attendance for all meetings includes: general group meetings, farmwork, and meetings of the group's rotating savings and credit association (ROSCA).
[b] Calculated for the first half of 1998.

contribution when compared to the value of agricultural inputs these groups received. The inputs received by groups were a complement rather than a substitute for labor: the planting of seeds and the application of fertilizer and pesticides all require higher labor input by members. The evidence suggests that program groups did hold more farmwork meetings than comparison groups in the first half of 1998. On average, program groups held 0.45 more additional meetings per week than comparison groups (column (2)). Attendance rates in program groups for farm work, however, are 9 percent lower than in comparison groups (column (3)), and thus agricultural labor input hours are only slightly higher in program groups.

There is no evidence that members in program groups contributed more time and labor in nonagricultural activities, although it is difficult to ascertain the total time input of members in all nonagricultural activities. Attendance rates at general meetings (where "absenteeism" is defined as missing a meeting without advance notice or permission) are not significantly different in groups that received funding, conditional on a meeting being held (table 7.9, columns (5) and (6)).[8] The point estimate is actually lower. Program groups are no

---

[8] Rates of attendance were ascertained by randomly selecting six members and tracking their attendance at the two most recent meetings.

Table 7.10 *Community interaction*

Dependent Variable	Number of times groups gave assistance to members (1)	Number of contributions to community fundraising event (2)	Number of visits outside by groups/ individuals (3)
Program groups	0.13	−1.85	5.46**
	(0.48)	(1.97)	(2.42)
R^2	0.15	0.05	0.23
Observations	80	80	77
Mean of dependent variable in comparison groups	11.9	4.20	13.40

Notes: $^*p \leq 0.1$. $^{**}p \leq 0.05$. $^{***}p \leq 0.001$.
OLS Regressions with robust standard errors in parentheses. All regressions include indicator variables for the geographic division in which a group is located.

more likely than comparison groups to visit a member's home to give emergency assistance, nor do they meet more frequently for their ROSCA activities (not reported).

There are no other signs that group solidarity was enhanced by program participation. Groups that participated in the program do not give assistance more frequently to members (table 7.10, column (1)) nor do they support members with higher amounts of cash assistance (not reported).

Community interaction

Participation in the women's group program does not appear to strengthen the internal solidarity of program groups relative to comparison groups in any way we could measure. Participation could nonetheless have facilitated the groups' ties to external groups and access to outside resources. However, program groups neither have greater participation in community fundraising events (table 7.10, column (2)), nor do they give higher amounts at such fundraising on average (not reported). We find that program groups do receive more visits from external groups and individuals, including other self-help groups, nonprofit organizations, government officials, and neighbors (table 7.10, column (3)). Program groups received an average of five additional visits as compared to groups that did not receive funding. These visits include technical assistance and advice, field days, and general "inspection" tours. Given that program groups do not receive more non-ICS assistance than comparison groups (not reported), it is unclear whether these visits indicate greater support for groups, or attempts by outsiders to claim credit for, or capture, program group funding.

Table 7.11   *Group composition*

Dependent variable	Change in group size 1997–8 (1)	Number of new entrants (2)	Number leaving the group (3)	Probability of electing new officials in 1998[a] (4)
Program groups	0.47	1.54**	1.23	0.19
	(0.98)	(0.59)	(0.80)	(0.12)
R^2	0.04	0.20	0.04	—
Observations	80	80	80	74
Mean of dependent variable in comparison groups	−1.76	1.70	3.70	0.43

Notes: $^*p \leq 0.1$. $^{**}p \leq 0.05$. $^{***}p \leq 0.001$.
Columns (1)–(3): OLS regression with robust standard errors in parenthesis. Column (4): Probit regressions with robust standard errors in parentheses. All regressions include indicator variables for the geographic division in which a group is located.
[a] Represents the change in probability of holding an election with program participation.

Group composition

Turnover of membership was higher in program groups than in comparison groups (table 7.11). Program groups accepted more new members, and more members left these groups during the project period (columns (2) and (3)), though only the coefficient on new entrants is statistically significant. The evidence suggests that composition of new membership changed with program participation. New members are more likely to be younger, unmarried, and to have a formal sector job (Gugerty and Kremer 2000).

Provision of agricultural inputs and training also appears to increase the likelihood of groups changing leadership relative to comparison groups, though this result is not quite significant at the 10 percent level (table 7.11, column (4)). In 1997, only ten groups held elections for officials; forty-four groups held elections in 1998. Comparison groups were only 5 percent more likely than funded groups to hold an election in 1997 (though the difference is not statistically significant). At the end of the project period in 1998, funded groups were almost 20 percent more likely than comparison groups to hold an election, though again this result is not statistically significant. The composition of leadership also changed in program groups. New leaders in program groups had higher levels of education and were more likely to be men (Gugerty and Kremer 2000). The increasing role of men, more educated women, and women with formal sector employment in program groups suggests that donor assistance may lead to changes in the very characteristics that originally made the groups attractive to donors. It is also consistent with the hypothesis that outside assistance to women's groups spurs rent seeking.

Conclusions

Among the three projects we examine, we find no evidence that donor concern with social capital was linked to measurable social capital outcomes, though the time frame of our evaluation was relatively short and effects may change over the medium or long run. A top-down project distributing a predetermined set of textbooks had similar effects to a participatory project providing grants which school committees could use as they wished. A women's groups project that focused explicitly on building social capital and which included a large element of organizational training did not improve social capital indicators and in fact may have allowed less disadvantaged outsiders to increase their role in the groups at the expense of the women who were the original members.

While projects' effect on social capital is not correlated with training or participatory project design, it is correlated with the form of assistance. The agriculture program provided substantial private benefits to group leaders, such as reimbursement for transport to town for training sessions at relatively generous rates. Agricultural project inputs could be relatively easily diverted to leaders' farms. Thus the form of assistance may have encouraged individuals to invest in rent seeking as much as in genuine service to the group. In contrast, the inputs provided to textbook schools were not easily diverted to private use. Resale of textbooks would involve substantial transaction costs, especially as books are stamped as having been provided by ICS. In the grants program, ICS supplied actual inputs rather than cash, leaving less room for kickbacks or favoritism in construction contracts.

Although individuals may invest more in institutions receiving outside assistance, that investment may take the form either of rent seeking or of productive investment. Project design may influence this choice. Where programs try to impose collective decisionmaking on what is more naturally an individual or household activity, such as agricultural production, they may promote rent seeking as much as social capital. When program inputs are less easily diverted and beneficiary institutions have a clearer collective rationale, program participation may more naturally produce effective programs and social capital.

REFERENCES

Coleman, J., 1988. "Social Capital in the Creation of Human Capital." *American Journal of Sociology.* Supplement 94: 95–120

1990. *Foundations of Social Theory.* Cambridge, MA: Harvard University Press

Colletta, N. and Perkins, G., 1995. "Participation in Education." Environment Department Papers, Participation Series, Paper 1. World Bank, Washington, DC

Glewwe, P., Kremer, M., and Moulin, S., 1999. "Textbooks and Test Scores: Evidence from a Prospective Evaluation in Kenya." Department of Economics, Harvard University, Cambridge, MA

Gugerty, M. K., 2000. "You Can't Save Alone: Testing Theories of Rotating Savings and Credit Associations." Program in Political Economy and Government, Harvard University, Cambridge, MA

Gugerty, M. K. and Miguel, T., 2000. "Community Participation and Social Sanctions in Kenyan Schools" Harvard University Department of Economics, Cambridge, MA

Gugerty, M. K. and Kremer, M., 2000. "Outside Funding of Community Organizations: Benefitting or Displacing the Poor?" National Bureau of Economic Research Working Paper 7896. <www.nber.org>

Heying, C., 1997. "Civic Elites and Corporate Delocalization: An Alternative Explanation for Declining Civic Engagement." *American Behavioral Scientist.* 40(5): 657–668

Minkoff, D., 1997. "Producing Social Capital" *American Behavioral Scientist.* 40(5): 595–605

Narayan, D., with Patel, R., Schafft, K., Rademacher, A., and Koch-Schulte, S., 2000. *Voices of the Poor: Can Anyone Hear Us? Voices from 46 Countries.* Washington, DC: World Bank

Putnam, R., 1993. *Making Democracy Work.* Princeton, NJ: Princeton University Press

Schulman, M. D. and Anderson, C., 1998. "The Dark Side of the Force: A Case Study of Restructuring Social Capital." *Rural Sociology.* 64(3): 351–372

Wood, R., 1997. "Social Capital and Political Culture." *American Behavioral Scientist.* 40(5): 595–605

Woolcock, M., 1998. "Social Capital and Economic Development: Towards a Theoretical Synthesis and Policy Framework." *Theory and Society* 27(2): 151–208

8 Induced social capital and federations of the rural poor in the Andes

Anthony J. Bebbington and Thomas F. Carroll

Poor people's organizations in the Andes embody an important form of structural social capital. As such they constitute a potentially important asset in people's livelihood strategies and may therefore have important roles to play in poverty reduction strategies. However, such organizations vary widely in scale, role, effectiveness, and degree of inclusiveness and exclusiveness. This diversity means that we must be careful before invoking simple conceptions of "social capital in the Andes" and before making generic (and perhaps romantic) assertions about organizations of the rural poor.

Given the diversity of interests of the rural poor, federated forms of organizations that are able to bridge some of these differences are of particular interest. This chapter reports on a study comparing such organizations in the Andes of Bolivia, Ecuador, and Peru. It presents findings on the different dimensions of social capital embodied in these organizations, the impacts that this social capital may have on local development, and the forms of external intervention through which it might be built.

The importance of organizations of the poor

National governments and multilateral organizations have only recently begun to recognize what nongovernmental organizations (NGOs) have long accepted as an article of faith – that organizations of the poor may have an important role to play in development and that empowerment is an important poverty reduction goal in its own right.[1] The social capital debate has been one of the more important vehicles through which this case has been made in these spheres,

The authors express their appreciation for the support provided by the Social Capital Initiative at the World Bank, and by the Pacific Basin Research Center at the John F. Kennedy School of Government, Harvard University. They also thank Alvaro Cobo, Mary Garcia Bravo, Leonith Hinojosa, Luciano Martínez, Diego Muñoz, Tom Perreault, Galo Ramón, and Victor Hugo Torres for conducting and commenting on this research; Sandy Davis, who task-managed the project from within the World Bank; and Jim Robb, who provided the map.

[1] A World Bank report (1999) identifies empowerment as one of four key poverty reduction outcomes (the others are economic opportunity, capabilities, and security). The importance of empowerment also permeates the *World Development Report 2000–2001*.

because it has suggested the importance of social relationships and organizations in influencing patterns of economic and social change and determining the quality of development, as experienced by poor people.

This emerging interest in poor people's organizations generates a series of important questions: Which types of organization might be best able to contribute to the quality of life and well being of poor people? Do different organizations of the poor make different types of contributions for different people? Do some organizations benefit their members while excluding nonmembers? Which organizations might be most socially inclusive and effective in addressing poverty and marginalization? Assuming that important organizations can be identified, how can their capacity be assessed and strengthened where it exists or induced where it does not?

This chapter attempts to answer some of these questions. It argues that one particularly important type of organization is the supracommunal, or second-order, federation, which links community-based groups around shared economic, political, and cultural interests. These federations are important because they are closer to the grassroots than, say, national confederations and are better able to be participatory and accountable. They have a potentially critical role to play in shifting the relationships between poor people, states, markets, and more powerful interests in society. Functioning at a level between community organizations and distant national social movements, such federations have the potential to transcend the limits of very localized forms of base organization and to foster more regional and strategic forms of collective economic, political, and sociocultural action. However, to be effective in this regard they need to be grounded in – and build on – particular types of social relationships.

External intervention can play an important role in the emergence and effectiveness of such federations. Put another way, this form of social capital can be *constructed* (cf. Bebbington 1997; Grootaert and Narayan 2001). Indeed, the federations reviewed in this chapter owe their origins and current form to some degree of external support. Their effectiveness in building bridges across their member groups and to external actors varies considerably, as does their contribution to local development. So while intervention can construct social capital, its effectiveness in doing so varies greatly according to the style of intervention, prior conditions, and the wider policy environment.

In this chapter, social capital is understood in structural rather than cognitive terms.[2] Federations are understood as embodying a particular type of structural social capital – a set of social relationships that facilitates access and collective action of different forms. We argue that a structural conception of social capital facilitates attempts to link the concept with development practice (see Evans 1996).

---

[2] See chapter 3 in this volume for a further discussion of structural and cognitive social capital.

Following a brief definition of second-order organizations, we discuss the different forms of structural social capital that exist among the rural poor of the Andes. These different forms play important roles for their members, but they also pose the problem of how to mediate across differences and foster more regional forms of collective action that might address more generally shared interests and allow more coordinated relationships with external actors.[3] In the following section we present a brief case study from an Ecuadorian municipality. That example illustrates the types of change that can occur when such regional forms of collective action do emerge and identifies the types of intervention that facilitate the process. We then suggest a methodological framework that might be used to discuss and differentiate among forms of social capital in a more analytical and quantitative fashion. That methodology is applied in the following sections, which present some results on the capacity of the organizations studied and assess the extent to and ways in which these organizations were induced by external action. The last section draws some implications for theory and practice.

Defining second-order organizations

Sociologically, second-order organizations are social systems that have the capability to combine strong intragroup ties with weak extragroup networks in a way that can develop positive synergies between the two types of ties (Woolcock 1998). While smaller-scale interest groups may help resolve local collective action problems, they do not address regional issues that might affect many localities – for instance the emergence of new product markets; the installation of large-scale, lumpy infrastructure, such as irrigation canals; the creation of new organizations, such as financial or marketing services; and policy changes affecting regional development. For such regional interests to be represented – and for patterns of regional governance and political economy to be changed in any significant way – more inclusive and regional forms of collective action are necessary (Fox 1996; Foley and Edwards 1997, 1999). Similarly, for a more regional vision of development to be articulated, it is necessary to build structures that go beyond narrow interest group specificities and that are able to nurture the identification of, and then act on, more broadly shared concerns. Federations, which link a range of community-based groups, potentially constitute one such mechanism.

The label "second-order organizations" thus refers to organizations with a particular structural characteristic – namely, organizations that unite several base groups at a supracommunity level. This definition of second-order

---

[3] Coordinated responses are important because all too often (sometimes unwittingly in the name of efficiency and ease) external actors have controlled local populations through a strategy of divide and rule.

organizations leaves great room for variation in form, function, and orientation. Here we offer a relatively simple classification. Andean second-order organizations (or OSGs)[4] can be understood as existing along a broad continuum. At one extreme are more political organizations, concerned primarily with lobbying and mobilizing to protect and promote the concerns of their members. These concerns may be related to ethnic identity, access to land, human rights, or other issues. At the other extreme are more economic and developmentalist organizations, concerned with fostering and implementing local livelihood initiatives. They may engage in: social enterprise-type activities (marketing, credit provision); joint implementation of development projects; or facilitation of service delivery by other actors. Whatever the strategy (and organizations often use several at once), these organizations are characterized by a more pragmatic, less confrontational stance.

Organizations may start at any point along this continuum, and they may mix roles (social enterprise organizations, for example, may lobby for better commodity prices). Over time, however, there appears to be a tendency for organizations to move toward the more developmentalist and productive roles as a result of pressure from members to make more tangible contributions to local development.[5] In the cases we study, most of the second-order organizations have, or are in the process of moving toward, a more developmentalist orientation, although some still maintain some radical discourse and exert pressure for basic services.

Social difference, social capital, and organizations of the poor in the Andes

It is important to distinguish between two types of relationships embodying social capital: *bonding* and *bridging* relationships. Bonding relationships strengthen links between people, facilitating forms of intragroup interaction and collective action. Bridging mechanisms strengthen links between groups and other actors and organizations (see Bebbington 1997, Woolcock 1998, and Narayan 1999; the distinction between bonding and bridging social capital is explored further in chapter 9). In some sense the distinction is more apparent than real: both types of relationships are about bridging differences. Indeed, a successful bridging relationship can ultimately break down more pronounced distinctions and so become a bonding relationship.

---

[4] OSG is the acronym for Organizaciones de Segundo Grado, the translation of 'second-order organizations'.

[5] This shift also reflects an important process observed among the case study organizations – namely, that over time they assume more and more functions, not necessarily performing them well. As a result, all organizations take on some sort of service-provision and – to a lesser extent – enterprise and natural resource management roles.

These definitional quibbles notwithstanding, the distinction between bonding and bridging is helpful for thinking about the potential importance of peasant federations as well as the challenges confronting them. On the one hand, these federations exist within a wider universe of more interest-specific organizations. Some of these organizations include some poor people and exclude others; others include both poor and not-so-poor people. These organizations can thus not be thought of as simply "organizations of the poor." On the other hand, these organizations exist within a political economic context in which peasant (especially indigenous) populations have been disadvantaged or largely ignored by government and market actors. They therefore need to be effective in building both bonds among different local groups and bridges with external actors. In this section we focus primarily on the challenge of building bonds among rural people in the Andes, largely in order to highlight the need for care in using the term "organizations of the poor."

Challenges of internal bonding

Categories such as "indigenous," "peasant," and "poor," though commonly used, hide a great deal of the diversity that exists within rural populations in the Andes. This diversity exists along many axes – kinship, ethnicity, class, gender, generation, and resource control, to name but a few. Federations reflect an effort to bridge across some of these differences in order to facilitate forms of collective action that would otherwise be impossible. They never succeed in bridging all these differences, however, or in turning every difficult relationship among organized subgroups into a more harmonious one. In this sense, federations must be seen as organizations that represent just some of the rural poor. This is not to wrest legitimacy from them; it is to suggest that care be used before talking generically of organizations of the rural poor.

Kinship.   Andean ethnography has long emphasized the importance of kin-based networks in resolving problems of resource access and collective action. These networks may involve labor mobilization; others exist as informal and formal governance structures. For instance the *ayllu*, a kin-based group, regulates access to and use of natural resources and mediates intracommunity and intercommunity conflicts. Other kin-based networks are far less visible and less formal but still play important roles in families' and individuals' attempts to access land, water, seed, or institutional resources.

Just as kinship can bind tightly, it can also exclude. In certain parts of the Bolivian Andes, for instance, *ayllus* have come into conflict with one another over efforts to gain exclusive use of land and water resources. Kinship can also complicate efforts to operationalize formal rules and sanctions within poor people's organizations. In several of our case studies, the formal leadership of federations were wary of applying sanctions because to do so would have contravened the kin-based solidarities linking the individuals involved. Though quite understandable, such behavior can easily be perceived as favoritism and corruption.

Thus while the formal structure of Andean organizations is one of legally recognized communities, cooperatives, associations, and other divisions, cutting across these divisions are networks of nonformalized social capital based on kin-based solidarities. These solidarities may be forms of power – mechanisms through which individuals and groups gain access to positions of authority and privilege (including in second-order organizations).

Ethnicity and class.   Another source of tension among organizations can be the organization's identity as an ethnic or a class-based organization. Some of the earliest efforts to reach out into the countryside and foster organizations were, for instance, initiatives of an emerging communist and socialist left, linked to particular parties and to particular groups of workers, such as miners in Bolivia. In Bolivia in the 1950s and Peru in the early 1970s, "revolutionary" governments likewise tried to reach out to these organizations. As a result, new forms of rural organization were often laid on top of existing ones (*sindicatos* laid atop *ayllus* in Bolivia, cooperatives laid atop *comunidades* in Peru). Because of the link to broader institutions (the state, parties), new confederated forms of organization also emerged at the national level (examples include the Federaciones Departamentales de Sindicatos in Bolivia and the Federación Nacional de Organizaciones Campesinas [FENOC] in Ecuador).[6] These organizations were based on more syndicalist notions of organization and cast the peasantry as a class.

Many have argued that class-based concerns differed in important ways from ethnic claims, and indeed in the past twenty–thirty years, there have been efforts to develop organizations around notions of both class and ethnic identity. As a result, both subnationally and nationally, different organizations exist side by side, with differing claims, languages, procedures, and emphases. This multiplicity of organizations has at times been a source of tension, and it has affected interventions. For instance, national confederations with differing orientations have jockeyed to gain greater control of the resources and management of the Indigenous Peoples Development Project (PRODEPINE) in Ecuador. The disputes have been accentuated by the fact that the different organizations are grounded in different networks and different cadres of leadership, so that debates and differences as often reflect struggles for prominence as they do differences of opinion over the forms that development should take. While these differences

---

[6] FENOC is now called FENOCIN (the Federación Nacional de Organizaciones Campesinas Indígenas y Negras).

are often more pronounced at the supracommunity level (where struggles for power are more pronounced), they are also apparent at the community level in some areas. For example, tensions between *sindicatos* and *ayllus* exist over which group represents the more legitimate grassroots indigenous organization in Northern Potosí, Bolivia (Rivera-Cusicanqui 1992).

Gender and generation.   While notions of gender have been criticized by some as Westernized concerns imposed on Andean views of the world, gender nonetheless constitutes an important axis of difference in the Andes, influencing access to resources and decisionmaking processes (Deere and Léon 1987). Indeed, many Andean organizations have traditionally been dominated by men, and they tend to promote men's concerns and access to resources. It cannot be assumed that these organizations represent poor rural women.

Generation is another dimension of difference in the countryside, primarily because younger people encounter far greater difficulty than do older people in gaining access to some of the resources necessary to build a rural livelihood. Indeed, rates of out-migration are far higher among younger generations. To the extent that organizations prioritize productive and claim-making advocacy activities linked to agriculture and rurally based livelihoods, they can fail to represent adequately the concerns of younger generations. This exclusion can have several effects. In some cases it can mean that younger people gravitate toward certain types of organizations in which they might have more authority. (In Northern Potosí, for example, the tension between *ayllus* and *sindicatos* is also in some measure a tension between generations.) In other cases it can simply mean limited interest and participation by younger people in these organizations.

In several areas studied (such as Cotocachi and Guamote in Ecuador) one of the most important activities for younger adults is sports. Young migrants return home periodically for sports tournaments, forming organizations around soccer, for instance. Some federations, such as the Unión de Organizaciones Campesinas de Cotaca (UNORCAC), in Cotocachi, have thus decided to make sports activities explicit concerns of their organization as a means of sustaining the interest of young people in both the organization and in local development more generally.

Resource control.   Differential patterns of access to and use of natural resources also lead to divergent interests. The resulting differences in cropping systems and options leads to differences in the types of livelihood support that families prioritize. As patterns of resource access generally vary across space, these differences can translate into geographic tensions within federations: different sectors have different priorities, and the links among communities within a sector may often be far stronger than those in other sectors, even if they exist within the same federation. In other cases, different groups (at times belonging to the same federation) struggle for access to and use of the same resource. Where communities span a number of cropping systems within a single organization, or where there are conflicts among and within communities within the same federation, the challenge of elaborating inclusive proposals is thus all the greater.

Challenges of external bridging

Even second-order organizations whose exclusive purpose is to foster collective action for internal purposes (such as the management of an irrigation canal) must at certain moments build external relationships. The most common of these is a relationship with a donor agency that supports the federation with finance, technical cooperation, or materials. Indeed, the difficulty that second-order organizations have mobilizing financial resources internally means that these types of external links are essential. Although these relationships provide support, they are also some of the most difficult because they involve dependency, which external actors can use to influence and manipulate the organizations. Being able to manage and cope with this manipulation requires leadership capacities and the possibility of switching to other sources of support should the organization chose to terminate the relationship.

A second type of link – developed most often by more representative, lobbying-type organizations – is with institutions and interinstitutional forums through which organizations can pursue their concerns. One of the principal challenges that second-order organizations face is to gain the legitimacy they need in order to have access to these institutions. In Ecuador and Bolivia (far less in Peru) a series of policy reforms have increased the ease with which organizations can gain such access to decisionmaking and planning processes. In Ecuador these reforms derive from the strength of the indigenous movement and so reflect the cumulative effect of support to organizations in that country. In Bolivia the reforms were initiated by government.

A third type of bridge involves working with another actor to "co-produce" an activity. We found many examples of this kind of bridging in the cases we studied. Indeed, many more activities are co-produced than performed by single organizations, and the cases show partnerships with a range of governmental and nongovernmental institutions (and also with some organizations from the fair trade sector). Examples include the following:

- The joint provision of preschool centers by UNORCAC and the central government in Ecuador.
- The joint provision of market outlets and housing materials in Ecuador by the Unión de Organizaciones de la Parroquia de Ayora y Cayambe (UNOPAC), NGOs, and the local church.

- The joint provision of coffee processing services by Corporación Agropecuaria Campesina (CORACA-Irupana) and an NGO in the Bolivian Yungas.
- The joint provision of coffee-processing services by the Central de Co-operativas Agrarias de La Convención y Lares (COCLA) and a United Nations-supported project in the Peruvian Yungas.

The nature of these co-production relationships is not static. In some cases (UNOPAC, for instance), the organization has assumed progressively more responsibility for the activity over time. In other cases, responsibility has not increased, suggesting that internal capacities have not been adequate (or that the external actor has been unwilling to transfer control).

Dimensions of social capital within federations

In the light of these observations, we can identify five types of relationship that represent variants of structural social capital within federations (box 8.1). All of these relationships need to exist if the organization is to be effective in fostering local development, increasing inclusion and fostering changes in patterns and processes of governance.

Box 8.1   Dimensions of social capital within a second-order organization

Social capital within second-order organizations can be thought of along five dimensions: local and kin-based networks, intercommunity linkages, external linkages, municipal and regional linkages, and linkages with support agencies.

Local and kin-based networks

In the Andes, traditional communities, while always embodying both vertical and horizontal networks, tend to have strong bonds of mutual help, based on kinship, symbolic patronage (*compadrazgo*), and spatial propinquity. These bonds facilitate collective action and problem-solving, as well as ritual and other social activities. Promoting these bonds may not lead to higher-level cooperation, but once a second-order organization is established, it can draw strength from this collective experience and representation of constituent grassroots groups.

Intercommunity linkages

Intercommunity networks are usually project groups within a second-order organization in which members from various and more heterogeneous communities participate. Typical and important examples include *juntas de agua*, or irrigation associations, along canals that cross several community boundaries. The rules underlying the degree of trust and cooperation necessary for the functioning of such groups are much more rigorous and difficult to establish than at the community level.

A second-order organization is itself a system of regional or multi-communal cooperation. To make such a system work, many factional interests as well as clientelistic vertical networks have to be overcome or harmonized. In the more traditional second-order organizations, this has often been accomplished by stressing ethnic identity and culturally cohesive activities and rituals. In more modern organizations, it is achieved by identifying strong common economic and service interests (such as access to capital, markets and technology).

Linkages to higher-level indigenous organizations

The main challenge in establishing linkages with indigenous organizations at regional and national levels is to build relationships through which these higher organizations can effectively represent, respond to, and be accountable to the second-order organization. These relationships are more hierarchical than internal linkages. They are important, though, for fostering more significant forms of political participation and advocacy.

Municipal and regional linkages

While federations have developed links to other local organizations for some time, more territorially based sets of relations with state, civil society, and market actors are a relatively recent phenomenon. These relationships reflect national policy shifts in which increasingly the municipality is becoming the foundational unit for development planning, and in which power and resources have gradually been shifted to this level. The primary challenge in establishing these links is to build synergies for the local co-production of development.

Inter-institutional linkages with support agencies

These tend to consist of more dependent relationships with donors and other external agencies that channel support to OSGs. The primary purpose of these relationships is thus to gain access to resources, though in some cases the purpose is also to gain access to markets and decisionmaking fora.

Some of these dimensions of structural social capital refer to internal relations within the federation. These include the quality of the relationships between the federation and its member organizations (indeed, one of the greatest challenges is to develop responsive and transparent relationships with these constituent groups).

Other relationships are more external, bridging with different actors, and allowing access to institutional resources, decisionmaking forums, or the umbrella services and support of higher-level representative indigenous organizations. These external linkages tend to be with NGOs and reform-minded bureaucrats, but they are increasingly being formed with decentralized municipal and provincial government units.

If federations embody a form of social capital in each of these different dimensions, assessing their capacity must include indicators for each of these dimensions. However, federations' capacity to perform their functions depends not only on these relationships but also on other assets, such as financial capital, produced capital (such as infrastructure), human capital, management systems, and even cultural capital (the extent to which their practices resonate with the cultural practices of their members). Put another way, assessment of the significance of the social capital constituted by these organizations must also include an assessment of the other resources that those relationships harness and mobilize.

We address this challenge of measurement below. First, though, we discuss a short case study from the canton of Guamote in Ecuador that suggests the types of change in patterns of local development and governance that *can* occur when local organizations are able to develop linkages along these five different dimensions.

Peasant federations and local development in Guamote[7]

Guamote is one of the poorest *cantones* (cantons) of highland Ecuador, with a population of some 28,000, 90 percent of whom are rural and indigenous Quichua. The canton was one of Ecuador's last bastions of the traditional hacienda – large rural estates characterized by a system of tied Quichua labor, technical backwardness, and abusive labor relationships between owners/managers and the local Quichua population. In 1954 just nine haciendas owned more than 61 percent of the land in Guamote; even as late as 1974, 87 percent of the land was owned by landowners owning at least 20 hectares. Organizationally and politically, Guamote was dominated by the hacienda, which controlled both the local population and the local state (Casagrande and Piper 1969; Sylva 1986). Indeed, there were very few independent indigenous communities until the 1960s and 1970s. For many households the most important relationship for survival was the vertical link to the hacienda, rather than horizontal ties among families.

[7] For a detailed description of this case study, see Bebbington and Perreault (1999).

In a period of four decades, this situation has changed remarkably. Today no large haciendas remain, the local state is in Quichua hands, land use has intensified, and much of the previous pasture land has been turned to agricultural use. A far wider group of people now has rights of access to natural capital and education (human capital formation). One of the critical factors in this transformation has been the steady formation of social capital in the form of new civil society organizations.[8] The past forty years in this region have witnessed what is in a sense a three-layered process of social capital formation. The earliest and "lowest" layer of this process was the creation and consolidation of community-level organizations. The subsequent middle layer involved the emergence and consolidation of federations of these community organizations. Both processes contributed to, and were reinforced by, a third type of change: the emergence and consolidation of larger-scale movements of indigenous people in Ecuador that together have national reach and significance.

These processes have meant a steady knitting together of networks linking families, communities, and localities and the establishment of links to other actors in the state, the market, and civil society. In the process, the dominant vertical patronage relations of the hacienda and the land use system associated with them have been replaced by more horizontal sets of relationships and new land use systems. This has allowed the Quichuas of Guamote to renegotiate relationships of resource control, market participation, and political power in different and largely complementary ways, reshaping the ways in which people manage resources and make a living, and changing the nature of sociopolitical relationships in the region.

By the 1960s the dominance of the hacienda as the principal institution of highland rural Ecuador was increasingly challenged, both nationally and locally. As a result of labor withdrawal, land occupations, and other forms of peasant resistance, some haciendas in Guamote began to sell their land to Quichuas. Land reform legislation was passed in 1964 and 1973, and Guamote was identified as a priority area because of the coordinated indigenous mobilization there. Communities had to be formally constituted entities in order to benefit from land reform law, and also to gain access to subsequent development projects. Language and negotiating skills were also required to gain access to institutions. Such community formation and legalization was facilitated by the church in Guamote and especially by state programs, which had worked in the area since the 1970s. Likewise, both the church and a team of committed reformists in the provincial government launched highly successful programs of bilingual education in the province. Many of the contemporary leaders of indigenous

---

[8] Conducting research over the past ten years in Guamote has allowed us to reconstruct, and in part witness, the processes through which this social capital has been built and transformed in the form of rural people's organizations. It has also allowed us to monitor the extent to which this process has had direct and indirect impacts on livelihoods, resource use, and the political landscape.

organizations in the province were trained in these programs (Bebbington *et al.*, 1992). Together these processes helped build organizational and human capacity to link communities to the state, which in turn allowed expanded community access to resources and development services.

The mid-to-late 1970s saw the beginning of a new process of social capital formation – the knitting together of organizations and networks that began to link communities and establish ties with other actors. These federations have assumed various roles: negotiating for resources and development investment in the region, co-managing the implementation of development programs, mobilizing to protest on political and administrative issues, and increasing the capacity, albeit imperfectly, of rural communities to engage in regional and national political economic processes. These federations owe their emergence and consolidation to a process in which both external interventions and community-based processes have played a role. Two of the principal federations in the canton have been Organización Jatun Ayllu de Guamote and the Unión de Organizaciones Campesinas Indígenas de Guamote. Their activities and impacts demonstrate some of the ways in which the emergence of such organizations can change patterns of local development and governance.

Jatun Ayllu

Jatun Ayllu traces its origins directly to the work of Guamote's Catholic Church. In many ways created by the church, this federation has gradually become more independent over the course of two decades. The organization grew out of the church's social justice and leadership training programs for community-level catechists, later assuming related activities. It first managed a rural development program funded by the state (and negotiated by the church). Later it began managing a credit program funded by an NGO (the Fondo Ecuatoriano Populorum Progressio [FEPP]) and developed links with provincial-level indigenous organizations. In each case, the church played an important role in facilitating these relationships, but Jatun Ayllu began to link communities with brokers who in turn had links with external resources.

Until the early 1990s, the federation's principal impact on livelihoods was through a church-led program fostering community access to land. Other credit and service projects had more modest impacts, but they enabled the organization to broaden its membership base and they laid the ground for a later, credit-based land purchasing program. Following national indigenous mobilizations in 1990 which brought parts of the Ecuadorian highlands to a standstill, the church responded with a debt buyback program that funded a credit line that allowed indigenous communities to purchase land from larger farms and haciendas. This program was managed at the national level by FEPP; as links were already established with Jatun Ayllu, the two organizations agreed to work together in the land purchase program for Guamote. Jatun Ayllu identified communities with needs and possibilities for land purchases; FEPP dealt with the technical and financial aspects of the purchases. This expanded the federation's member base and its political significance within the canton. It also widened community access to land and dealt the final blow to all remaining haciendas there. Through its links with the local church and FEPP, Jatun Ayllu has thus played a significant role in changing resource access for many communities and households in Guamote.

Unión de Organizaciones Campesinas Indígenas de Guamote

The Unión de Organizaciones Campesinas Indígenas de Guamote (UOCIG), was created in 1989 under the influence of a national government rural development program (the Programa de Desarrollo Rural Integrado [DRI]). The DRI had been unable to establish links with Jatun Ayllu because of differences of opinion with the priest who worked closely with the federation. In 1989 the DRI proposed the creation of UOCIG, to serve as an interface between the project and the sectors of Guamote in which it concentrated its work (sectors in which Jatun Ayllu was largely absent).

Despite its initial links to the DRI, UOCIG almost immediately assumed some autonomy, in part because the DRI's resources were already declining. Its more developmentalist outlook (deriving from its origins in the DRI) facilitated its access to resources dedicated to the technical dimensions of development. As a result, by 1990 UOCIG was implementing an agricultural program funded by a large Ecuadorian NGO, whose access to UOCIG was facilitated by the DRI. The NGO's own links and wider dissemination of its positive experience with UOCIG subsequently facilitated the federation's access to financial resources from other sources. Like Jatun Ayllu, UOCIG developed a network of relationships strongly influenced by those of the external actors present at the federation's origins.

Impact of federations in Guamote

The emergence of horizontal networks linking communities – networks formalized in the federations – has shifted the way external actors view Guamote, leading them to coordinate development activities with one or other of the federations. At the same time, the political mobilization embodied in the federations, coupled with the shifts in landholding that have accompanied this mobilization, have together led to a profound shift in the power relationships that determine how Guamote is governed. Thus, an indigenous mayor and town council were elected in Guamote for the first time in 1992 and again in 1996; by 1998, six of its seven town councilors were indigenous. The federations have played an important role in these changes. Members of the leadership of both Jatun Ayllu and UOCIG serve as elected councilors in the municipality, and one federation officer became the first indigenous councilor in the provincial government of Chimborazo. In 1992 a UOCIG official ran successfully for mayor, continuing to serve as Secretary of UOCIG. In 1996 his re-election was supported by Jatun Ayllu and his vice-mayor was also a former Jatun Ayllu official.

These changes have radically altered the political landscape and the nature of development in the canton. They have blurred the distinction between local state and organized civil society, as federation leaders breeze comfortably in and out of municipal offices. The changes have also meant that the municipal government has assumed a more active role in development projects in the canton, particularly in rural areas in which the municipality traditionally had no real presence. External development actors increasingly engage with the municipality, which coordinates with the two federations.

As long as the municipal government retains its rural community bias and political base, in time the federations may become the implementing arm of the municipal government, widening the reach of its programs. Indeed, the municipality has created a formal committee to coordinate relationships with all the federations in the county. As part of this effort, federations will take charge of municipality-wide afforestation and community investment programs that the municipal government has negotiated.

While the two federations have had many impacts on local development and governance, the longer-term organizational sustainability of these processes is nonetheless in doubt. The strength of the organizations waxes and wanes with the resources they handle: the wider the networks of the organizations, the greater their strength, as the likelihood of them accessing resources grows. But as long as these resources come as grants, the federations do not escape the problem of low member contributions. Indeed, their community-level support rises and falls with the external resources available. Furthermore, the justification for funding these federations is weakened if the local state is now far more responsive to (and to a degree controlled by) the local indigenous population.

Such caveats notwithstanding, it remains the case that Jatun Ayllu and UOCIG have helped resolve certain collective action problems in Guamote, and have enhanced the capacity of indigenous people to deal with state, market, and other actors in civil society as a means of accessing resources and local political power. This combined process of forming organizations and networks has clearly changed social relations and development processes, and it has influenced how, and by whom, different resources are used.

These changes have without doubt been a result of the cumulative impact of external interventions by NGOs, the Church, and the state. In addition to injecting technology, training and money into the region, these interventions have also helped build up networks, relationships, and organizations, at times deliberately, at times inadvertently. Also critical has been the human capital formation that has occurred as a result of both bilingual education programs and the involvement of young adult leaders in emerging indigenous organizations and development projects. The strengthening of organizations and networks has meant that this human capital has to some extent been held socially accountable. This expansion of human and social capital has widened household and community access to resources through the mechanisms of the federations, their networks, and most recently the local state.

Finally it must be reiterated that the impacts of these activities has been further enhanced, and in some cases made possible, by the parallel processes of social capital formation occurring elsewhere and at broader geographical scales in Ecuador. These activities coalesced into the creation of indigenous people's organizations and networks with national reach, changing the national political landscape in myriad ways that enhanced opportunities for indigenous organizations and families in Guamote. At the same time, these national political changes were made possible by a range of local organizing experiences, similar to those in Guamote, occurring in many other parts of the country.[9] Thus, to explain the steady thickening of civil society in Guamote we need to understand how sociopolitical and development processes interrelate among regions, changing the wider national policy and institutional context.

Measuring structural social capital in peasant federations

Guamote's experience illustrates the impact that federations can have on local development and governance. The case is largely descriptive, however. More specific measures of the different dimensions of social capital and organizational capacity in federations are needed if notions of organizational capacity are to be acted on more strategically – both by the organizations themselves and by those interested in understanding and supporting their role in local social transformation.

With this measurement challenge in mind, the research for this chapter aimed to assess two things: (i) the capacities of OSGs in terms of different dimensions of social capital and the other assets available to the organization; and (ii) the relationship between capacity and forms of external support to the OSG. The method used was intensive case study analysis. We completed six case studies in Ecuador, two in Peru, and two in Bolivia (table 8.1 and map 8.1). We

---

[9] Carroll (1998) analyses the well-coordinated national indigenous protests that occurred between 1990 and 1995, which for the first time called wide attention to the capacity and power of the "nested" federation system. In Guamote, UOCIG helped catalyze the national uprising in 1990 and soon after used its leverage to occupy the old Ministry of Agriculture office as its own headquarters.

Table 8.1 *Cases studies*

Organization	Date founded	Initial stimulus	Number of base groups	Sources of support	Function	Orientation
Bolivian cases						
Asociación de Productores Lecheros de la Provincia Aroma (ASPROLPA)	1992	Government dairy development program	36	State	Enterprise and services	Developmentalist
Corporación Agropecuaria Campesina-Irupana (CORACA)	1984	Economic programs	85	Peasant federation/NGO	Enterprise and claim-making	Radical ≫ developmentalist
Ecuadorian cases						
Organización Jatun Ayllu de Guamote (OJAG)	1975	Church social program/land	42	Church	Claim-making and services	Radical ≫ developmentalist
Tucuy Cañar Ayllucunapac Tantanacuy (Tucayta)	1984	Water project	19	Peasant federation	Natural resource managing (water)	Developmentalist
UCCOPEM	1984	Cultural/mediate intercommunal conflicts	About 30	NGOs	Claim-making and services	Radical ≫ developmentalist

Organization	Year	Activity	No.	Institutional base	Function	Orientation
Unión de Organizaciones de la Parroquía de Ayora, Cayambe (UNOPAC)	1989	Earthquake response	17	Church	Enterprise and services	Developmentalist
Unión de Organizaciones Campesinas de Cotocachi (UNORCAC)	1977	Cultural defense	45	Peasant federation and cultural group	Claim-making and services	Radical >> developmentalist
Unión de Organizaciones Campesinas Indígenas de Guamote (UOCIG)	1989	State IRDP	13	State	Service accessing and resource accessing	Developmentalist
Peruvian cases						
Central de Co-operativas Agrarias de La Convención y Lares (COCLA)	1967	Market coffee	7	Campesino federation/public programs	Enterprise	Developmentalist
Sociedad Agrícola de Interés Social Marangani (SAIS)	1973	Receive and manage land and land reform enterprise	11		Enterprise	Developmentalist

Country	Towns/Cities	Indigenous Organization
Peru	Ilave	Multi-Comunal Ilave
	Juli	Multi-Comunal Juli
	La Convencion	COCLA
	Sicuani	SAIS Marangani
Bolivia	Irupana	CORACA-Irupana
	Aroma	ASPROLPA
Ecuador	Juan Montalvo/	
	Cayambe	UNOPAC; UCCOPEM
	Guamote	Jatun Ayllu; UOCIG
	Cotocachi	UNORCAC
	Canar	Tucayta

Map 8.1   Federations in Ecuador.

intentionally worked with less well-known groups rather than some of the highly successful federations in order that our conclusions be more representative – and because the very successful federations have already been subjected to various studies (including several by ourselves). In addition, two larger surveys were conducted in collaboration with other organizations. Originally we had also been encouraged to find pairs of organizations, one strong and one weak, in the same locality – with a view to making controlled comparisons of federations operating in the same small-scale region. This effort to control for regional agroecological and political economic effects was not possible, however, for two reasons. First, it was difficult to find comparators within the same locality, and second, simple notions of strength and weakness were not easy to operationalize *ex ante*. While for purposes of *ex post* analysis we have compared organizations, these comparisons do not hold all other conditions constant.

The study aimed to derive scoreable indicators of the different forms of social relations (and other assets) that constitute organizational capacity. The intellectual origins of such an approach go back to the longstanding concerns of Norman Uphoff and the local organizations group at Cornell University to develop measurements that reflect the capabilities of membership organizations (Uphoff 1991, 1997). In one effort, for instance, Uphoff developed a set of 87 indicators, which he grouped into nine categories: decisionmaking, resource mobilization and management, communication and coordination, effectiveness, conflict management, accountability, sustainability, linkages, and problem-solving. Other researchers have created similar measurement tools to assess the strength of membership organizations, but there are few reports on how these methods have worked in practice.

Another interesting precursor has been the attempt by the Inter-American Foundation (IAF) to measure the organizational development of its grantees. The eight organizational variables constructed by the IAF are similar to the Cornell categories (Ritchey-Vance 1998). The indicators are largely proxies for patterns of organized collective action and interaction (c.f. Ostrom 1990). The variables can be used to measure the process itself (e.g. the degree of rule compliance or sanctions) or the outcome of the process (e.g. the degree of sustainability as a result of member contributions). This is consistent with the duality that social capital represents in a membership organization: organizational capacity is the institutional source of social capital accumulation, but it is also the institutional embodiment (at any given time) of the social capital that has already been accumulated by the membership.

One of the purposes of our study was to experiment with different instruments to further develop such measures of organizational capacity. Originally, using both inductive and deductive reasoning, we compiled a list of fifty-five indicators, which we divided into eight categories. We piloted these measures in the first two case studies in Peru. Scoring was based on a four-point scale, with scores established by the field team. We also tested the measures in the context of two programs in Ecuador, the National Rural Development Program (PRONADER) and the Indigenous Peoples Development Project (PRODEPINE) (van Nieuwkoop and Uquillas 1999). For PRONADER we used fewer indicators and a method in which federation members themselves generated scores against the indicators. In PRODEPINE, on the other hand, the project's technical staff developed measures based on twenty of our original indicators (some in adapted form). These indicators were grouped into five clusters of variables for a nation-wide rapid survey of the 155 second-level peasant (*campesino*) federations and eleven Amazonian third-level federations.[10] These indicators were of an objective numerical nature that could be obtained from federation records supplemented by short interviews with a few leaders. These indicators were measured on a 100-point scale (Ramón 1999).

[10] In essence these variables were proxies for human capital, financial capital, social capital, and administrative capacity (Ramón 1999).

These experiments and further field testing ultimately led to the decision to use three separate instruments.[11] The first, administered to five federation staff and leaders per federation, primarily assesses the quality of the federation's social relationships and certain types of assets (such as financial and human resources). The second, administered to five people per community in five communities served by each federation, assesses the quality of the federation's community relationships and community perceptions of the federation's effectiveness. The third is a data sheet for basic quantitative information obtainable from federation organization records and other documents.

Together these instruments gave us 124 separate indicators, which we grouped into forty-four variables. Half of the indicators were objective and half subjective. About 12 percent of the indicators were scored by the researcher, with the rest constructed from the interviews. The variables were clustered into seven dimensions of capacity: leadership, participation, organizational culture, resource mobilization and use, sustainability, intermediation and negotiation, and linkages/alliances.

The capacities and limits of federations

Not surprisingly, our results suggest wide variation in the capacities of second-order organizations in the Andes. Much of this variation is related to the quality of the social relationships within the organization and with those linking it to external actors. These in turn appear to be related to the context within which the federations operate. Within this variation, several patterns are apparent, each of which we review here.

As we noted, sub-sets of the variables were used in two separate surveys in Ecuador. One of these surveys was a rapid baseline assessment of the entire universe of highland and coastal indigenous second-order organizations in Ecuador and regional third-order organizations in the Amazon (Ramón 1999). The results showed that 26 percent of the federations had capacity scores above 80 (out of a possible 100), 55 percent had scores between 50 and 80, and 19 percent had scores below 50. The general image is one of a reasonable number of relatively solid organizations but many more that are not especially strong. The greatest strength of the second-order organizations appears to be the quality of their internal and external relationships; administrative, financial, and human capacities appear to be much more variable. This might suggest that these organizations are indeed carriers of important forms of social capital on which to build. In some instances, the organizations emerge as having capacity in all the dimensions; in other cases the survey demonstrated capacity limits that would require initial support to build capacity before program implementation.

---

[11] This iterative approach also had the effect that we reassessed some of the variables in the course of the work. Hence the tables in the text for different organizations' scores are not always comparable across countries.

Table 8.2 *Organizational capacity indicators for fifteen federations in Ecuador*

Variable	High	Mean	Low	Range of difference
Participation	63	47	40	23
Management	56	52	27	29
Satisfaction of members	73	60	40	33
Sustainability	55	45	30	25
Benefit distribution	44	17	7	37
Self-initiative	69	33	10	59
Overall capacity	60	39	26	34

Note: In this scoring system, the maximum score possible for any variable was 100. The "High" column records the highest score achieved by any one federation against that variable; the "Low" column the lowest score; the "Mean" the average score; and the final column notes the difference between highest and lowest scores.

The second survey was a smaller sample of fifteen second-order organizations that had worked with PRONADER. In this survey, more indicators were used, and they were clustered in slightly different ways. A similar picture emerges, however, of very variable organizational capacity and significant variation in the extent to which members are satisfied with their organizations (table 8.2). Satisfaction of members is closely related to the overall capacity indices (suggesting a close relationship between capacity and quality of contribution to local development). It is also notable that the indicators on which there was most variation in scores were self-initiative and benefit distribution, suggesting that these are two particularly good predictors of overall organizational capacity. Overall, the results suggest the usefulness of the instrument in identifying both generic and particular areas of organizational strength and weakness as a precursor to any capacity building initiative.

In addition to administering the two surveys in Ecuador, we studied twelve federations, six of which we report on in this chapter (see map 8.1). Each of the six organizations has different origins, with some initiated by the national *campesino* movement, some by NGOs, some by government land reform programs, and some, in a sense, by market possibilities. Some are more enterprise-oriented, others are more political. All of these groups, however, aim to link base groups and build bridges with external actors and spheres.

Case studies from Peru

We studied two federations in Peru.[12] The Central de Co-operativas Agrarias de La Convención y Lares (COCLA) was strong and prospering. The Sociedad Agricola de Interés Social (SAIS) was in crisis.

[12] The case studies on Peru draw on fieldwork coordinated by Leonith Hinojosa.

Central de Co-operativas Agrarias de La Convención y Lares.
Located on the eastern slopes of Peru's central-southern Andes, in the department of Cuzco, COCLA is a federation of small and medium-size coffee growers integrated by twenty-five cooperatives and two production committees. The 5,450 families that belong to the organization represent about 15 percent of the producers in the valley.

COCLA collects and markets members' coffee to internal and export markets and provides related services, including an input store, technical assistance, coffee processing, and production of small-scale coffee hulling machines. Its origins date back to a radical social movement in the late 1950s and 1960s that organized to gain access to land in the La Convención valley. This movement – which led to the redistribution of land in La Convención – was consolidated in 1958 in the Federación Provincial Campesina de la Convención y Lares (Fepcacyl).[13]

In the face of coffee marketing problems and the creation of grassroots cooperatives aiming to address some of these problems, the Federación proposed the creation of an economically focused second-level "central" of cooperatives in 1967. During the 1970s this organization subsequently received support from national programs supporting agricultural reform, rural mobilization, and the establishment of cooperatives.

These programs began to unravel as national policy changed under more conservative regimes in the late 1970s and 1980s and COCLA failed to consolidate itself. In the mid-1980s, however, the government and the United Nations initiated a special development project in the valley, with the primary goal of finding substitutes for coca, which is used to produce cocaine. This program, called CODEVA, promoted coffee as an alternative to coca, providing COCLA with significant technical assistance. This support created tensions with Fepcacyl, which sought to defend the interests of coca producers and thus resisted substitution programs. Notwithstanding these tensions, the period of CODEVA's presence (which ran until 1995) saw COCLA's consolidation, its success in gaining access to new international markets, and its entry into alternative organic markets.

COCLA has been able to strengthen both its services to members and its internal operational processes, largely because of the external assistance CODEVA provided from 1985 to 1995. While much of CODEVA's work was focussed on technical issues of producing and marketing quality coffee, it also paid attention to socio-organizational issues. It helped to train people in COCLA in business administration, create an organizational structure that facilitated a more entrepreneurial orientation, and introduce technical improvements in both production and processing.

---

[13] The federation initially covered only La Convención; Lares was added in 1961.

COCLA has become a strong regional economic actor, and it has helped develop new market relationships for its members, who, in turn, contribute to the organization. Member contributions cover 90 percent of normal administrative and operating costs. The remaining funding, and the recurrent need for extraordinary finance (to cover special technical assistance needs, credit or new project development costs), comes from external finance, largely in the form of subsidized loans.

Although COCLA is a relative success, it nevertheless suffers from some weaknesses. The fact that it is a commodity-specific organization limits the extent to which it builds bridges to different local organizations and different types of producers. Its focus on coffee producers and producing organizations leaves the building of wider and more inclusive intercommunity networks to other organizations. At the local level, this role falls to community-level governance structures (*sindicatos*) and at the regional level to Fepcacyl. Indeed, one key challenge is to build better linkages between local cooperatives and *sindicatos* and between COCLA and the regional federation. While this has not always been easy – largely because of political differences over how to respond to state efforts to restrict coca production – over time these actors have come closer together. Two factors appear to explain this. First, COCLA's contribution to the *campesino* economy has become more accepted by the regional federation. Second, COCLA's experience of external threat (primarily from the government) has made it more aware of its need for the political voice of the regional federation. The result is that, although the political and economic federations remain separate in organizational terms, their mutual respect and recognition of each other's role has grown.

Sociedad Agricola de Interés Social (SAIS-Marangani). The Sociedad Agricola de Interés Social (SAIS-Marangani) is located in the highlands of Cuzco, near the town of Sicuani. During the course of field work, the organization was in crisis and its members were discussing the possibility of dismantling it. A federation of twelve communities of alpaca herders (about 2,000 families), the SAIS organized sales, shearing, carding, and other processing activities. It sold its members' output to only one export company – a measure of its inability to engage with its external environment.

Unlike COCLA, which existed before the government began supporting reform enterprises, the SAIS was created by the government land reform program out of a hacienda, a wool-processing plant, and a variety of neighboring communities. These communities had not shared common concerns before SAIS was established. Indeed, the lower slope communities, which owned better lands and more water, were more oriented to agriculture than to alpaca production. When it was created, in 1973 the SAIS received support from the same government programs as COCLA. As these programs dwindled because of national policy

Table 8.3   *Organizational capacity indicators for COCLA and SAIS-Marangani*

Variable	COCLA Percent of total score possible	SAIS-Marangani Percent of total score possible
Leadership	59	34
Participation	80	63
Internal processes	78	48
Financial management	86	32
Autonomy and self-sufficiency	67	63
Demand analysis and vision	80	45
Representation/negotiation	95	55
Linkages	62	25
Total	76	43

Note: The scores mark the percentage of the highest possible total score that could be achieved for that indicator.

changes, the SAIS began to receive less and less external assistance. The only assistance it received, in fact, was sporadic visits from the Ministry of Agriculture.

Measuring and interpreting organizational capacity.   Consistent with these more qualitative interpretations of capacity in the two organizations, the survey results also suggest that COCLA has much greater organizational capacity than the SAIS (table 8.3). The difference in total score is 33 percentage points, with the greatest differences appearing in financial management (54 percentage points), representation/negotiation (40 percentage points), and linkages (37 percentage points). Differences in leadership, internal processes, and participation, while somewhat less extreme, are still very substantial.

As we noted, at the time the survey was conducted, the SAIS was on the verge of bankruptcy and about to be dissolved. Exogenous causes (a fall in wool prices, largely due to national trade policies) may have contributed to the organization's demise. But the consistently poor organizational performance in recent years documented by the indicators also clearly contributed to the federation's decline, as the greater resiliency to these problems by other alpaca-based federations in Peru suggests. The SAIS' failure to respond strategically to changing market circumstances – by identifying alternative markets and products, contacting sources of external support, or improving internal efficiency – was a reflection of more deeply seated problems of social cohesion and collective consciousness within the organization.

The SAIS' organizational weakness is reflected in the fact that its leaders increasingly used the organization for their personal benefit. This shows up in weak indicators for accountability, honesty, vision, conflict of interest, conflict management, and poor discipline in rule compliance in addition to the low ratings in the financial management cluster. In this context, two communities had already withdrawn from the SAIS (the exit option). It is not clear why, until the drastic decision to dismantle the organization, communities failed to use internal procedures (the voice option) to try to offset this progressive decapitalization. Indeed, the implicit loyalty option adopted suggests that the relationship between the base organizations and the federation was essentially one in which member organizations merely took turns decapitalizing the federation.

The SAIS developed neither the internal nor the external dimensions of social capital to become effective and develop a self-reproducing collective commitment to the organization. This failure apparently reflected the structural problems inherent in the organization from the start (especially the diversity of community interests and the rapid creation of the federation by the state), as well as the lack of sustained external support, which might have offset these problems and turned the organization into a vibrant entity for eliciting collaboration (rather than cannibalism) from its members.

It should be noted that the SAIS' failure as an organization – and COCLA's relative success – also has much to do with wider policy and market issues. The SAIS' demise reflected a change in government policy toward land reform enterprises from one that was more supportive to one of neglect. It also reflected problems in the alpaca export market. COCLA was never as dependent on government sponsorship and received organizational support from another source (CODEVA). Furthermore, its product enjoyed a more stable (if far from ideal) export market. As a result, household incomes were more stable and COCLA was able to generate its own revenue.

Case studies from Ecuador

Two organizations were studied in the northern highlands of Ecuador.[14] The Unión de Organizaciones Campesinas de Cotacachi (UNORCAC) is more concerned with ethnic politics and revindication. The Unión de Organizaciones de la Parroquía de Ayora y Cayambe (UNOPAC) focuses on social services and productive enterprise.

Unión de Organizaciones Campesinas de Cotacachi.   UNORCAC is an ethnic federation of forty-five communities (about 2,500 families). Founded in 1977, it traces its roots to programs of bilingual education and indigenous

---

[14] These case studies draw on field work conducted by Mary Garcia Bravo, with some support from Alvaro Cobo, Leonard Field, and Luciano Martínez.

Table 8.4   *Organizational capacity indicators for UNOPAC and UNORCAC*

Variable	UNOPAC Percentage of total score possible	UNORCAC Percentage of total score possible
Leadership	68	66
Participation	80	64
Internal processes	73	64
Financial management	77	54
Autonomy and self sufficiency	62	45
Representation and negotiation	76	76
Linkages	76	63
Total	73	63

Note: The scores mark the percentage of the highest possible total score that could be achieved for that indicator.

cultural revitalization. Reflecting these roots, it has focused primarily on socio-cultural activities, only recently getting involved with livelihood issues. Since its founding, UNORCAC has maintained a certain distance from NGOs. Although at times it has collaborated with them, it has also been quick to separate itself when it felt that NGOs were interfering in the internal processes of the organization. This slightly confrontational style is observable in its recent relationship with the municipal government of Cotocachi, even though it is controlled by an indigenous mayor affiliated with one of the national indigenous organizations.

Unión de Organizaciones de la Parroquía de Ayora y Cayambe. UNOPAC, a smaller federation of seventeen communities (about 750 families), is considered a relatively successful social enterprise. It has received resident technical assistance from an NGO since it was founded in 1989. Since that time, organizational capacity has gradually been transferred from the NGO to UNOPAC. Technical staff, once paid by the NGO, are now paid by UNOPAC. Indeed, UNOPAC is one of a very few federations in Ecuador that self-finances most of its activities.

Measuring and interpreting organizational capacity. The indicators confirm the initial impression that there was a notable difference in capacity between UNORCAC and UNOPAC – a pattern that also emerged in the qualitative appraisal (see Garcia 1998). Indeed, while UNORCAC is more visible in regional and national politics, UNOPAC consistently reveals higher organizational capacity in the measures used in the study (table 8.4). The average difference in scores is about 10 percentage points, with substantial differences

Table 8.5   *Ratings^a of community perceptions of participation in decisionmaking^b in UNOPAC and UNORCAC*

	UNOPAC		UNORCAC	
Indicator	Case 1	Case 2	Case 1	Case 2
Dissemination of information before decision	4	4	2	1
Consultation with bases	5	3	2	1
Intensity, openness and scope of debates	5	3	2	2
Dissemination of information about decisions	5	2	4	2
Total	19	12	11	6

Notes: ^aRatings are based on a five-point scale ranging from very good (5) to very poor (1).
^bRather than ask generically about participation in decisionmaking, the study asked specifically about levels of participation in two recent important decisions made in the organizations. These two decisions are referred to as Case 1 and Case 2 in the columns of the table.

in financial management (23 percentage points), participation (16 percentage points), and linkages (13 percentage points). Only the cluster scores for representation and negotiation are similar, reflecting UNORCAC's relatively well-developed ability to represent its members in their dealings with the outside political environment.

The community-level interviews show further weaknesses in UNORCAC and its relationships with its member organizations (even though UNORCAC is ostensibly the more representative of the two organizations). Community-level perceptions suggest that involvement of community-level members in decisionmaking appears to be greater in UNOPAC, which scores high in terms of two-way communication between the federation and its bases and the intensity and transparency of the decisionmaking process (table 8.5).

UNOPAC's higher level of participation translates into a far greater sense of accountability and community ownership: twenty-three out of twenty-five community-level people interviewed reported feeling a sense of ownership of UNOPAC. In contrast, only sixteen of the twenty-five people interviewed felt a sense of ownership of UNORCAC.

While one cannot infer a direct causal relationship between community perceptions that they own their organizations and financial management, it is notable that UNOPAC is also far more sustainable in financial terms, covering 61 percent of core costs from its revenues and member contributions. In contrast, UNORCAC depends almost entirely on external grant resources.

This greater sustainability may have much to do with the nature of the two organizations: while UNORCAC mostly fosters social, cultural, and political actions, which inevitably do not generate economic returns, UNOPAC is engaged in a range of enterprise activities that generate economic returns both for its members and for the federation. UNOPAC has endeavored to ensure the sustainability of its core physical facilities and human resources by maintaining some of its own central income-producing projects and by allocating some share of the income from other decentralized activities to the operation and maintenance of the federation's headquarters. A good example is the income from 17 hectares of communal cropland acquired by the federation. Communities share revenues in proportion to their contribution, but 15 percent of revenues goes to the central organization. Meanwhile, the federation tries to counterbalance the tendency of its economic programs to exclude certain people by cross-subsidizing certain services, such as legal advice, and fostering greater women's involvement in a range of decisionmaking processes. Indeed, there are twice as many women in leadership positions in UNOPAC as there are in UNORCAC.

Overall, the comparison between UNOPAC and UNORCAC tends to support the argument that once critical claim-making concerns (such as access to land) have been addressed, communities and their members tend to value productive, income-generating activities more than activities related to cultural strengthening and political representation. While it is the case that UNORCAC does sponsor sporting events and radio programs, as well as some programs that improve education, health, and the quality of drinking water, these activities seem secondary to its concerns for political representation. Furthermore, such service activities do little to generate income for the federation: members are generally far less willing to pay for social services than economic ones. With its current suite of activities it is therefore unlikely that UNORCAC will reduce its dependence on external support, or elicit more sustained involvement from its members.

Case studies from Bolivia

We examined two commodity-based organizations in Bolivia.[15] The Corporación Agropecuaria Campesina-Irupana (CORACA) focuses on providing economic services to members. It is structurally linked to the regional *campesino* organization, which in turn focuses more on issues of representation and politics. The Asociación de Productores Lecheros de la Provincia Aroma (ASPROLPA) likewise provides some services to members and also coordinates and represents their interests as they pertain to the dairy sector. Unlike CORACA, it is independent of the wider regional campesino movement. CORACA-Irupana was perceived as the stronger organization, ASPROLPA as the weaker – impressions that were confirmed by the indicators.

---

[15] These cases draw on field work conducted by Muñoz (1999).

Corporación Agropecuaria Campesina-Irupana. CORACA-Irupana was created within the context of a nation-wide attempt by the national *campesino* movement in 1983 to supplement the movement's more representative and political organizations with social enterprise entities (to be called CORACAs) across Bolivia. A Bolivian NGO, Qhana, and a donor organization encouraged the more politically oriented and claim-making Federación Regional de Campesinos de Sud Yungas (a coca-producing area of Bolivia) to create a regional CORACA, offering funding and technical assistance. Thus was born CORACA-Irupana in 1984 (earlier attempts to build cooperatives in the region had been unsuccessful). It focused on coffee marketing as its core activities, receiving technical, financial, and administrative assistance from Qhana. Over time the organization has moved from simply marketing coffee to installing processing facilities, establishing a technical assistance program (implemented largely by a Qhana team inside CORACA), and most recently initiating an organic production and marketing program. While the national CORACA movement has largely been a failure, CORACA-Irupana is one of its few successful organizations.[16]

CORACA-Irupana (like all CORACAs) was organically linked to the regional federation. Indeed by statute it had to have many of the same leaders. While this overlap helped keep the actions of the two organizations relatively consistent, it also left the identity of CORACA-Irupana uncertain: was it a social enterprise concerned with only production and marketing concerns or a representative organization willing to speak out on a range of issues of concern to its members? This close link between the regional federation and CORACA-Irupana was encouraged by Qhana, but *campesinos* in the region have apparently dedicated greater effort to consolidating CORACA-Irupana than the regional federation. As a result, CORACA-Irupana has gained some independence from the regional federation. This independence was spurred in the early 1990s by the joint elaboration of a regional development plan that required all actors working in Yungas to specify their roles. Today CORACA-Irupana's leaders assess its success in terms of the increased farmer awareness of the need to improve the quality of coffee production, marketing, and processing.

Asociación de Productores Lecheros de la Provincia Aroma. ASPROLPA, a federation of thirty-six base groups, located in the province of Aroma in the high plains (*altiplano*) of La Paz, has quite different origins. Indeed, it is unique among all the cases in that it was established in some

---

[16] CORACAs were supposed to be created as economic arms of all levels of the *sindicato* movement, something that has happened only rarely, particularly at levels lower than that of the federations. Many CORACAs have suffered serious management and corruption problems. Today only a few CORACAs function well. Nevertheless, some leaders still see the creation and restoration of CORACAs as an important task.

sense in response to the emergence of a market (rather than created in order to open a market). In the 1960s the Bolivian government initiated a program of dairy development in various parts of the country, including the *altiplano*. The program combined the establishment of government-owned milk-processing plants (*Plantas Industrializadas de Leche*, or PILs) with technical assistance and the collection and marketing of milk. As a result, communities and groups of communities specializing in milk production began to emerge. In time these communities were grouped by the PIL program into modules based around a milk collection center.

ASPROLPA was founded in 1992 as a second-order organization grouping together the modules that had been created in the province of Aroma during the 1980s. In 1997 – when it began to receive more direct technical assistance from an externally financed dairy development project – it began service activities and widened its relationships beyond those related to the PIL. Its primary objective was always (and remains) to aggregate *campesino* voices in negotiations with the government over milk prices, credit, and other services. ASPROLPA thus represented private sector interests in negotiating with the government.

As a result of recent structural reforms of the Bolivian economy, milk-processing plants have been privatized, and the plant supplied by ASPROLPA members is now owned by a Peruvian company that is itself a subsidiary of a multinational. Consequently, ASPROLPA now represents one set of private sector interests in negotiating with other (more powerful and globally mobile) private sector interests. This type of negotiation has proven to be far more difficult for ASPROLPA, because the criteria for legitimate complaints have changed. No longer can equity or "rights" be invoked; with the PIL able to shift its sources to other suppliers, arguments are now won or lost on grounds of economic viability.

Measuring and interpreting organizational capacity. The indicators of organizational capacity helped identify several key differences between ASPROLPA and CORACA. Interestingly, unlike in Ecuador, the differences in Bolivia relate less to the quality of social relations within the organizations (indeed, in each case there is a relatively solid relationship between the federation and its base organizations) than in differences in other assets (in particular managerial capacity) and external social relationships. CORACA-Irupana, for example, has a relatively well-established accounting system; ASPROLPA has none. CORACA-Irupana has a technical staff; ASPROLPA has one part-time account keeper. Particularly now that ASPROLPA has to deal with a company whose criteria are purely financial, these deficits represent important weaknesses, as they greatly reduce its capacity to enhance the quality, quantity, and competitiveness of members' milk and thus to make them attractive suppliers to the newly privatized PIL.

This comparison highlights the fact that organizational capacity involves more than social capital. CORACA-Irupana's far stronger administrative and technical capacity and resource endowments owe very much to its close links to Qhana, which has close links to European NGOs that can provide financing and links to alternative trade organizations in Europe. Sustaining this web of relationships and the activities it makes possible is not, however, straightforward. The growing complexity involved in introducing new services and accessing new markets may encourage the organization to seek external resources (in this case the human and financial capital of Qhana), with the view to building CORACA-Irupana's capacities over time. The day-to-day immediacy of other tasks, however, all too easily crowds out this dimension of patient, cumulative capacity building.

Structural problems in federations

Several general issues emerge from the case studies. This section identifies three of the most important issues.

Lack of ownership

Perhaps one of the principal problems facing all the organizations studied here is the issue of ownership by members. Even in an apparently strong organization, such as UNORCAC, which has placed councilors in the municipal government and spawned national figures, leaders recognize that most people in the base organizations see it as a sort of NGO rather than a second-order organization. As a result, members perceive it as a source of free services rather than an object of ownership and make no financial contributions to its maintenance.

This raises a series of problems for the organization. One is clearly financial sustainability and independence: without member contributions or payments for services, loans, or other benefits, the organization will never be able to become independent of external financing. Indeed, such dependence is significant in most of the cases studied.

A second problem is at the level of leadership. If the organization is not engaged with its bases, only a few leaders will emerge, and leadership positions will be held by a small and apparently eternal cadre. Internally, this concentration of leadership creates the sense that the organization belongs to others, not the bases, and is therefore more like an NGO than a true federation of the bases. Externally, it can lead to problems of legitimacy in the eyes of others, who argue that the federation is a phantom organization, or at best an undemocratic one. This, indeed, is a recurrent argument used to bypass such organizations or justify why they should have only limited voice in development planning.

This set of problems may be less important in enterprise-oriented organizations, which are often seen by members as providing important market and economic services for which members are prepared to pay (often in the form of a percentage of the final price of marketed products). In organizations such as these, the problems of concentrated leadership are less severe, both internally and externally. Internally, the concentration of leadership may not be perceived as greatly different from the structure of management in normal businesses; as long as the leadership is accountable and does a good job and the organization is economically successful, such permanence and concentration may actually be deemed desirable. Externally, similar criteria may apply. Indeed, continuity in leadership may be seen as an asset, because it allows the accumulation of market skills and contacts necessary for successful entrepreneurial activities.

Exclusion

Enterprise-oriented federations have had a greater impact on rural incomes than any other type of second-order organization. By dealing with markets collectively rather than individually (which would have been impossible), these organizations have secured new outlets through which members can sell their products, have added value to products, and have improved product quality. Overall they have enhanced their members' access to and position in new markets.

These federations have succeeded by accumulating strong management capacities over time. Design factors have also been important. In particular, these organizations have concentrated on a single or restricted number of products. Enterprises *can* work in a wider range of activities in order to meet the needs of a more diverse membership, but doing so is administratively complex. Many federations that have tried to diversify their membership have had disappointing impacts, have lost money or have ultimately suffered from tensions among different types of member. The SAIS, for instance, was supposed to be a collective agricultural enterprise formed out of agricultural communities in the lower areas and herding communities in the higher areas. In practice, the enterprise always paid more attention to the processing and sale of alpaca wool. The agricultural communities came to see relatively little benefit from the SAIS, especially in recent years, when it ceased even attempting agricultural development and product marketing. By 1998 the agricultural communities were lobbying for the closure of the SAIS, while the alpaca communities wanted it to continue.

In addition to production system-based mechanisms of exclusion, some enterprises establish financial membership requirements, such as the initial capital contributions that base cooperatives have to pay in order to join federations of cooperatives. These fees are not easily met by all, meaning that members tend to be drawn from the middle-class and rich peasantry.

Overall then only certain parts of the local population are members and are able to benefit from the services provided by successful enterprise federations. This is not something to criticize: indeed such exclusion and focussing is fundamental to the economic success of the federations. However, it must always be born in mind that *campesinos* who primarily produce crops not covered by the federation, or who cannot afford entry requirements, do not benefit – or benefit only indirectly – from the existence of the federations.

Tensions between political and economic organizations

The limits on inclusion in economic organizations point to a recurrent theme across the cases: the awkward relationship between economic and political organizations. Economic organizations tend to be less inclusive (although they do build linkages among producer groups in different communities). Political organizations tend to be more inclusive in principle, although in practice they tend to have weaker relationships with their bases, except during short periods when base organizations express acute political concerns or face emergency needs and so mobilize behind their political organizations more massively than they would for the more social enterprise-oriented federations.

The tendency for social enterprise-oriented organizations to explicitly exclude certain types of producers from membership, coupled with their inclination to be politically pragmatic, frequently attracts criticism from more political federations. This can lead to difficult relationships – as, for instance, in the relationships (until recently) between the more political peasant organizations and ASPROLPA and COCLA. Political organizations complain (with some justification) that they initiate activities, such as cultural activities, that are more inclusive or aim to include those excluded by the economic organizations but are unable to sustain these activities because they have no claim over the income generated by the economic organizations. The weak ties of these organizations to their bases and a tendency toward partisanship in the more representative organizations (such as UNORCAC) likewise attract criticism from economic federations and other observers that the organizations are politicized and detached. These same characteristics can also undermine the economic integrity (and solvency) of any social enterprise initiative conducted from within the organization, as political criteria become mixed up with economic criteria in resource allocation decisions (as in the case of CORACA-Irupana in its early years).

This problematic relationship between economic and political organizations is clearly recognized within the organizations and has been addressed in different ways. In some cases, the two types of organizations remain independent of each other (as in COCLA and ASPROLPA's relationships with their regional representative organizations); in others they are linked as two semiautonomous arms of the same organization (as in CORACA-Irupana); in yet others they are combined in the same organization (as in UNORCAC). The evidence here and in other studies we have conducted suggests that the solvency of the social enterprise federation and its ability to build sustainable bridges with new economic actors does require a degree of independence from more representative, political organizations (Bebbington 1996; Bebbington, Quisbert, and Trujillo 1996). At critical moments, however, the enterprise organizations need the political muscle of the representative groups to defend rights, negotiate adverse macro policy frameworks, and so on.

Finding the best balance in this relationship depends as much on the quality of the relationships among economic and representative organizations as it does on the formal structuring of this relationship. The emphasis must be on building bridges between different types of organization, so that they are able to respect one another's roles and benefit from them when necessary. How far it is possible to build such a relationship will depend greatly on the political and leadership dynamics at work in a region.

Inducing effective social capital: the role of external actors in building effective federations

Perhaps the most important message to emerge from the case studies is that the stronger second-order organizations have received sustained support from and maintained long-term relationships with other actors, in particular NGOs and religious activists. This is not to say that such longstanding relationships are in every sense healthy: they can at times involve a paternalism in which the external actor never lets go and fails to support the development of capacities within the organization so that it may become more self-reliant.[17] Several of the cases involve organizations that have deliberately broken with third parties because of this type of dependency.

Organizations that have not had longstanding stable support have fared less well. In particular, they have not developed the administrative capacity or external linkages to deal effectively with market or policy changes (as in the cases of SAIS and ASPROLPA) or to build constructive relationships with other actors (as in the case of UNORCAC).

Three important dimensions to this role of external actors emerge from the case studies. First, external actors provide much assistance in accessing resources and in using them to build up other capital assets of the organization by investing in human capital formation, training, infrastructure, and the development of administrative systems. Second, external actors can help build external

---

[17] The relationship between CORACA-Irupana and Qhana is a case in point. In another case, a priest continued to control the finances of a second-order organization and delayed its legal registration for more than twenty years (Bebbington and Perreault 1999).

social capital by building bridges between the second-order organization and other actors, with their capacity to do so depending greatly on the quality of their own relationships with other actors. Third, external actors can help build internal social capital in the second-order organization. Doing so takes much skill, sensitivity, and intimate knowledge of the second-order organization and its local context. There are two particularly important ways in which this can be done. One is to identify and help mediate conflicts as they arise, so that they are addressed but do not explode to the detriment of the organization. The external actor can also ensure greater transparency and honesty by the federation in its dealing with its bases or at least instill among base organizations the sense that the organization is being managed well and cleanly. Clearly, getting the balance right in such a role is crucial; frequently external actors can intervene too much, distorting the relationship between an organization and its members.

Different actors can play this external capacity building role. In some cases it is played by the church or religious orders (UNOPAC), in others by NGOs (CORACA-Irupana) or special development projects (COCLA). The government generally plays such a role less frequently and less successfully than other actors. In large measure this is because state agencies and policies lack the autonomy and above all the continuity to be able to sustain a supportive relationship in the long term. It is also harder for public institutions to justify concentrating resources in a small number of counterpart organizations for an extended period.

The most dramatic example of the risk of depending on public institutions for long-term support is the SAIS, which was created by a radical land reform program that unraveled shortly after the federation was created. As a result, the SAIS has received almost no attention from the state and has had to develop its own capacities (social and human), with very little success. These observations are not to refute Fox's (1990, 1996) claim that state actors can play important roles in helping such organizations consolidate themselves. But these roles appear to take the form of shorter-term support rather than long-term capacity building.

External actors and federation accountability

External actors can also play an important role in eliciting the emergence of more accountable membership organizations (Carroll 1992). Indeed, common to all the cases studied is the sense that accountable and transparent organizations do not emerge spontaneously or even easily (just as accountable and transparent NGOs, government programs, and multilateral development agencies are few and far between). Indeed, building accountability is complicated by the very nature of second-order organizations, which are removed from the day-to-day interactions through which accountability is exercised at the community level. Creating mechanisms and a culture of accountability is something that has to be worked at. The presence of external actors can help in several important ways.

The presence of certain types of external actors can exert a form of moral accountability: members may feel more comfortable with a federation that is linked to a church or NGO. The presence of an external actor may be seen as a guarantee that resources will be used efficiently and honestly. Of course, this type of relationship can cause some tension between the leadership of the federation and the external actor. As noted, we found instances in which the federation and external actor had parted company because the federation believed the NGO or church interfered too much in its affairs, denying it the autonomy and independence it needed.

A second way in which external actors have helped create accountability has been by consolidating professional capacities inside the federations – something that is much more common in social enterprise and production-oriented types of federation than in the more political federations. External actors can (and have) played several roles in this process, not only by providing financial resources and technical assistance but also by helping institutionalize this professional capacity within the federation. These professional groups, made up of people who are often not of *campesino* or indigenous origin, can then serve as a counterweight to other resource-allocation criteria used inside the organization, such as favoring the communities or political parties of those in the directorate. This is a difficult balance to strike, for excessive influence by this technical unit disembeds the federation from local social relationships. Furthermore, elected leaders and paid staff often disagree over strategy, due process, and salaries, and technical staff can have as many inappropriate inclinations as leaders. Nonetheless, it does seem that in cases where there is insufficient counterweight to the leadership from the bases, the presence of such technical units *can* serve to offset the possible emergence of corrupt, partisan, or inequitable forms of resource allocation. The creation of such units depends very much on the support of external actors.

These observations are not meant to imply that indigenous and *campesino* federations must always be watched over by non-*campesino* organizations or individuals, nor that such organizations are inherently any more transparent or honest than the leadership of a federation. Rather, the studies suggest the value (and possibility) of a form of synergy, in which relationships between federations and external actors can elicit greater accountability in each. Horizontal relationships between organizations and between technical units and leadership committees within organizations can to some degree substitute for inadequate vertical relationships between organizations and communities/households as mechanisms for exercising accountability. In doing so they can help create a culture of trustworthiness in and around the organizations, that helps them become more effective.

External actors, grants, and credit

An important theme running through the cases is the issue of credit as opposed to grants as a mechanism for building social capital and organizational capacity. Leaders and observers of UNOPAC claim that much of its current strength lies in the fact that its initial work involved the use of credit (for building materials provided for reconstruction after an earthquake). COCLA and CORACA-Irupana also have credit arrangements with financing organizations and members.

Support for using credit is based on the notion that it creates a healthier institutional culture than do grants. The implication is that the use of credit helps build relationships of reciprocal obligations between the organization and members, limiting the extent to which the bases view the organization as a provider of free services. Credit thus becomes a way of tying the organization into its bases and vice versa. Providing credit rather than grants also helps prevent excessive patronage politics between leaders and base organizations.

Creating a culture of repayment is not easy, however, especially in environments in which many other loans have not been repaid. It is certainly difficult to do after the organization and many other donors have worked on a grant basis. It is also difficult where the organization has initially been a claim-making one in which the discourse was based on (often anti-capitalist) solidarity. A further problem is that credit programs (especially those that disburse credit to individual borrowers) are in general exclusionary, in part because there is often insufficient money to offer many loans, in part because eligibility criteria rule some people out. Of course, the success of a credit program also depends on the accountability (and administrative capacities) of those managing it. If ties between the community and the federation are weak, pressure for accountability is unlikely to come from below. Exercising pressure for such accountability thus becomes an important role for third parties until such control comes from members.

Preconceptions about organizational models

Successful capacity building is more the exception than the rule. Of the many reasons for this, one that merits comment is the problem of preconceptions about what constitutes the right organizational arrangement. Among the cases considered here, the imposition of a design on the SAIS and CORACA-Irupana caused considerable tensions and (in the case of the SAIS) failure.[18] Even in the more successful cases there is often an early period in which external actors attempt to push a particular organizational model and as a result build little

[18] For other examples, see Rivera-Cusicanqui's (1992) discussion of the ways in which external interventions based on preconceived models of rural social organization aggravated tensions between *ayllu*s and *sindicato*s in North Potosí in Bolivia.

capacity – and in the worst cases can even set capacity-building efforts back. Indeed, perhaps one of the benefits of a long-term relationship is that it allows actors to get beyond the stage of such preconceptions and begin to work on design issues in a more process-oriented way.

This is not to say that design is unimportant[19] but rather that social capital – and organizational capacity more generally – are best built inductively rather than ideologically, based on a sound knowledge of local history, culturally patterned social relationships, and expectations. Such considerations are especially important if successful bridges across different interest groups and existing informal and formal institutions are to be built. If rigid designs are imposed where there are a multiplicity of interests and informal institutions already working (that is, the normal scenario), the intervention may well bring about social conflict rather than help create social capital.

Conclusions

On the basis of the preceding analysis and discussion we can draw both empirical conclusions about the relationships between second-order organizations and social capital formation, as well as more strategic conclusions of relevance (we hope) for the practice of development. We take each in turn.

Social capital, empowerment, and second-order organizations

Second-order peasant federations in the Andes embody a specific and important type of structural social capital. As such, they make possible regional forms of collective action of various types – economic, political, natural resource management, cultural. They also facilitate more coordinated forms of engagement with government, civil society, and market actors.

One of the more remarkable patterns to emerge from the cases is that these federations seem to be at once enduring but also fragile (cf. Hirschmann 1984). Several of these organizations have existed for more than twenty years, thus outliving other efforts to create social capital, such as interinstitutional roundtables or working groups. Yet they have also experienced ups and downs. Even when successful, federations and their partners constantly struggle with problems of representation, accountability, financial viability, and so on. There are many reasons for this, but some seem to derive from the very nature of such regional membership groups. As regional organizations, federations necessarily depend on less frequent face-to-face interactions, reducing the extent to which reciprocal accountability can be exercised among members. This increases the importance of developing other accountability mechanisms, such as a relationship with an

---

[19] See Ostrom (1992) on the importance of design.

external actor or the existence of a professionalized mini-bureaucracy inside the federation. These mechanisms appear to be surrogate forms of accountability that in turn elicit greater member trust (though not always: see the case of the SAIS). To the extent that these alternative mechanisms are not developed, the federation is less effective in fostering supracommunal collective action.

While second-order organizations embody a special form of structural social capital, a wide range of other forms of social capital exists within the geographical reach of the federation. These may be based on spatial propinquity, shared natural resources, kinship, generational groups, or other shared characteristics. These different types of social capital can pull in different directions. One of the challenges facing second-order organizations is to find ways of co-existing with these other forms of collective action so that rather than divide the organization, they feel comfortable with its existence, actions, and prominence in a particular domain of activities.

A related design problem is whether the second-order organization aims to include some or many of these other forms of structural social capital within its own organization (as some of the more representative organizations aim to do) or instead restrict its role to specific functions (as the more social enterprise-oriented organizations tend to do). In some cases – albeit not necessarily by design – sporting, cultural, and other ritual events sponsored by second-order organizations can help dissipate some of the tensions that can emerge among different groups.

If the inherent qualities of the social capital embodied in *campesino* federations makes them fragile, why are they often so persistent? We suggest that this persistence can be explained by the unique role that this type of social capital can play and the potential benefits it can have. The cases identify various types of impact: economic, sociocultural, and political. Some of the economic payoffs are associated with the creation of social relations that allow new markets to emerge or help create marketing arrangements that bypass established arrangements and increase members' income. Others relate to the accessing and management of new types of natural resource inputs to production, in particular land (in earlier years) and irrigation water (more recently).[20] Impacts in the political sphere have included the emergence of more inclusive and responsive forms of municipal government (Irupana, Guamote). Impacts in the sociocultural sphere have included the resurgence of cultural identity (as a result of efforts by UNORCAC) and the broadening of access to a series of human development programs made possible by the federations' ability to influence and extend government initiatives (as in the case of the preschool programs managed by UNORCAC).

---

[20] Irrigation groups were integral parts of several of the cases we studied but are not described here. See Perreault, Bebbington, and Carroll (1998) and Martinez (2000). Federations are involved with obtaining water rights and collectively managing water as a common good.

Of course, we cannot know that these impacts would not have occurred in the absence of the federations. However, the co-existence of federations and many of these impacts and institutional innovations and the relatively clear evidence that the federations helped extend the coverage of government programs (across space and over time) suggests that synergy is at work (cf. Evans 1996). Given that many federations already exist in the Andean region, the potential for reproducing similar experiences elsewhere seems real. But it is also clear that the mere presence of a federation is not sufficient to bring about any significant change in local development.

Federations of community-based organizations have an important role to play as agents of development. By creating extracommunity linkages and access to other sources of power and resources, they overcome the limitations of community-based approaches. They exist close enough to the community level to foster participatory processes of change, but as regional organizations they can exercise more power than local groups. As a result, federations have altered, albeit only partly, the political and economic relationships that have hurt indigenous *campesinos* in the Andes for so long.

Perhaps the greatest potential of these federations is that, beyond any specific role they might play in development programs, they also have the potential to create more constructive bonds and bridges among different parts of the rural population. To the extent that they succeed in doing so, they may make an important and enduring contribution to the empowerment of rural populations and to a change in the deeper structures of economic and social exclusion in the Andes.

Implications for practice: inducing and reinforcing social capital through intervention

This study adds to the accumulating evidence that structural social capital can be induced and reinforced by purposeful intervention and that trust, cooperation, shared identity, and reciprocity can be enhanced and replicated through sensitive and persistent support.[21] Invariably, these strategies involve building on existing (or latent) social resources, finding incentives of strong common interest, and gradually transferring responsibilities for management and problem-solving. In most of the cases we studied, building and consolidating second-level federations took a decade or more.

The study also suggests that there are different dimensions of social capital within the federations and that each requires attention if synergies are to be achieved. In particular, the results suggest that the internal and external dimensions of organizational capacity are complementary. External capacity

---

[21] See Durston (1998) for a similar finding in postconflict Guatemala.

is needed to access resources, shift power relationships, and enter new political and economic spheres. But sustained success in these external spheres requires that the organization develop capacities of collective action, resource management, administrative competence, problem-solving, and rule enforcement. Ultimately, success in the external sphere depends on the legitimacy of second-order organizations, which in turn derives from the quality of internal relationships, the accountability of the second-order organization to its members, member satisfaction, and organizational transparency.[22]

Several more specific implications for external cooperation emerge from our results. We would emphasize three. The first is the familiar "precautionary principle" – that intervention can do as much harm as good, and therefore requires great care, perhaps especially in this realm. The second emphasizes the importance of building partnerships among actors. The third emphasizes the complementary importance of building capabilities within the federation itself.

Do no harm and be alert to possibilities.   Many second-order organizations have been weakened by particular types of interventions. External actors have bypassed them, imposed models on them, competed with them, politicized them, or made them excessively subject to government regulation. One of the lessons from this experience is that careful social analysis continues to have an important role to play, particularly in identifying possible tensions that exist within and among organizations or between them and other actors.

Social analysis (especially local institutional analysis) can also help identify organizational opportunities, in three ways. First, it can identify the capacities and deficiencies of existing organizations and suggest the potential role of interventions to support second-order organizations and the types of impact that those interventions may have. Such studies (if done appropriately) can also serve as baselines against which impacts on such forms of social capital can be assessed. Second, social analysis could identify the possibilities for fostering relationships among federations and other actors that might create synergies, improving the effectiveness of organizations and creating more effective forms of reciprocal accountability.[23] Third, analysis of existing, emerging, and defunct organizations can throw light on the influences of different policy and political economic changes on second-order organizations. Such organizations in Peru, for instance, have suffered from abrupt changes in land reform and economic policy (as well as rural violence), while those in Ecuador have benefited from

---

[22] We argue elsewhere (Carroll 1998) that the self-confidence and dignity acquired through internal collaboration and problem-solving is essential for successful external engagements.

[23] A study of local-level institutions in Indonesia was used as an input in a new social investment project aimed at building such relationships between community organizations and district government (Scott Guggenheim, Principal Social Development Specialist, World Bank, personal communications, 1998, 1999).

a largely supportive policy environment that has in varying forms recognized their legitimacy and potential role in local development.[24] To some extent it may also be possible to illuminate the local conditions that will determine the types of institution most likely to thrive in a particular context. In a number of the cases studied, for example, the emergence of a federation was preceded by a relationship between an external agency and a network of what might be called potential leaders in the rural population (literacy trainers, church activists, social promoters).

Build partnerships.   The strongest federations studied here (and in previous work) had longstanding relationships with external actors (churches, NGOs, special projects). These relationships, which often revolve around key individuals, create reciprocal accountability, in which the presence of each actor promotes slightly more transparency in the other. In sum, the joint action of the different actors leads to greater impacts than would have been possible had either organization acted alone. Results in areas in which sustained partnerships have functioned have been impressive. UNOPAC facilitated postearthquake reconstruction programs and the emergence of new economic activities in Cayambe. COCLA and CORACA-Irupana facilitated the emergence of new agricultural product markets. And second-order organizations in Guamote helped turn it into one of the most interesting experiments in municipal governance in Ecuador (Bebbington and Perreault 1999).

Building and sustaining such partnerships requires sensitivity, dedication, and above all flexibility; the absence of one or other of these qualities has sometimes led to the rupture of relationships. This implies that donors should design flexible instruments and be open to the possibility of change in the course of a project. This may mean supporting new partnerships and relationships even where they were not initially identified in project documents.

Build intra-organizational capacities.   Building technical expertise inside the federation is critical to its success. COCLA, CORACA-Irupana, and other federations all benefited from a long period of investment in internal management capacity. While the resources implied are relatively modest, they need to be invested over an extended period of time.

One of the mechanisms through which an external intervention might build social capital is through the use of credit relationships. While most NGOs (and government programs) have preferred to use grants, one of the most

---

[24]   During the review of this chapter, the government of Ecuador had declared a state of emergency, imprisoned indigenous leaders, and more generally targeted federations and national organizations as opponents of the regime. Although this moment has since passed, it only demonstrates that supportive policy environments do not endure.

successful institution building NGOs in the Andes, the Fondo Ecuatoriano Populorum Progressio, has long used credit in its relationships with *campesino* organizations, and it has encouraged the federations to extend credit to their members.

REFERENCES

Bebbington, A., 1996. "Organizations and Intensifications: Small Farmer Federations, Rural Livelihoods, and Agricultural Technology in the Andes and Amazonia." *World Development* 24(7): 1161–1178

1997. "Social Capital and Rural Intensification: Local Organizations and Islands of Sustainability in the Rural Andes." *Geographical Journal* 163(2): 189–197

Bebbington, A. and Perreault, T., 1999. "Social Capital, Development and Access to Resources in Highland Ecuador." *Economic Geography* 75(4): 395–418

Bebbington, A., Quisbert, J., and Trujillo, G., 1996. "Technology and Rural Development Strategies in a Small Farmer Organization: Lessons from Bolivia for Rural Policy and Practice." *Public Administration and Development* 16(3): 195–213

Bebbington, A., Carrasco, H., Peralvó, L., Ramón, G., Torres, V. H., and Trujillo, J., 1992. *Los Actores de una decada ganada: tribus, comunidades y campesinos en la modernidad.* Quito: Abya Yala

Carroll, T. F., 1992. *Intermediary NGOs: The Supporting Link in Grassroots Development.* West Hartford, CT: Kumarian Press

1998. "Indigenous Organizations, Protest, and Human Rights in Ecuador." In John D. Montgomery (ed.), *Human Rights: Positive Policies in Asia and the Pacific Rim.* Hollis, NH: Hollis Publishing Co.

Casagrande, J. B. and Piper, A. R., 1969. "La transformación estructural de una parroquía rural en las tierras altas del Ecuador." *América Indígena* 24(4)

Deere, C. D. and Léon, M., (eds.), 1987. *Rural Women and State Policy: Feminist Perspectives on Latin American Agricultural Development.* Boulder, CO: Westview Press

Durston, J., 1998. "Building Social Capital in Rural Communities (Where It Does Not Exist)." Paper presented at the Latin American Studies Association Annual Meetings, Chicago, September 24–26

Evans, P. (ed.), 1996. *State–Society Synergy: Government and Social Capital in Development.* Berkeley, CA: Institute for International Studies

Foley, M. W. and Edwards, R., 1997. "Escape from Politics? Social Theory and the Social Capital Debate." *American Behavioral Scientist* 40(6): 550–561

1999. "Is It Time to Disinvest in Social Capital?" *Journal of Public Policy* 19(2): 141–173

Fox, J. (ed.), 1990. *The Challenge of Rural Democratisation: Perspectives from Latin America and the Philippines.* London: Frank Cass

1996. "How Does Civil Society Thicken? The Political Construction of Social Capital in Mexico." *World Development* 24(6): 1089–1103

Garcia, M., 1998. *La UNORCAC: Proceso organizativo y gestión.* Quito. mimeo

Grootaert, C. and D. Narayan, 2001, "Local Institutions, Poverty and Household Welfare in Bolivia." Policy Research Working Paper 2644. World Bank, Washington, DC

Harriss, J. and De Renzio, P., 1997. "'Missing Link' or Analytically Missing? The Concept of Social Capital: An Introductory Bibliographic Essay." *Journal of International Development* 9(7): 919–937

Hirschmann, A., 1984. *Getting Ahead Collectively: Grassroots Experiences in Latin America.* Oxford. Pergamon Press

Martinez, L., 2000. *El Capital Social en La Tucayta. Estudio de Caso de una Federación Campesina, Provincia de Cañar-Ecuador.* Quito. Mimeo

Muñoz, D., 1999. *Análisis sobre capital social y las organizaciones campesinas. Caso Boliviano.* La Paz. Mimeo

Narayan, D., 1999. "Complementarity and Substitution: The Role of Social Capital, Cross-Cutting Ties, and the State in Poverty Reduction." World Bank, Poverty Group, Poverty Reduction and Economic Management Network, Washington, DC

Ostrom, E., 1990. *Governing the Commons: The Evolution of Institutions for Collective Action.* New York: Cambridge University Press

    1992. *Crafting Institutions for Self-Governing Irrigation Systems.* San Francisco: Institute for Contemporary Studies

Perreault, T., Bebbington, A., and Carroll, T. F., 1998. "Indigenous Irrigation Organizations and the Formation of Social Capital in Northern Highland Ecuador." *Conference of Latin American Geographers Yearbook* 24: 1–16

Ramón, G., 1999. *Informe acerca de los resultados de la consultoria sobre el indice institucional de las organizaciones de segundo grado, OTGs, y nacionalidades.* Quito: PRODEPINE

Ritchey-Vance, M., 1998. "Widening the Lens on Impact Assessment: The Inter-American Foundation and Its Grassroots Development Framework (The Cone)." In J. Blauert and S. Zadek (eds.), *Mediating Sustainability.* West Hartford, CT: Kumarian Press

Rivera-Cusicanqui, S., 1992. *Ayllus y Proyectos de Desarrollo en el Norte de Potosí.* La Paz: Hisbol

Sylva, P., 1986. *Gamonalismo y Lucha Campesina.* Quito: Abya Yala

Uphoff, N., 1991. "A Field Methodology for Participatory Self-Evaluation." *Community Development Journal* 26(4): 271–285

    1997. "Local Organizational Capacity: What Is It? How to Measure It?" Cornell University, Ithaca, NY. Mimeo

    1999. "Understanding Social Capital: Learning from the Analysis and Experience of Participation." In P. Dasgupta and I. Serageldin (eds.), *Social Capital: A Multifaceted Perspective.* Washington, DC: World Bank

van Nieuwkoop, M. and Uquillas, J., 1999. "Defining Ethnodevelopment in Operational Terms: Lessons Learned from the Ecuador-Indigenous and Afro-Ecuadorian Peoples Development Project." World Bank, Latin America and the Caribbean Region, Environmentally and Socially Sustainable Development Sector Management Unit, Washington, DC

Woolcock, M., 1998. "Social Capital and Economic Development: Toward a Theoretical Synthesis and Policy Framework." *Theory and Society* 27(2): 151–208

World Bank, 1999. "Building Poverty Reduction Strategies in Developing Countries." Poverty Reduction and Economic Management Network, Washington, DC

9   Social capital and social cohesion: case studies from Cambodia and Rwanda

Nat J. Colletta and Michelle L. Cullen

The Cold War, in which superpowers sought to maintain a global balance of power without resorting to nuclear arms, masked many local, intrastate conflicts by internationalizing them. What were really civil wars among indigenous peoples contending for local power were turned into "virtual" international conflicts fought by proxy. Externally financed economic growth and outside support for authoritarian regimes concealed deeply rooted internal ethnic, religious, social, and economic cleavages. With the end of the Cold War, this virtual bubble burst: of the ninety-six violent conflicts that occurred between 1989 and 1995, ninety-one are considered civil conflicts (Wallensteen and Sollenberg 1996).

Unlike interstate conflict, which often mobilizes national unity and strengthens national social cohesion, violent conflict within a state weakens its social fabric. Intrastate conflict divides the population, undermines interpersonal and communal group trust, and destroys norms and values that underlie cooperation and collective action for the common good, decimating social capital stocks – and, thus, exacerbating communal strife. This damage to a nation's social fabric impedes the ability of states and communities to recover after hostilities cease. Even if other forms of capital are replenished, economic and social development will be hampered unless social capital stocks are restored. Ideally, this restoration of social capital will support bonds within communities, build bridges between communities, and link state and community levels, hence strengthening the society's cohesiveness.[1]

This work was funded by the World Bank's Social Capital Initiative. Guidance was provided by Christiaan Grootaert and Thierry van Bastelaer. The research project was designed and managed by the authors. The Cambodian research team was led by Veena Krishnamurthy under the auspices of Cambodian Social Services, which also prepared the final report for the study. The Rwandan literature review was conducted by Lindiro Kabirigi, Jean Rugagi Nizurugero, and Gérard Rutazibwa. Field research was carried out by Callixte Kayitaba, Anecto Hanyurvinfura Kayitare, Christine Kibiriti, and Speciose Mukandutiye. Elizabeth Acul, Antoinette Kamanzi, Therese Nibarere, and Anna Rutagengwaova provided organizational assistance. Toni Ntaganda Kayonga and Markus Kostner contributed valuable input and guidance throughout the study. We gratefully acknowledge the contributions of those mentioned above and especially Markus Kostner, Peter Uvin, and Michael Woolcock for their insightful input and suggestions. This work was based on a more extensive comparative study that also examined violent conflict and social capital in Guatemala and Somalia (see Colletta and Cullen 2000).
[1] The concepts of bonding, bridging, and linking social capital are extrapolated from Michael Woolcock (2000) and chapter 7 in the World Bank's (2000) *World Development Report 2000/2001.*

279

A growing body of research has examined the phenomenon of social capital in an attempt to define the concept and the forms it may take and to describe how it may influence and improve the development process. Efforts have also been made to develop indicators for measuring social capital and to provide recommendations on how to encourage and support it. Few studies, however, have actually analyzed social capital and how it interacts with violent conflict – an important issue considering the rise in the frequency of intrastate conflict and the importance of social capital for social and economic growth and development (Grootaert 1998; Collier and Hoeffler 1999; Rodrik 1999; Easterly 2000a, 2000b). Understanding this phenomenon could enhance the abilities of international actors and policymakers to more effectively build peace through reconciliation, reconstruction, and development.

This chapter examines the interaction among social capital, social cohesion, and violent conflict; changes in social capital resulting from violent conflict; and ways in which governments and international actors can foster the socially cohesive relationships necessary for conflict prevention, rehabilitation, and reconciliation. The findings and recommendations are based on case studies of violent conflict and social capital in Cambodia and Rwanda. The results are preliminary, as each case study was conducted on an exploratory basis only. Study results are specific to those countries analyzed, although some broad generalizations may apply more globally. Further research is needed to confirm and solidify the results.

Conceptual framework

Categorizing and analyzing social capital is difficult, for there are many definitions of the term and what it encompasses. In general, *social capital* refers to systems that lead to or result from social and economic organization, such as worldviews, trust, reciprocity, informational and economic exchange, and informal and formal groups and associations. Although there is much contention over what interactions and types of organization constitute social capital, there is little disagreement about the role of social capital in facilitating collective action, economic growth, and development by complementing other forms of capital (Grootaert 1998).

The definitions and indicators used in the Rwanda and Cambodia case studies focus primarily on informal and local horizontal relationships, such as trust and cross-cutting networks, and to some extent on certain aspects of vertical relationships, particularly state and market penetration, as important factors in fueling conflict and influencing the formation and transformation of social capital. The concepts and definitions of social capital used for field-work stem primarily from the works of Putnam, Coleman, Fukuyama, and Uphoff. Putnam's work emphasizes the horizontal aspects of social capital, while Coleman's definition enables the examination of both positive and negative aspects of the phenomenon. Fukuyama's work stresses the importance to social capital formation of trust – a grossly depleted commodity during warfare. Uphoff's work facilitates the analysis of social capital by separating its cognitive and structural aspects.

Social capital consists of "the features of social organization, such as networks, norms, and trust, that facilitate coordination and cooperation for mutual benefit," according to Putnam (1993, p. 36). Communities with positive economic development and effective governments are those supported by "networks of civil engagement," or citizenry linked by solidarity, integrity, and participation. These civic networks, Putnam states, foster norms of reciprocity that reinforce sentiments of trust within a society and improve the effectiveness of communications and social organization.

Coleman's (1988) definition of social capital broadens Putnam's and includes vertical associations that can be characterized by hierarchy and an unequal distribution of power among members. These relationships mean that social capital can be beneficial to some and useless or harmful to others, depending on its characteristics and application.

As a key measure of social capital, trust, as described by Fukuyama (1995), "arises when a community shares a set of moral values in such a way as to create expectations of regular and honest behavior" (p. 153). Reciprocity, civic duty, and moral obligation, according to Fukuyama, are essential to a successful and stable society and are the behaviors that should emanate from a thriving civil society.

Uphoff (2000) breaks social capital down into structural and cognitive components. *Structural* social capital refers to relationships, networks, and associations, while *cognitive* social capital refers to norms and values as the driving forces behind these visible forms of social capital.

To enrich the analysis of field results and better understand the interrelations of social capital, social cohesion, and violent conflict, social capital definitions from the work of North, Olson, and Narayan were also employed (although macro-level interactions were not the main focus of either country case study). This broadening of the definition of social capital permits the inclusion of government, market, and development actors, which have a direct impact on the social capital environment facing actors at the local level, and helps identify measures for policy and operational recommendations.

Macro aspects of social capital are well described by North (1990) and Olson (1982), who define social capital to include not only trust, norms, and networks but also the sociopolitical environment that shapes norms and social structures. In addition to the largely informal and often local horizontal and hierarchical relationships in the concepts of Coleman and Putnam, this view encompasses more formalized institutional relationships and structures, such as the government, the political regime, the market, the rule of law, the court system, and civil and political liberties (Grootaert 1998).

Narayan (1999) emphasizes the importance of inclusion of the state in social capital analysis in her work examining the dynamics of complementarity and substitution. She argues that focus must be not only on civic engagement, ideally characterized by inclusive ties that link different individuals and groups, but also on the effectiveness of the state. A strong, civil society founded on cross-cutting ties that operate in a weak state environment substitutes for the state's inadequacies and hence is not a model case for growth. A high level of civic engagement, combined with a well-functioning state, complements the state's abilities and produces the fertile soil necessary for social and economic development.

Social capital, social cohesion, and violent conflict

The field studies in Cambodia and Rwanda examined the changes in social capital resulting from violent conflict. When attempting to develop policy and operational recommendations from study findings, however, it became clear that the relation of social capital to the cohesiveness of a society had to be examined in order to better understand the emergence of violent conflict and the role social capital can play in a conflict-ridden environment. This relation between social capital and the cohesiveness of a society can be expressed in the construct of social cohesion, or the nexus of well-integrated horizontal (bonding and bridging) and vertical (linking) social capital. As Berkman and Kawachi (2000) note:

Social capital forms a sub-set of the notion of social cohesion. Social cohesion refers to two broader intertwined features of society: (1) the absence of latent conflict whether in the form of income/wealth inequality; racial/ethnic tensions; disparities in political participation; or other forms of polarization; and (2) the presence of strong social bonds – measured by levels of trust and norms of reciprocity; the abundance of associations that bridge social divisions (civic society) and the presence of institutions of conflict management, e.g., responsive democracy, an independent judiciary, and an independent media. (2000, p. 175)

Income and wealth inequality, racial and ethnic tensions, and disparities in political participation and weak civic engagement all are associated with poor social cohesion. This lack of cohesion stems from poor community relations with the government (linking) or polarization among people within (bonding) and between (bridging) communities (Woolcock 2000; World Bank 2000). In this manner, social cohesion is the key intervening variable between social capital and violent conflict. The more bonding and bridging horizontal social capital link with vertical social capital, the more likely it will be that a society is cohesive and thus possesses the inclusive mechanisms necessary for mediating

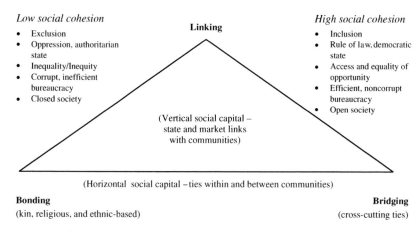

Figure 9.1   Social cohesion: integration of bonding, bridging, and linking social capital.

or managing a conflict before it turns violent. The weaker the social cohesion, the weaker the reinforcing channels of socialization (value formation) and social control (compliance mechanisms). Weak societal cohesion increases the risk of social disorganization, fragmentation, and exclusion, potentially manifesting itself in violent conflict (figure 9.1).

The work of Johann Galtung (1996) captures the intersection of bonding, bridging, and linking social capital by characterizing the structure of violence in three basic social and economic phenomena: exclusion, inequality, and indignity. In many developing countries, unequal patterns of development – in terms of investment as well as access to its opportunities or fruits – have been a major source of societal cleavage. The process of globalization integrates markets and values, facilitating growth. Yet it is also a source of increasing exclusion and marginalization, widening the gap between rich and poor within and among societies and exacerbating the conditions that can give rise to violent conflict. The consequent exclusion and inequality have been compounded by the struggle for identity in a rapidly changing world; traditional values, roles, and institutions are continually under assault as a result of the communications revolution and the penetration of markets and raising of expectations in even the most remote parts of the globe. The impact of market penetration has been intensified by the weakening of the state in the face of dwindling resources, endemic corruption, and the rise of civil society, which can complement the state's role but can also compete with it for legitimacy. As a consequence, wars are increasingly fought over control of resources and power by social groups within states rather than between states.

Conflict resulting from exclusion, inequality, and indignity does not in itself necessarily lead to the eruption of widespread hostilities; the tolerance and coping capacities of the poor and marginalized are legend and manifold. However, conflict often engenders large-scale violence if various structural conditions are present, such as authoritarian rule and a lack of political rights (as in Rwanda), state weakness and lack of institutional capacity to manage conflict, and socioeconomic imbalances combined with inequity of opportunity and a weak civil society (as in Cambodia). The risk of an outbreak of violent conflict increases when these conditions exist concurrently or are exacerbated by other problems, such as the manipulation of ethnic or other differences (in religion, culture, and language), which can further fragment society and intensify the conflict (Carnegie Commission on Preventing Deadly Conflict 1997; Collier and Hoeffler 1999; Nathan 1998; Reno 1999).

Social capital can be readily perverted to undermine social cohesion and fragment society for individual and group gain, potentially resulting in violent conflict. Under the guise of the Cambodian government, the Angka used inclusionary social capital within the group to strengthen its resolve and weaken those excluded from the group. In Rwanda the political and economic elite used identity to mobilize and contort social capital in order to achieve their own ends.

Within this complex matrix of factors underpinning violent conflict, two main features of social capital become increasingly relevant as potential kindling to fuel the fire of hostility. Vertical relationships plagued by inequality and an unequal distribution of power and opportunity (and thus often accompanied by exclusion and indignity) can instigate violent conflict. Horizontal relations, or the lack of ties between unlike groups in a multicultural society, can erupt into hostilities if one group is seen as monopolizing resources and power to the disadvantage of the others. If within these groups, high levels of bonding social capital link only like members, differences in access to resources and power may worsen relationships and heighten tensions between those in control and those excluded (Narayan 1999). Thus violent conflict can be triggered by the presence of strong exclusionary bonds combined with a lack of horizontal bridges within communities and vertical links between communities and the state.

These precepts describe the possible underlying causes of conflict and reveal the interfaces among various forms of social capital, social cohesion, and violent conflict with several conditioning factors (inequality, indignity, exclusion, poor governance). While the community studies touch on issues relating these factors to violent conflict, the indicators used to assess violent conflict (the number of people killed, loss of access to markets, damage to biodiversity, and disregard for peace accords) tend to correspond with violent conflict as manifested in social, economic, environmental, and political conditions. The indicators assess violent conflict rather than conflict *per se*, which may include intrahousehold conflicts or common disputes over property or legal matters.

In all of the communities studied, violent conflict is viewed as both an independent and a dependent variable (a cause and an effect) in its relation to social capital. That is, social capital can be constructive and support societal cohesion and the mitigation of conflict, but it can also be perverted to hasten social fragmentation and the onslaught of violent conflict.

Cambodia: state absolutism and social capital transformation

Throughout Cambodia's twenty-year conflict, the state targeted communities and individuals, virtually waging war against its own constituents while concurrently destroying the social foundations that traditionally serve as the girders for state building and cohesion. To compound matters, encroaching globalization, hastened by postwar reconstruction and rehabilitation interventions, have interfaced with social capital stocks, further transforming Cambodian society.

Methodology

The Cambodian study, conducted by Social Services of Cambodia, included a literature review and six months of field work. Field research was conducted by an international research director and five local field staff (three men and two women). The research team trained the local field staff extensively in research methods and skills.

Field research incorporated information from more than twelve weeks of village stays and participant observation. During this time, various research techniques were employed, including participatory group exercises (village mapping, resource flow analysis, wealth ranking, and trend analysis) and semi-structured interviews with individuals and groups. This approach to field research allowed good relationships to develop between staff and villagers, greatly contributing to the quantity and quality of the information obtained.

Social Services of Cambodia works in more than 300 different villages in the Kompong Speu province of Cambodia. Twelve of these villages were randomly chosen as potential study sites. The two villages ultimately chosen, Prasath and Prey Koh, were of the same size (about 650 people) but had different experiences of conflict. Prasath, the control village, experienced displacement only once. In the variable village, Prey Koh, villagers were displaced twice, and more people seemed to have been killed there than in Prasath.

In addition to village stays and participant observation, two household surveys were conducted, one to establish baseline socioeconomic information and one to explore social capital issues. The baseline survey collected demographic information and information on landholdings, household occupations, and each household member's place of residence before and during the conflict period.

The survey was conducted in all households in each village (130 households in Prasath, 114 in Prey Koh).

People under the age of fifteen make up about 43–44 percent of the population in each village, about 33 percent of the population is between fifteen and thirty-five, and about 23–24 percent is over thirty-five. Most people were born in their village. Only a very small percentage of the population of either village could remember details of life during the preconflict period.

The survey targeting social capital issues was conducted in about 30 percent of all households (thirty-nine randomly selected households in Prasath, thirty-four in Prey Koh). It examined the following behavioral aspects of social capital in the preconflict, conflict, and postconflict periods:

- Problems in improving livelihood and economic activities.
- Sources of information on livelihood and economic activities.
- Borrowing and lending practices.
- Ownership of and lending practices for livestock, household equipment, and tools.
- Labor exchange.
- Participation in groups and associations.
- Availability and use of services.
- Sources of assistance during crises.
- Participation in activities for the common good.
- Welfare of vulnerable individuals and families.

The definition of social capital used in the Cambodia study was based primarily on the works of Coleman, Putnam, and Uphoff. Horizontal and vertical aspects of social capital were studied, using a modified paradigm derived from Uphoff's work. Structural aspects of social capital were emphasized, although inferences to underlying cognitive social capital that buttressed these structural forms were woven into the analysis when possible.

Social capital was measured by examining levels of trust, as evidenced by measures to secure livelihood and exchange (economic, informational, and so on), and levels of social cohesion, as indicated by collective action and the provision of social services and welfare. Social capital was broken down into five structural components: community events, informal networks, associations, village leadership, and links with external agencies.

Community events are activities that increase feelings of solidarity, strengthen social cohesion, improve communication, provide a learning ground for coordinated activities, promote civic mindedness and altruistic behavior, and through shared experiences help form a sense of collective consciousness. Weddings, funerals, and pagoda activities are classified as community events.

Informal networks – such as rice and water sharing groups – are manifested in innumerable informal exchanges of information and resources within communities. These exchanges – for the most part spontaneous, informal, and unregulated – are the outcome of individual initiative and entrepreneurship. They are thought to be shaped by various factors within the communal environment, predominantly market forces, kinship, and affinity (natural bonds that exist between individuals who live close together or have shared interests and concerns). Informal networks represent efforts to cooperate, coordinate, and provide mutual assistance, and they help maximize the utilization of available resources. They are valuable in providing individuals with support mechanisms in economic and social endeavors. These same informal networks, however, can be based on exploitative relationships in which gains are unevenly distributed.

Associations unite people, frequently from differing kin groups, who work together for a common purpose and have a visible identity. For the most part, these groups have clearly delineated structures, roles, and rules within which group members operate. Associations nurture efforts toward self-help, mutual help, solidarity, and cooperation. They are regarded as the building blocks of civil society and are usually horizontal. The main example of an association illustrated by the study was *provas dei*, an exchange group that trades goods and labor.

In this study, vertical social capital includes the relationships and interactions between a community and its leaders and extends to wider relationships among the village, the government, and the marketplace. Village leadership includes official, traditional, and informal leaders. Official leaders include the communal chief and the local government administration. Traditional leaders are usually people revered for their religious or spiritual attributes (*achars*) or for their age, experience, and knowledge. Informal leaders wield influence because of their wealth, special skills, or charisma. Official and traditional leaders play key roles in the political, social, religious, and welfare activities of the village while shaping networks within the community and between the community and the outside world. The nature and quality of leadership in the community determine the level and quality of development in the village. To a lesser degree, unequal exchanges in resources or information establish patron–client relationships, adding another vertical dimension to village dynamics. Virtually all external links to the villages are considered vertical. External community links include vertical relationships with the government, nongovernmental organizations (NGOs), and the private sector or marketplace.

The indicators of violent conflict used in this case study assess the impact, intensity, and duration of the conflict (table 9.1). Cambodia's experience with violent conflict was manifold, as evidenced by the fact that interviewees discerned different conflict eras. The period of conflict as defined for the study entailed three separate eras distinguished by changes in leadership: Lon Nol (1970–5), Khmer Rouge (1975–9), and the Vietnamese rule, or Heng Samrin (1979–89).

Table 9.1   *Indicators of violent conflict in Cambodia*

Effects on the population	Physical damage	Nature of the conflict
• Number of people killed • Number of people physically disabled • Number of people mentally affected • Extent to which violence is a way of life and is used to solve problems • Number of family members enrolled in the army • Number of people who left the village during the fighting • Changes in composition and size of the population	• Extent to which infrastructure (houses, wells, roads, trees, temples) was destroyed • Physical traces of war (damaged buildings, craters, and so on) • Area of land infested with mines • Number of times village was relocated or dispersed	• Duration of fighting in the village • Types of groups perpetrating the conflict

State-sponsored warfare and citizen victims

Thirty years of warfare all but destroyed most forms of social capital in Cambodia. But the threads of violence predate the recent conflicts and are woven deep in the country's past. Political disruption and successive conflicts have plagued Cambodia since the fall of the Kingdom of Angkor. Relative stability was not achieved until the imposition of French rule, which began in the 1850s and ended with Cambodia's creation in 1954 as a new constitutional monarchy. The Kingdom of Cambodia, led by Premier Prince Norodom Sihanouk, experienced political stability and economic growth as Sihanouk pushed for advances in health, education, and industry. Toward the end of the 1960s, however, the country began to become destabilized, as a result of economic difficulties, corruption, and the increasing threat of communism. As a result, support for Sihanouk declined (Becker 1998).

In 1970 General Lon Nol overthrew Sihanouk, who fled to China, where he publicly formed an alliance with the communist Khmer Rouge. Lon Nol's soldiers terrorized the countryside, dividing and destroying villages within combat zones. Concurrently, regional issues compounded the turbulence. The Vietnam War spilled over into Cambodia, and a growing contingent of communists continually clashed with Lon Nol government soldiers. In response, US planes repeatedly bombed Cambodian territory in an attempt to oust Vietnamese communists supposedly in the area. This campaign killed thousands of innocent people, destroyed numerous villages, and rendered much of the land unusable because of unexploded ordnance, chemical defoliation, and landmines (Ebihara, Morland, and Ledgerwood 1994; Nee 1995).

Lon Nol was subsequently ousted by the Khmer Rouge, which in April 1975 formed Democratic Kampuchea. Under the guise of communism, the Angka ("the organization," the secretive team of Khmer Rouge leaders), headed by "Brother Number One," Pol Pot, initiated a radical agrarian revolution. This break with the past marked Year Zero, when many aspects of Cambodian life were figuratively and literally wiped clean. People were forced from their homes in the cities into rural areas, where they and their rural counterparts were organized into work brigades and coerced into forced labor. Entire villages were relocated; families lost their homes and possessions and were often separated and assigned to different camps. Opposition to the Khmer Rouge was not allowed: dissidents were tortured or killed.

People who lived in cities, along with those who had been affiliated with the Lon Nol government or military, were classified as "new" people, as were their families. "New" people were treated much more severely than "old" people, rural peasants and those who earlier had fallen under the Khmer Rouge. Fragmentation between "old" and "new" split not only neighboring communities but also villages and, at times, families, thus breaking both bonds of kinship and bridges of association. Although both "old" and "new" people generally lived under unbearable conditions – overworked, underfed, and terrorized by fear on a daily basis – the preferential treatment given to "old" people created much resentment.

The four years of totalitarian Khmer Rouge rule resulted in the genocide of roughly 2 million Cambodians, who were murdered or killed by overwork, starvation, and disease (Bit 1991; Nee 1995; van de Put 1997). Any remnant of vertical social capital between the state and civil society was shattered in the wake of a perverse accumulation and use of social capital formed by select communist intellectuals and a vanguard of unemployed, uneducated youth, who pitted themselves against the urban, educated, professional and business segments of society and the older traditional rural peasantry.

Vietnamese troops overcame the Khmer Rouge and formed the People's Republic of Kampuchea in January 1979. The new Vietnamese government, largely viewed by Cambodians as a continuation of external domination over Cambodia, continued to fight the Khmer Rouge throughout the next decade, perpetuating instability throughout the country. Despite this insecurity during the ten years of Vietnamese rule (the Heng Samrin period), recovery gradually began as conflict and insecurity waned. Progress remained slow, however, and was continually hampered by noncommunist governments world-wide who were wary of the Vietnamese occupiers and kept Cambodia in relative isolation (Chandler 1992; Nee 1995).

With the Vietnamese withdrawal in 1989, the state of Cambodia was formed. Prince Sihanouk returned after thirteen years of self-imposed exile. A transitional government was established until the Paris Agreements in October 1991, which temporarily formalized the government structure. The United Nations

Transitional Authority in Cambodia (UNTAC) oversaw the peace process, reconstruction, and rehabilitation, with mixed results (Ebihara, Morland, and Ledgerwood 1994). Elections were finally held in 1993, instituting a new coalition government headed by Prince Ranarridh, with Hun Sen as co-premier. In 1997 an attempted coup disrupted the dual government, leading to a strengthening of Hun Sen's control. The July 1998 elections left Hun Sen in control of the recovering state.

The social outcomes of ideological and regional war

During the Lon Nol regime, traditional sources of social capital were severely eroded throughout Cambodia. Many villages were split up, and villagers were forced to relocate due to warfare, bombings, and recruitment. Within villages, exchange slowed and solidarity around the temple dissolved. Some families did manage to stay intact, however, despite massive dislocation (Nee 1995).

The Khmer Rouge ushered in another era of organized violence, which included systematic attacks on traditional Cambodian society – on norms, culture, religion, organizations, networks, and even the family. Community and family members were encouraged to spy and report on each other, destroying trust and planting the seeds of deeply rooted fear. A war against class distinctions was waged, as attempts to level economic status were instituted by making everyone unpaid agricultural laborers. By destroying all social, political, and economic institutions in this extreme communistic experiment, the brutal Khmer Rouge regime transformed and depleted what little social capital had remained from the Lon Nol period (Bit 1991; Nee 1995).

After a decade of destruction, forms of social capital gradually began to re-emerge during the Heng Samrin period, despite the turmoil that continued to fester. This turmoil was marked by skirmishes between the guerrillas and invading troops, internal migration, and the disruption of agriculture, which resulted in widespread famine. The Khmer Rouge had used collectivization as a strategy to transform the economy and had broken up families to work in cooperatives. Vietnamese efforts to rebuild Cambodia in the early 1980s paralleled this philosophy by focussing on collectivist cooperatives, such as the solidarity group *krom samaki*, which forbade private ownership and encouraged development through communal efforts. Although some progress and recovery occurred under the Heng Samrin government, Cambodians greeted the end of the Vietnamese regime with relief.

The postconflict forms of structural social capital and its composition do not differ greatly from those that existed before the wars. In both of the villages studied, community events, particularly pagoda activities and religious ceremonies, mirror practices of the period before the conflict. Village meetings are also conducted in much the same way they were before the conflict.

Informal networks continue to be organized by kinship and affinity, just as they had been before the fighting erupted, but they are increasingly beginning to be shaped by market forces. Nonfarm activities, particularly small business and trade, are promoting new networks that go beyond the circle of relatives and friends. These networks have increased the need for mobility and information, putting people in touch with the world outside their villages. Networks formally based on the concept of mutual aid are giving way to new networks based on rigid reciprocity and the need to earn cash income, as is evident in the decrease of *provas dei*. Informal networks are thus not dissolving as a result of the ravages of violent conflict, but are changing in composition in response to the power and permeating influence of external market forces.

Visible changes after the conflict were not noticed in associations sponsored by the government or initiated by village leaders or the pagoda. Local associational initiatives – such as rice banks, funeral associations, and water users' groups – did not alter drastically either. Prey Koh exhibits more associational involvement than Prasath, primarily because of its higher level of economic activity. Prey Koh suffered more from conflict than did Prasath, but associational activity increased, despite the deeper schism between "old" and "new" people and the consequent more prominent threat of the breakdown of trust among villagers. This suggests that the conflict did not necessarily diminish the willingness of people to work together, which perhaps remained strong as a result of the communities' Buddhist tradition.

There is little difference between the preconflict and current village leadership (including traditional, informal, and official leaders) with regard to type, role, and nature. In general, village leaders are more visible in Prey Koh than in Prasath, primarily because of their greater resources and better links with the outside world. Prasath's narrow resource base has resulted in poor links with the outside world; village leaders, preoccupied with problems within their own households, are consequently less active. Pagoda activities are more or less at the same level in both villages, and elders and *achar*s appear to be equally active in both.

Various factors seem to have supported the revival of social capital, which began under Heng Samrin rule. These factors include community members' resilience (an inner strength that allows people to continue to cope and to rebuild their lives), community members' strong desire to help themselves, the powerful role played by the pagoda and Buddhist traditions in shaping identity and the need to re-establish this identity, the need to restore basic village infrastructure that had been destroyed, and the knowledge that the government would not be able to provide what was needed.

In the preconflict period, no agencies other than the government operated in the two villages. Government-provided services and resources were very basic, but they may have been of better quality than they are now, particularly in education and health. In both communities, state penetration remains weak and the substitutional effects of emerging civil societies, particularly in the provision of basic services, are only beginning to emerge. NGO involvement in village development and in providing services is a relatively new phenomenon, which began in the Heng Samrin period. NGOs, particularly international bodies, have been highly visible in Cambodia. In the study villages, however, their role has been intermittent. Development of links with external agencies in both villages currently depends largely on initiatives from outside. A more recent phenomenon has been the increasing involvement of the business community, especially in Prey Koh, where businesses, clearly driven by the profit motive, are highly exploitative of the environment and villagers.

The Cambodia case illustrates how the ebb and flow of horizontal social capital can vary according to the relative penetration of vertical state and market forces. As the conflict waned, integrative bonding relationships were supplanted by external bridging ties. Despite Prey Koh's higher level of exposure to conflict, its proximity to market-penetrating forces transformed and strengthened certain types of social capital, mainly more development-oriented, bridging social capital, in the postconflict period. In contrast, Prasath, which remains isolated, is marginalized from market penetration, and social capital has remained encapsulated in insular, kin-oriented bonds. The research team posited that this difference reflected deeper market penetration in Prey Koh, which is closer to the highway and has easier access to market activities than Prasath, which is located near the foot of the hills and until recently had been plagued by sporadic violence from Khmer Rouge attacks. The implication is that while violent conflict often shapes social capital in favor of bonding relationships and a survival orientation in the emergency period, postconflict market penetration may easily reverse this pattern and lead to more outward-focussed, bridging social capital in the medium-to longer-term transition to peace.

Rwanda: hate, fear, and the decay of social relations

Although Rwanda seemed to become unglued rapidly in April 1994, the weakening of bridging social relationships between Tutsi and Hutu and the increasing penetration, grasp, and span of the state over communal affairs had been occurring for decades. In an attempt to better understand the conflict and its interactions with social relationships and norms, the Rwandan study examined how social capital interacted with conflict, both in terms of the unraveling of the social fabric between Hutu and Tutsi and the strengthening of social dynamics among Hutu that facilitated the genocide. While problematic vertical and horizontal relationships within Rwanda led to the civil war, external factors, such as international interventions and changes brought about by modernization also affected social capital stocks.

Methodology

The Rwandan study was conducted by local consultants and entailed both field and desk research. The first phase of the study, the literature review, assessed pertinent historical information and outlined traditional forms of Rwandan social capital. Field research in the selected communities was conducted by two teams, each consisting of one man and one woman. The research included a three-week period of participant observation, six weeks of survey implementation, and three weeks of interviews with associations, focus groups, and key informants in two communes.

Both communes are of comparable size: Giti's population is 48,000, Shyanda's is 39,000. The two communes share the same language, religion, and culture and have similar modes of subsistence and socioeconomic status, although Giti has been and remains marginally more prosperous. Intermarriage between Hutu and Tutsi was and remains common in both areas. Giti, the control site, experienced low levels of violence. Shyanda, the variable site, experienced high levels of organized killing.

As in Cambodia, surveys were conducted at the household level, targeting 1.5 percent of randomly selected households in three sectors of each commune. The average household contained five people. The team administered 114 surveys in Giti and 144 in Shyanda. Focus groups of five–fifteen participants were made up largely of mixed groups – widows, orphans, politicians, intellectuals, associations, and businesspeople. Key informants were chosen from these groups. Question and issue guides for both group and individual interviews were developed based on the initial survey findings.

Social capital was measured by the density and nature of organizations and networks (both vertical and horizontal) and by members' sense of commitment and responsibility to these groups. The propensity for cooperation and exchange (material, labor, ritualistic, and informational) served as a proxy for trust. In addition, the study attempted to develop indicators and measures of both vertical and horizontal social capital that were specifically tailored for war-torn societies. Indicators for measuring social capital were based on social capital concepts as described by Putnam, Coleman, and Fukuyama and were adapted to the particularities of Rwandan society. Related measures examined as proxies for social capital and trust included the following:

- Channels and mechanisms for the exchange of information.
- The existence and nature of associations and the reason for their creation (shared interests or prescribed commonality, such as familial relations).

- Intermarriage and extended family relations.
- Intercommunity relationships and mechanisms for conflict resolution.
- Availability and functioning of infrastructure.
- Types, nature, and organization of exchange and interdependence.
- Nature and organization of assistance, mutual aid, and cooperation (including sharing of basic necessities, such as food, water, firewood, and salt).
- Social protection and welfare; collective responsibility.

To confirm that these factors were considered representative of social capital not only by the researchers but also by those being interviewed, survey questions and focus group interviews sought to elicit what social capital meant to each participant. Throughout survey implementation and with each focus group, it became clear that participants and researchers had roughly the same definition of social capital. Although each focus group had its own interpretation, the combined concepts covered almost all facets of social capital as defined for the study. Participants in both communities viewed social capital as including mutual assistance, trust, solidarity, civic duty, collective action, protection of the vulnerable, peaceful cohabitation, and a just political system engendered by the state.

The original goal of the Rwandan study was to assess how conflict depleted social capital and how social capital was restored following the war's end. After the initial findings from the field were submitted, however, it became evident that conflict transformed rather than simply depleted stocks of social capital and that new forms of social capital emerged during the conflict. The study was therefore broadened to encompass these transformations.

Indicators of violent conflict in Rwanda included social, economic, environmental, and political factors (table 9.2). Changes in social capital were assessed before and after the conflict. The period of conflict was defined solely by the interviewees, who equated it with the genocide of April–July 1994. However, it should be noted that violence and conflict have plagued Rwanda for decades and that the civil war officially began in October 1990. Since the end of the genocide, widespread violence has continued, with revenge killings and civil war occurring along Rwanda's borders and within the Democratic Republic of Congo.

Throughout the study, difficulties emerged because of the sensitivity of the topic and the recentness of the war. Unlike Cambodia, where much time had passed since the genocide and few people were still around to provide details, the Rwanda genocide was fresh in people's minds, and the unsettling presence of *génocidaires* living amidst victims created an atmosphere of fear and intimidation. The research teams therefore spent more time than originally scheduled in each commune to build relationships, trust, and acceptance by residents. After the field teams strengthened their relationships with communal members,

Table 9.2   *Indicators of violent conflict in Rwanda*

Effects on the population	Physical damage	Nature of the conflict
• Number of people killed • Number of communities and families destroyed • Number of people physically disabled • Number of people relocated • Destruction of economic infrastructure • Loss of access to markets	• Damage to resources necessary for production • Extent to which crops were lost and fields destroyed • Damage to biodiversity • Area of land laid waste due to mass migration • Area of land infested with mines	• Duration of fighting in the village • Types of groups perpetrating the conflict

discussions broadened to encompass details of the respondents' conflict experiences.

Anatomy of genocide

The 1994 massacres killed more people more quickly than any other mass slaughter in history – more than 800,000 people died at the hands of their brethren within a three-month period (Berkeley 1998). Historically, the ethnic hatred that fueled this armed eruption did not exist between Hutu and Tutsi: during precolonial times the two groups coexisted symbiotically, engaging in complementary modes of subsistence. Yet in this coexistence, Hutu and Tutsi were neither similar nor equal. Most important, group membership was not static (Newbury 1988; Prunier 1997). Distinctions between the groups stemmed from membership of different classes, not from dissimilar ethnic backgrounds. Being labeled "Hutu" or "Tutsi" simply meant belonging to a loosely defined category based on occupation or class – Hutu were cultivators and Tutsi were pastoralists and generally belonged to the ruling and warrior classes.

Relationships between Hutu and Tutsi deteriorated under Belgian colonial power. By supporting the minority Tutsi rule, colonization further entrenched socioeconomic disparities and solidified the divide between the groups along "ethnic" (rather than class) lines.[2] The arbitrary distinctions between the groups were sharpened by colonial mythology, which relegated the Hutu cultivators to a lower status and treated the pastoral Tutsi as the superior ruling class. The Belgian census of 1926 forced Hutu and Tutsi to choose an "ethnic" identity. What had once been a dynamic system of classes became a static system based

[2] Hutu represent approximately 85 percent of the Rwandan population, Tutsi roughly 14 percent, and the Twa 1 percent.

on "ethnicity," which later became a (much abused) tool for manipulation of the masses by elite ruling groups (Lemarchand 1970; Newbury 1988; Prunier 1997).

The ruling Tutsi government was overthrown in 1961.[3] In retribution for the former discriminatory systems put in place to exclude Hutu, the new Hutu government began to focus on marginalizing the Tutsi community. Traditional social and political systems were replaced by the central administration, as the state penetrated ever deeper into the lives of the citizenry (Lemarchand 1970; Prunier 1997). Skirmishes between Hutu and Tutsi spread throughout Rwanda, killing thousands and forcing a massive Tutsi migration – a tragic pattern that continued over the next thirty years. As the violence between the groups persisted, the government became increasingly repressive against Tutsi, abridging their rights and institutionally excluding them from educational and employment opportunities. Falling commodity prices, increasing debt, and government corruption led President Juvenal Habyarimana's regime to deflect attention from the compounding crises by fueling the flames of ethnic hatred (Prunier 1997).

Tutsi rebel forces of the Rwandan Patriotic Front (RPF) invaded northern Rwanda in October 1990, unleashing increased insecurity and killings in the area. In response, Rwandan security forces distributed arms to local civilian officials, and the national army was expanded. The RPF continued its attacks within Rwanda's borders throughout 1991 and 1992, exacerbating hate politics and rhetoric against Tutsi. Concurrently, President Habyarimana took small steps toward liberalizing the political system, mainly in an effort to maintain his power. More strident steps to retain control were implemented in late 1992, when the Habyarimana regime began to train Hutu extremist militia groups, known as the Interahamwe and the Impuzamugambi. This training continued while the government pursued peace talks with the rebel forces in 1993 and early 1994 (Prunier 1997; Uvin 1998).

On April 6, 1994, President Habyarimana's plane was shot down over Rwanda's capital, Kigali. Government forces and militia immediately began attacking Tutsi and moderate Hutu. Within the next three months, brutal killings of Tutsi erupted throughout the country. While some Hutu willingly participated in the massacres, others were ordered or forced to kill. A campaign of Tutsi elimination forced roughly 2 million refugees to flee the country, while displacing about 1 million people internally. During the genocide, Rwandan society collapsed completely. Business and agricultural activities ceased, skilled people and the intelligentsia were slaughtered or fled, the infrastructure was purposely destroyed, and government operations, including legal, educational, and health activities, were dissolved (Des Forges 1999).

---

[3] Ironically, former Belgian colonial forces who had propped up the Tutsi regime assisted Hutu in ousting the ruling Tutsi party.

After the Tutsi rebel forces of the RPF took Kigali in July 1994, hundreds of thousands of Hutu fled to neighboring countries, many of them destroying everything in their path as they left. Meanwhile, Tutsi refugees from the 1994 exodus and earlier migrations spilled back into Rwanda. Chaos ensued during this massive return, with much looting, pillaging, and squatting taking place. Government attempts to repatriate Hutu refugees were unsuccessful, for many feared widespread reprisal killings.[4] More than 1 million Hutu finally returned home in 1996 from neighboring Burundi, Tanzania, Uganda, and the Democratic Republic Congo (Prunier 1997).

The perversion of social capital

During the genocide, social capital atrophied, as the country, communities, and families fell prey to hatred and violence. Yet integrative forms of social capital increased within families fighting for survival, among individuals attempting to save or rescue Tutsi, and in the small Muslim community within Rwanda, which never took part in the genocide. High levels of bonding social capital also emerged among Hutu extremists, with very negative ramifications for those excluded, revealing that violence can be the result of strong bonding social capital among its perpetrators.[5]

As the formal Hutu government dissolved, a primary operating unit emerged that coordinated the genocide. Communities split as orders calling for Hutu to kill Tutsi originated from the central government and were spread throughout Rwanda by way of local leaders, who helped mobilize the masses. Although some Hutu hid and saved Tutsi, many participated in the killings out of a sense of perceived ethnic duty, out of loyalty to the Hutu-controlled state, and because of threats against their or their families' lives. Once the killing began, Hutu killed not only Tutsi they did not know but also their neighbors and, in some cases, even family members. To make matters more complex, some Tutsi with Hutu physical characteristics killed Tutsi to save themselves. These indiscriminate but intimate killings led to the disintegration of communes and families and fragmented social cohesion (Gourevitch 1998; Des Forges 1999).

Ironically, the genocide was also a powerful community building exercise, at least among participating Hutu. Seeking to preserve their control and resources, Hutu power groups achieved their ultimate success by mobilizing exclusionary and divisive social capital that bonded (primarily) unemployed, uneducated

---

[4] Many revenge killings did take place throughout the genocide and in the period immediately following it, as Tutsi slaughtered Hutu in retaliation for deaths in their families. The exact figures are not known, but the numbers of Hutu killed by no means match those of Tutsi killed (Prunier 1997; Des Forges 1999).

[5] For a similar conclusion on social capital dynamics within militias, gangs, and guerrilla groups, see Moser and McIlwaine (1999).

Hutu youth to form the Interahamwe. High levels of social capital existed both vertically and horizontally among Hutu ranks, while bridging social capital linking the Hutu with the Tutsi was all but eliminated. Within Hutu extremism, state-driven vertical social capital fueled communal-level Hutu groups' success by providing excellent information networks, reinvented past traditions, and a sense of solidarity and civic duty (Prunier 1997).

In the initial weeks of the genocide, lists of Tutsi addresses helped expedite the killings and ensure thoroughness. The media were used to spread hate propaganda against Tutsi. *Radio et Télévision Libre des Mille Collines* broadcasts listed Hutus in each commune who had not participated in the killings, publicly pressuring them to join the genocide. These information networks also kept the Interahamwe informed on the identity of those who had been killed, who had not yet been removed, and who had helped facilitate the killing process. By spreading hate, fear, suspicion, and greed via newsletters and radio, Hutu extremists were able to whip Hutu masses into a murderous frenzy. For those who joined in the killings, the hate propaganda against the Tutsi justified their actions and eased their consciences (Gourevitch 1998; Des Forges 1999).

Extremist Hutu also gained following in part by invoking precolonial Rwandan traditions and applying them in a new vein. For instance, the nomenclature for extremist Hutu groups was similar to that of precolonial militias and blood brotherhoods. Propaganda used to fuel Hutu actions referred to the former tradition of cooperative labor (*umuganda*), which had evolved into forced labor and was seen as abusive to Hutu. The slogan of the 1959 massacres reflects this reference – *tugire gukora akazi* ("let us go and do the work") (Prunier 1997; Gourevitch 1998).

Génocidaires were united by the collective action of killing, which helped create feelings of collective consciousness, commonality, and shared goals. *Interahamwe* means "those who attack together;" *impuzamugambi* means "single-minded ones," or "those who have the same goal." With mass participation in the killings, it became difficult to assign guilt to individuals. In the words of a participant in the genocide, "No one person killed any one person" (Des Forges 1999, p. 770).

The success of the genocide depended in part on civilians' sense of civic duty and on the historical strength of the central government. Historically, vertical social capital, manifested in almost absolute state power, penetrated Rwandan society so deeply that it superseded horizontal relationships or loyalties. Officials from the police, local administrations, and military forces went door to door requisitioning men to partake in their "national duty" of eliminating Tutsi, and Hutu voluntarily or grudgingly followed these orders. Killing Tutsi was portrayed as a Hutu obligation; such phrases as "it is your duty to help clear the field" and "eradicate the cockroaches" were current. The image of killing as a means of self-defense against the RPF invasion was also employed, with the resounding urgency of kill or be killed (Prunier 1997).

This perverse manipulation of social capital made possible the mass recruitment of Hutu; yet real social and economic gains proved an added incentive to Hutu involvement. Roughly 60 percent of Rwandans were under the age of twenty before the genocide, and few had hopes of acquiring land or obtaining jobs. Population density in Rwanda was also very high; in Shyanda, for example, it had reached 668 people per square kilometer by 1989 (Prunier 1997). Scarcer land, drought, and low crop prices combined to create an economic crisis. Tutsi elimination would benefit Hutu who participated in the killings by decreasing the number of competitors for land, homes, cattle, and other possessions.

Social capital in the aftermath of violence

Violent conflict and the political and economic disintegration of the Rwandan State profoundly destroyed whatever broad-based forms of social capital had existed. The conflict negatively affected most manifestations of horizontal social capital, such as exchange, mutual assistance, trust, and protection of the vulnerable. In the postwar period, however, they are being revived in various forms to help regain some sense of normalcy. Traditionally bridging activities, such as exchange and associations, have re-emerged in both Giti and Shyanda, yet have been reduced or transformed due to the conflict, its legacy, and modernizing factors. Bonding social capital has also suffered, and trust remains an extant issue for rebuilding both bonding and bridging social relations.

Exchange, reciprocity, and mutual assistance have all diminished in Giti and Shyanda in the aftermath of the war, mainly due to decreased levels of trust, abject poverty, environmental degradation, and a scarcity of goods and labor. With fewer men to contribute to the financial and physical needs of community, as many have been killed or are in prison, and with fewer resources on which to draw, the burden on women and children has increased tremendously. This increased burden has not, however, been offset by mutual assistance, for people are struggling to meet their own needs, let alone provide for the needs of others. Although Giti experienced less violence than Shyanda, it did experience much devastation due to the large number of refugees who sought shelter in the commune, damaging crops, land, and buildings. In addition, Giti commune members have isolated themselves from neighboring communes that participated in the genocide, which has negatively affected intercommunal trade.

According to interviewees, increasing modernization, monetization, and individualism, as well as widespread and worsening poverty, are also to blame for the decrease in mutual assistance and gift giving within communes. The majority of those interviewed viewed "traditional" social capital as localized, bonding relationships among extended family and small communities that provided welfare mechanisms and social protection. Moves toward bridging social capital, which engenders developmental and economic linkages and is often accompanied by monetization and individualism, were seen to have eroded these bonding relations.

Associational groups were also transformed by the conflict. New types of associations have emerged to deal with the legacies of the war. Whereas pre-war associations strove to better the welfare of people internal and external to the group, the new organizations are predominantly exclusive, although they include both Tutsi and Hutu. These new groups comprise the most vulnerable, who focus on meeting the group's internal needs. One association has arisen to provide funds for schooling Hutu and Tutsi orphans in Giti, with graduates from this program contributing to keep it active. In Shyanda, widow associations have emerged, and despite the commune's genocidal experience, members include both Hutu whose husbands are in prison and Tutsi whose husbands were killed during the war. This seemingly stunning example of bridging social capital between Hutu and Tutsi, however, is flawed. Group members feel that they cannot communicate openly, and that there are underlying feelings of mistrust and resentment. The women say that they cooperate to meet each other's needs, but only for their survival and not due to altruism or trust.

The family and intermarriage were also affected by the warfare. Many of the Rwandans interviewed felt that the dissolution of families, which occurred in both communes, has led to increased membership in these new types of associations, who can provide assistance when there is no family to turn to, or when the family is too vulnerable to provide. The nuclear family has failed to a degree – fathers and brothers are dead or in jail; mothers, struggling to fill their role, often cannot meet their children's needs. Some children are sent away from home to live with extended family or to wander the streets in hopes that aid or religious organizations will assist them. Respondents also noted that relationships between families joined by marriage have been greatly weakened: in-laws can no longer rely on one another for support and assistance. Although intermarriage still occurs between Hutu and Tutsi in Giti and Shyanda, it is often criticized in the wake of the genocide. Commune members in Giti are even reluctant to marry those outside their own commune for fear of marrying into a murderous family.

Adding to the strain on bonding and bridging social capital between Hutu and Tutsi, the genocide has created new social cleavages that run within these groups. Tutsi, for example, are divided both by the duration of their stay abroad and by where they sought refuge: those returning from Uganda are perceived as being more elitist than those from Burundi, who have a higher status than returnees from the Democratic Republic of the Congo. Tutsi who remained in Rwanda and survived the genocide are suspected of collaboration with the *génocidaires*, for it is doubted that any Tutsi could have survived on his or her own. There are also divisions among the Hutu who participated in the killings, those suspected of being involved, and those who did not participate (Prunier 1997; Gourevitch 1998).

The war also has affected vertical relationships in Rwanda, which traditionally have had great influence over Rwandan society. This strong vertical influence may have helped spare Giti during the genocide, thanks to the actions of its burgomaster (communal head), who forbade killing in his commune. In contrast, in Shyanda, which initially escaped violence and in fact served as a Tutsi refuge, killings began soon after orders were dispatched by the acting prime minister, a Hutu from the region, who visited the commune to check on its lack of genocidal response (Des Forges 1999). In this case, strong vertical alliances overpowered horizontal allegiance with tragic results.

Since the war, the official communal leadership, which is still appointed by the centralized government, has maintained high levels of control over the communes, although efforts toward decentralization are being made. Communal elections have been held to elect local community development committees (CDCs), which have autonomy in planning and decisionmaking over development efforts in their respective communes. It is hoped that these decentralization efforts will help restore the populace's faith and trust lost during the war. Through development interventions utilizing the CDCs, efforts are being made to fortify and augment existing bonding and bridging social capital within and between the communities so that progress made is sustainable.

Policies and programs for strengthening social capital and social cohesion

Physical rehabilitation and reconstruction cannot be achieved without social reconciliation. Participation and decentralization can empower people to take over development; they can give people a sense of control over their future, while also building and augmenting bonding, bridging, and linking ties. An inclusive community-level approach to development founded on the concepts of participation and decentralization will put the beneficiaries themselves in control of managing their own affairs and will give local administrative structures primary responsibility for development activities. This thereby not only empowers the groups but also encourages them to work together to build their connected futures, strengthening bonding and bridging relations. Efforts by international actors to build and strengthen civil society must be accompanied by efforts to improve respect for pluralism, tolerance, and participatory, democratic principles, in other words to forge better links between government and communities. Equality among social groups that promotes ties cutting across ethnicity, clans, gender, age, religion, and political ideologies is necessary if civic engagement is to flourish. Such civil society binds together potentially disintegrative elements, building new, cohesive social identities while keeping bonding elements of communal identity in balance. Based on the findings from the Cambodian and Rwandan studies, recommendations specific to these countries and the above approaches to building social capital and cohesion can be made.

Cambodia: nurturing associations for economic growth and development

Despite the wars' devastation to the Cambodian social fabric, communities have remained resilient. Current forms of social capital in Cambodia ensure basic survival and a livelihood for some people but also allow exploitation of people and resources by others. Reconstruction efforts should build on the extant bonding and bridging relationships, while expanding the role of social capital to more responsible management of available resources, based on principles of equity and sustainability.

The United Nations Development Programme's CARRERE Project and the World Bank-financed Northeast Village Development Project are good examples of efforts to build local capacity and social capital into the development process. These are second-generation community fund or social development approaches in which community resources are managed not through intermediary agents but by the village itself, building on existing institutions and relationships and creating new ones through project development and implementation. The aim is to connect to markets and create a form of social capital that arises from community traditions and cultural and familial solidarity but also creates and is created by repeated and predictable economic and social exchanges, thus connecting people of diverse backgrounds to each other in numerous overlapping and reinforcing relationships. In this manner, the project will build on extant bonding and bridging social capital relations, while forging and augmenting new ones.

Efforts to encourage village participation in development interventions, however, can be supported externally yet must originate internally. If external actors try to forge new social capital relations and increase participation simply by convening meetings in villages, these efforts may be counterproductive. Villagers may attend meetings out of perceived coercion, not out of free will. Meetings called by external actors are reminiscent of the days of Pol Pot, when villagers expected to listen to political propaganda, not participate. Furthermore, these types of meetings tend to alienate the poor, who spend the meetings thinking about how they will get their next meal and resent this use of their time (Nee 1995). Ownership of initiative is critical to building sustainable crosscutting social capital.

In addition, attempts to support cooperation, participation, and group solidarity may not be immediately appropriate during initial development efforts. The dissolution of trust within Cambodian society was a direct consequence of the societal fragmentation brought about by the Lon Nol government and the Khmer Rouge's campaign to manipulate people and retain control through coercion, suspicion, and fear. True reconstruction cannot take place if this dissolution of trust is not acknowledged and addressed. Until trust is rebuilt, attempts to encourage solidarity and group cooperation may backfire by reminding Cambodians of the Khmer Rouge's communal works and the collectivism of the *krom samaki* under the Heng Samrin regime (Nee 1995). External interventions must be sensitive to these issues and allow cooperation to occur spontaneously, by supporting efforts that network people and build a responsive and responsible civil society.

External actors may not be able to overtly create new networks and groups or actively pursue increased participation from an external impetus, but they can work on developing the conditions that will foster the creation of networks and increase participation. In part, this effort to create a more conducive environment for social capital formation and participation stems from the rebuilding of the economic and social infrastructure, mitigating threats to social capital, and not doing damage to social relations by the development interventions themselves.

Cambodians lack the economic and social infrastructure needed to crack the shell of poverty, while they also lack the community participation and grassroots institutions needed to build this infrastructure. Decentralization, local ownership, and participation work only if communities are socially cohesive, appropriately organized, and inclusive. Development actors should capitalize on existing associations, such as the pagoda networks, which are organized and cohesive, and work to complement, not substitute for, these local efforts (Cambodia 1999).

The creation of a more conducive environment for social capital requires the ability of development actors to identify threats to social capital, such as acute poverty, increasing population pressure, degradation of resources, and the emergence of a market economy in the absence of proper regulation, the rule of law, and safety nets for poor households. Any external development efforts in these areas should be designed to enhance the state's capacity and its ability to relate to citizens and communities in a participatory manner.

As social capital does not necessarily benefit all, development actors should avoid or minimize interventions that reinforce the negative elements of existing social capital. In Cambodia, this implies shunning efforts that focus on vertical planning and that implement structures without putting in place accompanying horizontal structures and accountability to lower levels. Given current circumstances, it is equally important to strengthen Cambodia's horizontal social capital, encompassing both bonding and bridging relations, as to focus on vertical social capital, such as efforts to strengthen government capacity and accountability.

Rwanda: rebuilding family, community, and state interrelations

Although Rwanda has made much progress since the war, many Rwandans remain haunted by its terror. Securing food and shelter has been difficult for many survivors. As a legacy of the genocide, homeless orphans wander the streets, and widows and wives of men in prison struggle to make ends meet. Widespread poverty and severely damaged infrastructure hamper growth and development. Interahamwe incursions into northwestern and southwestern Rwanda have kept these regions relatively unstable and caused them to lag in development. The March 1999 local elections were a major step forward for the government, for they helped mute criticism of its legitimacy (Prunier 1997; Gourevitch 1998).

The shaping of social capital in Rwanda is clearly at a crossroads. The challenge is to balance economic development with social development in a manner that simultaneously enables the nation to find its way out of the darkness of poverty while encouraging social relationships that cross class, ethnic, and gender divides while preserving bonding ties that serve as the foundation of societal life. Inclusive state institutions and conflict management mechanisms need to be encouraged and supported for a cohesive society to thrive. Many positive signs of steps in this direction have already emerged, such as the cross-cutting widows and orphan associations; the revival of *gacaca*, a traditional form of dispute mediation and distributive justice; government moves toward decentralization and increasing participation; and a more accountable civil administration.

In light of the perceived ineffectiveness of the International Criminal Tribunal (ICT) for Rwanda and the common view that it will be unable to administer justice, efforts have been made to reinstate *gacaca*, a traditional system of justice exercised by a group of community elders to help handle allegations of genocide. The specifics of how this mechanism would work in conjunction with the tribunal are still under discussion, however they would be seen as a legal venue that would complement the ongoing ICT. Many Rwandans see this procedure as the only hope for reconciliation. It would provide a much-needed venue for both Hutu and Tutsi to relate their experiences and voice their concerns. International actors should find some means of supporting this process – but with caution. Elders and sages chosen from the commune may be better able to handle rulings and sentencing of those convicted of genocide, since they are familiar with the situation and the people. There is, however, a danger of subjective rulings and the inability to conduct fair trials in certain communes. Nevertheless, attempts should be made to seek individual accountability, thus helping to diminish the tendency to ascribe collective guilt to all Hutu (Des Forges 1999).

Another key factor in the reconstruction of intracommunity and intercommunity relationships is the establishment of free and objective media. Genocide was committed so quickly and effectively in Rwanda because of propaganda issued by biased, extremist radio programs, journals, and weekly papers. By once again linking Hutu and Tutsi by creating a Rwandan identity, fair media may help prevent a recurrence of violence and help keep the government in check.

Efforts to build civil society in Rwanda failed in the past, as the rapid explosion of genocidal killings showed. Extreme poverty, inequality, clientelism, and poor information networks, compounded by the social, economic, and political marginalization of the rural populace (the majority of Rwandans) made the emergence of an autonomous, highly developed civil society all but impossible. Thus despite the abundance of these associative groups during the 1980s, social capital was not sufficiently inclusive or potent to counterbalance the hate politics generated by Hutu extremists (Uvin 1998). Facilitating the creation of NGOs is not just a matter of freeing the space necessary for their existence but also of using these groups to go beyond the boundaries of family, ethnic group, and location as the basis for group cohesion. Social learning and social change, not just the presence of numerous types of organizations, are needed to create a healthy civil society.

The process of developing social capital within communities and between constituents and the state takes a long time. It must be initiated internally, and it requires the gradual increase in the ability and willingness to shape the political sphere. Pluralism and participation must be promoted along with social capital initiatives. Through this process, people gain confidence in their ability to operate within the public arena. As the society becomes more open, networks of communication and cooperation arise across communities, as divisions based on ethnicity, religion, gender, and region are overcome. Knowledge of politics and political workings increase, as do skills in conflict mediation, compromise, and negotiation.

Projects that decentralize state power and increase participation by civil society actors and individuals should be implemented to help rebuild faith in the central government and encourage cooperation among constituents. Community-based reconstruction approaches, such as the World Bank Community Reintegration and Development Project, are attempting to create the space for development of social capital that can transcend "ethnic" lines through increased participation. Programs like these not only unite groups within communities, they also link communities to the state through decentralization. Community decisionmaking to assess and prioritize community needs and determine and manage the allocation of resources to address these needs can be a powerful source of reconciliation through reconstruction. A central goal is to build local institutions that promote inclusive development by giving people a voice and that are capable of creating the social infrastructure necessary for conflict mediation.

Designs for sustainable peace and development

As seen in both the Cambodian and Rwandan case studies, social capital can take many forms and serve many functions, depending on its nature and use. It can contribute to social cohesion or spur social fragmentation. It can be a source of mutual aid and protection in the face of violent conflict, or it can be perverted to mobilize groups such as unemployed youth for violent ends. Social capital can help bridge and mitigate the exclusive relationships that create the conditions for conflict, or it can reinforce highly exclusionary bonds, such as those that exist within gangs or extremist ethnic groups. It can substitute for state and market failures or complement their successes by providing basic protection or safety nets.

Thus social capital is a double-edged sword with regard to conflict and development. Violent conflict can destroy primary bonds, undercutting indigenous social capital as a form of social protection. But by weakening such primary bonds, conflict can create opportunities for bridges to other networks, and it can displace relationships that tend to create dependency, limit access to new information and opportunities, and retard change. Under such conditions, social capital can serve as a key source of reconciliation and reconstruction in divided societies through the formation of broad and diverse networks. The development of civic institutions that cut across traditional bonding social capital to form new links that cross ethnic, religious, age, income, and gender lines can provide the basis for the mediation, conflict management, and conflict resolution mechanisms that all societies require to sustain peace and development. A new government presents the opportunity to improve government capability and deepen community relations (Gittel and Vidal 1998; see Martin 1996a, 1996b for further discussion).

The goal of development policies and operations in conflict-affected countries is to respond to the needs of those affected by war, who cry out to be free from oppression, fear, hunger, and violence and long to be rich with opportunity and security that empowers them to make decisions that affect their own lives. Socially cohesive communities rely on all forms of social capital: bonding ties for protection and survival in time of crisis, bridging links for action and development in time of hope, and dynamic government–community relationships that allow civic engagement to thrive as the ultimate guarantee against violent conflict. External policies and programs needs to nurture and transform social capital in order to create and maintain the mechanisms and institutions necessary for strengthening social cohesion, managing diversity, preventing violent conflict, and sustaining peace and development.

REFERENCES

Becker, E., 1998. *When the War Was Over: Cambodia and the Khmer Rouge Revolution.* New York: Public Affairs
Berkeley, B., 1998. "Judgment Day." *Washington Post Magazine* October 11: 10–15, 25–29
Berkman, L. and Kawachi, I., 2000. *Social Epidemiology.* New York: Oxford University Press
Bit, Seanglim (ed.), 1991. *The Warrior Heritage: A Psychological Perspective of Cambodian Trauma.* El Cerrito, CA: Seanglim Bit
Cambodia, Kingdom of, Ministry of Planning, 1999. *Cambodia Human Development Report 1999: Village Economy and Development.* Phnom Penh
Carnegie Commission on Preventing Deadly Conflict, 1997. *Preventing Deadly Conflict: Executive Summary of the Final Report.* New York
Chandler, D., 1992. *Brother Number One: A Political Biography of Pol Pot.* Boulder, COL: Westview Press
Coleman, J. S., 1988. "Social Capital in the Creation of Human Capital." *American Journal of Sociology* 94 (Supplement): S95–S120
Colletta, N. J. and Cullen, M., 2000. *Violent Conflict and the Transformation of Social Capital: Lessons from Cambodia, Rwanda, Guatemala, and Somalia.* Washington, DC: World Bank
Collier, P. and Hoeffler, A., 1999. "Justice-Seeking and Loot-Seeking in Civil War." World Bank, Washington, DC
Des Forges, A., 1999. *"Leave None to Tell the Story": Genocide in Rwanda.* New York: Human Rights Watch; Paris: International Federation of Human Rights
Easterly, W., 2000a. "Can Institutions Resolve Ethnic Conflict?" World Bank, Development Research Group, Washington, DC
    2000b. "The Middle Class Consensus and Economic Development." World Bank, Development Research Group, Washington, DC
Ebihara, M. M., Morland, C. A., and Ledgerwood, J. (eds.), 1994. *Cambodian Culture since 1975: Homeland and Exile.* Ithaca, NY: Cornell University Press
Fukuyama, F., 1995. *Trust: The Social Values and the Creation of Prosperity.* New York: Free Press
Galtung, J., 1996. *Peace by Peaceful Means: Peace and Conflict, Development and Civilization.* Thousand Oaks, CA: Sage Publications
Gittell, R. and Vidal, A., 1998. *Community Organizing: Building Social Capital as a Development Strategy.* Thousand Oaks, CA: Sage Publications
Gourevitch, P., 1998. *We Wish to Inform You That Tomorrow We Will Be Killed with Our Families.* New York: Farrar, Straus & Giroux
Grootaert, C., 1998. "Social Capital: The Missing Link?" Social Capital Initiative Working Paper 3. World Bank, Washington, DC

Kawachi, I. and Berkman, L., 2000. "Social Cohesion, Social Capital, and Health." In L. Berkman and I. Kawachi (eds.), *Social Epidemiology.* Oxford: Oxford University Press

Lemarchand, R., 1970. *Burundi and Rwanda.* New York: Praeger

Martin, K., 1996a. "New Measures in Conflict Prevention." *Canadian Foreign Policy* 4(1): 139–143

1996b. "Rethinking Foreign Policy: From Managing to Preventing Conflict." *Policy Options* 17(3): 30–34

Moser, C. and McIlwaine, C., 1999. "Urban Poor Perceptions of Violence in Colombia." World Bank, Environmentally and Socially Sustainable Development Department, Washington, DC

Narayan, D., 1999. "Social Capital and the State: Complementarity and Substitution." Policy Research Working Paper 2167. World Bank, Poverty Division, Poverty Reduction and Management Network, Washington, DC

Nathan, L., 1998. "Crisis Resolution and Conflict Management in Africa." Paper presented at the conference "The Nexus between Economic Management and Civil Society in Countries Emerging from War in the SADC Region," sponsored by the Centre for Conflict Resolution and the World Bank Post-Conflict Unit, Cape Town, South Africa, October 11–13

Nee, M., 1995. "Towards Restoring Life: Cambodian Villages. Told by Meas Nee; with Joan Healy as Listener and Scribe." Melbourne, Australia: Overseas Service Bureau

Newbury, C., 1988. *The Cohesion of Oppression: Clientship and Ethnicity in Rwanda 1860–1960.* New York: Columbia University Press

North, D. C., 1990. *Institutions, Institutional Change, and Economic Performance.* New York: Cambridge University Press

Olson, M., 1982. *The Rise and Decline of Nations: Economic Growth, Stagflation, and Social Rigidities.* New Haven, CT: Yale University Press

Prunier, G., 1997. *The Rwanda Crisis: History of a Genocide.* New York: Columbia University Press

Putnam, R. D., 1993. "The Prosperous Community: Social Capital and Public Life." *American Prospect* 13: 35–42

Reno, W., 1999. *Warlord Politics and African States.* Boulder, COL: Lynne Rienner

Rodrik, D., 1999. "Where Did All the Growth Go? External Shocks, Social Conflict, and Growth Collapses." *Journal of Economic Growth* December (4): 358–412

Uphoff, N., 2000. "Understanding Social Capital: Learning from the Analysis and Experience of Participation." In P. Dasgupta and I. Serageldin (eds.), *Social Capital: A Multifaceted Perspective.* Washington, DC: World Bank

Uvin, P., 1998. *Aiding Violence: The Development Enterprise in Rwanda.* West Hartford, CT: Kumarian Press

van de Put, W., 1997. "Community Mental Health Program. Facts and Thoughts on the First Years: 1 February 1995–1 October 1996." Phnom Penh: Transcultural Psychosocial Organization

Wallensteen, P. and Sollenberg, M., 1996. "Armed Conflict, Conflict Termination, and Peace Agreements 1989–96." *Journal of Peace Research* 33(3): 339–358

Woolcock, M., 2000. "Managing Risk and Opportunity in Developing Countries: The Role of Social Capital", in G. Ranis (ed.), *The Dimensions of Development.* New Haven, CT: Center for International and Area Studies, Yale University

World Bank, 1998. "Project Appraisal Document on a Proposed Learning and Innovation Credit in the Amount of SDR 3.7 Million (US$5.0 Million) to the Rwandese Republic for a Community Reintegration and Development Project." World Bank, Africa Region, Washington, DC

1999. "Project Appraisal Document on a Proposed Learning and Innovation Credit in the Amount of SDR 3.6 Million Equivalent to the Kingdom of Cambodia for a Northeast Village Development Project, April 30, 1999." World Bank, East Asia and Pacific Region, Rural Development and Natural Resources Sector Unit, Washington, DC

2000. *World Development Report 2000/2001.* New York: Oxford University Press

10   Ethnicity, capital formation, and conflict: evidence from Africa

Robert H. Bates and Irene Yackovlev

Ethnicity plays an ambiguous role in the great transformation from societies that are rural and agrarian to those that are urban and industrial. On the one hand, ethnicity creates: by providing incentives that organize the flow of resources across generations, it provides the capital for urban migration and the acquisition of skills for industrial employment. On the other hand, ethnicity destroys: ethnic conflict leads to costly acts of violence. On the one hand, ethnic groups promote the forces of modernization; phrased more fashionably, they constitute a form of social capital (Coleman 1990; Putnam 1993). By promoting urban migration and education, they advance the private fortunes of their members. On the other hand, ethnic groups organize politically; occasionally they engage in acts of violence (as illustrated in chapter 9), destroying wealth and discouraging the formation of capital. Ethnic groups can thus both generate benefits and inflict costs on societies.

In advancing this first theme, this chapter advances a second: that the political dangers of ethnicity are imperfectly understood. Every modern industrial country contains urban centers in which politics are organized in significant part by ethnic groups. In the modern world, ethnic politics are normal politics. This being the case, ethnicity need not, in general, be feared. Clearly, however, ethnic rivalries can fuel political violence. To understand fully the significance of ethnicity, it is therefore important to identify the conditions under which ethnic competition can lead to political conflict. In seeking to identify those conditions, we turn to the distinction between *necessity* and *sufficiency* in causation. To straightforwardly equate ethnicity with violence is to ignore this distinction. Put another way, as will be shown below, it is to ignore the information contained in all but one cell of a fourfold table.

Ethnicity and modernization

Increases in urbanization, education, and *per capita* income constitute the social and economic attributes of development. Political participation constitutes the major political correlate. As people move to towns, obtain higher levels of schooling, and earn higher incomes, they also become more active politically.

They more frequently possess and offer political opinions, seek and exercise the right to vote, and join and participate in associations, rallies, demonstrations, and strikes. (See Lerner 1958 for findings based on surveys, Deutsch 1961 for findings based on aggregate data, and Milbraith 1965 for a review and synthesis.)

Many students of development appear to believe that modernization implies the end of ethnicity. With education, some argue, nationalism would supplant less cosmopolitan political identities, such as those of ethnic groupings. With the growth of markets and the rise in *per capita* income, others argued, class interests would supplant ethnic identification. Modernization would lead to the politics of nationalism and class action (Shils 1957, 1981; Rostow 1961).

Scholars soon encountered facts that were at odds with such expectations. Many were driven to recognize that rather than weakening the power of ethnicity, modernization strengthened it.

Events in Northern Rhodesia (now Zambia) provide an apt illustration. Following the discovery of rich copper deposits, Northern Rhodesia rapidly became one of the most urbanized territories in Africa (Davis 1969). By the late 1950s, the mining companies had hired more than 30,000 people and constructed a score of townships. Investing in schools, social facilities, and medical services, the companies promoted the creation of a permanent labor force. One of the last regions in central Africa to be colonized, Northern Rhodesia rapidly became its most urbanized.

As modernization theory would predict, urbanization generated class consciousness, and political activism soon followed. By the late 1940s, the African mineworkers had formed a trade union, and labor organizers were promoting strikes and sometimes violence in the mine compounds. In the early 1950s, the more educated, white-collar workers formed an independent Mines' African Staff Association. The creation of the staff association represented the assertion of the interests of a growing urban middle class. It included the most modern members of the newly industrialized population, whose interests differed from those of manual laborers (Epstein 1958).

If the Mines' African Staff Association contained the most modern segments of the population in Northern Rhodesia, the royal court of the Lozi contained the most traditional. The Lozi kingdom had joined Northern Rhodesia under the terms of a special treaty with Great Britain. The Lozi resisted integration into the broader colony. By emphasizing its distinctive "special relationship" with the Colonial Office in London and remaining deeply skeptical of the nascent nationalist movement while at the same time celebrating and preserving tribal traditions, the royal court sought to preserve the Lozi's special identity and parochial interests.

This juxtaposition of the formation of the Mines' African Staff Association with the activities of the Lozi kingdom renders significant the behavior of one

Godwin Lewanika. Founder and leader of the staff association, Lewanika was a charter member of the modern elite. Nonetheless, in the early 1960s he chose to resign his post in the Staff Association and to assume the throne of the Lozi. Despite his high level of education, urban-based occupation, and leadership in a class-based association, Lewanika remained loyal to his ethnic group. Rather than treating ethnicity as rivalrous with modernity, he treated it as complementary.

The pattern exhibited in Northern Rhodesia finds its parallel in other regions of the world, where the educated took the lead in building ethnic associations. Lonsdale (1970) describes how the "Christian establishment" of mission-trained Africans helped form the Kavirondo Taxpayers' Welfare Association in Western Kenya. Twaddle (1969) describes the launching of the Young Bagwere Association by "the 'new men' created by missionary education" in Eastern Uganda. Those who founded these organizations held top jobs (as clerks, traders, professionals) in the modern sector. Ottenberg (1955) describes the role of urban traders in organizing the Afikpo Ibo in Nigeria. Sklar (1967) stresses that throughout Nigeria ethnic associations were created by "lawyers, doctors, businessmen [and] civil servants," whom he characterizes as the representatives of a "new and rising class" in African society.

More often than not, these associations originated in towns. The Ibo associations in Nigeria first emerged in Lagos (Abernethy 1969). Abako, a once powerful political movement of the BaKongo, was first formed in Kinshasa, only later recruiting support from the countryside (Young 1965). And it was in the railway towns, rather than in the villages, that the Luo Union enrolled its first members in eastern Africa (Grillo 1969).

As with the formation of ethnic associations, so, too, with ethnic conflict. In Nigeria, for example, disputes among Ph D-holding administrators at distinguished universities fanned the tensions that culminated in civil war. Members of different ethnic communities rallied behind their own for appointments to top academic posts. General Chukwuemeka Ojukwu, the leader of the Biafran succession, and Moise Tshombe, the leader of the independence movement in Zaïre, were college graduates. So, too, are Mangosuthu Buthelezi, the leader of South Africa's Inkatha Freedom Party, and the heads of the warring factions in Southern Sudan. As these examples show, modernization does not extinguish ethnic ties. Rather, it appears to impart new vitality to them.

Rural origins: the family and contracts between generations

Sociologically, modernization refers to the expansion of education and the rise of cities. Economically, it refers to rising levels of *per capita* income. Improvements in education, urbanization, and income require inputs of capital, particularly investment in human beings. In most societies, such investment takes place within families. This is particularly the case in developing societies, where, for the most part, only formal institutions have access to markets for capital.

While ethnic groups are not merely scaled-up forms of kinship, kin groups nonetheless constitute their primary units. People "join" ethnic groups by proving their membership in families that share common ancestry. A major argument of this chapter is that ethnic groups render credible the implicit contracts between generations within constituent family units, thus strengthening the incentives that enable families to serve as instruments for the formation of human capital and agencies for the modernization of societies.

The family, modernization, and investment

People can and do join ethnic groups. But in contrast with most other groups, not just anyone can join. As Horowitz writes, "[t]here is no bright line to be drawn between kinship and ethnicity, especially in societies where the range of recognized family relationships is wide and the importance of kinship ties is great" (1985, p. 60). While membership is an entitlement that can be activated, the entitlement is restricted by family membership.[1] A search through records of descent and marriage or sponsorship by a family in good standing may be required to enroll.

Recognizing the central role of families in ethnic organizations enables us to better grasp the relation between modernization and ethnicity. To a significant degree, modernization is achieved through the formation of human capital. This process is organized privately, by families, rather than by the state. Families organize the flow of resources between generations and sectors, promoting the acquisition of skills and urban migration (and thus the modernization of societies). Ethnic structures of power help preserve the contract between generations within family units.

The markers of modernity – urbanization and education – are closely linked, for people often acquire education in order to prepare themselves for urban employment. To become urban and educated, people bear certain present costs in order to secure uncertain future payoffs. Financing such investments often takes the form of intergenerational transfers within families, in which the older generation – parents or relatives by marriage – channel resources to the younger, helping family members relocate to sectors of the economy in which they can secure higher incomes (Sjaastad 1962; Sahota 1968).

The benefits of such sacrifices include the emotional rewards of having secured a better future for one's offspring. The benefits also take material form. Children in towns dispatch a flow of goods to relatives in the countryside,

[1] The substance of this right, like that of most other rights, is negotiable. As is frequently pointed out, there is a plastic quality to ethnicity. It is not rigid, as is sometimes argued by people who stress the role of primordialism or tradition.

Table 10.1   *Effect of family structure on remittances from town*

Item	Coefficient
Number of children	3.228*
	(2.509)
Average age of children	0.5753*
	(2.225)
Average education of children	8.161
	(1.527)
Constant	0.1685
R^2	0.17
F	4.206*
N	105

Notes: t-statistics are shown in parentheses.
*$p \leq 0.01$.
Source: Bates (1976).

including clothing, shoes, and household products that may be in short supply or difficult to purchase on rural incomes. They also send money, to help finance consumption by their relatives or to invest in buildings (shelter for people, animals, or farm equipment), to upgrade stocks of trees or cattle, or to purchase or clear new lands.

A useful illustration comes from research Bates conducted in a village in Luapula Province, Zambia, that supplies labor to mining centers (Bates 1976). Bates focused on links between town and country and found that the income rural dwellers derive from town varies systematically with the structure (size, age composition, education) of their families (table 10.1). The coefficients suggest that having an additional child increases remittances by an average of 3.23 *kwacha*. (The *kwacha*, the local currency, was worth about $1.40 in 1966, when the study was conducted.) They also suggest that adding a year to a child's education results in an increase in remittance income of 8.16 *kwacha*. Interviews indicate that a year's schooling cost 40 *kwacha* (20 *kwacha* in fees and 20 more in clothing and other expenses). Supporting a child through secondary school (twelve years of education) was therefore expensive; but it would, by these estimates, yield more than $100 a year in future income. The costs incurred by the parents in the village thus generated a stream of income from urban relatives. And they yielded a rate of return that was competitive with that on many other investments.

Rates of migration vary by district in Zambia, and differences in the level of education vary significantly with levels of net out-migration (table 10.2). As would be expected, so, too, do differences in measures of rural prosperity. Of particular interest is the coefficient on the cattle *per capita* variable. Herding

Table 10.2 *Factors affecting out-migration in Zambia, 1963–1969*

Item	Coefficient
Percent schooled, 1963	0.6613**
	(3.625)
Male/female ratio, 1963	33.57*
	(1.769)
Cattle *per capita*	−10.55
	(1.527)
Brick rooms *per capita*	−16.95
	(1.612)
Constant	27.06
R^2	0.6464
F	6.398**
N	105

Notes: t-statistics are shown in parentheses.
** $p \leq 0.01$. * $p \leq 0.05$.
Source: Bates (1976).

cattle in Zambia is possible only in parts of the country that are free of the tsetse fly, which spreads a disease fatal to domesticated livestock. As the coefficient for the cattle *per capita* variable suggests, in districts in which families can accumulate cattle herds, the rate of urban migration is significantly lower than in districts in which families cannot. Probing the meaning of this coefficient deepens our understanding of the role of the family in the modernization process.

The natural rate of increase of cattle yields a return on the cost of initial acquisition. Where urban centers are expanding and *per capita* incomes are rising, the demand for meat – and the value of livestock – increases. Interviews with people who manage family herds in Zambia indicate that they have a keen understanding of the investment opportunities that livestock offer. As expressed by the Ila, a cattle-keeping people in central Zambia, "[c]attle are our bank" (Fielder 1973, p. 351). Livestock not only yield a monetary return, they also generate social returns through their use in payment of bride price, hospitality, or in the cementing of long-term relationships or alliances. As Fielder concludes, "[c]attle are regarded very much as shares or investments." Where such an alternative exists, individuals face fewer incentives to organize the transfer of resources between generations. We may therefore expect less spending on the education of children, less preparation for the urban job market, and less migration to town.

Cattle keepers throughout much of the rest of Africa behave much the way they do in Zambia. Their behavior contrasts with that of agriculturalists, who

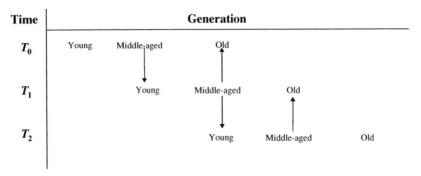

Figure 10.1   Intergenerational transfers over time.

educate their children and migrate to town, where they secure jobs in the modern sectors of the economy. Much of the literature portrays cattle keepers as "conservative" and "resenting change" (the classic study remains Herskovitz 1926). Our understanding of the behavior of families suggests another explanation: that cattle constitute an alternative form of investment, which competes favorably with investment in children.

For a schematic representation of the argument, families can be thought of as consisting of three generations: the young, the middle-aged, and the elderly (figure 10.1). Children and young people are supported by the middle-aged, who are economically active; when children become middle-aged, they, in turn, support the next generation. They also support the elderly, who once nurtured them. Insofar as the contributions of the young yield later streams of income, this intergenerational transfer of resources thus serves as a means of family investment – one that promotes urbanization, education, and thus the process of development (see Samuelson 1958; Hammond 1975).

Political power and social reciprocity

Because of lack of collateral (as a result of the lack of individual land rights), the lack of information about potential borrowers, and the lack of effective legal systems, which allows opportunistic borrowers to renege with impunity, capital markets often do not exist in developing societies. In such settings, nonmarket mechanisms often provide the primary means for providing savings, credit, and investment services (Posner 1980; Binswanger and McIntire 1987; Bardhan 1989). A social organization, the family, comes to serve an economic function, eliciting savings and organizing investment in people.

There are obvious opportunities for defection from the system shown in figure 10.1 The parties are separated by distance. Living in town, younger family members are "abroad."[2] Literally and figuratively, they are beyond the reach of their parents. Monetary exchanges are also separated by time: adult children are expected to reciprocate for benefits received when they were young. Given the opportunities for defection, the system appears fragile. What keeps it intact?

Sentiment plays a major role, of course. Parents gain satisfaction from the success of their children and are therefore willing to devote resources to their upbringing. Children take pride in their ability to provide for their parents. The existence of such sentiments conditions expectations, so that people are willing to channel savings to children because they believe that their children will return these savings to them in the future.

Additional mechanisms, involving the use of power, are also at play. And it is here that ethnic groups become important. Ethnic groups strengthen the role of the older generation, particularly elders and family heads in rural areas, providing them with sanctions over younger relatives. Knowing that they can sanction opportunism by members of the younger generation, the older generation has reason to believe the younger generation's promises to repay for investments made in their education and emigration from their rural communities.

Land rights

In many agrarian societies, individuals often cannot freely transfer land. Constraints on land use empower elders, thereby strengthening the credibility of intergenerational contracts and the capacity of families to create capital.

At the end of their work lives, urban residents often seek to return to their rural homes. They do so because housing and food are less expensive in rural areas, because village life is less dangerous, and because they have relatives in the village, who may assist them in their declining years. When land is not allocated through the market, it is allocated politically – by elders, clan heads, chiefs, or headmen – to members of the community. To remain a member in good standing, future retirees must therefore retain a social presence in these communities, even when living "abroad." Many do so by providing gifts and money to their rural relatives. By fulfilling their obligations to their families, they retain friends in court, so to speak, who affirm their membership in the rural community during deliberations over land rights.

The political allocation of land rights thus gives the elders of the family, who have stayed at home, a mechanism with which to secure resources from the middle-aged, who work in town. This privileged position of the rural elders in the political allocation of land lowers their risk of securing a return from their investments in the careers of the young. Given the power of the older

---

[2] Thus the title of the fine paper by Hershfield (1969).

generation, it would be foolish for members of the younger generation not to repay the debts they incurred in their youth. Knowing that, the middle-aged can rationally invest in the departure of the young to the towns. The political control of land rights strengthens the bargain made between the generations.

In the phenomenon of ethnicity, there is thus not only a close tie between the economic and the sociological; there is also a close relation between the sociological and the political. Because families are embedded in ethnically based systems of governance in which the elders possess power, resources flow between generations.

Cultural rites

Ethnicity mobilizes not only sociological but also cultural forces that safeguard contracts between generations. The older generation, based in rural areas, exploits its position as the custodian of the "true" culture of the community. Its members lay claim to this position in order to control the behavior of their offspring. Rural elders emphasize the significance of bringing up children in the ways of their forefathers. Children who do not know the rituals, who have not been properly initiated into the secrets of the tribe, who did not know their elders, their forefathers, or their family's history – such children, rural dwellers realize, pose a danger. By shirking in their obligations to their families, they undermine the capacity of the family to act as a means of investment. And that threatens the role of kinship in underpinning the fortunes of rural-based kin.

When assuming the role of interpreters of culture and tradition, rural leaders target both the young and the elderly. In eastern Africa, for example, the Luo have long ventured from the inland savannas to the forest zones around Lake Victoria, to the coast of the Indian Ocean, and to the towns along the line of rail. For many years, these elders were buried where they died. In recent years, however, rural leaders have "revived" a "tradition" of burial in the rural homelands (Cohen and Odhiambo 1992). As the elders control the allocation of rural lands, they possess power over the burial of the dead. To secure a proper burial, people who have migrated to other destinations must remain on good terms with their rural-based kin. The tradition of rural burial thus strengthens the power of rural families to extract resources from "sons abroad." In so doing, it reinforces the incentives that render the family a means of forming capital.

The formation of capital in families involves a contract between generations. As shown in figure 10.1, those actively employed invest in the young at time T_0 in anticipation of receiving a stream of profits in a subsequent period (time T_1), when they become elderly and the young people middle-aged. Ethnic groups consist of congeries of families. They accord power to elders, who exercise political control over the allocation of "tribal" land and the interpretation of culture and tradition. By empowering elders, ethnic groups create a political framework that renders credible the expectation that the young will honor their debts.

Ethnic groups thus provide a structure of power that underpins intergenerational contracts within their constituent unit, the family. They shape expectations in ways that enable them to underpin the formation of capital. Ethnic groups strengthen incentives to educate and train the young; they strengthen the forces that render the young a source of enhanced family well-being for all members of society. In so doing, they also promote the flow of people from rural areas to towns and from agriculture to industry. By helping shift people from sectors in which diminishing returns constrain the possibilities for higher incomes into sectors in which increasing returns are possible, ethnic groups have promoted the modernization of societies and the development of economies throughout the globe.

Urban origins of ethnic groups

While anchored in rural areas, ethnic groups are often organized by elite members of urban communities that find themselves disadvantaged in the urban labor market. They are formed in an attempt to alter expectations – and thus patterns of remuneration – that are viewed as discriminatory by ethnic minorities but as normal by employers of labor.

Social correlates of leadership

In an intriguing study of Eastern Nigeria, David Abernethy (1969) describes the behavior of what he calls "ethnic missionaries." Because of their proximity to Lagos, the Yoruba were among the first people in Nigeria to be educated by missionaries. By dint of their location, they faced low costs migrating to town. They therefore possessed a competitive advantage in the labor market in the colonial capital. Only decades later did mission schools spread among the peoples of Eastern Nigeria. As a result, when Ibo job seekers arrived in Lagos, they found the best jobs taken by the Yoruba. As Abernethy writes:

The struggle for employment was bound to produce frustration, and those not chosen for the best jobs found it easy to blame their plight on the advantages possessed by members of other groups. Of course, different groups clearly did have differential access to education, which in turn was the key to job mobility.

What was the best course of action open to the urban migrant who was acutely concerned lest his ethnic group fall behind others in the struggle . . . ? Certainly the rural masses had to be informed of the problem. If the masses were not aware of their ethnicity, then they would have to learn who they really were through the efforts of "ethnic missionaries" returning to the homeland. These "missionaries" would also have to outline a strategy by which the ethnic group, once fully conscious of its unity and its potential, could compete with its rivals. Clearly, the competition required enrolling more children in school, particularly at the secondary level, for the graduates of a good local secondary school would be assured of rapid . . . mobility within modern society. (1969, pp. 107–108)

The behavior of these "ethnic missionaries" finds its parallel elsewhere. In his typically pungent and informative fashion, Gellner (1983) portrays a similar role in the fictive nation of "Ruritania."[3] Covering a wide range of cases from throughout the world, Horowitz (1985) cites the case of French-speaking Canada, where the incessant message that the people are "weak, unprogressive, too backward" comes not only from their ethnic competitors but also from the ranks of their own elites.

Enhancing the stock of skills held by members of their communities is in the private interest of "advanced" members of "backward" groups, for several reasons. Among the most important is information. Markets for labor suffer from high levels of uncertainty. Because it is difficult to assess individuals' job skills before hiring them, employers often select employees based on expectations. They offer wages and benefits that reflect the average (expected) value of applicants of a given kind. The category may be defined based on past encounters with people who attended a particular school, completed a particular course of study, or came from a particular area. In the absence of a formal education system, social, rather than formal, criteria become the basis for reputations. People from a given social category find it advantageous to seek a particular kind of job because their prospects are maximized by offering their services in occupations in which they are perceived as best qualified. Where information is costly, occupational specialization by ethnic groups may occur.

Perry (1993) documents the sorting of people into crafts and industries by region in Shanghai and the manner in which the resultant diversity disrupted the attempts by the Communist Party to form class-based workers' movements. Horowitz (1985) notes that in South Asia the British regarded the Gurkhas as martial and targeted them for military recruitment, the Sikhs as mechanical and recruited them as artisans. Brahmins were considered skilled administrators and therefore prized as candidates for jobs in the public service. Documenting the existence of "a dogma of ethnic skills," Horowitz also notes the existence of "ethnic specialists" in Southeast Asia (Chinese tin miners and traders, Indian rubber tappers, Ceylonese railway workers).

Informational constraints in labor markets result not only in occupational specialization but also in stratification. On average people from groups or

---

[3] The analysis in this chapter provides micro foundations for Gellner's classic analysis of the behavior of the "blues" (Gellner 1983).

regions poorly endowed with schools and training facilities lack the skills of those from better endowed groups or regions. They therefore receive fewer good job offers on average. As a result, their incomes tend to be low.

In Central Africa missionaries established schools in Malawi (then Nyasaland) and Barotse (now part of Zambia) before entering the northern parts of the region. The mining companies and colonial authorities soon came to prize the educated migrants from those areas, with the result that Malawians and Lozi came to hold the top jobs in industry and public administration. Bemba-speakers, being from the north, were less likely to possess formal education. As a result, they came to "specialize" in manual labor.[4]

Within such patterns of stratification, people in the lower-ranked groups who possess above-average skills suffer most. Because of imperfect information, their skills are evaluated based on expectations. To the extent that bids for labor reflect social reputation, these individuals are discriminated against in labor markets. The inferior average endowment of their group lowers their individual earnings. Educated and skilled members of "inferior" groups therefore pay the highest costs of discrimination – and therefore possess the strongest incentives to end it.

Keying wage offers to expectations leads to a canonical encounter, one that lies at the core of the history of many, if not most, ethnic revivals. Skilled people from a "backward" group suffer because they receive salaries reflecting employers' observations of the average performance of employees from that group. Poorly qualified members of an "advanced" group benefit from the reputation of their group by earning high salaries, based on the reputation of those who belong to their group. In the work place, then, talented people from "backward" groups find themselves laboring under poorer conditions of service than less qualified people from "advanced" groups. The resultant ire sparks ethnic protest.

Ethnic groups are often seen as traditional or atavistic; they are regarded as vestiges of societies now eclipsed by the forces of modernization. From such a perspective, it is therefore anomalous that the leaders of such groups come from the highly educated elements of urban-based communities. But these patterns are what is to be expected, given the initial conditions – the uneven spread of education in the rural sector and the high costs of observing human skills – and an assumption of rationality on the part of employers and migrants.[5]

---

[4] One result was that members of the Mines' African Staff Association, which organized the better-paid mine employees, saw their interests defined not only in economic but also in ethnic terms. This mixture of interests helps explain why Godwin Lewanika could experience continuity in moving from the head of the staff association to the chieftancy of the Lozi.

[5] Becker's (1957) analysis differs from that offered here in that it assumes perfect information, employs trade theory, and emphasizes the patterns of opposition that take place between people competing on the same side of the labor market. Suppose, Becker argues, that of two ethnic

Strategies of leaders

"Moderns" therefore turn to ethnic protest. Highly skilled members of ethnic groups with poor skills are likely to demonstrate in order to publicize the presence of articulate and capable people of their kind and the costs inflicted on people like themselves. By demonstrating, activists seek to alter expectations in the labor market and provide evidence of the benefits to be gained from modifying the prevailing system of employment.

When rural areas are unequally endowed with educational opportunities, it is almost inevitable that rural out-migration will result in urban ethnic protest. Urban ethnic protest leads to rural political activism as well, as urban activists build political awareness among their rural kin. This fuels a cultural awakening, with the creation of reading groups and correspondence societies, the building of schools, and the training of teachers. This revival is often accompanied by political conflict, as urban migrants intervene in the selection of rural councilors, headmen, or chiefs in an effort to put in place "progressive" local leaders who will transform their native communities.

Urban elites strive to prepare their rural kin for the new world that awaits them – or rather the one that they themselves have encountered – be it in Lagos or Dakar, in the mining towns of central or southern Africa, or in New York, London, or Marseilles. Preaching the virtues of schooling, education, and training, they seek better to equip their brethren for competition for jobs in town.

While urban elites often engage in secular evangelism out of a sense of public service, such activism serves their own interests as well. Given the significance of reputation in the determination of employment contracts, they find their own prospects tied to the assessment of the average quality of job candidates from their region. By altering the distribution of skills in the pool of candidates from which they themselves are drawn, they thus improve their own prospects in the marketplace. They seek to dispel the belief that people like them might not be well qualified.

Ethnic groups thus emerge as an alliance between urban elites and rural residents. They blend the talents and aspirations of the urban cosmopolitans with the desire for material gain – and political respect – of rural provincials. While the result is often a conflict for leadership between "moderns" and "traditionals,"

groups, one possesses (and is widely perceived to possess) more human capital than the other. Absent discrimination, this group would "export" services intensive in the use of human capital, while the other group would "import" such services and "export" services intensive in the use of unskilled labor. The least skilled members of the skilled group and the most skilled members of the unskilled group would be interested in "protection" (discrimination that impedes such trade). Becker's argument thus leads us to expect activism among the elite members of the disadvantaged group. But it predicts separatism, rather than ethnic revival. The analysis we offer is superior, in that it not only accounts for the social identity of the activists but also for their demands, which are more often activist and transformational than separatist. Bates thanks Ronald Rogowski for pointing out the contrast with Becker's argument.

their interests are as often in concert as in conflict. The incentives to compete are sufficiently strong that, joined in movements of ethnic revival, the two can secure the transformation of their societies.

Conditions in urban markets connect the interests of urban elites to the collective standing of their rural homelands; they find it privately advantageous to invest in the collective advancement of their village communities. And although urban elites may experience conflict with rural leaders, they find it in their interests to respect their power over cultural traditions and the lands of their birth. Their power underpins the relation between generations that fuels investment in the modernization of their societies.

The movement toward protest

From the moment of their creation, ethnic groups are political. They organize wards and neighborhoods in cities; politicians cannot resist seeking to incorporate them into their political organizations. Urban leaders, by inserting themselves into the selection of chiefs, headmen, mayors, and school boards at home, charge into the political fray in rural areas as well.

For a variety of reasons, ethnic groups may seek to transform local political influence into national political power. Some of their leaders possess private political ambitions. Others seek to influence the distribution of government funding to the advantage of their home constituencies. Whatever their motivation, urban-based elites seek to build organizations that allow them to participate in policymaking at the national level. Some do so by brokering their influence in the towns and urban centers into influence over national political agendas. In the United States, for example, New York, Miami, and Chicago control large blocs of votes in states that loom large in presidential contests. Exploiting their influence within state delegations, urban political elites gain influence over national political outcomes. Others find it useful to organize more broadly, forming larger organizations that cover broader geographic areas. They are driven to once return "home" and to tend to the interests of their rural communities.

The rise to national power of urban blacks in the United States was marked by the building of ties between black political leaders in the north and the rural leadership of the south. Black leaders in Chicago, Cleveland, or Detroit long influenced the behavior of national political candidates, particularly within the Democratic Party. To gain control over the national political agenda, they had to champion not only the interests of their urban constituents but also the interests of blacks in other regions, in particular, the agrarian south. By transforming local protests against job discrimination into a national crusade for civil rights, they forged political links between urban destinations and rural points of origin, built a national political movement, and gained the capacity to engrave their political preferences into national legislation.

Similar dynamics mark the developing world. In Zambia, for example, urban elites first built associations in the towns formed by the mining industry or along rail lines. They subsequently transformed these organizations into improvement associations, which focussed on the welfare of rural communities. With the formation of political parties, they transformed these associations into ethnically based factions of the nationalist movement (Rotberg 1965). The political organization of "country" by "town" occurred in the post-independence period as well. When Vice President Simon Kapwepwe challenged Kenneth Kaunda for the presidency of Zambia, for example, he first cultivated Bemba-speaking members of the urban elite in the copperbelt. These elites then traveled back to the rural areas, where they put forward their demands for roads, schools, and government projects. They sought to use their power in ways that compelled the government to bring jobs to them, rather than their having to migrate to the city in search of jobs (Bates 1976).

The search for national political influence thus leads to efforts by urban-based political elites to secure the backing of rural dwellers. The result is the empowerment of rural elites. When the urbanites return home in search of political backing, the rural elites extract a price. They secure backing for their private positions of leadership in the rural community and the ethnic association, and they use their positions to extract benefits for their communities as well.

In seeking rural support, urban elites compete with one another, if only for positions of leadership within their own communities. Rural leaders find ways of exacerbating and exploiting this competition. In Kenya, for example, rural leaders seek donations for community projects from those urban-based elites who seek political support from their rural communities. They also seek political services, such as help from the government in supplying materials or "regularizing" the legal status of schools and clinics constructed by members of the community. Not daring to be seen as niggardly or impotent, those seeking political prominence are driven to contribute to and work on behalf of the projects initiated by the rural leaders. In this manner, rural elites have been able to secure the construction of schools, cattle dips, roads, and clinics (Barkan 1986).

Political incentives thus join economic interests in promoting ethnic ties between urban elites and rural communities. To some scholars, the politicization of such ties represents the transformation of "ethnicity" into "tribalism" (Gluckman 1960; Berman and Lonsdale 1992). As the connotation of the words suggest, this transformation is often viewed as threatening. The word *tribalism* suggests the dark side of the processes analyzed here. Ethnicity may yield the benefits of education, urbanization, and rural development. But it may do so at too high a price – one that yields the possibility of violence.

The discussion here casts doubt on such views, for it suggests that ethnic politics are normal politics. Ethnicity is linked to the rise and development of communities in all regions of the world; it shapes political relations in all major urban centers, including those, such as Shanghai, Manchester, or New York, that have transformed the contemporary world. When ethnic politics is so pervasive and political violence is not, surely ethnic politics cannot pose the dangers often attributed to it.

Do ethnic tensions lead to political violence?

To determine whether ethnic tensions lead to political violence, we return to Africa, a continent whose politics are widely viewed as dominated by ethnic groups and pervaded by political violence. On the one hand, the findings strengthen the skepticism regarding the dangers of ethnicity. On the other, they point to a danger zone, in which political relations among ethnic groups may in fact turn violent.

To investigate the relation between ethnicity and violence, we use a data set containing economic, social, and political information on forty-six African countries between 1970 and 1995. These data cover every country in Sub-Saharan Africa except South Africa, whose politics remained *sui generis* throughout this period.[6] To capture the properties of ethnicity, we use data on the size distribution of ethnic groups from Morrison, Mitchell and Paden (1989), data on linguistic diversity from Gunnemark (1991), and data on the presence (or absence) of an ethnic minority at risk from Gurr (1999). For data on political protest and violence, we use data collected by Banks (1996) on the number of riots and demonstrations and the frequency of revolts and assassinations.

We start with some simple tabulations of the incidence of violence in communities with and without minorities at risk (table 10.3). These calculations are based on roughly 1,200 country years of data (forty-six countries over twenty-six years). As the conventional wisdom would suggest, ethnic tensions are indeed pervasive in Africa: roughly two-thirds of the observations reveal the existence of a minority at risk. But the data also show that, notwithstanding the conventional wisdom, acts of protest and violence are relatively rare. Between 1970 and 1995, for example, only fifty-two assassinations are reported. Only in the case of revolts, a measure compounded from other measures, did more than 12 percent of the observations record acts of protest and violence. (For a description of the variables used, see annex table 10A.1, p. 331.) Most of the time when minorities were at risk and ethnic tensions high, however, political

---

[6] Many of these data can be downloaded from <*http://www.gov.harvard.edu/research/rbates*>.

Table 10.3   *Incidence of demonstrations and violence in communities with minorities at risk*

Minority at risk?		Demonstrations		Riots		Revolts		Assassinations	
		Yes	No	Yes	No	Yes	No	Yes	No
Yes	Number	80	572	82	569	183	468	42	609
	Percent of column	79.2	63.3	83.7	62.8	76.3	61.3	80.8	64
	Percent of row	12.3	87.9	12.6	87.4	28.1	71.9	6.5	93.5
No	Number	21	332	16	337	57	296	10	343
	Percent of column	20.8	36.7	16.3	37.2	23.8	38.7	19.2	36
	Percent of row	3.2	51	2.5	51.8	8.8	45.5	1.5	52.7
Total		101	904	98	906	240	764	52	952

Source: Authors' tabulations based on data from Gurr (1999) and Banks (1996).

Table 10.4   *Sufficiency of minority at risk as a cause of violence*

Minority at risk	Violence	
	Yes	No
Yes	+	0
No	+	+

violence did not occur. Clearly, politicians devoted more effort to promoting ethnic violence than ethnic conflict.

Were the presence of a minority at risk a sufficient cause of political violence, violence would occur whenever a minority was at risk (table 10.4). Were the presence of a minority at risk a necessary cause of violence, violence should not exist where no minority is at risk (table 10.5). The data in table 10.3 strongly suggest that while the presence of ethnic minorities may approximate a necessary condition for political violence, it does not constitute a sufficient condition.

Observers of political violence note the association between the occurrence of violence and the existence of ethnic minorities. But failing to take into account the full array of data, they fail to note that in most instances in which minorities are at risk, there is no warfare. And by confusing sufficiency with necessity, they overestimate the dangers of ethnicity.

Table 10.5 *Necessity of minority at risk as a cause of violence*

	Violence	
Minority at risk	Yes	No
Yes	+	+
No	0	+

Table 10.6 *Sign and significance of key independent variables affecting protests and violence*

	Measures of protest				Measures of violence			
	Riots		Demonstrations		Revolts		Assassinations	
	Sign	Significance	Sign	Significance	Sign	Significance	Sign	Significance
Education	−	High	−	High	+	High	−	Low
Urbanization	+	High	+	High	−	Low	−	Low
Income	−	Low	−	Low	−	Low	+	Moderate
Language	−	Low	−	High	+	Moderate	+	Low
Ethnicity/ Ethnicity[2]	+/−	Moderate	+/−	Moderate	−/+	Low	−/+	High
Youth	+	High	+	High	+	Low	+	High

Although a straightforward link between ethnicity and violence is not found in Africa (the one region where we might expect to find it if we were to find it at all), a danger zone exists in which the politics of ethnicity appear to change.

The literature on participation and development suggests a relation between modernization and instability (Huntington 1968). While exploring the impact of ethnicity, we control for the impact of urbanization, education, and *per capita* income. We also include a measure of the size of the cohort of young men in the population, a variable whose importance has been stressed in recent years (Goldstone 1991; Mesquida and Wiener 1998).

Because measures of ethnicity do not change over time, annualized data cannot be used. For the dependent variables, we instead use the total, or average, number of acts of protest and violence over the twenty-six-year period, or the number or proportion of years in which such acts occurred (table 10.6).

For the independent variables which vary over time, we use annual averages. Limitations in the data, especially on education, result in the dropping of several countries from the sample. The small number of observations that remain (about twenty) severely limits the information that can be extracted from the data.

Of particular interest are the coefficients associated with language and ethnicity. The variable *language*, which captures the percent of the population that does not speak the official language at home, provides a measure of linguistic diversity. Whereas linguistic diversity is associated with reduced levels of protest, when controlling for the impact of other variables, *language* is associated with higher levels of violence. *Ethnicity*, or the size of the largest ethnic group, enters quadratically. When the coefficient for the linear term is significant, so, too, is the coefficient for the quadratic. As the size of the largest ethnic group grows, the level of violence initially decreases but then increases. In contrast, the level of protest initially increases but then decreases. (Results of regressions using the number of years in which assassinations occurred, the proportion of years in which revolts occurred, the number of riots, and the number of demonstrations are shown in appendix tables 10A.2–10A.5 and appendix figures 10A.1–10A.4.)

It is important to emphasize the low quality of the estimates. Many of the coefficients are imprecisely estimated, and the models tend to overpredict infrequently observed events and underpredict frequently observed events. In the case of violence, significant factors have been omitted from the models. Nonetheless, the estimates do offer insight into the role of ethnicity that is of considerable interest to social scientists, as well as to students of Africa.

The histogram in figure 10.2 shows the size of the largest ethnic group across the forty-six African nations. It underscores the high level of ethnic diversity in most African countries.

The data suggest that as the largest ethnic group increases in size, the level of protest mounts; the coefficients of the control variables indicate that protest is most intense in highly urbanized societies. As the quadratic form of the relation between ethnicity and protest suggests, the data also indicate that beyond a certain point, as the largest group increases in size, the frequency of protest declines. In contrast, as the largest ethnic group increases in size, the level of violence at first declines before rising again (figure 10.2).

The patterns in the data suggest that as the largest ethnic group reaches 50 percent or more of the population, people confront the possibility of permanent political hegemony or permanent political exclusion. In the face of such prospects, they may change their preferred form of political action, switching from protest to violence. That people are more likely to use violence the wealthier is the country (and therefore the greater the spoils of victory) lends credence to this interpretation. In the face of the prospects of large gains or large losses, people may be more willing to "go for broke" and take the riskier actions that violence entails.

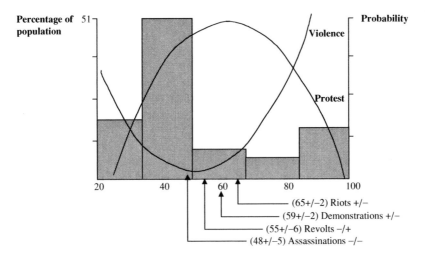

Figure 10.2   Effect of size of largest ethnic group on number of protests and level of violence.

The difference in the behavior of the measure of linguistic diversity is also noteworthy. A high value implies cacophony in town – and therefore high costs of political organization. But high levels of linguistic diversity need not imply high costs of organizing in rural settings. Given the geographically concentrated distribution of language communities in Africa, high levels of national linguistic diversity, as measured by the *language* variable, can coexist with high levels of linguistic homogeneity in rural settings. The switch in the sign of the coefficient on linguistic diversity when moving from protest to violence, along with the loss of significance for the coefficient on urbanization, may thus signal a change in the structure of politics, as political competition shifts from the urban to the national level and as urban organizers leave the towns and move into the countryside.

Policy implications

Ethnicity has been viewed as posing problems for national development. In the study of Africa, for example, ethnic diversity is commonly viewed as either directly associated with slow growth (Easterly and Levine 1997) or retarding growth through its impact on violence. This chapter argues that the forces of ethnicity, and the social capital it represents, provide a means of both rendering intergenerational contracts binding, thereby promoting private investment, and mobilizing private resources for public purposes, thereby promoting the formation of public goods. Ethnicity, we argue, elicits investment and the formation of capital and thus promotes growth in developing societies. It structures incentives at the micro-level, in ways that promote macro-level transformations.

Like Laitin and Fearon (1996) and others, this chapter casts doubt on a second tenet of the conventional wisdom: that ethnic diversity promotes violence. While violence may often have ethnic roots, even in societies with strong ethnic tensions, diverse ethnic groups can peaceably co-exist.

Under some conditions, ethnic differences can promote violence. Ethnic politics appear to be most volatile when an ethnic bloc is large enough to permanently exclude others from power. Such a group may then be in a position to privatize the state, as it were. Politics may then be redefined as a redistributive, or zero-sum, game that is fundamentally conflictual in nature. The remedy would appear to be to avoid strengthening the incentives to exclude and to institutionalize incentives to promote interethnic cooperation.

Some researchers, such as Van Evera (1995), have explored the politics of minorities at risk and advocated the creation of states within countries, the better to ensure their security. The results presented here suggest, however, that when groups become ascendant within jurisdictions, violence may replace protest as a preferred political strategy. As we have seen, the prospects of political capture of the polity and the fear of the resulting permanent political exclusion, may drive ethnic leaders to wager on violence. Put another way, it is diversity, not homogeneity, that lowers the probability of conflict. Separatist solutions may therefore exacerbate, rather than ameliorate, the problem.

The same findings cast doubt on another common political prescription: the creation of federal systems, with ethnically homogeneous regional units (Laitin 1998). If the incentives driving our findings be correctly understood, such a remedy would only transfer the locus of violence to the local level.

In cautioning against some forms of remedy, the analysis underscores the value of others. In particular, the analysis lends support to the argument advanced by Horowitz (1985) that in ethnically diverse societies, we should seek to avoid the adoption of winner-take-all institutions for the choice of governments. Plurality-based elections would exacerbate the fears of permanent exclusion that appear to drive the relations we observe. Proportional representation, in contrast, helps ensure representation in legislatures, where minorities can join in the bargaining over the formation of governments. In particular, transferable voting encourages the formation of political alliances, as parties can benefit from agreements over the pooling of votes. Insofar as policymakers seek to reduce fears and strengthen incentives to form political alliances, they may therefore want to adopt proportional representation with transferable votes, thereby dampening the tensions that arise in multiethnic societies.

Our results offer reason to welcome rather than fear ethnic diversity in developing societies. They provide insight into the kinds of institutions that might allow us to reap the economic benefits and avoid the political costs of cultural diversity. They suggest that the most desirable institutions would be those that weaken the prospects of winner-take-all outcomes and assuage minorities' fear of permanent political exclusion, thereby countering the logic that leads political violence to replace political protests in ethnically diverse settings.

APPENDIX: SUPPLEMENTARY FIGURES AND TABLES

Table 10A.1   *Variables employed*

Variable	Definition	Source
Education	Average number of years of secondary education of people twenty-five and older	Barro and Lee (1994)
Urbanization	Urban population as percent of total population (in logs)	World Bank (1998)
Income	Real *per capita* GDP, purchasing power parity, chain index	Summers and Heston (1995)
Language	Percentage of population that does not speak official language at home	Gunnemark (1991)
Ethnicity	Percentage of population in largest ethnic group	Morrison *et al.* (1989)
Youth	Percentage of males fifteen–twenty-nine in adult male population	World Bank (1998)
Demonstrations	Any peaceful public gathering of at least 100 people for the primary purpose of displaying or voicing opposition to government policies or authority, excluding demonstrations of anti-foreign nature	Banks (1996)
Riots	Any violent demonstration or clash of more than 100 people involving the use of physical force	Banks (1996)
Revolts	Any illegal or forced change in the top governmental elite, any attempt at such a change, or any successful or unsuccessful armed rebellion whose aim is independence from the central government	Banks (1996)
Assassinations	Any politically motivated murder or attempted murder of a high government official or politician	Banks (1996)

Table 10A.2   *Results for number of years in which assassinations occur*

Independent variables	Coefficient	Robust std error	t-stat.	$P > |t|$
Education	−1.472	1.190	−1.236	0.216
Urbanization	0.848	2.246	0.377	0.706
Income	1.050	0.628	1.671	0.095
Language	0.941	0.775	1.215	0.225
Ethnicity	−10.349	3.265	−3.170	0.002
Ethnicity^2	9.186	2.744	3.348	0.001
Youth	25.297	8.897	2.843	0.004
Constant	−17.966	6.787	−2.647	0.008

Source: Authors' tabulations based on data from Gurr (1999) and Banks (1996).

Table 10A.3   *First difference effects of number of years in which assassinations occur*

Variable	Estimated coefficient	Change (from, to)	First difference
Education	−1.472	(0.035, 0.8)	−0.739
Urbanization	0.848	(0.05, 0.74)	0.517
Income	1.050	(5.8, 8.2)	2.956
Language	0.941	(0.05, 0.95)	0.547
Ethnicity	−10.349	(0.19, 0.563)	−1.229
Ethnicity^2	9.186	(0.036, 0.317)	
Ethnicity	−10.349	(0.563, 0.99)	2.047
Ethnicity^2	9.186	(0.317, 0.98)	
Youth	25.297	(0.41, 0.55)	3.285
Constant	−17.966		

Table 10A.4 *Results for proportion of years in which
revolts occur*

Independent variables	Coefficient	Robust std error	t-stat.	$P > |t|$
Education	5.202	2.375	2.190	0.029
Urbanization	−7.011	5.336	−1.314	0.189
Income	−0.776	1.104	−0.703	0.482
Language	3.698	2.329	1.588	0.112
Ethnicity	−12.272	10.411	−1.179	0.238
Ethnicity^2	11.412	9.319	1.225	0.221
Youth	−4.741	8.459	−0.56	0.575
Constant	9.457	9.039	1.046	0.295

Source: Authors' tabulations based on data from Gurr (1999) and Banks
(1996).

Table 10A.5 *First difference effects of proportion of years
with revolts*

Variable	Estimated coefficient	Change (from, to)	First difference
Education	5.202	(0.035, 0.8)	61.668
Urbanization	−7.011	(0.05, 0.74)	−16.938
Income	−0.776	(5.8, 8.2)	−7.525
Language	3.698	(0.05, 0.95)	8.752
Ethnicity	−12.272	(0.19, 0.538)	−6.497
Ethnicity^2	11.412	(0.0361, 0.289)	
Ethnicity	−12.272	(0.538, 0.99)	20.385
Ethnicity^2	11.412	(0.289, 0.98)	
Youth	−4.741	(0.41, 0.55)	−2.829
Constant	9.457		

Table 10A.6   *Results for number of riots*

Independent variables	Coefficient	Robust std error	t-stat.	$P > |t|$
Education	−3.670	1.087	−3.375	0.001
Urbanization	8.573	4.025	2.130	0.033
Income	−0.144	0.751	−0.191	0.848
Language	−1.110	0.740	−1.500	0.134
Ethnicity	13.240	7.663	1.728	0.084
Ethnicity^2	−10.686	5.927	−1.803	0.071
Youth	19.859	4.691	4.234	0.000
Constant	−11.513	4.026	−2.859	0.004

Source: Authors' tabulations based on data from Gurr (1999) and Banks (1996).

Table 10A.7   *First difference effects of number of riots*

Variable	Estimated coefficient	Change (from, to)	First difference
Education	−3.670	(0.035, 0.8)	−6.857
Urbanization	8.573	(0.05, 0.74)	191.676
Income	−0.144	(5.8, 8.2)	−1.050
Language	−1.110	(0.05, 0.95)	−4.143
Ethnicity	13.240	(0.19, 0.62)	5.187
Ethnicity^2	−10.686	(0.036, 0.384)	
Ethnicity	13.240	(0.62, 0.99)	−4.636
Ethnicity^2	−10.686	(0.384, 0.98)	
Youth	19.859	(0.41, 0.55)	9.231
Constant	−11.513		

Table 10A.8   *Results for number of demonstrations*

Independent variables	Coefficient	Robust std error	t-stat.	$P > |t|$
Education	−2.751	0.768	−3.584	0.000
Urbanization	7.618	2.900	2.627	0.009
Income	−0.494	0.643	−0.768	0.442
Language	−1.406	0.491	−2.861	0.004
Ethnicity	9.023	5.168	1.746	0.081
Ethnicity^2	−7.517	3.868	−1.943	0.052
Youth	19.489	4.691	4.155	0.000
Constant	−7.634	3.234	−2.361	0.018

Source: Authors' tabulations based on data from Gurr (1999) and Banks (1996).

Table 10A.9   *First difference effects of number of demonstrations*

Variable	Estimated coefficient	Change (from, to)	First difference
Education	−2.751	(0.035, 0.8)	−4.758
Urbanization	7.618	(0.05, 0.74)	111.091
Income	−0.494	(5.8, 8.2)	−3.317
Language	−1.406	(0.05, 0.95)	−5.291
Ethnicity	9.023	(0.19, 0.60)	3.180
Ethnicity^2	−7.517	(0.0361, 0.36)	
Ethnicity	9.023	(0.60, 0.99)	−3.016
Ethnicity^2	−7.517	(0.36, 0.98)	
Youth	19.489	(0.41, 0.55)	8.285
Constant	−7.634		

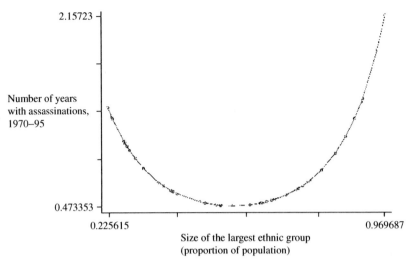

Figure 10A.1   Ethnicity and numbers of years with assassinations.

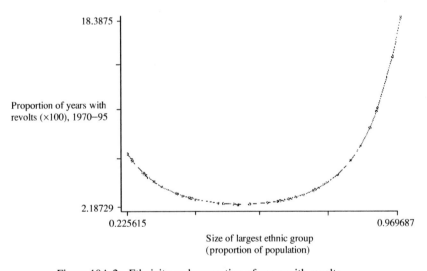

Figure 10A.2   Ethnicity and proportion of years with revolts.

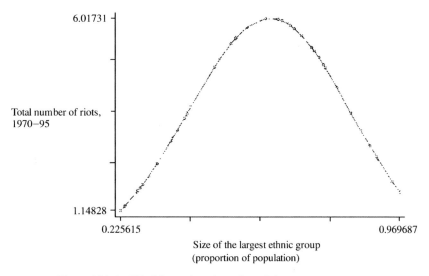

Figure 10A.3   Ethnicity and total number of riots.

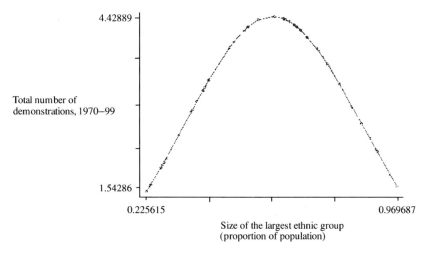

Figure 10A.4   Ethnicity and total number of demonstrations.

REFERENCES

Abernethy, D., 1969. *The Political Dilemma of Popular Education: An African Case Study.* Stanford, CA: Stanford University Press

Banks, A. S., 1996. *Cross-National Time-Series Data Archive.* Binghampton, NY: State University of New York, Center for Social Analysis

Bardhan, P. (ed.), 1989. *The Economic Theory of Agricultural Institutions.* Oxford: Clarendon Press

Barkan, J. D., 1986. *Politics and the Peasantry in Kenya.* University of Kenya, Institute for Development Studies, Nairobi

Barro, R. J. and Lee, J.-W., 1994. "International Comparisons Data Set." National Bureau of Economic Research, Cambridge, MA

Bates, R. H., 1976. *Rural Responses to Industrialization.* New Haven, CT: Yale University Press

Becker, G., 1957. *The Economics of Discrimination.* Chicago, IL: University of Chicago Press

Berman, B. and Lonsdale, J., 1992. *Unhappy Valley: Conflict in Kenya and Africa.* London: J. Currey

Binswanger, H. and McIntire, J., 1987. "Behavioral and Material Determinants of Production Relations in Land-Abundant Tropical Agriculture." *Economic Development and Cultural Change* 36: 73–99

Cohen, D. W. and Odhiambo, E. S. A., 1992. *Burying SM. The Politics of Knowledge and Sociology of Power in Africa.* Portsmouth, TX: Heinemann

Coleman, J. S., 1990. *Foundations of Social Theory.* Cambridge, MA: Harvard University Press

Davis, J. M., 1969. *Modern Industry and the African.* New York: Negro Universities Press

Deutsch, K. W., 1961. "Social Mobilization and Political Development." *American Political Science Review* 55(3): 493–510

Easterly, W. and Levine, R., 1997. "Africa's Growth Tragedy: Policies and Ethnic Divisions." *Quarterly Journal of Economics* 122 (November): 1203–1250

Epstein, A. L., 1958. *Politics in an Urban African Community.* Manchester: Published on behalf of the Rhodes-Livingstone Institute by Manchester University Press

Fielder, R., 1973. "The Role of Cattle in the Ila Economy." *African Social Research* 15 (June): 327–361

Gellner, E., 1983. *Nations and Nationalism.* Ithaca, NY: Cornell University Press

Gluckman, M., 1960. "Tribalism in Modern British Central Africa." *Cahiers d'Etudes Africaines* 1: 55–70.

Goldstone, J., 1991. *Revolution and Rebellion in the Early Modern World.* Berkeley, CA: University of California Press

Grillo, R. D., 1969. "The Tribal Factor in an East African Trade Union." In P. H. Gulliver (ed.), *Tradition and Transition in East Africa.* Berkeley, CA: University of California Press

Gunnemark, E. V., 1991. *Countries, Peoples, and Languages: The Geolinguistic Handbook.* Gothenberg, Sweden: Geolingua

Gurr, T. R., 1999. *Minorities at Risk.* Washington, DC: United States Institute of Peace Press

Hammond, P., 1975. "Charity: Altruism or Cooperative Egoism?" In E. Phelps (ed.), *Altruism, Morality, and Economic Theory.* New York: Russell Sage Foundation

Hershfield, A. F., 1969. "Ibo Sons Abroad: A Window on the World." Paper presented at the Annual Meeting of the African Studies Association, Montreal

Herskovitz, M. J., 1926. *The Cattle Complex in East Africa.* Washington, DC: American Anthropological Association

Hodgkin, T., 1956. *Nationalism in Colonial Africa.* New York: New York University Press

Horowitz, D. L., 1985. *Ethnic Groups in Conflict.* Berkeley, CA: University of California Press

Huntington, S. P., 1968. *Political Order in Changing Societies.* New Haven, CT: Yale University Press

Laitin, D., 1998. *Identity in Formation.* Ithaca, NY: Cornell University Press

Laitin D. and Fearon, J., 1996. "Explaining Interethnic Cooperation." *American Political Science Review* 90(4): 715–735

Lerner, D., 1958. *The Passing of Traditional Society.* New York: Free Press

Lonsdale, J. M., 1970. "Political Associations in Western Kenya." In R. I. Rotberg and A. Mazrui (eds.), *Protest and Power in Black Africa.* New York: Oxford University Press

Mesquida, C. G. and Wiener, N. I., 1997. "Population Age Composition and Male Coalitional Aggression." York University, Department of Psychology, Toronto

Milbraith, L. W., 1965. *Political Participation.* Chicago, IL: Rand McNally

Morrison, D. G., Mitchell, R. and Paden, J., 1989. *Black Africa: A Comparative Handbook*, 2nd edn. New York: Paragon House

Ottenberg, S., 1955. "Improvement Associations among the Ifikpo Ibo." *Africa* 25(1): 1–22

Perry, E., 1993. *Shanghai on Strike.* Stanford, CA: Stanford University Press

Posner, R. A., 1980. "A Theory of Primitive Society with Special Reference to the Law." *Journal of Law and Economics* 23 (April): 1–53

Putnam, R., 1993. *Making Democracy Work.* Princeton, NJ: Princeton University Press

Rostow, W. W., 1961. *The Stages of Economic Growth.* Cambridge: Cambridge University Press

Rotberg, R. I., 1965. *The Rise of Nationalism in Central Africa.* Cambridge, MA: Harvard University Press

Sahota, G. S., 1968. "An Economic Analysis of Internal Migration in Brazil." *Journal of Political Economy* 76(2): 218–245

Samuelson, P. A., 1958. "An Exact Consumption–Loan Model of Interests With or Without the Social Contrivance of Money." *Journal of Political Economy* 66(6): 467–472

Shils, E., 1957. *Political Development in the New States.* Gravenhage, Netherlands: Mouton

1981. *Tradition.* Chicago, IL: University of Chicago Press

Sjaastad, L. A., 1962. "The Costs and Returns of Human Migration." *Journal of Political Economy* 70(5): 80–93

Sklar, R. L., 1967. "Political Science and National Integration: A Radical Approach." *Journal of Modern African Studies* 5 (May): 1–11

Summers, R. and Heston, A., 1995. *The Penn World Table, Version 5.6.* Cambridge, MA: National Bureau of Economic Research

Twaddle, M., 1969. "Tribalism in Eastern Africa." In P. H. Gulliver (ed.), *Tradition and Transition in East Africa.* Berkeley, CA: University of California Press

Van Evera, S., 1995. "Nationalism and the Causes of War." In C. A. Kupchan (ed.), *Nationalism and Nationalities in Europe.* Ithaca, NY: Cornell University Press

Varshney, A., 2000. *Ethnic Conflict and Civic Life: Hindus and Muslims in India.* New Haven, CT: Yale University Press

World Bank, 1998. *World Development Indicators.* New York: Oxford University Press

Young, C., 1965. *Politics in the Congo.* Princeton, NJ: Princeton University Press

Conclusion: measuring impact and drawing policy implications

Christiaan Grootaert and Thierry van Bastelaer

The notion that social relations, networks, norms, and values matter in the functioning and development of society has long been present in the economics, sociology, anthropology, and political science literature. Only in the past ten years or so, however, has the idea of social capital been put forth as a unifying concept embodying these multidisciplinary views. The concept has been greatly stimulated by the writings of scholars such as James Coleman (1988, 1990) and Robert Putnam (1993). They, and many other writers, have attempted to define social capital rigorously and to identify conceptually sound and practically useful bounds of the concept (see the reviews in Grootaert 1997, Portes 1998, Woolcock 1998, Narayan 1999, Serageldin and Grootaert 2000, and Woolcock and Narayan 2000). The success of these efforts has been limited. While some progress has been made toward achieving consensus on the bounds of social capital, diversity of definitions across authors remains large. A general framework for thinking about social capital and for relating it to development has emerged, however (see Introduction and overview, p. 2).

In parallel with these conceptual endeavors, a growing number of efforts have been made to measure social capital and its impact on development and on various dimensions of well-being. These efforts have been hindered by the lack of consensus on how to define the concept. Researchers engaged in measurement exercises have therefore taken a pragmatic position on how to define and delineate social capital in order to facilitate its measurement. The Social Capital Initiative, on which this volume is based, was set up with that philosophy in mind. Each of the authors in this volume has taken a practical approach that falls within the emerging general framework of social capital.

This framework recognizes that social capital is a genuine asset that requires investment to accumulate and that generates a stream of benefits. It also embodies an integrating approach toward defining social capital and tries to bridge the segmentation in some of the literature between the micro and macro views. It shies away from creating a dichotomy between institutions (as used in the "new institutional economics") and networks (as used in social network theory) or between institutions and networks on the one hand and the more abstract

341

notions of trust, values, and norms on the other. It recognizes that all of these concepts are relevant manifestations of the same underlying asset and that a functioning society must inevitably embody these different types of social capital as they reinforce one another (Serageldin and Grootaert 2000).

The conceptual framework on which the measurement exercises in this book are based is anchored along two dimensions. First, it views social capital along a micro to macro continuum. At the micro level, social capital is manifested in the horizontal associations that Putnam made famous in his seminal book on democracy in Italy (1993) and the vertical associations and related social structures to which Coleman (1990) referred. At the macro level social capital refers to the institutions about which Mancur Olson (1982) and Douglass North (1990) wrote. A constructive interaction between these two spheres means that the state and its institutions have the ability to provide an enabling environment in which local institutions can blossom and bring together local constituencies. At the same time, local institutions lend a measure of validity and stability to the democratic institutions of the state as well as those that enforce the rule of law.

The other important dimension of social capital, developed by Norman Uphoff (2000) spans the range from structural manifestations of social capital to cognitive ones. *Structural* manifestations refer to the more visible and perhaps more tangible aspects of the concept, such as local institutions, organizations, and networks among people, which can be set up for cultural, social, economic, political, or other objectives. *Cognitive* social capital refers to more abstract manifestations, such as trust, norms, and values, which govern interactions among people. Whereas an organization can be directly observed and is subject to some measure of direct counting (the size of its membership, the number of times members meet, the activities they undertake), norms and trust must be observed indirectly, through the perceptions of the people that act based on those norms.

The ideal approach to measuring social capital would embody all four quadrants of figure 11.1. In practice, however, the state of the art has not advanced to that stage. Most of the chapters in this volume focussed on one or two of these quadrants. Most of the studies are situated at the micro level and focus on institutions or norms that are relevant for households, villages, and communities. The main exception is Robert Bates and Irene Yackovlev's study (chapter 10) of ethnic social capital and conflict in Africa, which takes a macro perspective, examining how the size of different ethnic groups in a country is related to that country's ability to reach closure on policy decisions in a peaceful manner. In the same vein, the review by Stephen Knack (chapter 2) uses the country as the unit of analysis to try to identify correlations between various measures of social capital at the country level and performance indicators of growth and poverty alleviation.

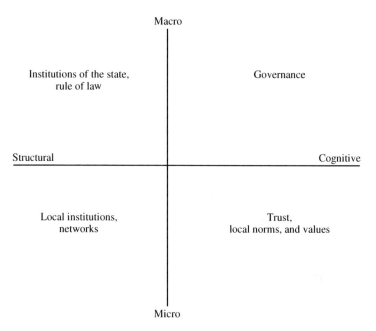

Figure 11.1   Dimensions of social capital.

Most of the studies in this volume try to incorporate aspects of both structural and cognitive social capital, although measurement is often more advanced for structural social capital. Indicators that formally capture both structural and cognitive social capital are found in Anirudh Krishna and Norman Uphoff's study of watersheds in India (chapter 3), Jonathan Isham and Satu Kähkönen's analysis of water supply systems in Indonesia (chapter 5), and Sheoli Pargal, Daniel Gilligan, and Mainul Huq's study of waste management in urban neighborhoods in Bangladesh (chapter 6).

Two questions arise naturally from the studies in this volume. First, how much progress have we made in measuring social capital and its impact? Have we learned enough to conclude that measuring social capital is feasible, and that it can be measured as successfully as natural, physical, and human capital? And if social capital can be measured, what problems remain in measuring it, and what are the priorities for future research?

The second, and undoubtedly more important, question concerns policy recommendations. The fact that *social capital* is called *capital* suggests that one can invest in it, just as one can invest in human and physical capital. Is this the case, and if so, how is it to be done? Which actors are involved in such investment – the state, the private sector, civil society, households, or individuals?

Measuring social capital and its impacts

The overriding lesson that emerges from this book is that it is possible to measure social capital and its impact. The empirical studies indicate that social capital has a profound impact in many different areas of human life and development: it affects the provision of services, in both urban and rural areas; transforms the prospects for agricultural development; influences the expansion of private enterprises; improves the management of common resources; helps improve education; can contribute to recovery from conflict; and can help compensate for a deficient state. More generally, it helps alleviate poverty for individuals and for countries as a whole. Lest this sound excessively simplistic or overly generalized, we note that the extent to which social capital matters varies tremendously across settings, as do the aspects of social capital that are effective.

We cannot help but be impressed by the consistency of these findings across both the quantitative and the qualitative studies in this volume. Methodological diversity is both a strength and a challenge of research on social capital. The analysis cannot be conducted strictly within the economic paradigm, using quantitative methods. Nor can it be investigated solely through anthropological or sociological case studies. The studies in this volume convincingly illustrate the need for and importance of this methodological diversity. Some studies – such as Marcel Fafchamps and Bart Minten's analysis of traders in Madagascar (chapter 4) and Pargal, Gilligan, and Huq's study of waste management services in Dhaka (chapter 6) – rely almost solely on rigorous econometric methods to measure the role of social capital. Other studies, such as Anthony Bebbington and Thomas Carroll's investigation of farmer federations in the Andes (chapter 8) and Nat Colletta and Michelle Cullen's study of civil conflict in Rwanda and Cambodia (chapter 9), are based on case studies. The strength of the quantitative studies lies in their ability to determine a confidence interval within which the results hold. As they are usually based on representative data sources, they can say more about the geographic area or the groups of people for which these results are valid than can case studies. The case studies excel at investigating the in-depth causal processes that lead to certain outcomes, although they often must leave open questions about the statistical validity of the results. Of course, this interplay and complementarity between quantitative and qualitative methods is not limited to the study of social capital. If anything is unique about the analysis of social capital, it is perhaps the high degree to which it is essential to draw on both methods and multidisciplinary approaches to reach valid conclusions.

This volume is, we believe, an adequate rebuttal to those who have argued that too much conceptual diffusion (and perhaps confusion) about social capital remains, and that measurement efforts should wait until further conceptual clarity and convergence has been achieved. We do not accept this point of view. Instead, from the variety of concepts and approaches available, we chose those that we believe lend themselves to pragmatic approaches. The lessons learned from measuring social capital have provided useful insights for the conceptual debate. Specifically, the results in this book show that the conceptual debate must steer away from viewing different concepts of social capital as alternatives. They show that both cognitive and structural capital matter and that social capital is a relevant concept at both the micro and macro levels. Based on the results in this book, we firmly believe that the way forward is to pursue further the integrating view on defining and measuring social capital. Still, we must recognize that progress has not been the same in each of the four quadrants of figure 11.1. Most progress has been made in measuring the impact of structural social capital at the micro level. We are perhaps farthest away from reaching the measurement goal in the upper righthand quadrant, in which cognitive social capital is measured at the macro level.

When the results of these studies were presented at a conference at the World Bank in June 1999, some commentators voiced skepticism about the measurement exercise on the grounds that social capital really refers to an underlying social force that eludes measurement and that the various measures used in the studies were at best imperfect proxies. There is some validity to this point of view. Indeed, one must be careful not to equate the measurement variables with the underlying social capital. However, the fact that proxy indicators are being used to measure social capital does not, in our view, detract from the validity of the exercise. Human capital provides a useful analogy. Human capital theory, developed some forty years ago, claims that human capital embodied in individuals increases their ability to earn income over their lifetimes. Two convenient proxies were proposed to measure this ability: years of schooling and years of work experience. No one confused these proxy indicators with human capital *per se*. Rather, the proxies are input measures that measure the two most important ways in which human capital is acquired. Even forty years after the development of the human capital model, measuring human capital directly (through performance or aptitude tests) remains very difficult. But this difficulty has not prevented the empirical literature on human capital from blossoming and leading to many extremely useful results for developing and implementing education policy.

The social capital model may currently be at the same early stage that human capital theory was thirty or forty years ago. Several useful proxies have been identified for measuring social capital in a policy-relevant manner. The case studies in this volume demonstrate the usefulness of such proxies. The challenge is to test these and other proxy measures in further empirical work, in order to build a strong case for their general applicability.

Experience suggests that the focus should be on three types of proxy indicators: membership in local associations and networks, indicators of trust and adherence to norms, and an indicator of collective action:

- *Membership in local associations and networks.* Using membership in local associations as an indicator of structural social capital consists of counting the associations and their members and measuring various aspects of membership (such as internal heterogeneity) and institutional functioning (such as the extent of democratic decisionmaking). Which associations to include in the indicators is culture-specific: agrarian syndicates could be relevant in one country, rotating credit and savings associations in another, parent-teacher associations in yet another. In the case of networks, which are less formal, the key information is the scope of the network and the internal diversity of its membership. Indicators of membership in associations and networks proved of key importance in the studies of watershed management in India (chapter 3), access to water systems in Indonesia (chapter 5), solid waste collection in Bangladesh (chapter 6), primary schools in Kenya (chapter 7), and civil conflict in Cambodia and Rwanda (chapter 9).
- *Indicators of trust and adherence to norms.* Measuring trust and adherence to norms (cognitive social capital) requires asking respondents about their expectations about and experiences with behavior requiring trust. Key questions relate to the extent to which households received or would receive assistance from members of their community or network in case of various emergencies (loss of income, illness). Questions of this type were included in the data collection instruments of most studies in this volume. They were used extensively in the analysis of each of the four studies that focused on measuring the impacts of social capital (chapters 3–6).
- *An indicator of collective action.* The provision of many services requires collective action by a group of individuals. The extent to which this collective action occurs can be measured and is an indicator of underlying social cohesion (at least to the extent that the cooperation is not imposed by an external force, such as the government). Several studies in this volume successfully use such measures. They include the study on watershed management in India (chapter 3), water supply in Indonesia (chapter 5), and solid waste removal in Bangladesh (chapter 6).

As proxies, these three types of indicators measure social capital from different vantage points. Membership in local associations and networks is clearly an input indicator, since these are the vehicles through which social capital can be acquired. This indicator resembles perhaps most closely the use of years of schooling as a proxy for human capital. Trust can be seen as an input or output indicator or even as a direct measure of social capital, depending on one's conceptual approach. Collective action is clearly an output indicator.

Because of their different perspectives, we believe that these three types of indicators, taken together, provide a valid basis for the measurement of social capital and its impacts.[1] They provide a helpful framework for designing a measurement instrument. Of course, the exact questions and indicators for each analysis have to be adjusted to each social, economic, and cultural setting. The data collection instruments used in the studies in this volume (available upon request from the authors) provide many examples. The questionnaires have yielded lessons as to which types of questions work well or poorly in the field and yield or fail to yield useful information for analysis. Analysts and practitioners have expressed a demand to see these lessons brought together in a prototype data collection instrument, so that subsequent analysis can build upon the experiences of others. To that effect, we have designed the Social Capital Assessment Tool, which combines the best questions from all the studies in this volume and from selected other studies on social capital.[2] The existence of the Social Capital Assessment Tool is not meant to obviate the need for local adaptation of data collection but to embody the experience of past empirical research in order to facilitate future data collection.

Policy implications: can one invest in social capital?

If one accepts the empirical evidence that social capital affects the well-being of people and the development of nations, the question of investing in social capital naturally follows. The history of development is one of investing in physical and human capital in order to enhance economic and social growth; *a priori* it would seem obvious that investment in social capital would be beneficial as well. However, given the current stage of knowledge, the case is not clear. While studies have shown that no country has reached high levels of development without adequate development of its human resource base and without solid investment in human capital, the same empirical case has not yet been made for social capital. This partly reflects the difficulties of measuring social capital. The case is further complicated by the fact that, as economic development proceeds and markets develop, substitution takes place between different types of social

---

[1] The indicators are relevant primarily at the micro and meso level. As the review in chapter 2 indicates, a wide array of macro-level indicators of social capital is available, but the literature has not yet advanced to the stage that it has clearly indicated that certain groups of indicators perform consistently better than others. Still, two classes of measures come to the fore: those relating to the way the government functions (civil liberties, political freedom, lack of corruption, and so forth) and those relating to civil society (group memberships, generalized trust, social polarization, and so forth). Civil society measures are to some degree a macro aggregation of the first two micro indicators mentioned in the text.

[2] This tool was pilot tested successfully in Panama and India, where it proved to be a valid basis for deriving indicators of institutional membership, trust and adherence to norms, and collective action (Krishna and Shrader 2000). A practitioner's handbook for the tool is under production by the editors of the present book (Grootaert and van Bastelaer forthcoming).

capital. Typically, local and indigenous forms of social capital are replaced by more formal and larger-scale networks and institutions.

Let us review the lessons provided by the studies in this volume about creating social capital at the community, supracommunity, and state level. The studies show that there is significant variation in the level of social capital across communities or villages within even a relatively narrow geographic area. The studies of villages in Rajasthan and Indonesia (chapters 3 and 5) suggest that it is primarily the internal dynamics of the community that explain these differences. In many instances, the role of a specific village leader or other influential individual is acknowledged. These are factors that are unlikely to be stimulated through outside interventions. The study of women's groups and schools in Kenya (chapter 7) shows that providing cash or in-kind support to local groups yields ambiguous results. Donor concern with social capital was not linked to measurable social capital outcomes, at least in the short run. However, project design is likely to affect social capital outcomes. Specifically, where program inputs are not easily diverted to other uses, outside assistance may lead to more effective programs and social capital building. Studies such as these provide a hint at the way one could go about helping local institutions. Replicating this kind of study across the world in order to build a caseload from which recommendations can be generalized represents an enormous challenge.

A promising venue for the creation of social capital resides in supracommunal institutions. Local-level organizations (those operating strictly within a community) are very beneficial to the welfare of the households in the community, but their effectiveness is necessarily limited. Bebbington and Carroll's study (chapter 8) shows the value of second-level organizations, which act as an umbrella for organizations at the community level and allow them to combine forces in obtaining resources and engaging in a dialogue with the next level of government. More important, the study shows that outside intervention can stimulate this type of organization and in doing so bestow benefits on communities and their members. Further research is needed to determine the extent to which such organizations function effectively in different cultural settings.

Finally, at the level of the state, the studies in chapters 9 and 10 indicate that the way certain national institutions are set up affects policy formulation and can positively or negatively influence the maintenance of internal peace. These arrangements form part of macro-level structural social capital and can to some degree be changed directly by the state or its constituencies. An example would be the way elections are run and whether or not the government reflects a country's multiethnic composition. In many cases, however, macro-level institutions are the result of traditions going back generations or even centuries, and the practical scope for change in the short term may be limited.

On balance, it seems fair to claim that the social capital literature has been more successful at documenting the beneficial impact of social capital than at deriving policy prescriptions and providing guidelines about how to invest in it. Certainly, the case for massive investment in social capital has not been made. Investing in social capital is more difficult than investing in human capital, where a number of time-tested approaches are available (building schools, training teachers, developing appropriate curricula, and so forth). Equivalent recommendations for investing in social capital have not yet emerged.

A clearer case can be made in favor of less proactive, but no less consequential, approaches to social capital. As the evidence presented in this volume clearly indicates, analytical tools are already sufficiently developed to register the presence and forms of social capital in a community. Including this information in project design can lead to development activities that, at a minimum, do not negatively affect existing social structures and norms. Moreover, when faced with alternative project designs, development practitioners are now in a position to use information on the existence and forms of social capital in the community to select the design that will maximize the leveraging role of social capital in influencing project outcomes. The introduction of a social capital assessment exercise at the early stage of project design can thus facilitate and lower the cost of the project – and dramatically increase its likelihood of success.

Conclusion

The policy message derived from the empirical studies in this volume is one of bounded optimism. The studies demonstrate that social capital matters significantly, and that it should not be relegated to an afterthought in project design – something to consider when the technical and economic features of a project have been finalized. Social capital often matters more than technical or economic considerations, and there is an explicit interaction between them. Certain types of infrastructure should not be proposed for villages that lack the social capital to maintain them. The successful management of common resources requires minimum levels of human and social capital.

Our knowledge of the critical factors that contribute to successful investment in social capital is just beginning to emerge. This should be cause for action, not hesitation, however, in view of the large demonstrated potential payoff. We hope that the empirical evidence accumulated in this volume contributes to this call for action.

REFERENCES

Coleman, J., 1988. "Social Capital in the Creation of Human Capital." *American Journal of Sociology* 94 (Supplement): S95–S120
      1990. *Foundations of Social Theory.* Cambridge, MA: Harvard University Press
Grootaert, C., 1997. "Social Capital: The Missing Link?" In World Bank, *Expanding the Measure of Wealth: Indicators of Environmentally Sustainable Development.* Washington, DC

Grootaert, C. and van Bastelaer, T., forthcoming. *Understanding and Measuring Social Capital: A Multi-Disciplinary Tool for Practitioners.* Washington, DC: The World Bank

Krishna, A. and Shrader, E., 2000. "Cross-cultural Measures of Social Capital: A Tool and Results from India and Panama." Social Capital Initiative Working Paper 21. Social Development Department. World Bank, Washington, DC

Narayan, D., 1999. "Bonds and Bridges: Social Capital and Poverty." Policy Research Working Paper 2167. Poverty Reduction and Economic Management Network. World Bank, Washington, DC

North, D., 1990. *Institutions, Institutional Change, and Economic Performance.* New York: Cambridge University Press

Olson, M., 1982. *The Rise and Decline of Nations: Economic Growth, Stagflation, and Social Rigidities.* New Haven, CT: Yale University Press

Portes, A., 1998. "Social Capital: Its Origins and Applications in Contemporary Sociology." *Annual Review of Sociology* 24: 1–24

Putnam, R., 1993. *Making Democracy Work.* Princeton, NJ: Princeton University Press

Serageldin, I. and Grootaert, C., 2000. "Defining Social Capital: An Integrating View." In P. Dasgupta and I. Serageldin (eds.), *Social Capital: A Multifaceted Perspective.* Washington, DC: The World Bank

Uphoff, N., 2000. "Understanding Social Capital: Learning from the Analysis and Experience of Participation." In P. Dasgupta and I. Serageldin (eds.), *Social Capital: A Multifaceted Perspective.* Washington, DC: The World Bank

Woolcock, M., 1998. "Social Capital and Economic Development: Toward a Theoretical Synthesis and Policy Framework." *Theory and Society* 27(2): 151–208

Woolcock, M. and Narayan, D., 2000. "Social Capital: Implications for Development Theory, Research, and Policy." *World Bank Research Observer* 15(2): 225–249

Index